The Drive to
Industrial Maturity

Business and Politics in America from the Age of Jackson to the Civil War: The Career Biography of W. W. Corcoran
Henry Cohen

Business Depressions and Financial Panics: Essays in American Business and Economic History
Samuel Rezneck

Towards an Integrated Society: Reflections on Planning, Social Policy and Rural Institutions in India
Tarlok Singh

The Age of Giant Corporations: A Microeconomic History of American Business, 1914-1970
Robert Sobel

Samuel Gompers and the Origins of the American Federation of Labor, 1848-1896
Stuart Bruce Kaufman

Statistical View of the Trusts: A Manual of Large American Industrial and Mining Corporations Active around 1900
David Bunting

State and Regional Patterns in American Manufacturing, 1860-1900
Albert W. Niemi, Jr.

The American Banking Community and New Deal Banking Reforms, 1933-1935
Helen M. Burns

Gold Is Money
Edited by Hans F. Sennholz

The Drive to Industrial Maturity

THE U.S. ECONOMY, 1860–1914

Harold G. Vatter

Contributions in Economics and Economic History, Number 13

Greenwood Press
Westport, Connecticut • London, England

Library of Congress Cataloging in Publication Data

Vatter, Harold G
  The drive to industrial maturity: the U.S.
economy, 1860-1914.

  (Contributions in economics and economic history;
no. 13)
  Bibliography: p.
  Includes index.
  1. United States--Economic conditions--1865-1918.
  2. United States--Economic conditions--To 1865.
  3. United States--Industries. I. Title
  HC105.V37   330.9'73   75-16970
  ISBN 0-8371-8180-1

Library of Congress Catalog Card Number: 75-16970
ISBN:0-8371-8180-1

First published in 1975

Greenwood Press, a division of Williamhouse-Regency Inc.
51 Riverside Avenue, Westport, Connecticut 06880

Printed in the United States of America

Contents

64642

Preface

A new book covering a phase of U.S. economic history may be justified among other reasons because it is innovative in some sense. The intended innovation in the present work is the combination of the old and the new economic history. A work that attemps as this does, to integrate the best in the heritage of the old narrative history with the more analytical and quantitative approach of the new is very much needed today.

Some more specific features of this book may also warrant a prefatory comment. In addition to the attempt at integration just noted, I give attention to problems of distribution and equity and to the effects of economic variables on political and social behavior. Orthodox economists stress the fact that people are maximizers of the difference between benefits and costs. But we also know that people are many-sided, warm-blooded activists in the historical process, and that "maximization" is consistent with a considerable variety of behavior patterns.

Except for the heavy weight ascribed to the role of demand in the explanation of why the country industrialized, supply in general receives a more elaborate treatment than demand in the present work. I employ a strongly regional theme throughout, which I believe is most appropriate for the nineteenth century.

The old "sectional conflict" approach is largely subordinated, how-ever. The notion of countervailing power, based upon conflicting interest groups, is much more prominent in my treatment than the traditional economists' individual maximizing units. Although I find much historical continuity, there is rather more of discontinuity in the presentation of history here than the gradualistic new economic historians would likely prefer. Nothing happens "naturally." Neither are there leading or indispensable sectors (unless capital formation be viewed as such) functioning as prime movers in the economic development process.

The accumulation of capital, and the social and political domination of the business stratum, I consider to be central to the development process in the period treated, without necessarily implying that private investment was central before or, more definitely, afterwards.

The period is viewed as an era, in the limited sense of a phase of history, i.e., an extended period exhibiting a number of distinguishing features as compared with the time before and/or after. Also, I implicitly hypothesize that this phase endowed the U.S. economy *after* World War I with a quite different set of economic relationships. The end product of the era provides the necessary setting for the subsequent adoption of a mixed capitalist economy in the United States.

Harold G. Vatter

Acknowledgments

I am much indebted to several of my colleagues at Portland State for carefully appraising various chapters in the early manuscript stage. These include Professor James Ashbaugh, Department of Geography; President Joseph Blumel; Professor Giles Burgess, Russell Dawson, Richard Halley, and John Walker of the Economics Department, and in the Department of History, Professors Bernard Burke, Gordon B. Dodds, James Heath, and Tom Morris. Extensive comments and criticisms by Irwin Unger added greatly to the readability and general quality of the original manuscript. The most imaginative contribution to the technical preparation of the manuscript by Miss Patricia Chapman and Mrs. Lynn Major was unexcelled at any time in my experience.

Above all, I wish to express my deepest appreciation for the enormous critical and editorial contribution of Professor Sidney Ratner of the Department of History of Rutgers University.

The Drive to
Industrial Maturity

[1]

The u.s. economy on the eve of the civil war

Long before 1860 the American people had thrown off the economic dependency associated with their colonial period, and had advanced far along the road toward a modern national economy. An aggressive policy of territorial expansion had wrested, partly through diplomacy and purchase, partly through force or the threat of force, from the European powers, Mexico, and the Indians all the vast domain west to the Pacific Coast, south to the present Mexican border, and north to the forty-ninth parallel adjoining Canada. But except for California, most of the area west of Minnesota, Iowa, Missouri, Arkansas, and eastern Texas was very thinly populated and economically underutilized.

Although only one-fifth of the population lived in urban places of 2,500 or more people by 1860, over twice that proportion had left agricultural pursuits for a variety of activities in the industrial and service sectors of the economy. Farm output had been whittled down to rather over one-third of total production, whereas manufacturing output was already approaching one-fifth of the aggregate annual flow of newly produced goods and services. The farm sector, however, was affected by a major upsurge in agricultural technology and in the North there was impending an enormous expansion that was to raise its output from 133 percent of the South's in 1860 to 252 percent twenty years later.

One Economy or Two?

The sprawling regionally heterogeneous economy of those times does not lend itself to description by brute national aggregates. The aggregates are deceptive as indications of their geographical components. Regional differences were enormous. Although one can perhaps analytically obliterate the substantial differences between the East and the West, the fundamental differences between these two regions, on the one hand, and the South, on the other, dictate separate treatment by the historian. This is reflected in the legendary remark of an Ohio river ferryman, as the right bank of the river was approached, "we are nearing the American shore."[1] Of course, recognition of South-North[2] contrasts does not negate the usefulness of the national concept for many purposes. Consequently, both frames of reference will be interwoven here, together with further breakdowns where such seem appropriate.

We know that in the two or three decades before the war both the South and the North grew rapidly in total output, the former to an important degree by virtue of the spread of cotton cultivation, particularly in its expanding southwest areas. The output of cotton lint rose at a compound annual rate in excess of 5 percent—considerably faster than Southern gross regional product. Northern regional product grew faster than the South's, but because the North's population growth exceeded the South's, its rise in output per capita may have fallen slightly behind that of the South. Although output per capita in the whole South possibly grew faster than in the whole North, all great Northern subregions grew faster than all Southern subregions because, as pointed out by William Parker, the relative statistical weights of the westward movements *lowered* per capita income growth in the North and *raised* it in the whole South.[3]

The South's share[4] of total population declined from about 45 percent in 1810 to about 35 percent of the nation's 31 million people in 1860. Meanwhile its land area had expanded more rapidly than the North's as the land-hungry plantation system pursued its conquest of the Louisiana Purchase and eastern Texas. One important reason for the South's lag in population was the slow increase in the slave population. For example, in the United States as a whole, "while the whites, from 1850 to 1860, gained 38 percent, the slaves and free colored increased somewhat less than 22 percent, and the total increase of the free colored and slaves for 70 years was but 485 percent against 757 percent for the whites."[5] Nevertheless, the slave population of the *major* cotton producing states[6] kept pace with the white population of those states because of the "migration" (importation) of slaves from the areas of the Old South and border states.[7] Even so, the total population growth—white, slave, and free black—of the "cotton states" lagged behind that of the North, being 60 percent for the former and 100 percent for the latter between 1840 and 1860.[8] For one thing, the growth of employment opportunities in the North provided for the absorption of over 5 million immigrants between 1820 and 1860, almost all of whom resided in the North. For another, the cotton states were lacking in their share of the fast-growing city populations, having, by way of example, only one city (New Orleans) among the leading fifteen in 1860. It is significant that the North's more urban population was growing faster despite the typically slower *natural rate* of growth of urban as compared with rural populations. Probably the main reason that the North could do this was that it received not only its own rural-urban migrants but also almost all of the immigrants. The foreign-born population in 1860 accounted for 7 percent of the U.S. total; if 90 percent were in the North then they comprised about one in nine in that region.

The different results obtained by comparing gross regional product growth and regional output per capita growth in the case of the antebellum South and North shows that it is best to use both criteria in appraising the long-run growth performance of an economy or a region. The former measure is sometimes superior, for among other things, it indicates which is outstanding and which is lagging among economies viewed as engaged in an international competition of some sort. The per capita criterion is probably more useful, however, for a first approximation[9] to people's material welfare, or for addressing oneself to population phenomena.

Southern Growth Without Development?

Indeed, two economies coexisted within the political confines of the United States in 1860. Of course, they formed a sort of "common market" linked by regional specialization and an interregional flow of trade and finance (but not of people to any significant extent). The South's balance of payments, viewed somewhat simplistically, contained large exports of cotton, tobacco, etc., to foreigners and much smaller cotton "exports" to the North. With the receipts from these it imported fabricated and processed products, from abroad but mainly from the North, and some food-stuffs, largely from the West. The South also bought financial and marketing services largely from the North (e.g., New York City bankers and merchants), and to a much lesser extent from Great Britain. It was a debtor region also; its capital account, if available, would have shown net indebtedness to both the East and to Great Britain.

The South's pattern of *development*, or *structural and techno-logical change*, had been shaped largely by a consensus of private decisions dominated by profit-oriented cotton and tobacco plan-ters. The rapid growth of a single staple export, accounting for about 60 percent of all U.S. exports in 1860, had strongly influ-enced the South's impressive *rate of output growth*, but it is a moot question whether the associated *structural pattern* maximized either growth or welfare in the very long run. This matter will be examined further below in connection with regional differentia-tion after the Civil War, but since the antebellum heritage is essen-tial to the wartime and postwar performance, it should be glanced at here.

Comparisons of the South and North on the eve of the Civil War have traditionally been structured around the military potential of the two regions. Interwoven in these comparisons was the contrast between slavery and free wage labor, with all the associated ethical overtones. In recent years, largely under the stimulus of the new economic historians' critique of the older belief that the Southern economy was almost moribund, controversy has centered on the issue of the profitability of slavery and comparative per capita income levels and growth rates of the two regions.

The critique may be said to have begun with the pathbreaking and apparently conclusive demonstration by Conrad and Meyer that the slave system was profitable to both slave breeders and cotton plantation owners. [10] While Conrad and Meyer took no stand on the question whether slavery retarded economic growth or development, many drew an implication that if the institution was profitable it could not very well have been a retarding force. This latter issue, not by any means a new one, then came to the fore. Out-standing contributors in this controversy were Robert William Fogel and Stanley L. Engerman. These leading new economic his-torians, drawing heavily on earlier income estimates by Richard

Easterlin—estimates presently very much under scrutiny—maintained that in the two decades prior to the Civil War the Southern growth performance *as measured by income per head* (if Texas is included in the South) was better than that of the North. Fogel and Engerman agree that *total production* grew faster in the North.

On the basis of the criterion of per capita income in 1860 prices, Fogel and Engerman reiterate the earlier argument of Engerman that between 1840 and 1860 the South as a whole grew at an annual rate of 1.7 percent, whereas the North's yearly growth rate was only 1.3 percent.[11] In what the eminent Southern historian C. Vann Woodward called an "all-out assault on American slavery historians,"[12] Fogel and Engerman's *Time on the Cross* argue that the existence of a 25 percent gap between the North and the South in per capita income level in 1860 would not suggest that the South was a poverty-ridden, stagnant, semicolonial region.

On the contrary, they point out that the Northern advantage was attributable entirely to the exceptionally high per capita income of the Northeast, as can be seen in Table 1.[13] They note that income per head in the South in 1860 was substantially higher than in the North Central states. The South was "the fourth richest nation of the world in 1860," "a country as advanced as Italy did not achieve the southern level of per capita income until the eve of World War II," the South's per capita income was growing 30 percent more rapidly than the North's, the per capita railroad mileage was only slightly below the national average, and manufacturing was "the only area in which the antebellum South lagged seriously behind the North in physical capital formation," a phenomenon "fully consistent with . . . the South's comparative advantage . . . in agriculture."[14]

Critics of the Fogel-Engerman position, prominent among whom were Eugene D. Genovese, Douglas F. Dowd, Marvin Fischbaum, and Julius Rubin,[15] concentrated on the very long-run developmental, rather than the simple growth, factors in Southern economic evolution. In other words they maintained that the structure of the South's economy and society was so nondiversified, so dependent on a single staple export commodity, and so inimical to industrialization and urbanization that its long-run growth potential was either exhausted by 1860 or inhibited for decades after the War.

As for the postwar stagnation of Southern economic growth until the 1880s, Engerman contended this was primarily attributable to wartime destruction and postwar socioeconomic dislocation.[16] The

TABLE 1

PER CAPITA INCOME BY REGION,
1840 and 1860
(1860 dollars)

	1840	1860	Average annual growth
North	$109	$141	1.3%
Northeast	129	181	1.7
North Central	65	89	1.6
South	74	103	1.7
South Atlantic	66	84	1.2
East South Central	69	89	1.3
West South Central	151	184	1.0
National	96	128	1.4

Source: Robert William Fogel and Stanley L. Engerman, *Time on the Cross: The Economics of American Negro Slavery* (Boston: Little, Brown, 1974), p. 248, Table 4.
Note 1: Slaves are treated as consumers rather than capital goods.
Note 2: The reason the North grows more slowly than its component subregions is, as William Parker pointed out, the weight of the westward movement in the North pulled down the per capita income growth rate. The South grows more rapidly than its components because the statistical weights due to the redistribution of Southern population from the two older subregions to the high level incomes of the West South Central, particularly Texas, raised the average growth rate from the whole region.

failure of Southern per capita income to rise and converge toward the national level until sometime after 1900 (according to Easterlin [17]) poses a problem that has received much less attention than it has deserved. Further study of that period may well throw light on the question of the possible roles of slavery, and the related comparative advantage of the South in staple agriculture, as forces frustrating the long run developmental, and therefore growth, potential of the South. [18] Indeed, we shall revert to these matters below in Chapter 4.

As Douglass North and others have emphasized, whenever regional growth is linked strongly with a staple export as was the case with the South, this linkage is a necessary but not sufficient condition for development. Sufficiency requires that the exports stimulate varied economic activities within the region, activities that promote structural change and thereby promise more internally generated, self-sustaining development in the long run future. In the case of the South, these "spread effects" and "linkages" from cotton exports tended to stimulate to an inordinate degree the proliferation and specialization of diversified activities outside the region.

While the South in 1860 was not a "monoculture," it was an example of an underdiversified, [19] primary production, relatively non-urbanized economy, with a distinct lack of residentiary (local market-oriented) activities. The distribution of income, as described by William Parker, was characterized by a great gap at the middle levels. The South probably had a chronic negative balance of trade that, instead of contributing to development, largely financed imported consumer goods and business services, and there was little import replacement. The underlying population was, as compared with the North, illiterate. The economic potential for occupational diversity of the great majority of the black 36 percent of its population was eroded by the institution of slavery. Despite the substantial numbers of black craftsmen, slaves were generally considered uneducable chattel. The potentials and aspirations of the poor white yeoman farmer or town dweller were also repressed.

In contrast to the North (in areas other than the frontier), the transfer of processing and fabricating activities from the household or plantation to the market economy was still far from complete. Thus the advantages of specialization stemming from such transfer were not optimally exploited. Of course the paucity of non-household fabrication was part of the phenomenon of scarce non-farm business in general. In most long distance marketing activities Southern firms could not match the lower costs of Northern firms. And the South had no protective tariff against Northern products.

The Southern manufacturing labor force on the eve of the war accounted for between 8 and 10 percent of the U.S. total of 1.53 million manufacturing workers. If the South had one-third of the U.S. total labor force of 11.11 million, then its manufacturing labor force of about 138,000 amounted to less than 4 percent of its total employment! For the whole North the proportion would be nearly 19 percent (1.39 million out of 7.33 million). In linkage-creating cotton textiles, the South accounted for only 7 percent of total U.S. value of product. Moreover, while large-scale manufacturing in the South and West was quite similar, as pointed out by William Parker, the

Midwest had a distinct advantage in industries having average firms in the middle-sized category: [20]

Firm size	Firms per 100,000 total population	
	Midwest	South
Small	20.7	53.9
Medium	344.0	102.8
Large	17.1	15.9
Total	381.8	172.6

As Parker emphasizes, it was the large number of locally dispersed middle-sized enterprises that could be counted on especially for fruitful long run "learning effects," the generation of inland urban centers, and later large-scale industry and marketing.

The heavily agrarian character of Southern society was of course reflected in the low level of general urbanization as well as the lack of large cities. Except for Louisiana, the urban population (in places of 2,500 or larger) was about 5 percent of the total in 1860, whereas in the United States as a whole it was about 20 percent.

Although the dominant ideology in the South belittled industrialization, manual labor, and nonclassical education, some Southerners had long recognized the need for more developmental measures. This had been stressed in a number of "commercial conventions." The South Carolinian William Gregg was a strong advocate of greater industrialization, and his cotton textile factory in Graniteville would have given a fillip to further industrial expansion had not plantation profits and ideology, together with Yankee competition, frustrated it. Even the South Carolina State Agricultural Society, perhaps influenced by a pro-industry speech before it in 1841 by former Congressman James H. Hammond, resolved at its meeting in 1844 "that a combined system of Agriculture, Manufactures and Commerce are essential in promoting the prosperity and happiness of a community."[21] J.D.B. DeBow, founder and editor of the prominent *Commercial Review of the South and Southwest*, asks what has happened to the receipts from the South's and Southwest's cotton crop over a twenty-year period, and answers:

Much of it has been paid to the neighboring states for provisions, mules, horses, and implements of husbandry; much has been paid for clothing and other articles of manufacture, all induced by the system of applying *all*, or nearly all the labor of the country to the production of one staple only, and by neglecting the encouragement of manufactures . . . the labor bestowed in cotton growing . . . has served to swell the general commerce of the nation; the manufacture of the raw material has given employment to foreign capital and to foreign labor, and has also served to swell the volume of foreign commerce. But the country of its production has gained nothing, and lost much . . . it has not kept its relative position in the rapid march of improvement which marks the progress of other countries.[22]

De Bow thus clearly saw (1) that the "multiplier-accelerator" and "linkage" effects were largely located outside the region and (2) that the South had a high marginal propensity to import finished goods, i.e., that it represented a case in which the "expansion in domestic demand resulting from increasing exports is supplied by the higher imports which they make possible."[23]

Contrasting Levels of Development

It seems likely that this unbalanced growth pattern was the major factor in the South's military inferiority relative to the North, rather than its smaller population or lack of internal unity.[24] Growth *rates* are not too significant for military and economic power. *Levels* of income per capita and the composition of output are absolutely vital here.

The per capita income discrepancy on an overall basis is seen to be very large. Where the crude averages are about equally high—in the West South Central and the Northeast—we have a high-yield agrarian region compared with a vastly more populous, highly productive, industrialized region. Clearly the former region could carry very little weight in swinging the South's economic-military potential toward more equality with the North. This is emphasized by the overwhelming commitment of Texas to cotton and of the whole West South Central region to the manufacturing of the same product. Thus whatever the possibly more skewed *distribution* of income in the South may have meant for military potential and future economic development, the Northeast may be said to have militarily confronted the South Atlantic and East South Central, or "Old South"—an area with a per capita income only one-half its level. And the North Central agrarian region, although possessing a per capita income about equal to that of the Old South, was a much better food basket.

Insofar as food and agriculture affected the military potential of the two contestants, the South's position was not too unfavorable, however. It is true that the South relied on the West for some important foodstuffs, notably some meat products, wheat, flour, potatoes, and whiskey. Yet the deficiencies were not insurmountable so far as production and stocks in the aggregate were concerned. Data for 1859 and 1860 on the output and stocks of selected items may be found in Chapter 2, Tables 4 and 5. It will be seen from these tables that, aside from the problem of transporting goods within the region, the South was surprisingly well equipped with respect to corn, tobacco, milch cows, swine (although the Southern hog was much lighter than the Northern), sweet potatoes, rice, sugar, rye, mutton, poultry, and cattle. Corn, the South's major crop, was a reasonable wheat substitute for human consumption and indeed had long been a basic food for slaves and poor whites. Other substitutes were also possible on land not planted with cotton. It was not in food production potential per capita that the South needed to fear the most, but in other areas outside agriculture.

In the case of the social overhead sector, as represented by railroads, the South was reasonably well off, since it had almost 33 percent of the mileage and 29 percent of the railroad invested capital of the United States, the great bulk of it having been constructed during the 1850s. This left the South about on par with the North on a per capita basis, but rather below par on an area basis. The quality of the South's railroad facilities was particularly poor. The latter was offset to some extent by the South's many navigable streams.

How was it that the antebellum South came to deviate from the usual pattern of nondiversification and unbalanced growth through staple export, with respect to transport—probably the most important component of infrastructure at that time? Perhaps the answer lies in the Southern desire to move export crops more cheaply from the hinterland to the chief southern seaports[25] for coastwise shipment to New York or, hopefully, directly to foreigners. Paul W. Gates points out that the Gulf states' competition "induced residents of the older communities who felt their regions' economy was slipping, to advocate the construction of internal improvements...."[26] Some Southerners also hoped that overland rail shipments would help make their captive seaports independent of the New York coastwise shipping interests. These objectives were to some extent facilitated by state and foreign lenders and by

Federal railroad land grants beginning in 1850. Private business's contribution to railroad promotion in the South was distinctly modest. The development of some transport infrastructure is not unusual in less developed, staple export countries today, often financed by imported capital.

But it was in the manufacturing and education spheres that the non-South possessed the greatest lead so far as the level of development of these sectors is concerned. In the former sector the North enjoyed 90 percent of the nation's manufacturing labor force and about 92 percent of total value added by manufacture. The North at that time would be considered, on the basis of contemporary world comparisons and modern world historical experience, an already fairly industralized regional economy, with almost one-fifth of its labor force engaged in manufacturing activities.

Investment in Education

If education contributes to economic development, then it could not have played a strategic role, relative to other influences during the era preceding the Civil War, despite the observations of foreign visitors that Americans were the most generally educated populace on earth. The judgment that education was not developmentally strategic is undoubtedly safe so far as formal education is concerned, but it is perhaps less securely grounded with reference to informal private-venture education and experimentation. Outside ordinary schools, knowledge was advanced through mechanics institutes and lyceums, especially in the North. However, it is likely that the bulk of technical education, which was considerable, was conducted in the home, on the farm, and in the shop or factory, and took the form of learning by doing. Some of the latter was formal, as in the case of apprenticeship training, some of it informal, as in the case of the transmission of European know-how by immigrants on or off the job. Of total expenditures for formal education of about $35 million in 1860, Professor Fishlow estimates that $20 million was public,[27] the South exhibiting, as in other social overhead investment categories, the greater public emphasis.

However, literacy, defined as the ability to read and write, was comparatively widespread among the nonslave population, particularly in the North. Bowman and Anderson have suggested that a literacy rate of about 40 percent of the labor force was historically necessary "for sustained growth, a supportive base for the first firm stage of development" and added that "additional literacy (or its equivalent in limited and mediocre elementary schooling) seemed to bring little benefit until a level of 70-80 percent was reached. [28] The United States had no doubt advanced well above the 40 percent barrier by 1860, at least in the North. It is doubtful that the very vital nonsectarian, tax-supported public school movement had resulted in even a mediocre schooling by 1860. Although the social reform movements of the 1830s and 1840s and the public school agitation of the 1850s had "enrolled" 60 percent of the whites (and 2 percent of the nonwhites) by 1860, the average white of twenty-one had had only 434 days of schooling, or 27 days per year. Such an achievement no doubt contributed to the diffusion of literacy and the training of skilled workers, but is unlikely to have added much more to the creation of what Alan Batchelder has called "productive intelligence."

On the level of more advanced formal education, by 1860 there were several thousand secondary level academies (private), a few technical colleges, about 250 colleges of all types, a few mechanics institutes, a handful of very newly established agricultural colleges, and 17 new state universities. In the very important agricultural field the Superintendent of the Census complained that "we are greatly behind some of [the European countries] in institutions designed to teach the innumerable applications of science to agriculture, and to elevate and throw a charm around this noble employment." But it seems likely that the approximately 900 agricultural associations, boards, and societies in the country, many long-established, were important contributors to the diffusion of agricultural knowledge, as were numerous individual crusaders for farm betterment and the institution of the agricultural "fair."

The Level of Living

Aside from the misery and subsistence levels of living endured by the Indians, probably among the poorest Americans were the 4 million slaves. So many tangible and intangible factors enter into the level of living—diet, shelter, clothing, job security, old age dependency, freedom to change employers and location of work, and the larger matter of a worker being a chattel or a nonchattel—that only the crudest and simplest indicators are called for here. It should also be remembered that before the Civil War Northerners and Southerners vilified each other for their oppressive labor systems. The most devastating criticisms ever made of free wage labor, hardly to be surpassed by Karl Marx, were developed by the spokesmen for the Southern slaveholding planters.

The historian, Kenneth Stampp, has argued that "the great mass of Northern workers enjoyed, by and large . . . a standard of living considerably higher than that of the mass of Southern slaves.[29] However it is difficult to agree with Stanley Lebergott that free labor had a sixfold advantage over slave labor's real annual income.[30] Conrad and Meyer suggest $45 for the annual real income of a "prime field hand" in the 1840-1860 period.[31] Fogel and Engerman estimate that the "basic income" (the value of the food, clothing, shelter, and medical care furnished to slaves) of an adult male in 1850 was about $48, with extra income possible from the sale of cotton and garden products, raising chickens, etc.[32] In contrast, average monthly wages of free farm labor in Georgia in 1860 (after a decade of increases) were about $12.[33] Such data as these are of course highly superficial, but their direction seems correct in the light of work done by people studying the living conditions of the times.

The farm laborer should properly be selected for comparison with the slave because the overwhelming majority of slaves worked in agriculture. But the free farm laborer was generally the lowest paid category of free workers. Nonfarm male workers' wages in 1860 averaged a little over $1.00 per day while the average male farm worker averaged $13.70 per month, including board.[34] Since nonfarm workers averaged six days' work per week, if they worked steadily their monthly wage would have approximated $26 (almost twice the farm worker's wage) and their annual wage would have been about $300. This compares with Lebergott's estimate of $363 average annual earnings for full-time nonfarm employment based on a daily wage of $1.09,[35] and the average worker's annual wage in manufacturing of about $290, adjusted upward by Clarence Long to $297.[36] There were of course substantial regional variations in the *money* (not necessarily real) earnings; the rate was highest in the West and lowest in the South.

It is hard to interpret these estimates in terms of living levels. Habakkuk has emphasized that real wages (money wages divided by consumer prices) were higher in the United States than in Great Britain,[37] and cites William Nassau Senior to the effect that in 1829 laborers' wages in "North America" were 25 percent higher than in England. It is perhaps small comfort to know that U.S. workers were possibly faring better than their counterparts in the most advanced industrial country in the world in 1860. The *New York Times* in 1853, prior to most of the consumer price rise of the 1850s, published a minimum working man's weekly budget for a family of four that required an income of $12 per week.[38] Clearly very few workers, on the basis of the above estimates, received an income sufficient to meet this minimum, harsh as it was.

However, a comprehensive view would have to recognize the historical and internationally comparative fact that the material life of free workers was better than it had been and better than that of free workers in western Europe. The large immigration from Europe attests to this. Inadequate as the level of living of workers, small farmers, and free farm laborers was in the pre-Civil War period, it was higher than it had been in 1789 or 1820 or 1830, and it was definitely higher than in the places from which the immigrants came. What seems unendurable, scandalous, and lamentable from our point of view today was superior in terms of what could be obtained then for most people in even the advanced countries of western Europe and in Great Britain, as noted in a penetrating study of the living standards of U.S. workers made by the Frenchman Emile Levasseur at the turn of the century.

We can nevertheless say that life for the working-class family was still, despite the progress made prior to the Civil War, squalid, primitive, and short. The 66-hour week outside farming (longer in farming!), even at a lower intensity of labor than existed later, left workers without the leisure to be human beings. Fogel and Engerman, after noting that Southern agriculture was more efficient than Northern agriculture, report that both slaves and free farmers in the South averaged 70-75 hours of work per week during the peak labor periods of planting, cultivating, and harvesting, and that "black plantation agriculturalists" performed their work with "extraordinary intensity" that "was more like a modern assembly line than was true of the routine in many of the factories of the antebellum era."[39] The intensity of labor in the Northern factory was considerable, and apparently notably greater than in Europe. Harriet Martineau observed that "there seems no doubt among those who know both England and America that the mechanics of the New World work harder than those of the old."[40]

The "ten-hour day movement" among the workers that stretched back to at least 1827, was almost operative in the building trades, but was not achieved in private industry generally until 1887. It took an "eight-hour day movement" to achieve this! In farming it is doubtful that work hours changed very much over the decades before 1860.

Meanwhile, some advances on other fronts, such as educational protective legislation for women and children, had been made. But a significant welfare indicator—the expectation of life at birth (in "affluent" Massachusetts)—was still only 38.7 years for males and 40.9 for females. However, this was an improvement. Harold Somers has estimated that there was an increase of 10 to 15 years in life-span from the end of the colonial period to 1856.[41]

For slaves life expectancy was less than for whites. One study reports that the life expectancy of slaves at age twenty was 17.5 years, and of whites 19.2 years in antebellum Mississippi.[42] Yet this mortality rate had apparently decreased in 1860 compared with ten years earlier.[43] Fogel and Engerman aver, as part of their wide-ranging defense of the comparative level of living of slaves, that slaves had much longer life expectations than free urban industrial workers in both the United States and Europe. However, they note that in 1850 slave life expectancy was 12 percent below the white American average. Furthermore, the infant death rate for slaves was 25 percent higher than for whites, a "strange paradox" in view of the alleged solicitation in the treatment of pregnant women by planters. This high infant mortality no doubt contributed materially to the fact that 40 percent of the slaves died before age nineteen.[44]

In the field of health the population faced primitive conditions, with the South "less healthy than the North."[45] Hookworm helped to create and to maintain the class of impoverished "poor whites" in the South. Diseases such as malaria and yellow fever "took a fearful toll of whites," and "the mortality from tetanus was incredibly high among slaves of all ages."[46] Other deases such as dysentery, pneumonia, pleurisy, typhoid, tuberculosis, and various mental disorders were widespread, and most of these afflicted both blacks and whites. In the country as a whole the leading cause of death from illness was tuberculosis.

In the Northern cities health and sanitation conditions were poor for most people. According to George R. Taylor, in 1860 growth of the cities took place despite bad conditions of urban living, not because of appreciable improvements. Street and alleys, even of the largest cities, were typically not only rutted and full of mud holes, but frequently ankle-deep in garbage, ashes and filth. Everywhere, hogs, dogs, geese, and hordes of rats—and in the South vultures—acted as scavengers . . . Even in the largest centers of population, water closets were a luxury of the rich, and brimming outdoor toilets, especially in the slum areas, presented with every rain an offense to the senses and a threat to health which seem incredible to city dwellers of the mid-twentieth century . . . death rates were much higher for the cities than for the country as a whole and . . . New York City's death rate was nearly twice that for London. Down to the Civil War and beyond, epidemics of such diseases as cholera, yellow fever, typhus and, small pox swept devastatingly through the crowded and unsanitary urban areas. [47]

The vaccination of school children had been proposed, but had not yet been put into effect. The Superintendent of the Census commented that "in both town and country a vast amount of needless sickness exists."

Clearly a comparative good growth rate of income per capita, even when it represented the achievement, in 1860, of possibly the highest level in the world of this incomplete measure of welfare, did not assure to the average person much better than a small amount of income beyond subsistence that he could use at his discretion. From the viewpoint of prosperous Americans a century later, most people in 1860 lived close to absolute poverty (only marginally separated from hunger and malnutrition). It can be easily appreciated, given the conditions of life of working people then, why labor organization around the job, together with a broad movement for a more human existence for wage earners, including shorter hours and public education, had already taken root in society. This movement, that is usually dated from the 1820s, was to permeate society and exert an ever-growing power in the decades after the Civil War. Unfortunately the movement was generally unconcerned about or hostile to the human rights of certain minorities such as blacks, Indians, and later Mexican-Americans.

Economic Conflicts Underlying the War: The Role of the Federal Government

The economic controversies between the South and the North prior to the outbreak of the war reveal much about the state of the economy and the strategic position occupied by the West on the eve of that conflict. What these issues were are still, incredible as it may seem, a matter of debate. It may be that this continuing debate, as Professor John Sproat has commented, "serves as a stubborn reminder of the historian's inability to relate history 'as it actually happened.'" [48] Alternatively, it may be simply that past experience is always interpreted in different ways as new insights, new evidence, new theories, and new interests arise and cause historians to look at things in a new way. The debate, however, can at least be limited here to the *economic* issues, without asserting that these were the chief issues or the only ones.

The economic issues include the territorial limits of legalized slave labor and the struggle for control of Federal government economic policy. The latter constellation of issues is the most revelant to a review of the economy on the eve of the war. Here we touch upon the "thesis" of Charles and Mary Beard and Louis Hacker, who argued that the Civil War was in its essence a revolutionary struggle for control of the Federal government between Northern "industrial" capitalist interests and the Southern slave-owning, landed aristocracy. Obviously, the South, which had a long-established policy of giving the state governments important developmental (not welfare) functions, wished to allocate a smaller role to the Federal government and a larger role to the state governments. Many of the political spokesmen and the common people of the North wished for a different allocation.

Allan Nevins has critically advanced the alternative thesis that the main single conflict-creating force behind the war was the struggle between the planters' goal of legalized slave labor and the free soil farmers' goal of the exploitation of new Western land. It may well be argued that once the war was launched, perhaps largely over the question of territorial expansion of slave plantation interests as against free soil farmer interests, the results led to a triumph of Northern nonfarm business interests on matters dear to the hearts of the latter group.

In any case, the specific issues with which Beard and Hacker dealt provide convenient foci for any discussion of developments in this period. Beard and Hacker referred, among other things, to questions involving the disposition of the public domain, especially in the West, various internal improvements such as the transcontinental railroad issue, the secularly falling level of the tariff after 1828, the type of commercial banking system, and Federal aid to agricultural and mechanical education to speed "the absorption of agriculture into the industrial vortex, endlessly sustained by capitalism, science and machinery."[49]

On a number of these issues the Beard-Hacker thesis argues that Southern opposition before the Civil War inhibited the realization of pro-industrial laws and policies, policies that were effectively launched after secession in a wartime legislative packet containing among other things, the Homestead Act (1862),[50] the land grants for a transcontinental railroad (1862, 1864), increases in tariff rates (1862, 1864), and the National Bank Act (1863) together with a prohibitive tax of 10 percent on all state bank notes (1865).[51]

The Public Domain

By 1860 about 394 million acres of the public domain (excluding Alaska) of 1.442 billion acres had been disposed of. Possibly 215 million acres of this were sold for productive settlement, in some loose sense, directly or through speculative hands. About 115 million acres were sold in the last 15 years of the period ending 1860. The average annual acreage disposed of, 1845-1860, was 7.7 million, based on the above figures. However, patents for only 80 million acres of homesteads were issued between 1860 and 1900, i.e., about 2 million acres per year. As Fred A. Shannon summed it up:

> even if all the homesteaders had kept and lived on their holdings, less than a sixth of the new homes and a little over a sixth of the acreage would have been on land that came as a gift from the government. Eighty-four out of each hundred new farms had to be achieved either by the subdivision of older holdings or by purchase.[52]

The fact of modest material results is underscored by the knowledge that less acreage was patented under the Homestead Act before 1904 than after (although the land patented earlier in most cases was the better land).

All this should not obscure the fact that the Northern farm sector in 1860 was experiencing a technological revolution and was on the threshhold of a period of substantial output growth. This was particularly in the North Central region and westward therefrom. This growth was strongly geared in some lines of production to a burgeoning export market for Western products that kept farm exports in excess of 70 percent of total exports until the mid 1890s.

What was new in this export pattern was the beginning of the relative decline of cotton and the increasing importance of farm products originating in the West.

The Transcontinental Railroads

Before the Civil War there was strong sectional strife over the plans for locating a transcontinental railroad, a conflict that delayed the consummation of any plan. Had this inhibited the expansion of the North with respect to Western farming, for example? It is difficult to say, but total Northern farm output grew at least as fast as Southern farm output between 1840 and 1860. No one has researched the question: would the former have grown faster after, say, 1850, had there been a transcontinental railroad spanning the northern route? In the next twenty years Northern farm output grew at the unexcelled rate of about 4.75 percent per year, but it is doubtful that much of this should be attributed to the transcontinental railroad. The railroad network of the North in 1860 already totaled at least 32,000 miles.[53] This meant about 13 miles for every million dollars' worth of commodity output in agriculture, mining, and manufacturing.[54] By 1870 the ratio had risen to 18 miles and by 1880 to about 20 miles. Since the ratio fell back to 16 in 1890, thus commencing the elimination of long run excess capacity, the railroad mileage growth, *on this crude measure*, must not have been in need of any great spurt above the trend preceding 1860 in order to reach its long run optimum.

These are of course aggregative relationships, and they do not address themselves specifically to either the transcontinental railroads or the pace of Western development. But, if the transcontinental railroads via the northern route were of major importance for economic growth, their macro-effects should be discernible. In any case, the decade of the fifties, while leaving railroad technology and organizational unification with much still to be accomplished in the direction of modernization, had witnessed an enormous railroad expansion. This spelled the end of the dominance of internal waterways[55] and shaped the still somewhat primitive railroads of the time into a network that east of the Mississippi resembled the final spatial pattern. An 1860 railroad map suggests that the Western rail tentacles just approached the edge of the frontier in the region between the ninety-fifth and the one-hundredth meridians. Although handicapped by heterogeneous gauges, poor rails, and other physical defects, the old Northwest was reasonably well accommodated with rail lines. Hence it would seem that the opposition of the South to government subsidy of a transcontinental railroad via a northern route was not a great handicap to Midwestern agriculture. On the other hand, the further development of the Mountain West and the establishment of rail transport connections between the West Coast and the Northeast was an important developmental goal that lends credence to the Beard-Hacker argument.

Money and Banking

The Superintendent of the Census declared that during the 1850s "the bank movement in the United States . . . underwent great expansion without becoming less sound."[56] This sounds excellent, presuming the banks were "sound" at the outset, a judgment with which many would not concur. In any event, it was and still is argued that what was needed then was not so much soundness as stimulation of development. These might not be the same. Agrarian sectors always suffer from the possession of precisely that kind of collateral for which sound bankers have a special distaste—farm land, and products subject to climatic vicissitudes. In the case of the South, sympathy for the state system and hostility to a national system merged with other sectional issues.

The 1,562 state banks in 1860 were the largest number in U.S. history up to that time. Even so, "by 1852 resentment against the banks had grown so great that there were no incorporated banks in the seven states of Arkansas, California, Florida, Illinois, Iowa, Michigan, and Wisconsin; in the Oregon and Minnesota territories; and in the District of Columbia. In Indiana and Missouri, banking was a state monopoly."[57] The state banks, public or private, were the banks of issue and deposit, despite Constitutional strictures regarding the Federal government's exclusive right to "coin money, regulate the value thereof"—thanks to Chief Justice Taney and four other Jacksonian Supreme Court appointees.[58]

Edward J. Stevens[59] has estimated the total money stock in 1859 at $672.3 million, of which $399.7 million was bank notes and deposits and $272.6 million was specie (foreign and domestic coin and bullion), including an unknown amount, between 1 and 7 percent of total specie, held by the Treasury. Demand deposits were not yet larger than all other forms of means of payment taken together in the aggregate, but they would be soon after the war. In the New England and Middle Atlantic regions deposits were more important than in the West and South, where alleged currency shortages were as a result typically in the forefront. In the Eastern cities checks written against demand deposits were unquestionably the major medium of exchange.

With a GNP in 1859 of \$4,170 million, the income velocity of circulation of money was historically high at 6.2:[60]

$$V = \frac{PQ}{M} = \frac{\text{GNP}}{M} = \frac{4.17}{.672} = 6.2$$

where $MV = PQ$; M is the stock of money, V is the velocity or rate of turnover of the money stock in any period, P is the price level, and Q is the total physical output of goods in any period. PQ is the sum of all quantities of products exchanged times their unit prices, and thus equals GNP. This was reasonably on trend, for it had been about 8.5 the decade before, and was about 5 in 1869, falling after the early 1880s as 1914 approached. This is just another way of saying that the ratio of money to income rose secularly. Of course, the farmers complained that the means of payment were always in short supply, and this probably meant currency and coin both before and after the Civil War. This complaint was another way of saying that credit for farmers was tight. The record shows that the aggregate face value of state bank notes grew at an annual compound rate of almost 6 percent between 1845 and 1860. But after these notes were taxed out of existence beginning July 1, 1866, the substitute national bank notes grew at a much slower rate. For example, the volume of such notes reached its absolute peak of \$352 million in 1882, and had grown since 1866 at an annual rate of only 1.75 percent. And the volume of U.S. legal tender notes ("greenbacks"), first issued during the Civil War, meanwhile had been practically constant. In the 1880s the volume of national bank notes declined sharply, and the aggregate volume of currency would therefore also have declined had it not been for the increase in silver coins and certificates so vigorously fought for by the agrarian and silver-mining coalition. Even so, a very tight money policy, as far as the currency component was concerned, reigned until the end of the century.[61] Thus, almost all the increase in the money stock was in bank deposits.

Business Enterprise

If agriculture is seen as a field for business enterprise, then most business firms in the United States in 1860 were farm enterprises. Nevertheless, the bulk of gross output, over $2,600 million out of $4,200 million, was produced under the aegis of nonfarm firms. Entrepreneurial[62] opportunities in farming were still vast and would continue to be for decades to come. Yet the shift to nonfarm business opportunities, particularly opportunities in wholesaling, retailing, construction, and manufacturing in urban centers, had long been under way. The growth potential in these was to continue to be greater than in the natural resource activities. This shift gradually undermined the unique power of land speculation to induce prosperity and depression and substantially raised the importance of construction and industrial investment in the determination of cyclical fluctuations (expansions and contractions).

By 1830 the typical nonfarm enterpriser left behind his predominantly mercantile, commercial, or foreign-trading orientation, and by 1860 he tended increasingly to become wealthy through domestic trade, mining, specialized finance services, and manufacturing. New England commercial enterprise probably reached its zenith when Daniel Webster opposed the first protective tariff in 1816. Certainly by 1828 New England had moved decisively toward manufacturing and tariff protection. Meanwhile many functions formerly performed by merchants, such as transportation, shipping, and finance, had become the specialized functions of other entrepreneurs.

Like mobile farm labor, mobile business entrepreneurship during the early nineteenth century contributed to the expropriation of most of the Indian population of the North Central region and participated in the expansion of that region's population from a frontier element comprising only 9.2 percent of the nation's total population in 1820 to 29 percent forty years later. Vigorous, aggressive entrepreneurship in this region, blessed with an unorganized local migrant and immigrant labor supply, and with primarily local, and to a lesser extent Eastern and international capital supply,[63] had on the eve of the Civil War succeeded in employing 14 percent of the country's manufacturing labor force and was poised to raise this to 23 percent by the end of the war decade.

Meanwhile in New England and the Middle Atlantic regions the larger cities had become the commercial, industrial, and financial hub of the national economy. New York City had an overwhelmingly dominant position with respect to financing and marketing the enormous cotton crop. Both the South and the West were debtor regions, and the metropolises of the East were centers of that creditor region. Commercial banking was well developed. Many central banking functions were being performed by the Boston, New York, Philadelphia, and Baltimore commercial banks for their respective hinterlands. Interbank clearings were efficiently organized. No doubt the creation of a central bank in the United States was long delayed partly because of the effectiveness of these large city commercial banks in a still very regionalized economy. Also, a group of New York City banks had come to hold large bankers' balances of banks across the country, i.e., large portions of the latters' reserves. The chief element still lacking was a nonprofit institution to create reserves for the commercial banks—a "lender of last resort."

The provision of longer term credit and capital was in a more primitive stage of development, however. There was practically no mortgage market. The securities market, despite the existence of the New York Stock Exchange, was in its infancy. Mutual savings banks and insurance companies performed some intermediary function between saver and borrower on long term. Commercial or trade credit extended by one business (usually a middleman) to another was an established means of providing intermediate and short term credit. But the investment banker, with a few exceptions such as S. and M. Allen (1808-1837) and E. W. Clark of Philadelphia (1837-1857),[64] had hardly appeared. His function was frequently performed by "Anglo-American merchant bankers" who underwrote American securities and extended funds to U.S. importers. Here we have a reflection of the immaturity of U.S. financial enterprises and of the international debtor status of the economy.

Yet, with all the growth in the business population, the nation was moving rapidly toward its ultimate configuration: a nation one-third self-employed, two-thirds employees. Sixty years earlier the self-employed had made up roughly 57 percent of the labor force, but on the eve of the Civil War they comprised 37 percent; meanwhile employees, despite the comparative rarity of the corportion, had grown from a mere 12 percent to 40 percent. According to Stanley Lebergott, by 1910 the farm and nonfarm self-employed were to be down to 29 percent of the total labor force. The decline in the relative importance of farming was the main explanation for this trend before the Civil War, but thereafter the spread of the corporate form of business as well as the large firm, however organized, and to a lesser extent the increase of tenancy and the relative decrease of full ownership within farming, were additional factors. The shift from enterprise ownership to wage labor may well have gone largely unnoticed, since the increase in the percentage of workers was obscured to many by substantial absolute increases in business proprietorships, almost all of whom were held by men. The individual proprietors in both numbers and economic importance were, however, already by 1860 yielding ground to the employees and, to a much lesser degree, to the corporate form (the latter operated by salaried employees), which received a fillip between 1837 and 1860 from the passage of general incorporation laws in many of the Eastern states. And the "business elite," as William Miller has explained, was already destined to come predominantly from urban fathers, Episcopal or Presbyterian in religion, from a New England or Middle Atlantic residence of native-born and ultimately British ancestors, and occupationally engaged in business or one of the professions. David Bunting has found, however, that at least a significant minority came from the ranks of nonpropertied people.

The organization of the individual enterprise in the nonfarm sector cannot be described with a single model. In the case of manufacturing, however, the typical enterprise was a one-factory firm that employed the technology of fixed stations, with workers and materials centered in those parts of the plant where fabrication occurred (as contrasted with a moving production line), and turning out a narrow line of products. The major power sources were either flowing water (especially in New England) or steam engines fueled mainly by wood and, to a much lesser extent, coal. [65] Thus, manufacturers and workers were still in their iron age, constrained by ancient fuels for power but now enormously aided by the steam engine, which in England had long ago replaced water power and used coal as fuel. It should be remembered that "efficiency" involves relative costs, however, and if the factory (or railroad locomotive) used mainly wood-fired steam engines, the reason was that the short-run private cost of wood fuel was less in those regions than it was in Great Britain.

Business proprietors, as was then customary, maintained a hard, paternalistic discipline in the industrial plant. The long hours and intense work pace have already been referred to. In the absence of cost accounting, time and motion analysis, and personnel management, unit labor costs were presumably minimized precisely by such long, hard work, by the frequent employment of low-paid women and child labor (earlier advocated by Alexander Hamilton) and by employer combination to prevent the formation of unions. When such policies bore fruit in the form of profit, the entrepreneur then came into possession of "internally generated" funds that could be used for the expansion of fixed and working capital. Plant (and therefore firm) expansion had already produced units of considerable size, such as William Sellers & Co. in Philadelphia, a machinists' tools manufacturer, perhaps the first in the history of the industry in the United States with 190 "hands employed" (of course, a number of New England textile mills were larger). The average number of wage earners per establishment in the Middle Atlantic region for all manufacturers was then only 10. Having a fairly large establishment in a metal fabricating industry, William Sellers operated with a capital labor ratio of $1,470 per "hand," whereas the invested capital per worker in all manufacturing in his region was only $800.

This cross-sectional comparison also holds for changes through time. The growth in the size of manufacturing plants over the years required the firm's proprietor (or later, manager) to increase fixed capital both per unit of output and per worker during the ensuing decades. This growth in fixed capital explains in large part the demand for investment banking services after 1860. It also, together with the subsequent development of the multiproduct, multiplant firm, to a great extent accounts for the later growing need for cost accounting, including depreciation accounting.

The U.S. Foreign Balance in 1860

Since the eighteenth century American foreign trade had been an important, but probably a declining, activity relative to GNP and to domestic trade. We lack good estimates of GNP before 1840, however, and a rough calculation of the ratio of exports plus imports to GNP suggests only a slight drop in 1860 compared with 1840, approximately 14 percent from about 16 percent. This small change is not surprising when one recalls the rapid growth of cotton exports, together with the fact they constituted about 50 percent of the total. The years approaching the Civil War also brought no break in the characteristic negative balance on merchandise trade and witnessed no change in the average propensity to import, (imports relative to national income), a sharp contrast to developments in the decades following the war. The country's balance of international payments for 1860 is briefly summarized in Table 2.

TABLE 2

U.S. BALANCE OF PAYMENTS, 1860
(millions of current dollars)

Account	Credit	Balance
Merchandise		
Exports	+333.6	
Imports	-367.8	
Trade balance		-34.2
Specie flow (gold & silver)		
Exports	+ 66.5	
Imports	- 8.6	
Specie balance		+57.9
Freight earnings (net)		
Immigrant funds		+18.4
Brought in by immigrants	+ 12.5	
Immigrant remittances	- 4.7	
Immigrant balance		+ 7.8
Tourist balance		-18.5
Payments on international indebtedness (net)		-25.1
U.S. and foreign capital flow (net)		- 6.3

Sources: Douglass C. North, "The United States Balance of Payments, 1790-1860," in NBER, Trends, pp. 573-627 passim. The item on net capital flow is a residual, i.e., is as much a statistical discrepancy item as it is a measure of the elusive magnitude it purports to be. Historical Statistics of the United States, Colonial Times to 1957, estimates this item for 1860 at minus $7 million (p. 565).

It clearly shows the negative balance on the merchandise trade account (the excess of imports over exports), the large gold (and silver) outflow necessary to pay for this discrepancy together with the tourist balance, and the large net service charges (interest payments) of over $25 million to foreigners (mostly British) on net foreign obligations of about $377 million. The implicit average interest rate on the net was therefore over 6 percent. The earnings of American ships carrying cargoes from and to foreign nations, long a noteworthy credit item, were substantial in 1860 and continued to be fairly considerable until the 1880s.

The composition of the merchandise or commodity trade revealed the dominance of farm exports, particularly the heavy reliance on cotton exports to England and France. The latter accounted for 57 percent of total exports in 1860.

In the case of imported merchandise, we know that in our contemporary world the lower the income per capita of a country, the higher the relative importance of fabricated commodities. For example, in the 1950s manufactured consumer goods accounted for over 51 percent of total imports for the lowest per capita income countries and for about 30 percent for the highest. Moreover, the countries with high shares of their labor force in agriculture had the higher average share of manufactured consumer goods imports. [66]

In the United States in 1860 the heavy reliance on the importation of fabricated goods was shown by the fact that finished manufactures alone accounted for almost 50 percent of total merchandise imports, and crude materials for only 11 percent. This latter ratio almost doubled in the next twenty years, even as finished manufactures fell to 30 percent during those same two decades. [67] Trade reliance of the American economy on primary producing countries was clearly increasing, despite the continued trade with Western Europe and the vast natural resource frontier that came under increasing exploitation within the political borders of the nation.

The historical immaturity of the American economy in the international sphere was shown by its debtor status (net borrowings of $6.3 million and the aforementioned service charges), the dominance of crude materials in its exports, the dominance of fabricated products in its imports, and the fact that the most advanced manufacturing country in the world, Great Britain, in 1860, received over half of the exports of the United States and supplied 40 percent of its imports. Great Britain was the largest single "trading partner" of the United States. In contemporary times, the U.S. position of 1860 is occupied by Canada, a less industrialized country than its creditor, the United States; but Canada's relative importance in U.S. trade today is distinctly less important than America's relative importance in Britain's trade in 1860.

Summary

On the eve of the Civil War the United States was a semi-industrial country with a large, relatively unexploited and unsettled frontier. The stage had been set for increasingly large-scale industrialization and urbanization accompanied by a vast expansion of domestic farm output and productivity in the North. A fast-growing rail network, superimposed upon a well-developed system of internal waterways, marked an advanced stage of a transportation revolution that had powerfully contributed during the nineteenth century to the creation of a national economy.

The state and local governments had enormously facilitated economic growth in both the South and the North. Soon the Federal government was to add to its impressive record of territorial aquisition—in itself a large contribution to economic growth—by the creation of a more favorable milieu for capitalistic development through its Civil War legislation and attendant policies. Beyond this, the Federal administrations and Congress during the next two decades or more were committed in general to minimizing regulatory activities, current outlays, indebtedness, and governmental intervention with respect to the distribution of income, i.e., they were advocates of laissez faire. All these minimizing objectives were by no means achieved. But these commitments, plus the Federal government's positive actions in such spheres as public land disposition, the tariff, and hostility to labor organization were widely believed to foster the accumulation of capital and therefore, according to the prevailing ideology, to foster social progress as well.

Life for the underlying masses of the farm and nonfarm working people, including the chattel slaves, was no doubt unduly harsh, burdened with toil, and limited in culture. Although the work week was 66 hours in industry and even higher in agriculture, there seems to have been some time and energy to devote to the development of the personality. Making ends meet narrowed but did not completely suppress the articulation and implementation of the preference for leisure, social intercourse, and cultural amenities. Having perhaps the highest per capita income in the world in the mid-nineteenth century released only part of the human potential of even the free population of wage earners and dirt farmers, but more than in most other countries. The preconditions for a greater release involved a break in the population trend, a substantial rise in productivity, and a drastic shortening of hours on the job, but these preconditions were not to emerge until after the Civil War. Nevertheless, when one compares the American scene with that of Europe, one can understand why Alexis Tocqueville wrote that there was more general enlightenment and more widespread equality in the United States than "in any other country in the world or in any age of which history has preserved the remembrance."

The question of the contribution of economic factors to the causes of the Civil War has never been answered in the sense of the achievement of an overwhelming consensus among historians. Most would agree that the issues touched on above point to genuine sources of interregional economic conflict. In addition, there was the conflict emphasized by Marxists as the primary one, the economic contradiction between a system of free wage labor and a system of chattel slave labor. According to this view, slave labor is incompatible with a predominantly industrial (nonagrarian) capitalist economy. Certainly many people both in the South and the North at that time, all non-Marxists, believed such a proposition to be true; and such belief was all that was necessary to precipitate confrontation. The same was true of many other issues, such as free soil for the West, the northern transcontinental route, the tariff, etc.

But aside from the, in one sense spurious, question of whether these economic conflicts were "real" or "imagined," the achievement of an interpretive consensus among historians has continued to founder on the relative weight to ascribe to each economic factor. This problem cannot be solved here. In addition, the economic conflicts were closely intertwined with political controversy. For example, the Beard-Hacker thesis relies decisively on the developmental role of Federal economic policy, a politico-economic phenomenon. And when the political element is introduced, more floodgates of controversy are opened. For example, in the decades following the war the Federal government's policy of laissez faire meant that it performed only a modest developmental role. Is this consistent with the argument that a close struggle over who would control the power of the central government was the basic issue of the war? Was the Union victory so decisive that everything essential to Northern industrial capital (or financial capital) was accomplished by the war, and thereafter the exercise of state power could subside, leaving most matters to the semiautomatic operation of the private market? It is entirely possible that the postwar history traced in the following chapters will contribute to resolution of some of these questions, just as it may contribute to an understanding of the very long run developmental potential of the antebellum cotton economy. Related to these questions and their resolution is the matter of the long-run effects of the war. A discussion of this, structered around but not necessarily supporting, the Beard-Hacker thesis, is presented in the next chapter.

NOTES

1. U.B. Phillips, "The Central Theme of Southern History," in E. O. Genovese (ed.), *The Slave Economy of the Old South* (Baton Rouge: Louisiana State University Press, 1968), p. 273.
2. By "North." I shall mean the entire non-South, including the Midwest, the Great Plains, and where appropriate the Far West and Southwest.
3. "Slavery and Southern Economic Development: An Hypothesis and Some Evidence," in William N. Parker (ed.), *The Structure of the Cotton Economy of the Antebellum South* (Washington: The Agricultural History Society, 1970), p. 119.
4. Three census regions minus Delaware, District of Columbia, and West Virginia. Definitions of the South vary. A highly selective group of "cotton states" (i.e., South Carolina, Georgia, Alabama, Mississippi, Louisiana, and Texas) would show no decline.
5. U.S. Civil War Centennial Commission, *The United States on the Eve of the Civil War* (Washington: 1963), p. 5.
6. North Carolina, South Carolina, Georgia, Florida, Alabama, Mississippi, Louisiana, Texas, Arkansas, and Tennessee. This grouping is from Alfred H. Conrad and John R. Meyer, *The Economics of Slavery* (Chicago: Aldine, 1964), p. 70, Table 13.
7. Ibid., p. 69.
8. If slaves engaged in cotton production increased approximately 58 percent during this period, then cotton output per slave must have risen substantially, for the production of cotton rose about 175 percent. [See ibid., p. 76, and Marvin W. Towne and Wayne D. Rasmussen, "Farm Gross Product and Gross Investment in the Nineteenth Century," in National Bureau of Economic Research, Conference on Research in Income and Wealth, *Trends in the American Economy in the Nineteenth Century*, Studies in Income and Wealth, v. 24 (Princeton: Princeton University Press, 1960), p. 308. This latter volume will hereafter be referred to as "NBER, *Trends.*"]

9. "First approximation" because, among other things, output per head tells nothing about the *distribution* of that output among persons. Also, total product as calculated excludes external diseconomies and disutilities, as well as positive externalities. (Externalities are the beneficial or harmful effects of some economic transaction on persons who are not directly a party to that transaction.)

10. Alfred H. Conrad and John R. Meyer, "The Economics of Slavery in the Antebellum South," *Journal of Political Economy*, 66 (April 1958), pp. 95-130. Reprinted in their book, *The Economics of Slavery and Other Studies in Econometric History* (Chicago: Aldine, 1964). As to the question of conclusiveness, see note 11.

11. Robert William Fogel and Stanley L. Engerman, *Time on the Cross: The Economics of American Negro Slavery* (Boston: Little, Brown, 1974), p. 248, Table 4. Easterlin's estimates of South Atlantic and East South Central per capita income relatives for 1840, used by Fogel and Engerman, have been adjudged substantially too low in a scholarly paper by Gerald Gunderson ["Southern Ante-bellum Income Reconsidered," *Explorations in Economic History*, 10, no. 2 (Winter 1973), pp. 151-76.] To the extent Gunderson is correct, and if the 1860 Easterlin estimates are allowed to stand, the rate of growth estimates of Southern income per capita has been exaggerated.

12. "The Jolly Institution," review of *Time on the Cross* in *The New York Review of Books* (May 2, 1974), p. 3.

13. Reproduced from *Time on the Cross*, p. 248, Table 4. However, this point reminds us that the Southern advantage was due primarily if not entirely to the high per capita income of, and migration into, Texas.

14. Ibid., pp. 247-55, *passim.*

15. See the readings in Hugh G. J. Aitken (ed.), *Did Slavery Pay?* (Boston: Houghton Mifflin, 1971).

16. "The Economic Impact of the Civil War," in Ralph Andreano (ed.), *The Economic Impact of the American Civil War*, revised ed. (Cambridge, Mass: Schenkman, 1967), p. 193.

17. Richard Easterlin, "Regional Income Trends, 1840-1950," in Seymour Harris (ed.), *American Economic History* (New York: McGraw-Hill, 1961;, p. 528, Table 1.

18. We invoke here the empirical postulate that growth of output can occur without economic development, but that the latter almost always produces output growth.

19. The Southern economy was relatively undiversified (heavily agrarian) but Southern agriculture was, taken in the aggregate, reasonably diversified and, for those times, capital intensive. [See Emory Q. Hawk, *Economic History of the South* (New York: Prentice-Hall, 1934), pp. 265-71 *passim.*]

20. Op. cit., pp. 121, 125. Parker's "North" (our Midwest) is represented in this sample by Ohio, Indiana, Michigan, Wisconsin, and Illinois; his South by Georgia, Alabama, Mississippi, and South Carolina.

21. Cited in Ernest McP. Lancer. Jr., *The Textile Industry in Antebellum South Carolina* (Baton Rouge: Louisiana State University Press, 1969), p. 51.

22. Cited in Harold D. Woodman (ed.), *Slavery and the Southern Economy* (New York: Harcourt, Brace, and World, 1966), pp. 195-6.

23. Nathaniel H. Leff, "Brazilian Economic Development," *Journal of Economic History*, 29 (September 1969), p. 480.

24. "The new Southern nation suffered from incessant quarreling among its political leaders, as Jefferson Davis proved incapable of unifying states that were just ad defiant of his authority as they had been of that in Washington." Elbert

B. Smith, *The Death of Slavery* (Chicago: University of Chicago Press, 1967), p. 177.
25. See George R. Taylor, *The Transportation Revolution* (New York: Rinehart, 1951), pp. 169, 198.
26. *The Farmer's Age: Agriculture 1815-1860* (New York: Holt, Rinehart & Winston, 1960), p. 417. See also U. B. Phillips "Transportation in the Antebellum South," *Quarterly Journal of Economics*, 19 (May 1905); passages cited in Eugene D. Genovese (ed.), *The Slave Economy of the Old South* (Baton Rouge: Louisiana State University Press, 1968), pp. 165-6; and Merl E. Reed, *New Orleans and the Railroads* (Baton Rouge: Louisiana State University Press, 1966, pp. 65, 76-7.
27. Albert Fishlow, "Levels of Nineteenth-Century American Investment in Education," *Journal of Economic History*, 26 (December 1966) p. 420.
28. Mary Jean Bowman and C. Arnold Anderson, "Human Capital and Economic Modernization in Historical Perspective," paper delivered at the Fourth International Congress of Economic History, University of Indiana, September 5-9, 1965, p. 5 (mimeographed).
29. *The Peculiar Institution* (New York: Random House, Vintage Books, 1956), pp. 281-2.
30. NBER, *Trends*, p. 455. Such a high ratio is also viewed skeptically by Albert Rees in his "Comment," ibid., p. 499.
31. Alfred H. Conrad and John R. Meyer, *The Economics of Slavery* (Chicago: Aldine, 1964), p. 57. Option A (2) is selected here to obtain the $45 estimate.
32. Fogel and Engerman, op. cit., pp. 151-2.
33. Lebergott, NBER, *Trends*, p. 453.
34. Ibid., p. 462, Table 2.
35. Stanley Lebergott, *Manpower and Economic Growth* (New York: McGraw-Hill, 1964), p. 528.
36. See Clarence Long, *Wages and Earnings in the United States 1860-1890* (National Bureau of Economic Research; Princeton University Press, 1960), p. 41 Long discusses two famous government documents on the wage subject, the Aldrich Report (1893) and the Weeks Report (1880).
37. H. J. Habakkuk, *American and British Technology in the 19th Century* (Cambridge, Eng.: Cambridge University Press, 1962), esp. p. 11, n. 1.
38. Cited in George R. Taylor, *The Transportation Revolution, 1815-1860* (New York and Toronto: Rinehart & Company, 1951), p. 296.
39. Fogel and Engerman, op. cit., pp. 196, 208.
40. Cited in William A. Sullivan, "The Industrial Revolution and the Factory Operative in Pennsylvania," Harry N. Scheiber (ed.), *United States Economic History* (New York: Knopf, 1964), p. 213.
41. Harold Somers, "The Performance of the American Economy: 1789-1865," in Harold Williamson (ed.), *Growth of the American Economy*, second ed. (Englewood Cliffs, N. J.: Prentice-Hall, 1964), p. 331.
42. Cited in Stampp, op. cit., p. 319.
43. U.S. Civil War Centennial Commission, *The United States on the Eve of the Civil War* (Washington, D.C.: Government Printing Office, 1963), pp. 15, 19. A cholera epidemic had inflated the 1850 totals, however.
44. Fogel and Engerman, op. cit., pp. 123, 126, 154.
45. Ibid., p. 124.
46. Stampp, op. cit., pp. 301, 304.
47. Taylor, op. cit., pp. 391-2.
48. "The Causes of the Civil War," in H. H. Quint et al. (eds.), *Main Problems in American History*, v. 1 (Homewood, Illinois: The Dorsey Press, revised 1968), p. 409.

49. Charles A Beard and Mary R. Beard, *The Rise of American Civilization* (New York: Macmillan, 1946), v. II, p. 258. For a statement of the general thesis, see ibid., pp. 105ff.

50. On the Southern opposition to a homestead bill, see Walter P. Webb, *The Great Plains* (New York: Grosset and Dunlap, no date, paper), p. 406.

51. A point is also made of the Contract Labor Law of 1864 admitting immigrants under conditions of limited indenture. Its quantitative significance is belittled by most historians, however.

52. Fred A. Shannon, *The Farmer's Last Frontier* (New York: Farrar and Rinehart, 1945), p. 51.

53. Albert Fishlow's estimate for 1858 is 29,920 miles for the United States ["Productivity and Technological Change in the Railroad Sector, 1840-1910," in National Bureau of Economic Research, Conference on Research in Income and Wealth, *Output, Employment, and Productivity in the United States After 1800*, Studies in Income and Wealth, v. 30 (New York: Columbia University Press, 1966), p. 596], close to George R. Taylor's 30,636 for 1860 (op. cit., p. 79).

54. For the South the figure was 12.4 miles.

55. For example, in 1858, $21 million worth of exports left Chicago by water and $60 million by rail, and New York railroads carried more pork, beef, wool, cattle, hides, horses, and whiskey, as well as "merchandise and manufactured goods" than did the New York canals. [Alfred Chandler, Jr., "Entrepreneurial Opportunity in Nineteenth Century America," *Explorations in Entrepreneurial History*, Second Series, v. 1, no. 1 (Fall 1963), p. 121, n. 19.]

56. U.S. Civil War Centennial Commission, op. cit., p. 39.

57. Paul Studenski and Herman Krooss, *Financial History of the United States* (New York: McGraw-Hill, 1963), p. 121.

58. *Briscoe v. the Bank of the Commonwealth of Kentucky*, 1837.

59. "Composition of the Money Stock Prior to the Civil War," *Journal of Money, Credit and Banking*, 3 (February 1971), pp. 84-101.

60. The GNP estimate is from Robert Gallman, "Gross National Product in the United States, 1834-1909," in *Output, Employment and Productivity in the United States After 1800*, op. cit., p. 26.

61. The currency/income ratio (currency defined as the sum of national bank notes, U.S. notes, silver certificates, and gold certificates) was .096 in 1870, .068 in 1880, and .075 in 1890.

62. This term is only approximately accurate when used synonymously with "business enterpriser." As Stuart Bruchey has commented, "This quality [of entrepreneurship] is displayed not only by the private businessman in search of cost-savings via administrative or technological innovation but also by the government administrator seeking ways of widening the tax base for needed public improvements, by the kind of workers found by Nasymth and other students of American manufacturing methods, and by the kinds of communities whose insistent demands prodded governments into providing social overhead capital necessary to growth. It is a quality of alertness to the possibility of material betterment, and it inheres or fails to inhere in the value system of a culture, although economic change may pave the way for it." *Roots of American Economic Growth 1607-1861* (New York: Harper and Row, 1963), pp. 208-9.

63. Lance Davis contends that "significant barriers to domestic East-West capital flows continued to exist" through the 1850s. "Capital Immobilities and Finance Capitalism," *Explorations in Entrepreneurial History* (Fall 1963), p. 91.

64. The investment banking firm of Jay Cooke and Company was a descendent of these firms. See N. S. B. Gras, *Business and Capitalism* (New York: F. S. Crofts and Company, 1947), p. 221-2.

65. Total consumption of fuels in 1860, estimated in trillions of British thermal units was: bituminous coal, 243; anthracite coal, 275; crude oil, 3; fuel wood, 2,641.
66. See Nassau A. Adams, "Import Structure and Economic Growth," *Economic Development and Cultural Change*, 15 (January 1967), p. 145.
67. Finished manufactures would typically thereafter fluctuate around one-fourth of total imports. An economy with a high income per capita always imports a significant amount of finished manufactures. Advanced industrial economies are good customers of one another.

[2]

Economic change in the civil war period

Territorial expansion and its economic concomitants—control over additional resources and the creation of new markets—had characterized the policy of the Federal government from the time of independence. Simon Kuznets has accurately if somewhat euphemistically called this "extending the land base of the original sovereignty." The Civil War involved the same policy from the standpoint of those who then controlled the Federal government, for it assured that the Southern territory would not be alienated from the political borders that encompassed the U.S. economy. Minimizing potentially lost resources has the same impact for the economy as maximizing acquired or economically controlled resources.

Since the achievement of this goal by the North, given the secessionist policy of the South, involved war, there was a cost in human and material terms. Besides the 635,000 deaths, the millions of wounded and disabled, and the great suffering among the civilian population, the Civil War entailed the destruction of much physical wealth, and lowered the growth rate of output for the economy as a whole. Had the U.S. economy grown from 1860 to 1870 as fast as it had grown from 1840 to 1860, total commodity output in 1870 would have been $4,160 million instead of the actual $3,270 million (in 1879 prices) estimated by Gallman.

Professor Kuznets has pointed out that in addition to the destruction of human lives and goods by war, there is typically an interruption of the advance of technological knowledge in civilian activities. During the Civil War, with some exceptions in munitions and shipbuilding, there was not much technological advance in war industries either. Nevertheless, in the North technological advance did not cease altogether, as is attested to by developments in canning and preserving, machine tools and the application of the micrometer, the meat-packing industry, machine-made watches, clothing manufacture, news media, and agricultural machinery.

The War and Southern Production

The greater part of the retardation in output growth during the Civil War was suffered by the South. Indeed, the South and the North moved in opposite directions. The South suffered an absolute drop in total commodity output while the North experienced a moderate absolute increase, at least for the whole decade, as seen in Table 3. This shows that Southern agricultural production in 1870 was still 25 percent below its prewar level. Manufacturing, however, recovered with surprising vigor in the South, and fared better than the data of Table 3, which includes mining, might suggest. Manufacturing employment grew from 111,000 in 1860 to 144,000 in 1870, and deflated value of products was probably only moderately below the 1860 total, i.e., labor productivity in Southern manufacturing declined.

Nevertheless, the overwhelming importance of agriculture assured, in contrast to the North, a drastic fall in Southern regional product over the decade of the sixties. Eugene Lerner has calculated flows of important farm products and stocks of agricultural capital and capacity in the eleven seceding states. Table 4 reproduces some of Lerner's farm output data, calculated as ratios to 1859 output, with the North shown in contrast. In general, it took a decade and a half for the South to reach the prewar level in cotton and a few other crops, but in most crops this goal had not been achieved by the end of the seventies. The record for livestock, shown in Table 5, is slightly better. Expansion in the seventies brought stocks almost up to, or in several important cases moderately above, the 1860 total. Oxen at this time were being replaced by mules and horses.

TABLE 3

COMMODITY OUTPUTS BY REGION, 1860-1880
(millions of 1879 dollars)

Census year	North			South		
	Total	Agriculture	Manufacturing and mining	Total	Agriculture	Manufacturing and mining
1860	$1,674	$ 853	$ 821	$710	$639	$ 71
1870	2,337	1,246	1,091	534	477	57
1880	3,876	1,861	2,015	838	738	100

Source: Stanley Engerman "Economic Impact of the Civil War," *Explorations in Entrepreneurial History*, 3 (Spring 1966), p. 180.

The two tables show dramatically the acceleration in the wealth and in production differentials between Southern and Northern agriculture that began to develop during the war. Although the South began to close the gap in many cases during the seventies, it still lagged far behind the North in a number of instances that could not be justified by any regional specialization arguments, e.g., in the case of hay, potatoes, corn, tobacco, horses, mules, milch cows, and swine.

From the standpoint of Southern regional economic development, however, postwar rehabilitation was far enough along by 1880 to permit the judgment that whatever indigenous growth forces existed could now operate without the severe constraints inherited from the war years. And, too, any failures in development performance subsequent to 1880 could not be attributed in any important way to wartime calamities. Indeed, the interpretation to be stressed in what follows is that the character of the South's economic development after Reconstruction was shaped to a very important extent by the character of its antebellum economy.

The War Years in the South

Because the Civil War was largely fought by foot soldiers with elementary military hardware, it was possible for the South to fight

TABLE 4

AVERAGE CROP OUTPUTS BY REGION, 1859-1880

Crop and region	Output in 1859 (millions)	Ratio of 1866-1870 to 1859	Ratio of 1876-1880 to 1859
Cotton			
South	2,373 lb.	51.1%	100.9%
Non-South			
Tame hay			
South	1.045 ton	36.9	78.2
Non-South	18.038 ton	124.7	168.1
Potatoes			
South	6.600 bu.	75.3	108.4
Non-South	104.500 bu.	107.0	133.6
Corn			
South	283 bu.	66.4	103.7
Non-South	556 bu.	122.7	235.6
Wheat			
South	31 bu.	58.3	90.0
Non-South	142 bu.	152.3	278.6
Rye			
South	2.201 bu.	54.5	44.7
Non-South	18.900 bu.	86.8	102.8
Buckwheat			
South	0.572 bu.	36.5	38.4
Non-South	17.000 bu.	61.4	64.8
Tobacco			
South	204 lb.	43.8	65.2
Non-South	231 lb.	89.0	157.8

Source: Eugene M. Lerner, "Southern Output and Agricultural Income, 1860-1880," *Agricultural History*, 33 (July 1959), p. 117-25. Reprinted in Ralph Andreano (ed.), *The Economic Impact of the American Civil War*, second ed. (Cambridge, Mass.: Schenkman Publishing Co., 1967), pp. 118-19, table III.

on by performing, in a more or less efficient fashion, what today would be considered fairly simple logistical tasks of equipping, provisioning, and transporting troops, and providing minimum medical and hospital care. The civilian population also had to be pro-

TABLE 5

SOUTHERN[1] AGRICULTURAL CAPITAL,
1860-1880
(thousands)

	South	South/U.S.	Ratio to 1860	South	South/U.S.	Ratio to 1860
	Horses			Mules		
1860	1,743.8	27.1%	100.0%	822.7	71.5	100.0%
1870	1,246.2	17.4	71.5	613.5	54.5	74.6
1880	2,083.0	20.1	119.4	1,044.8	57.6	127.0
	Milch cows			Working oxen		
1860	2,705.7	31.5	100.0%	853.6	37.8	100.0%
1870	1,852.3	20.7	68.4	507.6	38.4	59.5
1880	2,817.9	22.6	104.1	517.6	52.0	60.6
	Swine			Other cattle		
1860	15,562.7	46.4	100.0%	7,554.0	57.1	100.0%
1870	10,122.6	40.2	65.0	3,623.8	26.7	48.0
1880	13,509.9	28.3	86.8	7,264.4	32.3	96.2
	Acres of farms			Improved acres		
1860	200,476.3	49.2	100.0%	56,832.1	34.8	100.0%
1870	156,791.1	38.5	78.2	46,987.1	24.8	82.7
1880	197,002.4	36.7	98.3	67,350.6	23.6	118.5
	Values of farms			Value of farm implements		
1860	$1,850,708.5	27.8	100.0%	$82,971.4	33.7	100.0%
1870	977,142.3	10.5	52.8	45,145.3	13.4	54.4
1880	1,234,958.4	12.1	66.7	57,637.4	14.1	69.5
	Value of livestock					
1860	$ 362,163.1	33.2	100.0%			
1870	279,685.0	18.3	77.2			
1880	276,708.1	18.6	76.4			

[1]The South is defined as the eleven states that seceded from the Union:
N.C., S.C., Ga., Fla., Ala., La., Miss., Tex., Va., Tenn., Ark.

Source; Tenth Census of the United States. Cited by Lerner, *op. cit.*, p. 111.

visioned, however, and a region that before 1860 depended partly on the West for foodstuffs and on the Northeast and abroad for clothing and many other manufactured products faced severe shortages. The civilian population suffered material declines in consumption because of the drastic reduction in imports, and the diversion of much of the best human resources to the military (including almost all of the white manpower of military age), the consequent reduction in civilian farm output, intraregional transportation difficulties, and the widespread reversion to inefficient household production of fabricated goods on a greater scale than existed even under prewar conditions.

The blockage by the Union navy seriously reduced the volume of imports into the South from England and France. The consequent scarcity of imported goods, exacerbated by the deterioration of the already poor Southern railroads that left goods piled up in the seaports while the hinterland suffered, contributed to inflation and dissatisfaction by the poor farmers and the urban workers against the wealthier businessmen and the planters. The resulting drop in morale was important to the final collapse of the South.

The squeeze on the civilian sector associated with the diversion of productive factors and output to the military was engineered chiefly by loans and inflationary infusions of paper money rather than by taxation. This was generally true of the states as well as the Confederate government. Out of the total of $2.3 billion made available to the Confederate Treasury between February 1861 and October 1864, about $1.4 billion was in the form of Treasury notes (paper money), $700 million in bonds and certificates, and only $126 million in taxes, mostly property taxes. The government instituted a progressive income tax that brought in small amounts, as well as taxes on real estate, slaves, and personal property. In the absence of price controls, together with the curtailment of civilian production and imports, prices rose after 1861 and particularly after 1863. Thus the price mechanism, rather than direct exaction and taxation, provided the chief vehicle for transfer of output from the civilian to the military sector.

Heavy reliance on inflation stimulated the withholding and concealment of goods by people. The small population of wage earners also bore a particular burden by virtue of the lag of money wage rates behind the cost of living. Moreover, without civilian sector rationing, the poor bore a differentially harsh share of the added burdens of wartime hunger, malnutrition, disease, destitution, and untimely death.

The War and Northern Production

In the North total production during the war years expanded slightly if at all, but foreign trade was sustained at a level remarkably high in view of the elimination of cotton exports.

We have no satisfactory measures of aggregate Northern production during the war years, and must rely upon data pertaining to specific industries. But this can become a rather unrewarding game. Historians once believed 1861-1865 were "boom" years in the North, but Thomas Cochran effectively exposed that error by bringing together a number of statistical series in important non-farm activities such as pig iron production, coal output, railroad and other civilian construction, and bank loans. It is true Cochran often relied on total U.S. aggregates and stretched out his data to prewar and postwar decades. But available data seem to show that the Civil War years were not years of rapidly rising nonfarm production. Stephen Salsbury's rebuttal of Cochran is stronger in its long-run emphasis than it is with respect to his brief statistical bout regarding the significance of the years of rapid expansion, 1865 to 1875.[1] It is not implausible that wartime disorganization, loss of civilian manpower, and waste hurt the nonfarm sector for a few years and temporarily dampened the forces of long-run development therein. For example, Frickey's index of manufacturing production on an 1899 base of 100 stood at 16 in 1861, rose to only 18 in 1864, and then dropped to 17 in 1865.

Apparently this dampening effect also operated in the Northern farm sector, where the drain of manpower cut overall output growth despite noteworthy expansion in some areas, particularly in the West. Some students of wartime farming believe, however, that the manpower shortage stimulated farm mechanization, and the statistics of farm machinery production bear this out. The increased use of equipment also hastened the changeover from the use of human muscle and oxen to the use of horses.

The volume of foreign trade for the revelent years, estimated on a "gold specie value" basis that makes the war years comparable with the prewar, is shown in Table 6. By comparison with the five years preceding the Civil War it can be seen that U.S. exports (essentially exports for the years after 1861) held up remarkably well. This can be appreciated when it is noted that exports of unmanufactured cotton averaged $149 million in the five years preceding the war, and if this figure were to be added to the export totals dur-

TABLE 6

U.S. BALANCE OF TRADE
(millions of dollars)

Year[1]	Exports[2]	Imports	Balance
1856	281	323	- 42
1857	294	362	- 68
1858	272	274	- 2
1859	293	345	- 52
1860	334	368	- 34
1861	230	298	- 68
1862	209	195	+ 14
1863	222	251	- 29
1864	182	326	-144
1865	191	246	- 55

[1]1856-1860 are fiscal years, 1861-1865 calendar years.

[2]Exports for 1861-1865 include sale of ships.

Source: For 1856-1860, Douglass North, "The United States Balance of Payments, 1790-1860," in NBER, *Trends*, p. 605. For 1861-1865, Matthew Simon, "The United States Balance of Payments, 1861-1900," in ibid., p. 699. Because the North went off the domestic specie standard at the end of December 1861 and adopted the "greenback standard" of inconvertible paper, for historical comparisons Simon converted the estimates from currency terms to gold equivalents (see ibid., p. 631).

ing the years 1861-1865 the result would compare favorably with the export totals for the five representative prewar years.

On the import side, it will be seen that imports fell short of the totals for 1856-1860, but only in amounts that could plausibly be explained by the absence of the South's import demand. Hence, the successful prosecution of the war by the North did not require an inordinate reliance on foreign supplies. The negative trade balance in four of the five years is in keeping with the general historical pattern into which the war years fit. In the five years before the war the country exported $256 million in specie, and from 1861 through 1865 the North lost $205 million in specie.

One factor that tended to sustain Northern wartime exports, although its effect was only moderate, was the increase of wheat exports. British overseas supplies from non-U.S. sources dropped off, and U.S. farmers filled the gap. These exports averaged about $40 million per year between 1861 and 1864. Some historians believe that the failure of the South to elicit British intervention on its side partly is because these wheat exports offset Southern cotton as a diplomatic weapon with the English.

Another factor favorable to exports and adverse to imports was the premium on gold, which rose faster after 1861 than did wholesale prices, according to Wesley Mitchell. This is not easily supported by Table 6, however, until 1865.

Farm exports, which did much to help win the war for the North, were immeasurably aided by the extensive rail network. This network was, of course, also generally strategic for the movement of civilian and military goods and people during those critical years. As one writer has expressed it:

> More than two thirds of the 1861 mileage and an even greater proportion of railroad transportation capacity lay in the states which adhered to the Union. Invasion soon reduced further even the small percentage of the railroad mileage in Confederate hands. It is not too much to say that relative railroad strength was a decisive factor in the "first railroad war". . . .
>
> More important than . . . spectacular shifts of large army units from one strategic field to another was the part played by the railroads in the day by day movement of men, food, ammunition, material and supplies from distant sources to the combat forces. Movements of this sort reached a climax in General Sherman's campaign for the capture of Atlanta in the summer of 1864, when his army of 100,000 men and 35,000 animals was kept supplied and in fighting trim by a single-track railroad extending nearly 500 miles from its base on the Ohio River at Louisville.[2]

Inflation in the North

Like the South, the North fought the war without general price control or rationing, policies that were possible but were never under public discussion. Northern GNP in current dollars in 1860 must have been about 70 percent of U.S. GNP of $4.17 billion, or about $2.92 billion. Total Federal government expenditures in the course of the war, as shown by Table 7, were about $3.42 billion. Since aggregate taxes and miscellaneous receipts were about $805 million, it can be seen that about three-fourths of Federal expenditures were financed by loans and new money, of which the fiat paper "greenbacks" were to become the most famous. Loans were predominant, however. Only one-fourth to one-fifth of expenditures were financed by taxes, suggesting that the people were reluctant during the early years to bear the burden of the war, although of course they had to in real terms. But this percentage was greater than in any previous war in American national history.

TABLE 7

CIVIL WAR PUBLIC FINANCING IN THE NORTH,
1861-1865
(millions of dollars)

Account	Subtotal	Total
Total Federal government expenditures		3,418
Total Federal government receipts		
Customs	345	
Income tax (1863-1865)	84	
Excise taxes (1863-1865)	273	
Sale of public lands	3	
Subtotal	705	
Other receipts	100	
Total	805	
		805
Aggregate wartime deficit		2,613
Gross debt, end of 1865		2,681
Interest-bearing debt		2,218
Currency		
Demand notes issued	60	
Legal tender notes (including greenbacks), maximum outstanding at any one time[1]	447	
Total	507	

[1]Total issues were $915 million.
Source: Paul Studenski and Herman Krooss, *Financial History of the United States*, second ed. (New York: McGraw-Hill, 1963), pp. 152, 155.

The income tax was passed by Congress, remarkably enough, as early as August 1861. Although at first it raised little revenue, this radical innovation in taxation is of considerable historical interest because it reveals that in times of war long-run patterns in public finance are often anticipated or instituted. The Internal Revenue Act of July 1, 1862 has been characterized by Sidney Ratner as "a momentous legislative act in its consequences and a tremendous extension of the revenue system."[3] It was the first income tax measure ever put into operation by the Federal government; it embodied the progressive principle, and it also instituted an inheritance tax, "the first actual precedent for later federal legislation along this line."[4] The income tax portion of the act even inaugurated the principle of tapping revenue at the source, i.e., withholding. The 1861 rate was initially a flat 3 percent, but *applied only to incomes over $800*. Rates were made more progressive in the Act of 1862 and again in 1864.

In these ways resources were diverted from the contracting (or nonexpanding) civilian sector in the North. The loans were partly monetized, that is, large banks accepted the government debt paper and gave the Treasury either bank currency or deposit credits against which the Treasury could write checks, and those government checks were just like money, as is the case today. Thus there was a large increase in the money stock above the 1859 level of about $700 million.[5] Greenbacks alone by 1864 totaled $415 million, well over half the total money stock of 1859. The total stock of currency "outside the Treasury and in circulation" increased during the war years from $484 million to $1.1 billion, so that the total money stock—assuming bank deposits rose in approximate proportion—also about doubled.

Hence, with the prevailing high level of employment and nearly full utilization of capacity, making it impossible to raise total production in the short run, the classical setting for price inflation due to "too much money chasing too few goods" was explosively present. Increases in the quantity of money were thus likely to bring about almost proportionate increases in general prices—an effect that could be accentuated if the public decided to use its money holdings at a faster rate, that is, increase the velocity of monetary circulation. However, it appears that the public was surprisingly constrained regarding its velocity behavior because general prices rose only in rough proportion to the rise in the money supply. The Warren and Pearson wholesale price index (1910-1914 average of

100), for example, increased from 89 in 1861 to 193 in 1864, then slipped back moderately to 185 in 1865. The consumer price index (Hoover) on an 1860 base of 100 rose from 101 in 1861 to 175 in 1865. Thereafter began the long, secular price decline lasting until 1896.

The Union government therefore "taxed by inflation" more than by taxation proper. By this is meant the government achieved command over the resources it needed to prosecute the war directly (issuing new money) and indirectly (converting its debt paper into money[6]) by augmenting the money supply under conditions that could only generate an overall price rise. This was a time-honored technique designed to circumvent the public's resistance to losing its command over goods through increased taxes.

Some tax increases clearly contributed to inflation. For example, increases in customs duties beginning with the Morrill tariff of 1861 and in domestic excises beginning in 1862 "raised the price of all goods and services relative to factor incomes."[7] Of course such price rises, due to the incorporation of the additional taxes in the costs of goods, was possible only because increases in the money supply "validated" those price rises by bolstering market demand for such goods.

So far as the increase in domestic excises and customs is concerned, the demand for most manufactured items other than food was price-elastic. That is to say, the price rises induced by the imposition of such indirect business taxes resulted in substantial decreases in the quantity demanded. This relationship may partially explain the apparent drop in total manufactures during the war years. This drop is not apparent in the decadal record shown in Table 3, but the rise is notably modest. Using state censuses in New York and Massachusetts for 1865, Stanley Engerman has estimated that manufacturing output was considerably smaller in 1865 than it was in 1860. Military demand by the nonmechanized Northern armies was apparently not sufficient to offset the decline in civilian purchases of manufactured commodities.

Wesley C. Mitchell established long ago that wage earners suffered a fall in real wages (paper wages per hour or per day divided by consumer prices) during the Civil War. Mitchell declared:

The data indicated that the advance of retail prices in 1861 put nearly nine-tenths of the wage-earners for whom we have data in a worse position than they had held in 1860. In 1862 the situation became a trifle worse and it did not materially improve until 1866. . . .the period of advancing prices must have forced painful economies upon the vast majority of workmen's families. The low level of relative real wages in 1865 explains why money wages should have continued to advance after the end of the war.[8]

A comparison of E. D. Hoover's consumer price index and Mitchell's index on money wage rates (in January) in the East for skilled craftsmen shows the following:[9]

Year	Prices	Wages	Real Wages
1861	101	100	100
1862	113	100	89
1863	139	105	76
1864	176	120	68
1865	175	150	85

Mitchell attributed the lag in money wages behind prices to the weak individual bargaining position of the workers, customary ideas about a fair wage for a job that weakened the wage earner's aggression and strengthened the employer's resistance, and above average hours that tended to sustain weekly or monthly wages. [10] Kessel and Alchian, however, have argued that the implicit corollary shift to profits in Mitchell's interpretation is weakened by the rising excises and import duties that "operated to widen whatever divergence existed between the value of final output and the sum of payments to the co-operating agents of production." This means that some of the fall in real wages Mitchell observed resulted from customs duties and excises and would have taken place "whether or not inflation occurred during the Civil War." Aside from the implication here that inflated profits were less of a culprit, [11] Kessel and Alchian draw the more dramatic conclusion that

if turnover taxes or higher tariffs are regarded as the alternatives to taxing through inflation, the Civil War inflation kept the real wages measured by Mitchell from falling more than they in fact did. Therefore, a rationale exists for a conclusion that is the converse of Mitchell's—were it not for the inflation he would have found that real wages would have fallen more than they did.[12]

In any case, there is no disagreement that real wages did fall and labor suffered a decrease in its real income. Farmers probably sacrificed less than workers, and businessmen as a group probably did almost as well or better, in a material sense, than in peacetime.

Long Run Effects of the War

It was noted earlier that according to historians such as Beard and Hacker the Civil War was a catalyst of capitalist development. Although this thesis is now in disrepute, the matters dealt with in connection with the controversy over it are relevant to any treatment of U.S. economic evolution in the nineteenth century. In particular, the thesis placed a heavy reliance on (1) the developmental role of government, especially the Federal government, and (2) the general political climate surrounding the market system.

Both of these forces come into focus in the Civil War legislative packet put together by the Northern Congress. Taken as a whole, it is a rather impressive packet, and one that certainly would not have received much support from Southerners had they been present. Prominent candidates for inclusion in this package are: the highly protective Morrill tariffs of 1862 and 1864; the Homestead Act of 1862 granting 160 acres of public land free to any family head after five years' residence or cultivation; the Pacific Railway Act of 1862, liberalized in 1864, authorizing a transcontinental railroad along a northern route; and the National Bank Acts of February 1863 and June 1864, establishing a system of federally chartered banks with a currency secured by federal bonds. Other less significant developmental legislation included the transfer of the Department of Agriculture from the Patent Office to independent status in 1862, the Morrill Agricultural Land Grant Act of 1862 encouraging the establishment of colleges devoted to education in "agriculture and the mechanic arts," and the Immigration Act of July 4, 1864, authorizing the importation of contract labor as a means of meeting the labor shortage created by the military drain upon manpower.

The Morrill tariffs are an example of the establishment of a long run pattern, in this case the reversal of a protracted prewar downward trend in rates, and fixation of new rates at a persistently high level, in the name of wartime exigency. F. W. Taussig once incisively declared that in both 1862 and 1864, "three causes were at work: . . . the urgent need for revenue for the war; . . . the wish to offset the internal taxes imposed on domestic producers; and finally, the protectionist leaning of those who managed our financial legislation." [13] The average rates on dutiable commodities that were taxed mainly by specific duties on the weight or quantity of various commodities rather than by *ad valorem* duties, were raised from the

average level of the 1857 Tariff Act of about 20 percent to 37 percent in 1862 and to 48 percent in 1864! These tariffs make a nice case
study in ideological bias: domestic excise taxes increased to raise
wartime revenue, which then provided the ostensible rationale for
protectionist measures advanced as a fair and necessary offset to
the excises! The tariffs were not reduced or abolished after the Civil
War except briefly in 1872-1874, whereas many of the excises and
the income tax were.

The wartime results of these tariffs suggest that the revenue
goals were served as well as, perhaps, the protective ones. Average annual duties "calculated" were $72 million during 1862-1865,
whereas they had been $46 million during the preceding four years,
which had been years of higher average value of total imports. The
protective aspect is more elusive. The average of the ratio of the
total value of dutiable imports to free imports rose from 3.5 during
1858-1861 to 4.8 during 1862-1865. The wartime drop in imports
could be viewed as more than might be expected in view of the elimination of Southern imports. However, one might also plausibly
hypothesize that in view of the rapidly rising domestic prices beginning in 1862 foreign goods would be in greater demand, and it
could be that the new tariffs prevented this effect from material-
izing.

From the long-run standpoint that counted was the fact that an
abiding protective rate structure was reestablished. The prewar
downward trend had carried the ratio of duties collected to dutiable imports to a low of 19 percent in 1861; beginning in 1865 and
continuing until World War I this rate fell below 40 percent only
twice, and in general ran well over 40 percent. Today fewer people
than previously doubt that such protection contributed to expansion of the industries affected and helped domestic producers to
substitute their commodities for imports in the home market (import substitution). But the questions of (1) how much they were
helped and (2) how much this help contributed to total growth of
GNP have not yet been comprehensively analyzed. Besides, the infant industry argument for tariffs is debatable, and full consideration needs to be given to the free trade argument denying that in-
terferences with comparative advantage could rise the rate of
growth above that which would have obtained without high tariffs.
And in the short run the consumer faced a regressive tax on imported goods and higher prices on both domestic and imported articles.
Of course, the propertied groups as high savers would look with

favor upon such a state of affairs. The effect of high protection on the business atmosphere was in all likelihood favorable.

Much the same may be said for the Homestead Act. This was discussed briefly in the preceding chapter. At this juncture it is appropriate to add only that free land undoubtedly contributed to the expansionist psychology of the post-Civil War decades. As a policy, free land represented a dramatic liberalization of a prewar trend in public land policy. It is noteworthy that the curve of final homestead entries in acreage terms continued to rise every decade to its peak of 10 million acres in 1913. The cumulative acreage total of final homestead entries between 1870 and 1910 approached one-fourth of the total increase of land in farms during that period.

The Pacific Railway Act was the largest and most concentrated Federal land grant for transport. From 1823 to the time of passage of this act the Federal government had granted about 35 million acres to aid transport construction. Practically all of this was in the more populated East and South. Congress granted about three times this total between 1863 and 1871, but this time practically all of the land was in the sparsely populated Far West. Although most narrative historians have regarded these grants as momentous, some quantitative economic historians argue that on the test of aggregative effects the transcontinental railroads by themselves, even in the absence of the Panama Canal which became operative in 1914, were of small importance. Robert Fogel has estimated that the increase in national income due to the productivity of labor and capital on the Union Pacific Railroad lands (the UP was a major land recipient), as of 1880 was some $16 million, i.e., 2 percent of the $9 billion net national product of that year. It is revelant to note that the population growth of the Pacific states greatly exceeded that of the rest of the country *before* the advent of a transcontinental railroad, as it also did afterwards.

The National Bank Act of February 1863 was revised in June 1864, together with the ultimately prohibitive taxes imposed on state bank notes in 1864 and 1866, established a nationwide banking system and a national bank currency limited to an amount no greater than $300 million. These national bank notes, along with the inconvertible greenbacks (U.S. notes) provided the chief paper currency of the nation until the emergence of the silver certificate in the early 1880s. The greenback issue after 1866 remained under $400 million, but the currency volume, together with its geographical distribution, in the growing, still heavily agrarian, economy of the later nineteenth century became a most controversial issue.

Secretary of the Treasury Salmon P. Chase, antislavery Whig, Free Soiler, Democrat, and Republican who at different times believed in states rights, hard money, wartime inconvertible paper, and free soil, proposed a national banking system in his annual report in 1861. His partiality toward a national currency had been revealed in his inaugural address as governor of Ohio in 1856. The wartime need of the Treasury to market its bonds was combined with the idea of a bond-backed national currency in Chase's proposal to set up a national banking system. After the passage of the National Bank Acts of February 1863 and June 1864, the system hobbled along as a partial substitute for a central banking system until the passage of the Federal Reserve Act in December 1913.

Although many prominent people in some of the Western states found the idea of a uniform national currency preferable to the welter of state bank notes, most bankers in the East, where checks and drafts had long superseded currency in importance, seem to have opposed it. Many political, social, and economic cross-currents flowed together around the issue of a national banking system. Many feared a central government monopoly. Owners of state banks feared loss of business and profits. The New York Clearing House banks, despite the fact the proposed law was based on the principles of the free banking system of New York, regarded a bond-secured note issue as government-sponsored wildcatting. The New York *Journal of Commerce* in the January 20, 1863 issue belittled the magnitude of the potential note issue under the proposed system.

Nevertheless, the public became alarmed by the sudden jump in state bank notes during 1862 as their managers attempted to cash in on the wartime premium on gold by using greenbacks as reserves. This concern apparently was sufficient to compound the pressures operating on behalf of the proposal and to swing Congress in that direction. Congressman Samuel Hooper (Rep., Mass.), among others, in a speech in the House on January 19, 1863, added the argument that such a system would provide a much-needed market for "United States stocks . . . at this time when the necessities of the public service require so large an amount of bonds to be issued."

It is the judgment of many students of the subject that the first or second National Banking Act would not have been passed in the absence of the war. As one authority has put it, "Congress . . . was neither anxious to legislate on banking nor conscious of the full significance of their action when they did legislate."[14] It is highly probable, however, that the exigencies of wartime precipitated a move that otherwise would not have been delayed for long—assuming Southern secession and the removal of Southern influence in the Congress. The degree of acceptance is attested to in part by the increase in the number of national banks from 66 in the first year of the act to 1,294 in 1865.

Customs duties and interest on Federal securities continued to be paid in gold, although the country (except for California) suspended the domestic specie standard at the end of 1861, and the National Banking System inaugurated a period of inconvertible money lasting until the resumption of specie payments in 1879. The "free" banking principle in the Act permitted anyone to establish a bank if the requirements were met: minimum capital (from $50,000 in smaller places of less than 3,000 population to $200,000 in communities of over 50,000), payment of at least 50 percent of subscribed capital, double liability on the part of the stockholders in case of bank failure, "deposit" of Federal securities (U.S. government bonds) with the Comptroller of Currency amounting to at least one-third of the bank's capital, etc. To protect their depositors, National banks held their own cash-in-bank reserves, in lawful money (specie, specie certificates, or greenbacks) equal to 25 percent, all in cash, in big, central reserve cities, 25 percent in medium-sized reserve cities of which one-half could be deposits in New York City banks, and 15 percent in country banks, against their "outstanding notes of circulation and deposits." Regulation and bank examination was much stricter than that practiced by the states with regard to state banks. *National banks could not make loans on mortgages and could not operate savings departments.* No wonder many of them arranged to set up state banks as "dancing partners"!

The individual bank was "entitled" to receive from the Comptroller national bank notes "in bank" equal to 90 percent of the par or market value of the government bonds "pledged," and these could be put into circulation after appropriate authorization and identification by bank management. They were also subject to a tax of 1 percent. It will be noted that banks had to buy a minimum of $30,000 of government bonds, thus assuring the Treasury a needed market. The financial magic involved in creating new currency may be described in terms of the "T" accounts of the Comptroller of the Currency and any new national bank (all other balance sheet items ignored):

Comptroller of Currency		National bank	
Nat. bank notes $ 90	Bonds $100	Bonds $100	Nat. bank notes $90
Lawful money 10		Lawful money -10	
$100	$100	$ 90	$90

The Treasury could then spend the currency, and it would thus find its way into the hands of the public and the banks.

A continuing struggle took place in the years after 1863 over the regional distribution of the meager total of approximately $300 million of these national bank notes and of the only moderately larger amount of greenbacks. Like all "sectional" conflict this struggle is of considerable significance as an indicator of the evolving power relationships between various social strata.

Adequate data on the regional distribution of the total money stock are not available and per capita money stock estimates are not as relevant to allegations of shortage as regional output would be. Davis R. Dewey criticized the unequal sectional currency distribution of state banks before the war, pointing out that the "circulation" in New England was $50 million, and in Ohio, with "three-quarters as large a population," it was only $9 million.[15] Since, according to Richard Easterlin, East North Central personal income per capita was about one-half New England's in 1860,[16] for "equality" Ohio's circulation should have been ¾ x ½ of $50 million, or roughly twice that estimated by Dewey. Perhaps there were grounds for complaint.

Apparently the National Banking System carried on the previous banking tradition of starving the Middle West and the South for currency — *regions in which the demand for currency relative to deposit money was considerably greater than in the East.* Robert P. Sharkey ascribes the regional maldistribution of the limited volume of national bank notes from 1863 to 1865 to Comptroller Hugh McCulloch, an Indiana State banker, opponent of the NBS (!) and gold standard advocate.[17] McCulloch's allocation gave $170 million of the authorized $300 million notes to New York and New England. This was 57 percent in the area that placed heaviest reliance on check money and that could not have accounted for much more than 40 percent of Northern income. Fritz Redlich estimates that as late as 1874 the malallocation of bank notes was as follows (in millions): 6 eastern states, $110.5; 5 middle states, 125.1; 9 western states, 78.0; 15 southern and southwestern states, 36.6.[18]

This gave two-thirds of the notes to the first two regions. Easterlin estimates that in 1880 the New England and Middle Atlantic regions accounted for 44 percent of total U.S. personal income.

If the West and South were kept in chronic short supply of the forms of money they needed most, then the price of money could be kept high, and indeed interest rates—a determinant of creditors' incomes—were higher in the West and South than in the East. Of course, many factors in addition to possible monopoly influences, such as credit risk considerations, go into the location of the supply schedule of loanable funds. Nevertheless, it is reasonable to entertain the thesis of numerous scholars who view the post-Civil War sectional and social conflicts as expressing creditor-debtor, or creditor-small entrepreneur, antagonism. Such viewpoints are certainly consistent with the "hue and cry in one section of our country against inflation while in another there seems to be an almost unanimous vote in favor of an expansion of the currency." [19] As the experience of later decades unfolds, it will be desirable to keep in mind the Sharkey thesis that "*laissez faire* conditions of enterprise in pre-Civil War America—in which the entrepreneur thrived and the position of the creditor was none too secure—gave way in the post-Civil War period to a new situation in which the creditor interest was dominant, large-scale instead of small-scale enterprise was favored, and the East held the whip hand over the less developed regions of the Country." [20]

Notwithstanding the complaints about currency shortages, however, it seems very likely that supplanting the chaotic state bank note with a uniform national currency, continuing the state bank commercial loan under conditions of a large long run increase in the number of state banks, and providing some types of commercial loans by national banks was of considerable consequence for economic development. Once the economy passed beyond the local market stage, local currency became increasingly obsolete.

Summing Up the Long Run Effects

It seems clear that the Civil War threw the South far off its long-run growth path during the sixties and left it as late as 1880 at a per capita income level below prewar. But the effects of the Beard-Hacker "second American revolution" on the secular growth of the North are less clear, and the present lowly status of the Beard-

Hacker thesis is not necessarily final. This matter was reviewed in some detail by Stanley Engerman in a notable essay in 1966. [21] Engerman pointed out that there was an increase in the North's growth rate of per capita income after the war, a "key index favorable to the Beard-Hacker thesis." [22]

Furthermore, the record of capital accumulation, which according to the theme of this book was the most vital single force in the growth and development process from 1865 to 1914, seems to show a break in trend at the Civil War decade. Using the percentage share of gross capital formation in GNP as an indicator, estimates by Robert E. Gallman and Edward S. Howle are as follows: [23]

Years	Capital/GNP
1834-1843	16%
1838-1848	14
1844-1853	14
1849-1858	16
1869-1878	24
1879-1888	23
1889-1898	28
1899-1908	28

Other data reveal a rising trend in the capital formation proportion before the war, but even these show a sharp upward shift from 14 percent to 22 percent between the fifties and the seventies.

However, annual growth rates for the stock of fixed capital show higher performance from 1840 to 1860, of course calculated on a smaller base, than from 1870 to 1900. [24] As for structural shifts in the economy, such as the very significant proportion of agriculture to all other activities, postwar changes again failed to outpace those of the two prewar decades—for the United States as a whole, at least.

Many other aspects, impossible to probe here, need to be examined to survey the possible long-run effects of the war. Some of these have already been mentioned, for example the change in the South from an economically efficient slave system in cotton to a probably less efficient sharecropper system after the war. Another aspect is the developmental role of the state in the light of the general laissez faire policy pursued by the Federal government.

The meaning of laissez faire becomes relevant here. "Laissez faire" is a generalization from the economic experience of a number of capitalist countries. In the case of the United States a workable definition of laissez faire seems to be that it involves a policy of central government aid to development of the business sector at home and abroad associated with minimum increases in government regulation, a decentralized hard money policy, and a classical fiscal policy. [25] There has of course never been any perfect laissez faire in the sense of no central government, or even in the sense of government as "night watchman." In the United States that policy was associated with positive Federal actions designed to stimulate, and establish favorable conditions for, the growth of private enterprise and private investment. Such developmental actions included tariff protection, a uniform currency, a hard money policy biased in favor of the financial and creditor strata within the business community, [26] land grants to railroads, liberal land settlement and immigration policies, a hostile stance toward labor organization, encouragement to business expansion abroad, and other probusiness measures discussed in Chapter 8.

Arthur Schlesinger, Jr., in referring to the role of government at all levels and relying heavily upon pre-Civil War examples, finds what is here viewed as laissez faire is a regime strongly tinged with mercantilist ideas of government direction of the economy. [27] But with respect to the post-Civil War decades and the *Federal* government, which is the essential context of laissez faire policy as viewed herein, there is little left of the mild but distinctly mercantilist phenomena found in American experience before 1860. In our period Federal intervention occurred *after* the age of the merchant capitalist, did not involve an overriding export or bullionist policy emphasis, never employed the specially chartered trading company or any other public corporation as a central government instrument, and was strongly domestic in its developmental orientation. It must be recognized that central governments in capitalist economies have always aided business, but such aid policies in all the different periods of capitalist development are not always called "mercantilism." Warren G. Harding expressed the laissez faire philosophy of government's role as well as anybody ever did when he said, "we must give government cooperation to business, we must protect American business at home and we must protect it abroad." The hallmarks of the subsequent decline in laissez faire in the domestic economy may be found in the proliferation of regulations created by the growing conflict of ever more powerful organized economic groups, and more importantly, in the rise of large government budgets, and in the development of monetary and fiscal policies specifically directed towards sustaining aggregate demand and shaping the performance of the business economy. The replacement of the laissez faire arrangement with this "mixed economy" arrangement has been called "neo-mercantilism" by Joseph Schumpeter, but it is certainly a new set of relationships between business and government. The old lingers on in the new throughout history, but it is the new that offers the clue to what is historically forthcoming.

NOTES

1. The Cochran-Salsbury debate can be found in Ralph Andreano (ed.), *Economic Impact of the American Civil War*, revised ed. (Cambridge, Mass.: Schenkman, 1967), pp. 167-87.
2. *Dictionary of American History*, James Truslow Adams (orig. ed.), v. VI (Supplement One), J. G. E. Hopkins and Wayne Andrews (eds.) (New York: Charles Scribner's Sons, 1961), p. 243.
3. Sidney Ratner, *Taxation and Democracy in America* (New York: John Wiley & Sons, 1967), pp. 73, 76.
4. Ibid., p. 73.
5. With a money stock in 1860 of about $700 million, and GNP of about $4.2 billion (Gallman), the income velocity of money, GNP/M_1 was about 6.
6. To the extent the government borrowed from the public, rather than from the banks, its debt was not monetized, and inflationary pressures were accordingly not generated.
7. Reuben Kessel and Armen Alchian, "Real Wages in the North During the Civil War: Mitchell's Data Reinterpreted," *Journal of Law and Economics*, 2 (October 1959), reprinted in Ralph Andreano (ed.), *Economic Impact of American Civil War*, op.cit., p. 22.
8. Wesley C. Mitchell, *Gold, Prices and Wages Under the Greenback Standard*, University of California Press Publications in Economics, v. I (1908), pp. 237, 245. Originally published by the University of California Press; reprinted by permission of the Regents of the University of California.
9. Ethel D. Hoover, "Retail Prices after 1850" in National Bureau of Economic Research, Conference on Research in Income and Wealth, *Trends in the American Economy in the Nineteenth Century*, Studies in Income and Wealth, v. 24 (Princeton: Princeton University Press, 1960), p. 142, and ibid., pp. 146-7.
10. Ibid., pp. 275-6.
11. Of course, profits are not merely a simple function of the relation between wage rates and product prices in any case. Productivity and other costs must also be considered.
12. Kessel and Alchian, op. cit., p. 23.
13. F. W. Taussig, *The Tariff History of the United States* (New York: Capricorn Books, 1964), p. 167.
14. Margaret F. Myers, *The New York Money Market: Origins and Development* (New York: Columbia University Press, 1931), p. 218.
15. This aspect is stessed by D. R. Dewey, *Financial History of the United States*, 12th ed. (New York: Longmans, Green, 1939), p. 324.

16. "Regional Income Trends, 1840-1950," in Robert W. Fogel and Stanley L. Engerman (eds.), *The Reinterpretation of American Economic History* (New York: Harper and Row, 1971), p. 40, Table 1.
17. Robert P. Sharkey, "Commercial Banking," in David T. Gilchrist and W. David Lewis (eds.), *Economic Change in the Civil War Era* (Greenville, Del.: Eleutherian Mills-Hagley Foundation, 1965), p. 28.
18. Fritz Redlich, "Comment," in ibid., p. 34.
19. Ibid., p. 34.
20. Loc. cit., pp. 29-30.
21. "The Economic Impact of the Civil War," in Ralph Andreano (ed.), op. cit., pp. 188-209.
22. Ibid., p. 193.
23. "Trends in the Structure of the American Economy since 1840," in Fogel and Engerman, op. cit., p. 31, Table 6. The data are in constant prices of 1860 and therefore purport to show "real output" phenomena. Capital formation includes both public and private, and GNP excludes government but includes the value of improvements to farmlands made with farm construction materials and value added by home manufacturing.
24. Engerman, in Andreano, *Economic Impact*, op. cit., p. 194. Jeffrey Williamson attributes the jump in capital formation rates after the Civil War to a jump in the rate of saving, together with a sharp drop in the relative price of producer durable goods. [See his *Late Nineteenth-Century American Development* (London: Cambridge University Press, 1974), pp. 104-12, *passim.*]
25. "Classical" means a small, annually balanced budget in peacetime, minimal debt, and regressive taxes that fall on consumption rather than savings.
26. As might be expected, the business community was by no means unified on these matters. Robert P. Sharkey and Irwin Unger have persuasively argued, for example, that certain elements in the entrepreneurial group, along with farm groups, strongly preferred, expansionist, easy money policies. See Sharkey's *Money, Class, and Party* (Baltimore: Johns Hopkins University Press, paperback ed., 1967); the previous discussion by him in "Commercial Banking," loc. cit., pp. 23-31; and Unger's *The Greenback Era* (Princeton: Princeton University Press, 1964).
27. Arthur Schlesinger, Jr., "Ideas and the Economic Process" in Seymour Harris (ed.), *American Economic History* (New York: McGraw-Hill, 1961), pp. 6-7.

[3]

Performance of the economy, 1865-1914

Although the process of growth and of structural change toward a nonagrarian economy was well under way by the Civil War, what occurred after the war was much more than a mere proliferation and elaboration of that same process. Industrialization, railroadization, and urbanization continued to spread throughout the economic fabric. Agriculture continued to experience a relative decline, and the typical farm outside the South was run by an active, commercial proprietor or tenant. But quite new features also emerged.

Alfred Chandler's thesis that as late as the 1870s the demand for the products of the major industries of the United States was predominantly from the farm sector does not seem plausible in view of the fact that farm gross income in 1870 was only $2.6 billion and GNP was about $6.6 billion. Indeed, gross value added in farming had fallen below one-half of GNP as far back as 1839. Thus the aggregate demand for the products of nonfarm activities had come for at least three decades chiefly from the nonfarm sector. Local and regional markets were increasingly being replaced by nationwide markets, and local monopolies disintegrated. Similarly, the decline in the population growth rate that began in the 1850s persisted throughout the period, despite the large immigration between 1880 and 1920 that was almost double the 1840-1880 influx. Population density began to rise significantly after 1820, and it continued to incease after 1865. Death rates fell and the life-span rose, just as it had before the Civil War. In the international sphere the United States continued to be a debtor economy. Finally, laissez faire, if viewed as a loose alliance between business and government, continued to characterize the relation of society and the economy in the case of the Federal government, although regulatory intervention by the government, such as regulation of transportation and antitrust laws, began to expand as the nineteenth century waned. When regulatory intervention did proliferate rapidly after the turn of the century, its objective was to restore a presumed market automaticity, i.e., "pure" laissez faire.[1]

Discontinuities in the Development Process

All these developments exhibited more or less continuity with the past. Yet, discontinuous changes such as new products or processes and the termination or reversal of trends and patterns were also a very prominent feature of economic evolution between 1865 and 1914.

For example, the industrial sectors of the economy were still in the iron age at the beginning of the period. About 1,300,000 gross tons of pig iron were produced in 1867, but only 20,000 gross tons of steel.[2] The conversion from iron to steel as the dominant metal product was a dramatically new feature of the modern industrial process emerging from the last quarter of the nineteenth century. Although in more recent decades the light metals and plastics have been substituted for steel in some uses, it is hard to imagine the twentieth-century economy without that conversion from iron.

The fuel base of the economy also experienced great historic transformations. Fuel wood provided the source for 73 percent of all inanimate energy consumption in 1870, and coal accounted for only 26 percent. In the following decades coal, and later also petroleum, almost completely replaced fuel wood. (Electricity, produced mostly from coal, accounted for only about 6 percent of the total horsepower of all prime movers[3] in 1910.) Although in the farm sector the horse and the mule dominated throughout, work animals in the economy as whole, which furnished rather more horsepower than all other prime movers combined as late as 1870, had declined to about 20 percent by 1910. The power sources in the manufacturing sector were overshadowed by steam throughout the period, water power being replaced by steam in the 1860s. In short, the energy basis of the production sector had moved from water power, wood fuel, and work animals to the coal-fired steam engine, and latterly to the threshold of the age of electricity.

One of the greatest discontinuities in the pattern of American development in the period 1860-1914 was the closing of the domestic agricultural frontier by 1910. The presence of a rapidly expanding frontier and the westward movement of farmers, cattlemen, miners, and lumbermen powerfully influenced the course of events in the economy and the society at large throughout the nineteenth century, and its termination profoundly altered the character of economic evolution. The farm labor force and the land in farms had grown absolutely during the century. After 1910, the farm labor force ceased to grow, and thus to a relative decline was added an absolute decline. Land in farms reached 909.6 million acres in 1914,[4] and for the understanding of the dynamics of agricultural economic development the land employed for farming may thereafter be considered as practically fixed in amount. Practically the same thing may be said of the number of farms.[5]

Our period also witnessed not only an enormous relative and absolute growth of the railroad, but also its maturation and the intimations of its relative decline as a transport sector. The great period of railroad construction had both unfolded and terminated between 1850 and 1914. Much the same can be said of manufacturing, the heart of the industrial economy. Manufacturing value added had already reached about one-fourth of GNP in 1914 and thereafter never exceeded about one-third of GNP. The urbanization rate also rose rapidly after the Civil War, reached a high point, and then tapered off after World War I. A so-called "logistic" curve can describe all three of these processes through time (see Figure 1). Indeed, such a curve describes the typical growth pattern of almost all industries. By the end of our period all three processes mentioned had moved well up on the growth curve toward a rate that spelled the end of whatever developmental role they had played in the latter half of the nineteenth century. *Development in the twentieth century would have to proceed on the basis of other stimuli.* The same results were of course associated with the end of the frontier, which had presumably sustained the rate of return on property by virtue of the continuous absorption of new, fertile lands, forests, and mineral sources. These declining or disappearing influences placed a new and heavy burden upon technological ad-

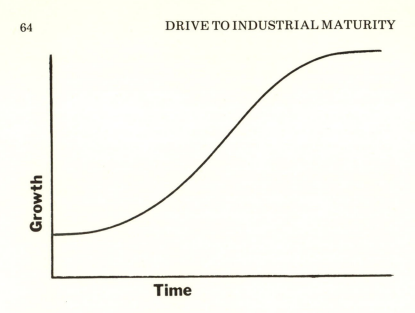

Figure 1 A logistic curve.

vance in all sectors to carry forward the development task of raising overall output and productivity in the economy after World
War I.

Another important change, in this case a change in policy ushered in soon after the end of the period under review, was the termination of the long era of open immigration, a policy that had contributed mightily to the development of the economic system in the
nineteenth century. The work of the patrician Immigration Restriction League, founded in the severe depression of 1894, the
organized labor movement, and various other more or less ill-
concealed nativist and chauvinist elements gradually overcame the
pro-immigrant influence of business and immigrant groups themselves. The rampant nationalism of World War I, bolstered by
antiradical nativism in 1919 and 1920 and a slump in 1920-1921,[6]
finished the job; after 1924 immigration was of little significance.

Some may agree with Alvin Hansen that the "disappearance of
great new private industries" also created a discontinuity in the
pattern of change. For those who believe that "leading sectors" of
the economy drive the development process like prime movers, the
end of railroadization, like the end of the canal era, meant the elimination of a strategic single source of growth. Joseph Schumpeter

shared this view with the early Douglass North and with Hansen. In Hansen's view, the automobile industry was the last great new private industry, and its rapid growth before World War I to maturation about 1927 was the "end of an era," like the disappearance of the frontier.

In the category of discontinuities, another reversal of historic patterns may also be discerned in the change from a negative to a positive balance on merchandise trade account in the U.S. balance of trade. This occurred in the middle 1870s and has remained a characteristic feature ever since. As a result, most Americans have probably come to believe that the economy cannot prosper unless the country exports more merchandise than it imports!

Another point of interest on the foreign balance is the fact that the United States was an international debtor country throughout the nineteenth century. But gradually, as the domestic frontier waned and the long-run rate of interest drifted downwards, U.S. private investors increasingly found foreign investments more attractive and exported capital funds in an ever-growing stream, most of these funds going into "direct investments in foreign plans, equipment, and land. The wartime liquidation of much European investment in the United States (most of it in securities, called "portfolio" investment) between 1914 and 1918 turned the tide and converted the U.S. into an immature (new long-term loans made greater than the annual returns on old loans) international creditor just after the end of the 1865-1914 period.

The record of discontinuities just called to mind is certainly impressive testimony that the development process and the accompanying changes in the modes of life pursued by people exhibit large upheavals that demand sweepingly new social decisions and techniques for meeting national and local goals. An example is the urbanization process, linked so strongly with the growth of the manufacturing and service sectors. Urban concentration proceeded without long-run planning, without effective recognition of the attendant diseconomies and disamenities, without awareness of many substantive social and psychological accompaniments. A prominent literary and journalistic school known as the "muckrakers" around the turn of the twentieth century called attention to many adverse aspects of the burgeoning industrial cities and won some noteworthy reforms. For example, this influence, combined with the Progressives (see below), helped introduce pure water, city sewage systems, some slum improvement, and better urban transit. But the problems continued to multiply after the muckraker agitation had subsided. But the muckrakers were perceptive anti-

cipators of the problems of a portion of the world that had just lost
its primarily agrarian character and become transformed into a
world of cities. More than a half century later society again began
seriously to attack the environmental problems wrought by an
overwhelmingly urban society.

Growth and Development Patterns

The GNP rose at a high annual compound rate of over 4 percent
between 1870 and 1914, while population increased at approximately a 2 percent rate. Since the participation rate (percentage of
population in the labor force) drifted upwards, the labor force
growth rate (1870-1910) was higher than the population rate—
about 2.5 percent per year. Both GNP and GNP per capita rose at
rates that exhibited long swings or waves. Using overlapping decades Simon Kuznets found peaks in long waves of the growth rates
in 1875-1884 and 1900-1909, and a trough in 1885-1894.[7]

To obtain the increase in output per capita, and output per person in the labor force, during these decades, it is necessary simply
to subtract the annual rates for population and persons engaged
from the GNP rate. Thus, if Q = GNP and H = population,

$$\frac{\Delta Q}{Q} - \frac{\Delta H}{H} = 4.0 - 2.0 = 2.0$$

the annual percentage rate of increase of output per head. Similarly,
if L is the labor force, we have

$$\frac{\Delta Q}{Q} - \frac{\Delta L}{L} = 4.0 - 2.5 = 1.5$$

the annual percentage rate of growth of output per person in the
labor force.

Average hours worked per week declined slightly, from 53.8 to
52.0 between 1869 and 1909. Hence manhours rose slightly less
than the labor force. Kendrick estimates the annual growth in
output per manhour as 1.65 percent.[8] This may be compared with
2.5 percent for the private, nonfarm economy, 1950-1972.

All these growth rates, which take GNP as customarily calculated—without considering associated "externalities"[9] and numerous nonmarket activities—compare well with other countries
favored by the Industrial Revolution in similar phases of development. Table 8 shows rough comparisons of the growth rates of

TABLE ·8

ANNUAL GROWTH RATES OF
INDUSTRIAL COUNTRIES
(percent)

Country	Output	Population	Output per capita
United States			
1840-1880	4.03	2.73	1.26
1880-1920	3.52	1.88	1.61
Great Britain			
1841-1881	2.54	1.19	1.33
1881-1921	1.77	0.91	0.86
France			
1871-1880 to 1901-1910	2.00	0.22	1.77
Germany			
1871-1875 to 1913	3.09	1.20	1.87
Sweden			
1881-1885 to 1921-1925	2.69	0.66	2.01
Japan			
1878-1882 to 1918-1922	4.14	1.05	3.05

Source: S. Kuznets, *Economic Growth and Structure* (New York: W. W. Norton, 1965), pp. 305, 307, Tables 1 and 2.

national product, population, and output per capita for the United States and a number of other industrial countries for approximately comparable long time periods. As Kuznets points out, the U.S. population rate was much higher than in the other countries shown. Consequently, although the total output record for the United States was comparatively good, its growth rate of output per head, for example over the decades from 1880 to 1920, did not outstrip most of the other countries. The United States was able to accommodate a high birth rate without significantly differing from comparable industrial nations in its production per capita performance. One conclusion from these comparisons is of interest. We know the level of the U.S. per capita income by the end of the first quarter of the twentieth century was substantially above that for most of the other countries shown. It therefore follows, as Kuznets asserts, from the roughly equivalent per capita income growth rates among them all over the long run, that the U.S. level of income per head at the beginning of the long period must also have been higher. The possible exception is Great Britain, and in that case the levels may have been roughly equivalent in the 1840s.

Except for output per worker or per manhour, the growth rates for GNP in the United States were generally higher in the nineteenth than in the twentieth century after World War I. Between 1860 and 1914 output grew to a great extent because of the growth of inputs of labor, capital, and in farming, land. In contrast, output after 1914 grew to a much greater extent because of technological and other productivity-raising changes, and to a much lesser extent because of the growth of inputs. This shift is attributable in large measure to the decline of the agricultural frontier, to changes in the quality and composition of capital goods, and to the secularly rising role of "human capital." These changes are certainly among the most significant transformations in U.S. economic history. Recognition of these transformations explains in part the great contemporary emphasis on education and research as factors in economic growth, as distinguished from, for example, capital investment, upon which people in the nineteenth century quite properly placed much emphasis. Indeed, the nineteenth century emphasis on private saving and tangible business capital formation was well placed, for such private saving and investment was and needed to be large and, until about 1900, a rising proportion of GNP. By the 1890s it accounted for well over one-fourth of total output (as was seen in Chapter 2) and assured a growth of aggregate demand sufficient to match the high growth rate of aggregate supply. This balance kept the economy "private" and was believed to call for no large government expenditures. Never before or after this period did private capital formation perform such an important role in economic growth. [10]

A striking feature of most of the last three decades of the nineteenth century was the secular decline of general product prices. It is often hard for twentieth century Americans to believe that the country once experienced a long period of substantial growth and development in the context of a falling price level. The wholesale price index (1910-1914 average of 100), which had risen to a high of 193 in 1865, reached pre-Civil War levels again at the bottom of the depression of the 1870s, and then continued the downward trend to a nadir in 1896. Average daily money wages continued at their Civil War high until a moderate drop occurred during the depression of the seventies; after 1880 they drifted upward to the end of the century. Thereafter money wage rates rose more briskly. Hence during the period of falling consumer prices after 1866, real wage rates in the long-run sense definitely rose, first catching up with wartime declines, then surpassing the prewar levels.

The nominal interest rate followed a secular downward trend, along with product prices at wholesale and retail (thus exhibiting the so-called "Gibson Paradox"). The money stock rose moderately faster than output (i.e., velocity, *GNP/M*, fell) for the whole period 1870-1896, and considerably faster after 1880. It would be expected that this would depress the interest rate, and indeed, as Gurley and Shaw point out, historically changes in velocity are associated directly with, for example, the corporate bond rate. The decline in interest rates was also no doubt facilitated by improved capital markets.

The Use of Natural Resources

Natural resources (e.g., land, minerals, fauna, flora) are potential productive inputs, as originally fashioned by nature rather than by society. It is not, however, their mere existence somewhere at any given time that counts from the standpoint of economic evolution. Rather it is their availability to human society, and this availability depends on the level of science and technology, together with the character of our social institutions. In the approach that emphasizes accessibility, "natural" resources are partly manmade, and it is in such a sense that the usual phase is employed here.

Changes in the pattern of natural resource use that typified the period have continued into the present day. If these natural resources (to the extent that they were used) be represented by the output of agriculture, timber products, and minerals, it can be said that the forty years from 1870 to 1910 were certainly years of most dramatic growth for the natural resource activities. The twentieth century exhibited distinctly slower rates for this extractive group taken as a whole. Among other features, this 1870-1910 period was the heyday of the lumber industry, the output of timber products reaching its all-time peak rate of expansion during the decade 1900-1910. Nevertheless, as the size of the American population kept increasing in the following decades, the *total* consumption of resources continued to rise, albeit at a slower rate. In this sense, the

TABLE 9

OUTPUT OF RESOURCES
(percent of GNP, 1954 prices)

Year	Total	Agriculture	Timber Production	Minerals
1870	36%	27%	4.0%	1.5%
1880	32	25	3.7	2.0
1890	29	21	3.9	2.8
1900	27	19	3.9	3.4
1910	22	15	2.8	4.2
1920	21	14	2.0	4.9

Source: U.S. Congress, Joint Economic Committee, *Staff Report on Employment, Growth and Price Levels*, December 24, 1959, p. 49, Table 2-8.

spectre of resource exhaustion was not dispelled. But in relative terms the trend for the total group was then and still is toward a decline. This may be seen in Table 9.

During the period 1870-1910 the output of minerals was a noteworthy contributor to U.S. economic growth quantitatively and especially qualitatively. But 1920 was the decennial peak for its relative quantitative importance. Until that date, the United States had usually been a net exporter of minerals and timber products, but after World War I, its increasing reliance upon imports suggests that domestic resource exhaustion in these categories is a foreseeable possibility. It is true that the pressure on forest resources was eased after World War I by virtue of the slow emergence of sustained yield forestry and the development of substitute structural materials, but this increased the pressure on the natural resource components of those substitutes.

Innovations

In the area of technological advance new developments were so substantive and manifold that even a cursory review seems almost impossible. Perhaps a simple classification with some outstanding illustrations for each category would give a fair impression of the progress in the "state of the arts."

Reference here is to innovations (*applied* inventions) rather than inventions. Institutional arrangements, such as corporation law, antimonopoly policy, immigration policy, municipal administration, and a host of other social constructs that may have furnished some incentive for innovations in production activity in its narrow sense are ignored at this point. A reasonable classification of innovations and their commercial exploitation in production might be:

New products
New processes
Growth of knowledge
— Education
— Pure and applied research

Of course, only new products and processes, which are intertwined, are technological advance in the narrowly defined sense. The growth of knowledge is indirect in that it is embodied in the former two. To the limited extent possible, however, it is perhaps useful to glance at this important determinant also, since it properly brings into focus the larger institutional forces primarily responsible for specific innovations in production and consumption.

The leading new product of this era, and one even more prominent since, was steel, together with the innovative processes associated with it. It is often said the "age of steel" was inaugurated in this period, and Abram Hewitt, a noted steel manufacturer, ringingly declared in 1892 that he looked upon "the invention of Mr. Bessemer as almost the greatest invention of the ages."[11] The commercial production of Bessemer steel began soon after the Civil War, and the firm of Cooper and Hewitt pioneered in this development. Bessemer was a *process*, just as open-hearth steelmaking was a process. The latter became the dominant process in the steel industry after 1907.

But new processes often employ new products. For example, open-hearth steelmaking employed the imported product, the Siemens regenerative furnace, that replaced the older reverberatory furnace. This was only one of a number of innovations in steelmaking itself. Blast furnaces for producing pig iron from ore increased in size so greatly that the late nineteenth century types may be considered different products from the 40-ton furnaces of Civil War days. The savings in fuel that occurred between 1865 and 1900 amounted to a minor revolution, not only in cost saving, but also in the determination of steel mill location.

In addition to steel there appeared a multitude of new steel products, from rails and barbed wire to machine tools, ball bearings,
and structured shapes for the construction industry. There was
scarcely any limit to the new world of steel products upon which
twentieth century industry came to depend to an almost unbeliev-
able degree. As in the case of basic steel itself, the new steel products also entailed new processes in both their fabrication (e.g., the
making of high-speed, carbon-alloy tool steel) and their use (e.g.,
the mechanization of metal working). Thus, many vital new products had steel as a major or minor component. Steel also revolutionized the railroads—in not only the making of rails, but also
freight cars (including refrigerator cars), air brakes (1869), automatic couplers (1873), and more powerful locomotives. Outstanding examples of modern steel machinery included machine tools,
such as Christopher Spencer's automatic turret lathe, electric
motors, electric generators, steam engines, steam turbines, shoe
machinery, earth working equipment, farm machinery, and the internal combustion engine. All these and many other types of machinery made partly of steel contributed greatly to the flood of
productivity, caused by product innovations that figured so prominently in the development of the economy from the Civil War to
World War I.

Steel thus had enormous "linkage effects" [12] chiefly *forward* to
steel products and to a lesser but important degree *backward* to industries serving it, such as coal, ore production, and transport facilities and services. The linked industries also vindicated their existence and growth by purchasing steel and steel products themselves. It is precisely such self-reinforcing development that
makes it so difficult to distinguish "autonomous" investment, i.e.,
business fixed investment stimulated by innovations and independent of changes in the level of income, from "induced" investment,
i.e., investment stimulated by increases in demand. All that can be
derived, in the absence of more research, is the rather unsatisfying
proposition that where the linkage effects of an industry are strong,
its contribution to a rise in autonomous investment is likely to be
noteworthy.

Steel widely permeated the web of technological imitation [13] and
innovation. But there were any other new products and processes.
Electricity, primarily in the form of alternating current, and its
long-distance transmission, a rival candidate for leading innovation (although more of a growth industry in the twentieth century
than in the nineteenth), were mainly dependent on copper, and only

indirectly dependent on steel. The infant electric utility industry reached backward to stimulate copper production, as well as steel products. It moved forward to the development of the carbon filament incandescent light, the telephone and telegraph, and the electric tramway as well as the replacement of leather belting by electric prime movers. The electric tramway, an important growth industry in its own right, revolutionized intra-urban transit between 1890 and 1914, with an attendant boost to transport investment and the growth of cities.

The petroleum derivatives industry was another innovative activity developed quite independently of steel or steel products. Although its historically most significant product had to await the rise of the motor vehicle, this industry made two noteworthy contributions in the form of kerosene and petroleum lubricants. Production of the former, much of it for home lighting, had reached 1.26 billion gallons in 1899 and had almost doubled that volume by 1919. But after that date, kerosene ceased to be a rapid grower until another resurgence occurred in the 1940s. While the output of refined petroleum lubricating oils was "only" 170 million gallons in 1899, their critical significance for modern industry and household operation has been incalculable. One can hardly imagine running the U.S. twentieth century machine economy with whale oil as chief lubricant! This is a fine illustration of the importance of something that started out as quantitatively unimportant. Yet by 1914 petroleum output had increased fivefold above its 1895 level.

But the list of noteworthy innovations is still far from exhausted. The spring-tooth harrow, the twine binder, the seed drill, the corn sheller, the combine, the steam tractor (there were 2,000 gasoline-engine tractors produced in 1909), the centrifugal cream separator and tester, the sulky plow, the chilled iron and steel plows, and commercial fertilizers all contributed to agriculture's modest productivity performance as new farmland all but disappeared.

Households witnessed, among other things, the emergence of commercial food canning and preserving, oleomargarine, the cigarette, electric refrigeration, the electric washing machine, and the indoor toilet. Although we are here primarily concerned with innovations in production, it is usually assumed that innovations contributing to the health and efficiency of the household have favorable effects on the efficiency of labor in production. Furthermore, technical facility in the production of consumer goods is transferable to the capital goods sector.

Spread widely through the nonfarm economy were numerous

other new products and techniques, notable among which were roller grinders in flour milling (a famous imported innovation), the use of sulfuric acid, wireless communication (another import), photography including "moving pictures," the Draper-Northrup automatic bobbin-changing loom for cotton weaving, the mechanical comb in the worsted industry, rayon (an imported innovation, the commercial production of which began in 1911), and the Owens automatic bottle blowing machine.[14]

The use of new products, and the adoption of new methods whether imported or domestically created, were not by any means inaugurated without undue caution or positive resistance by business, however, Resistance to innovation can be expected when obsolete plant and equipment embody large financial commitments that it is believed must be amortized either before a new method is installed or by the cost savings connected with the use of the new method. Furthermore, there was always some risk or uncertainty associated with innovation, and the normal aversion to it was increased by the rising average size of initial capital commitments. Moreover, in conditions such as those that obtained in the late nineteenth century United States there has always been a tendency for business to inhibit actual innovation, as compared with the optimal rate of innovation. Kenneth Arrow has argued for example,

> We expect a free enterprise economy to under-invest in invention and research (as compared with an ideal) because it is risky, because the product can be appropriated only to a limited extent, and because of increasing returns in use. This under-investment will be greater for more basic research. Further, to the extent that a firm succeeds in engrossing the economic value of its inventive activity, there will be an under-utilization of the information as compared with an ideal allocation.[15]

Although John Sawyer and some other scholars have stressed the speeding up of economic development by U.S. entrepreneurs, W. Paul Strassmann has asserted, on the basis of his study of the steel, textile, machine tool, and electric power industries that, although many Americans were highly speculative in real estate, canals, and railroads, in the field of manufacturing, excessive caution by entrepreneurs dampened the rate of innovation more than any other force. For instance, when the U.S. Navy in the 1880s offered the Bethlehem Iron Company guaranteed orders to institute production of heavy steel forgings using *established English hydraulic forging presses*, "the Bethlehem board of directors felt that the Navy did not understand practical steelmaking, that the plant would be too costly, that the process was *too different* and would require too much training of labor, and that the company was earning profits and there was no need to change. All these fears proved unwarranted."[16] Strassmann quotes Thomas R. Navin, Jr., to the effect that management attitudes in all the principal American textile machine shops were "merely accepting whatever changes were forced upon them from the outside."[17]

One of the most notorious nineteenth century cases of resistance to innovation was the refusal of the trunkline railroads and local butchers to build refrigerator cars. These persons feared the success of what seemed at the time to be a high risk innovation, and the adoption of a practical refrigerator car would destroy the asset values represented in cattle cars and stockyards. Hence, Swift had to build his own refrigerator cars, and they had to be run over the Canadian Grand Trunk line to the Eastern Seaboard. Another prominent case was the Selden patent on the Brayton internal combustion engine. Selden filed his application in 1879, but purposely delayed the granting of the patent until 1895 in an attempt to prolong the life of his patent monopoly so as to secure greater royalties in the long run.

The growth of production-related knowledge is connected with formal schooling, on-the-job training and discovery, informal interchange among trained people, the spread of technical journals, and pure and applied research—both individual and organized, private and public. Clearly this is a vast area of human activity, and the nineteenth century evidence is particularly scanty. Hence much of this activity has to be inferred by the use of treacherous proxy information. No adequate treatment of the subject is possible in a review discussion. Physical capital formation and the importing from abroad of new products and new processes no doubt had some innovation-promoting effects themselves. Nevertheless, it seems likely that the great bulk of innovations were the *result* of the production of new knowledge and the increased diffusion of that knowledge.

In the period between the Civil War and World War I, the growth of both public and private school enrollment with its attendant spread of general literacy and vocational education was probably the most important single factor in the growth of knowledge. Yet we do not know the extent to which the character of late nineteenth and early twentieth century improvements in production were complementary to such formal education. Hence, we can merely note, among other things, the increase in enrollments at all levels of education, the rising school expenditures per capita of school-age population, the greater number of days in attendance by the average pupil, the improvement in the average length of the school year, the increase in the number of engineering schools, and the establishment and growth of agricultural experiment stations subsequent to the passage of the Hatch Act in 1887. We can also point to the augmentation of industrial research activities by business firms, a development that was in its infancy compared to the later twentieth century effort.

Inventive activity was also on the rise, as suggested by the increase in patent applications filed, from 21,276 in 1867 to a nineteenth century peak of 45,661 in 1897. Most of this increase took place in the dramatic decade of the eighties, the only decade during which both patent applications filed and patents issued exceeded the growth of total output and about kept pace with the rise of manufacturing output.

Spectacular advances took place in science and technology between the Civil War and World War I that were considered in some cases as revolutionary. But from today's perspective these technological and institutional improvements made a relatively much smaller contribution to output growth in the 1866-1914 period than their successors have made during the twentieth century. In general, as pointed out by Nathan Rosenberg,[18]for the process of industrialization encompassed by this period, technological advance viewed from the supply side was heavily concentrated in metallurgy, machine tools, steam power, and engineering. The required skills were largely developed through mechanical ingenuity in association with the practical and crude empiricism employed by people in certain manufacturing activities and, as Albert Fishlow has emphasized, in the proliferating railroad repair shops. Such technological advances did not, as in the twentieth century, rely heavily upon either such science-based industries as chemical engineering or the higher education establishment, or elaborate experimental methods.

In the glance at innovations and their commercial diffusion little reference has been made to the appearance and spread of new, larger institutional arrangements. Yet institutional innovations may well have been as numerous and as important for economic development as were new methods in production. Of course, all such innovations did not necessarily stimulate growth or development, as one definition of the process by Douglass North and Lance Davis suggests, i.e., "an arrangement between economic units that governs the ways in which these units can cooperate or complete."[19] Railroad company pooling agreements, patent pools, "trusts," and other monopolistic arrangements to restrict output and/or raise prices were among the many types of "cooperative" innovations that probably inhibited development.

However, examples of the creation or spread of new institutional arrangements that probably contributed to economic advance were the introduction by the railroads in 1883 of standard time zones, the advent of investment banking, and the spread of the corporation under state general incorporation laws.

During the half-century between 1860 and 1913 the Federal government took limited interventionist action in the form of such measures as the protective tariff, the Homestead Act, an income tax law in 1894 that the Supreme Court invalidated, some conservation of natural resources under Theodore Roosevelt, and some antitrust and railroad rate legislation. But on most matters the Federal government, with some modifications under pressure from the Progressive movement after 1900, maintained a laissez faire institutional stance, refusing to intervent, except for regulatory measures, with policies to relieve poverty, redistribute income in favor of low income groups, forestall urban slums and blight, or initiate transfer payments to the unemployed, the ill and nonveteran disabled, or the aged. Caring for the destitute and aged was left to the local governments. Government purchases of goods and services at all levels persistently remained only about 7 percent of GNP, with no rising trend.

Developments in the Business Sector

The "captains of industry," including the more swashbuckling "robber barons," wielded enormous and almost unchallenged power over the shape of economic development in this era. The government was a willing helpmate. Labor organizations were growing, but still relatively weak, and for the most part narrowly focused on immediate working conditions, although the Knights of Labor in the early 1880s had broad social reform objectives and the small Industrial Workers of the World (I.W.W.) in the 1900s advocated abolition of the wage system and stressed direct action (the general strike, boycott, and sabotage) as the means of achieving their goal. The owners of small enterprises were unorganized and largely convinced that they, too, could find room at the top. But some succeeded in getting first state and then national antitrust and railroad rate legislation in the 1880s, 1890s, and early 1900s. Had it not been for a segment of militant farmers, pioneering unionists, and a handful of Progressive reformers and muckrakers, there would have been no "countervailing power" whatever to challenge the manipulation of the market system by the emerging coterie of wealthy enterprisers.

Despite the attacks on big business by the Grangers, the Populists, champions of small business such as Louis Brandeis, Socialists such as Eugene Debs, and radical labor groups such as the I.W.W., apparently the majority of Americans accepted on most matters the assumption by business leaders of power over the major economic decisions. Such acceptance, though shaken in the prolonged depressions following 1873 and 1893, and later by the criticisms of the Progressives, was buttressed by a widespread faith in the efficacy of the "automatic" market mechanism, and particularly the private investment process. On the ideological front, Social Darwinism and the doctrine of exclusively individual responsibility for one's material status were extensively employed to assure that the locus of decision making would remain in the hands of the rising corporate entrepreneurs. The dissent of social reformers and advocates of governmental intervention found some support, however, in the progressive legislation passed during the presidencies of Theodore Roosevelt, W. H. Taft, and Woodrow Wilson.

The corporate entrepreneurs wrought many changes in the structure and operation of the business sectors under their control. They made the corporate form of business dominant, and its use—or misuse— often became in their hands an instrument for the concentration of economic power and the taming of competition. Through the corporate form known as the "trust" the instability of the looser "pooling" agreements to set minimum or uniform prices and share sales or profits was largely overcome. In the trust, such as the American Tobacco or the Standard Oil Company, the controlling voting stock in a number of rival corporations was transferred to one corporation in exchange for the latter's trust certificates. Market policies were thus centralized in the hands of a small group.

When antimonopoly groups succeeded in making the trust un-popular and then legally untenable, the holding company was de-veloped, and notably abetted by the lenient corporation laws of New Jersey, to acquire the controlling shares of a number of com-peting corporations operating in various states. A famous example was the 1901 Northern Securities Corporation, combining the Great Northern and Northern Pacific railroads together with con-trol over the Burlington and a number of lesser enterprises. The heyday of the trust was the period 1879-1896; the holding company became popular with professional promoters between 1897 and 1903. This later period was also prominent for outright mergers—the first great merger movement in U.S. history, a movement that, in the words of Joe S. Bain, "basically altered the structure of American industry."[20] That structure was typically an industry with a leading core of oligopolists and a small firm fringe, creating a power dichotomy that generated the modern "small business problem."

The spread of the corporation was associated with a rise in the amount of fixed capital committed by investors in growing firms that increasingly operated more than one plant. The growth of fixed investment in plant and equipment in the multiplant firm prompted the modernization of long-term capital markets and their attendent financial institutions. It prompted the growth of inter-locks between industrial entrepreneurs and financial capitalists. It contributed to the separation of aggregate savings decisions and aggregate investment decisions in the economy. It also aggravated the fear of price competition, for when fixed costs are large, prices may be permitted to fall below total unit costs for periods so pro-tracted that bankruptcy can threaten. Price competition thus be-came increasingly "destructive" in the eyes of corporate mana-gers and the promoters of business combinations.

The reaction to the rate wars of the railroads and the price wars of manufacturers was an attempt to reduce or to eliminate price com-petition in all ways possible—from nonprice competition to an appeal to government to regulate market conditions. The results are to this day a matter of debate, although it is widely agreed among both experts and the lay public that the market results emerging from the development of oligopoly conform neither to the purely competitive model nor to the pure monopoly model of neo-classical economic theory. Moreover, from the standpoint of the history of economic thought, it is informative to note that in the twentieth century, neoclassical theory for all practical purposes ignored or minimized oligopoly, as it did unemployment, until the doctrines of imperfect competition were belatedly projected by Edward Chamberlin and Joan Robinson in the 1930s. Until then, theory and policy had to make do with the limiting case of pure monopoly or duopoly.

Regional Shifts

Whereas differing regional economies characterized the United States during the first three generations in the nineteenth century, the "nationalizing" of the country thereafter meant that original differences began to wither away. This homogenization and leveling off process was of course far from complete by World War I, and indeed is not complete even today. But, as ever, the chief differences were to be found between the North and the South. Within the North the great manufacturing belt came to stretch farther west to include the East North Central as well as the Middle Atlantic and New England states. In this great region agriculture continued to be very important outside New England, albeit experiencing the usual relative decline vis-a-vis industry. Absolute declines in the farm labor force were recorded in New England from 1860 on, and for the whole Northeast it came soon after the turn of the century, just as it did in the Lake States. [21] These absolute declines came later in the other regions of the North.

Probably the most dramatic regional change in the North was the enormous growth of Mountain and Pacific Coast states, especially California. The economic and population shift to the Pacific was to continue far into the twentieth century. While the area accounted for only 4 percent of total personal income in 1880, this had risen to 7 percent by 1920. [22] Nonfarm employment had reached 80 percent of the total in the Far West by 1910, the bulk of which was engaged in either manufacturing or services. [23]

Within the North the large interregional discrepancies in per capita personal income that obtained on the eve of the Civil War had been substantially reduced by 1920. During this period both the Northeast and the West moved downward toward the national average and the North Central moved upward as it became more industrialized. [24] This pattern of convergence attested to the interregional mobility of productive factors and to the achievement of greater uniformity in the sectoral diversity of economic activities within regions of the North.

The South suffered an enormous setback from the Civil War and conversion from the plantation system to the sharecropping system. The latter type of tenantry arose largely because of racism and a lack of fluid capital, and served as a means to share risk and assure landowners a stable labor supply. The system lent itself to abuse by the landlords and storekeepers to exploit both the poor black and the white farming population. But by $880 the South was in a position to develop in ways somewhat different from the antebellum pattern, with less reliance on cotton. Consequently, despite the burdens of the economic past, the South grew in per capita personal income about as fast as the rest of the nation between 1880 and 1900, and beginning sometime around World War I it grew rather faster. But economic growth is not necessarily economic development, and the South had a long way to go. Easterlin estimates that in 1920 its income per capita was still only 62 percent of the national average, a position only slightly bettered by the eve of World War II, sixty years after the end of Reconstruction.

Labor's Level of Living

Living levels are almost the equivalent of human welfare and the criteria of welfare selected by the historian always presume value judgments about what makes people better off. For example, only the living levels of employees or farmers are usually treated, because few are much concerned with the living conditions of the well-to-do. Humanists want to know how the great masses of manual workers and their families are faring materially and culturally, and we have a special interest in the poorest segment of this population. From a human standpoint we consider the progress of the majority of workers and self-employed farmers and businessmen to be the acid test of the ability of an economic system to justify its existence, its growth pattern and its allocation of resources to capital formation.

The 1860-1914 era was one in which there was still "not enough to go around" in the sense that even with a perfectly equal distribution of income, which was far from the actual situation, average incomes would have provided a rather poor material existence. For example, NNP (net national product) per capita in 1900, although notably above European levels, was in current dollars about $213 annually ($454 in 1929 prices) and the average annual money income of city families in 1901 was $651 in current dollars (about $2200 in 1957-59 dollars).

A glance at the distributive pattern shows that the "well-to-do" (family incomes of $1,200 or more) spent on the average $1,052 for current consumption, i.e., their consumption was 162 percent of the average city family's income. About 40 percent of all families spent for current consumption less than half that spent by the middle and upper income groups. [25] "Between 1900 and 1910, the estimates of the cost of a [simple but decent] budget for five persons ranged from $600 and $1,000 and the corresponding average incomes of wage-earner families ranged between $400 and $900 . . . . In 1901 more than 40 percent of the workers' families had incomes less than $600, Mitchell's and Ryan's estimate of the minimum standard for that time . . . and in 1918, some 30 percent of the workers' families surveyed by the Bureau of Labor Statistics had incomes less than $1,300, the lowest estimate of the minimum budget for workers' families." [26]

Progress had been made, however, in the overall sense. Although wages and salaries were only 42 percent of what they were to be half a century later, [27] real per capita consumption had risen about 85 percent in the quarter century between 1870 and 1896. Wage gains among different strata differed. In the same quarter century real farm labor wage rates (per month, with board) increased at a rate of only .42 percent per year, [28] whereas the real annual earnings of nonfarm employees increased 1.5 percent per year. [29]

With respect to real wage rates after the turn of the century, it was formerly believed that little advance was made. This conclusion was based on a study by Paul Douglas; but later research by Professor Albert Rees indicated a noteworthy rise, in the manufacturing sector at least, between 1890 and 1914. This matter will be referred to more explicitly in Chapters 10 and 11.

But there is much more to the level of living than average wage rates or averages of aggregate consumption. Conditions of employment and on-the-job environment are vitally related to the well-being of the working man or woman. Reduction in the hours of work alone provided an issue that absorbed much of the labor movement's energies for many decades. Almost 30 percent of the entire work force was on a seven day week as late as 1910! Intensity of work was a major consideration, as labor's resistance to Frederick

W. Taylor's "scientific management" movement (known as "speed up" by workers) mounted in the early twentieth century. The rate and nature of industrial accidents, together with protection therefrom, were of vital importance. The picture here would be considered scandalous in our time.

Real wages and job conditions do not completely define living levels, either. Conditions in a home and the larger social and economic environment must be included. There was very little income security against the incapacities of old age and infirmity, unemployment, ill health, and disability.

Life in the new industrial cities, despite its escape from agrrian drudgery, was associated with terrible environmental disamenities. Commutation was added to the workers' daily rounds. Slum housing without indoor toilets or bathrooms was widespread, if not typical. In Baltimore and Philadelphia a third of the population of the large slum areas slept four or more persons to a room; in corresponding areas in Chicago 70 percent slept in a room with only one or no outside window. [30] The general quality of low-income housing was poor, and the amount of household drudgery for housewives and mothers confirmed the time-honored quip that "woman's work is never done." The larger urban environment experienced by the working masses was a cultureless counterpart of the prevailing doctrines that labor was merely a factor of production—an "input."

In other aspects of the new urban life some progress had been made toward reducing infant mortality and providing a minimum of health care. But the provision of health services was then, as it is today, a relatively starved sector making inadequate provision for the delivery of health services to the low-income groups and to minorities. Great progress had been made in the diffusion and quality of primary and secondary education compared to pre-Civil War standards, especially in the South, but still greater progress was needed. Higher education was still by and large for the well-to-do only.

Clearly from the standpoint of the 1970s, life in America in 1914 was still "nasty, brutish, and short" on the eve of World War I for the mass of the working people, but the quality and length of that life, when measured by the conditions and length of life before the Civil War, seemed to many better than that of their parents or grandparents. Advances had been made during the past half century but the progress of industrialization and urbanization had been so rapid that very large proportions of annual production went to business capital formation. Workers' consumption levels and public services, although definitely rising over every decade, still did not rise as much as they might have, and hence workers paid the price for what was thought to be better material life to come in the long run. Social criticism was both stimulated and dampened by the continuous influx of immigrants who were conscious of the worse conditions left behind in "the old country." In the late nineteenth and early twentieth centuries the bulk of the immigrants came from southeastern Europe where levels of living were particularly low, as in the rural South, or Ireland at the time of the 1846 potato famine. The bad conditions in Europe made the contrast with American conditions appear favorable to the majority of immigrants. Furthermore, the doctrines of Social Darwinism, laissez faire, and business unionism helped to counteract, but not to nullify, the struggling social reform and public interventionist movements of the Progressive years between the turn of the century and the end of World War I. The latter saw the successful adoption of the Sixteenth (income tax) Amendment and the consequent enactment of progressive federal income and estate taxes under Woodrow Wilson, despite the fulminations of some of the mightiest captains of industry and finance. To most businessmen the income tax (in 1913) was a spearhead of socialism.

NOTES

1. See Harold U. Faulkner, *The Decline of Laissez Faire* (New York: Rinehart & Company, 1951), pp. 367-8.
2. Peter Temin, *Iron and Steel in Nineteenth-Century America* (Cambridge, Mass.: M.I.T. Press, 1964), pp. 266, 270. Imports of steel, in the form of rails, greatly exceeded domestic production.
3. Excluding the automotive.
4. The largest acreage ever reached was about 1.2 billion in the 1950s.
5. There were 6.5 million farms in 1914; the largest number subsequently was 6.8 million in 1935.
6. However, over 800,000 immigrants entered in 1921. And in 1924, the year of the ultimate in Congressional exclusion laws, over 700,000 entered. But this was the final reversal of the open immigrant policy.
7. Simon Kuznets, *Econimic Growth and Structure* (New York: W. W. Norton, 1965), p. 376, Table 15.
8. John W. Kenrick, *Productivity Trends in the United States*, National Bureau of Economic Research (Princeton: Princeton University Press, 1961), p. 310, Table A-IX; pp. 311-2, Table A-X.
9. Externalities are the utilities or disutilities experienced by others as a result of an economic decision made by any particular person or group.

10. Cogent analytical and empirical support for the strategic growth importance of private capital formation in our period may be found, e.g., in the impressive paper by Moses Abramovitz and Paul A. David, "Reinterpreting Economic Growth: Parables and Realities," *American Economic Review*, Papers and Proceedings, 63, no. 2 (May 1973), pp. 428-39.
11. Quoted in Elting E. Morison, *Men, Machines and Modern Times* (Cambridge, Mass.: M.I.T. Press, 1966), p. 124.
12. See Albert Hirschman, *The Strategy of Economic Development* (New Haven: Yale University Press, 1959), p. 106. The high score for steel was originally estimated by H. B. Chenery and T. Watanabe.
13. In addition to those innovations initiated in the United States, legions of innovations were imported, mostly from Europe.
14. The first aircraft was 1903 (the Wright Brothers). For omissions and some reference to the literature, see Harold U. Faulkner, op. cit., p. 120.

  Insofar as processes can be distinguished from products, the overlap having already been pointed out, reference should be made at least to the emergence of "scientific management," the reduction of the raw material content of fabricated products, the increased horsepower per worker, mineral tanning of leather, the Goodyear welt process in the shoe industry, the introduction of the rotary kiln in Portland cement production about 1900, oxyacetylene welding, hydraulic mining and the use of dynamite in mining operations, the Frasch process of sulfur mining, the oil flotation method of metallic copper concentration in the reduction of copper ore, the Solvay (Belgium) and electrolytic processes in the chemical industry, the system of standard sizes in ready-made clothing manufacture and—wave of the future—the adoption of continuous production technique in a number of industries such as flour milling and automobile assembly (Ford's first experimental, *manually operated* assembly line was instituted in 1913).
15. "Economic Welfare and the Allocation of Resources for Invention," reprinted in Douglass Needham (ed.), *Readings in the Economics of Industrial Organization* (New York: Holt, Rinehart and Winston, 1970), p. 423.
16. W. Paul Strassmann, *Risk and Technological Innovation* (Ithaca: Cornell University Press, 1959), p. 64. (Italics added.)
17. Ibid., p. 93.
18. See his *Technology and American Economic Growth* (New York: Harper and Row, 1972), pp. 53-5 *passim*.
19. "Institutional Change and American Economic Growth: A First Step Towards a Theory of Institutional Innovation," *Journal of Economic History*, 30 (March 1970), p. 133.
20. "Industrial Concentration and Anti-Trust Policy" in Harold Williamson (ed.),

20. "Industrial Concentration and Anti-Trust Policy" in Harold Williamson (ed.), *Growth of the American Economy* (Englewood Cliffs, N. J.: Prentice-Hall, 1964), p. 619.
21. See Alvin S. Tostlebe, *The Growth of Physical Capital in Agriculture, 1870-1950* (New York: National Bureau of Economic Research, Occasional Paper #44, 1954), p. 31.
22. Richard A. Easterlin, "Regional Income Trends, 1840-1950," in Seymour E. Harris (ed.), *American Economic History* (New York: McGraw-Hill, 1961), p. 535.
23. Harvey S. Perloff et al., *Regions, Resources, and Economic Growth* (Lincoln, Neb.: University of Nebraska Press, 1960), p. 182.

24. Richard Easterlin, "Regional Income Trends," op. cit., p. 528.
25. These data are from U.S. Department of Labor, *How American Buying Habits Change* (Washington, D.C.: Government Printing Office, 1959), p. 40.
26. Dorothy S. Brady, "Scales of Living and Wage Earners' Budgets," in Joseph T. Lambie and Richard V. Clemence (eds.), *Economic Change in America* (Harrisburg, Pa.: The Stackpole Company, 1954), pp. 487-9 *passim*.
27. U.S. Department of Labor, *Buying Habits*, op. cit., p. 28.
28. Calculated by applying a consumer price index on a 1914 base (from Stanley Lebergott, *Manpower in Economic Growth: The American Record Since 1800* (New York: McGraw-Hill, 1964), p. 528, to wage data in U.S. Department of Agriculture, Misc. Bulletin #26, "Wages of Farm Labor in the United States" (Washington, D.C.: Government Printing Office, 1903), p. 11, Table 2.
29. Lebergott, op. cit., p. 528.
30. U.S. Department of Labor, *Buying Habits*, op. cit., p. 10.

[4]

The south and the north: a half-century of regional contrasts

The economic contrasts between the South and the North were accentuated by the Southern devastation and military defeat in the Civil War. Although development in the North was slow during the war years proper, those years were nevertheless a seedtime for the subsequent diffusion of many agricultural and industrial innovations. In the fifteen years following the war all the major subregions of the North forged ahead, albeit at differing rates, and despite a long "depression" in the seventies. Meanwhile the landlords and country store merchants of the white South were establishing the sharecropper system (a halfway position between farm tenancy proper and hired labor service, considered by some a new form of peonage) for the 4 million freedmen and for many of the poor whites, rebuilding its agriculture more or less on the prewar model, and extending its railroad network. In Chapter 2 (especially Tables 4 and 5) it was seen that the South's farm sector had made substantial progress toward the achievement of prewar levels of output and stocks by 1880, but that even such progress left the South far behind the North's agriculture (except for cotton).

Richard A. Easterlin has estimated that per capita personal in-

come in the South as a whole was 72 percent of the national average
in 1860. Thereafter it was as follows:[1]

Year	South/U.S.
1880	51%
1900	51
1920	62

The deterioration in the South's position as late as 1880 largely resulted from the wartime destruction and postwar disorganization
experienced by the dominant agricultural sector.

It was during the decade following the war's end that the sharecropping system for tying the freedmen to the soil was gradually
imposed by the planters and reluctantly accepted by the freedmen
once they realized the government would not provide them with the
land and other tangible capital necessary for yeoman farming.
Hanumantha Rao has shown that sharecropping is likely to obtain where "the element of innovation management and entrepreneurship is minimized because of lack of significant substitution
possibilities among rival crops and factors, and the element of
uncertainty is thus reduced to negligible levels."[2] A system of
wage payments was widely tried at first. The planters favored this
because it was appropriate to the maintenance of the large plantation unit of production and made possible the organization of work
gangs similar to the slave system. But the lack of currency and
credit ruled out a money wage payment arrangement, and fragmen-
tation of plantation holdings along with payment by shares made it
easier for planters to tie their laborers to the land. This system of
land tenure, known anciently in Europe as metayage, long ante-
dates money economy. By forcing the sharecropper to procure foodstuffs and other personal items on credit through the year at the
merchant- or planter-owned store, the planter was able to retain de
facto much of the crop for himself and to maintain the sharecropper
family in almost complete subordination and at a subsistence level
of living. After a time the country store merchant, in cases where he
was not the landlord himself, became the key provider of credit and
supplies on credit for both the landlords and the sharecroppers.
This process of converting freedmen, as well as thousands of poor
whites, and their families to semivassalage took time, and the stabilization of contractual arrangements regarding the distribution of

output shares often involved conflicts that adversely affected productivity in a system that at best left little work incentive other than the threat of starvation.

Clearly not much can be said, therefore, about the South's post-war development pattern until after about 1880. On this matter Stanley Engerman has argued that the South developed after the Civil War (until 1900, at least) in essentially the same way it did before.[3] It is true that cotton remained the most important single crop (other than corn, perhaps), the South remained overwhelmingly agrarian, and the farm sector was slow to modernize. Significant changes, nevertheless, occurred after 1880 that cast doubt upon Engerman's thesis. Aside from the change from slavery to share tenancy for the blacks, and the increase in the proportion of the cotton crop produced by whites from 12 percent in 1860 to 50 percent by 1885,[4] cotton played a decreasingly significant role in the growth of Southern output after 1880. Before the war cotton exports and production grew much *faster* than Southern gross regional product, but from 1880 on, cotton exports and output grew much *more slowly* than southern GRP. Surely this striking relationship alone attests to a fundamental change in the pattern of Southern development. Total cotton production in the United States as a whole grew at an annual compound rate of only 2.25 percent between 1880 and 1900.

It was also after 1880 that the South for the first time experienced a strong downward secular trend in the relative importance of agriculture. In the populous Southeast, for example, about three-fourths of the regional labor force was still engaged in agricultural pursuits in 1880, a proportion that had changed little since 1800. This fraction, however, had fallen to 65 percent twenty years later and to 59 percent in 1910.[5] The region had also shifted to an important degree into logging and lumber production and mining. Furthermore, it had seriously undertaken the first-stage fabrication of primary materials. The great "migration" of the cotton textile industry from New England to the South also occurred after 1880. As a consequence the relative importance of manufacturing employment in the Southeast almost doubled between 1880 and 1910 (from 7.8 percent of the labor force to 14.5 percent).[6] Meanwhile, railroadization of the region proceeded rapidly: mileage doubled in the decade of the eighties alone! Finally, the Southeast began to urbanize. While only 9.5 percent of its population was "urban" (living in

places of 2,500 or more people) in 1870, over 19 percent was urbanized by 1910. This was an even faster rate than the rapidly urbanizing North exhibited. Hence, although the South still had a long way
to go, after 1880 it was at least taking the first steps toward an industrialized system, and seems to have undertaken to effect significant structural changes as compared with the antebellum cotton
economy.

Although the South's development pattern was different, and
the growth rate of personal income per capita first equaled (1880-
1900) and then exceeded (1900-1920) the national rate, the South in
1920, according to Easterlin, had a per capita income that was only
62 percent of the national average. This was still considerably below its pre-Civil War standing, and was probably about the level
that had been achieved by the rest of the United States thirty or
forty years earlier. Robert Fogel and Jack Rutner have estimated
that over the whole period 1839-1899 the income per worker in
Southern agriculture grew at a rate less than one-fourth that of the
national. Furthermore, Easterlin estimates that the South's average income was as low as 55 percent of the U.S. average in 1930 and
was only 65 percent of the national average as late as 1940! It is reasonable to conclude that, while the South demonstrated that it
could grow slightly faster than the nation after 1900, its modernization process was still too slow to produce a substantial degree of per
capita income convergence relative to the United States as a whole.
By contrast, the heavily agricultural North Central region, which
had started from a poorer relative position on the eve of the Civil
War, had slightly exceeded the national average by 1900.

It is the challenging and controversial thesis of Professor
Douglas Dowd that for many decades after the Civil War the people
of the South continued to pay a terrible price for the antebellum
heritage of slavery and cotton "monoculture." This heritage had
kept the Southern economy too agrarian, too limited by a single
staple export, too lacking in urbanization, too hostile to industrialization, too antithetical to popular education, too disdainful of
human labor, too racist, and too undemocratic.[7] Dowd and others
find the heart of the economic development process to reside in the
creation of appropriate institutional arrangements and related attitudes, and believe the South was particularly deficient in such facilitating vehicles. The adequacy of Dowd's thesis needs further examination; nonetheless, it is a research-productive and plausible
viewpoint.

The Beginning of the Great Black Migrations

Until the turn of the twentieth century the black people of the Deep South, and to a lesser extent the poor whites, were locked into a veritable prison, being economically, socially, and politically bound to the soil and to the locality of their forbears. Most economic considerations strongly suggested migration to the North, for incomes per person in both the farm and the nonfarm sectors were much higher in the North than in both the Southeast and the East South Central regions. But there was little such migration.[8] While the black population of the United States rose 82 percent, from 5.4 million in 1870 to 9.8 million in 1910 (compared to an increase of the white population of 140 percent), the proportion of the total U.S. black population in the South during that *forty* years fell only two percentage points, from 91 to 89 percent. But in the next *ten* years it fell four percentage points. The only noteworthy migration that did not occur in the forty years 1870-1910 was from rural to urban areas. In twelve southern states, the black urban population rose from 338,840 to 1,597,260.[9] There was also some intraregional migration even before 1890 within the South itself.[10] But there were only six cities of the North in 1910 with black populations in excess of 10,000.

The forced retention of blacks in Southern agriculture generated disguised unemployment and low productivity there. The institutional and related subjective barriers to mobility reduced the rate of growth for the entire U.S. economy. Most of these barriers were erected in the South. But large foreign immigration into Northern cities, discriminatory laws, and white racism in the North created an unfavorable environment in the latter region also and thus undermined the "pull" influences that otherwise might have overcome the incredible interregional immobility of the downtrodden Southern blacks. An analysis by W. E. B. Dubois, "The Philadelphia Negro, A Social Study," published in 1899, "revealed a problem in the North not unlike that in the South, one that was handled in much the same way."[11]

All the influences that ordinarily inhibit migration operated with differential harshness upon the Southern blacks. The small black population in the North prevented the emergence of a "reference group" outside the South to which Southern blacks could compare themselves and establish an affiliation having higher achievement levels. Fear of the unknown was thus intensified, and the "information gap" was widened by poor education, a distinct heritage of the antebellum period, and Southern propaganda portraying Northern conditions as worse than they actually were. Since there had as yet been little out-migration [12] there was little return migration to bring accurate information from the potential receiving areas in the North. Moreover, the extreme poverty of the Southern blacks made it impossible for them to incur any "search costs" or transportation and settlement costs. And prior to World War I Northern employers did almost nothing to recruit Southern blacks. Black migration required *both* geographical *and* occupational mobility, and this constituted a double barrier to black movement, which mainly had to be from the *rural* South. To all these differentially inhibiting influences must be added the terror associated with attempts to "desert" local employers in what was for most blacks virtually an authoritarian "apartheid" society like contemporary South Africa.

When migration did begin on a substantial scale, the Southern establishment exerted strong efforts to resist it. During a flurry of migration to Kansas beginning in 1879 (the "Pap Singleton Movement"), the Southern landlord group tried to prevent riverboat companies from transporting black migrants. During World War I Northern recruiters of black labor were frequently harassed, jailed, beaten, and shipped back North.

In the decade 1910-1920 the Southern blacks finally broke out of their regional imprisonment in a massive wave and began a great migratory movement which gained a momentum that continued into the 1960s. The great exodus has only in the 1970s fallen off to a moderate flow as Southern economic development has accelerated.

One major factor responsible for finally precipitating this vast migratory movement to the cities of the North was the acceleration of the expulsion of the black population from Southern agriculture, owing to the slow growth of the latter relative to the high rate of rural black population growth, the diversification of farming away from cotton, the stepped-up substitution of capital for labor, and the ravages of teh boll weevil, particularly in 1915-1916. [13] Other major factors were the increased pull from the North associated with improved transportation, World War I demand acceleration, active recruiting efforts by Northern employers, and the closing of immigration. These precipitating influences were superimposed upon the abiding income differentials between the South and the North and between Southern agriculture and Northern nonagriculture activities. For the closing of the frontier, among other things, meant that the migrating blacks would have additional barriers to entering farming in the North.

Overwhelmingly the blacks went into the cities to expand the emerging ghettos. Miserable as was Northern urban ghetto life, however, it was economically better than sharecropping and Southern urban ghetto life at that time. It was probably migration that accounted primarily for the material advancement of the black population between 1910 and 1930. In the very long run this migration also contributed to convergence of the South's per capita income toward the national average. By the end of World War I about one-fifth of the black population already lived outside the South. The formation of black ghettos was clearly under way by World War I. Two major factors lay behind that process. One was white racism in general and white real estate agents and homeowners in particular. The second was a strong feeling of cultural community, together with the need for mutual protection, on the part of blacks. [14]

Momentum and the joint effect of push and pull factors thereafter continued to draw blacks to the North, and, after the onset of World War II, to the West. At present about one-half the black population lives in the North. Because almost all live in cities, the great migration entailed the transformation of an essentially propertyless, agrarian population into a propertyless, urban employee class.

The Development of the North

Since the Civil War was mainly fought on Southern territory, the North was physically unscathed. Except for the tragic loss of manpower, the North faced no unsurmountable task of rehabilitation and reconstruction. The conversion from military to civilian production was a relatively minor adjustment, because food and clothing had made up such a large portion of wartime military demand. Manufacturing and construction in the civilian sector of the economy had suffered a wartime slowdown, but agriculture had forged ahead through the increased use of woman, child, migrant, and immigrant labor, and the application of new capital equipment. It has been said, with the usual grain of truth of such adages, that "the McCormick reaper won the war." Wheat production in the North rose from 142 million bushels in 1859 to 187 million in 1862 and 191 million in 1863. The *Report of Agriculture* in 1866 declared that

the agricultural condition of the Northern states was never more flourish-
ing. High prices, accessible markets and crops of average abundance have
assured good profits, and as a result mortgages have been paid, farm buildings erected, permanent improvements accomplished, farm implements and
machinery obtained, and in thousands of instances a surplus invested in
government funds.[15]

For the nonagricultural activities of the North the diversions of
the Civil War years represented merely a developmental pause.
Sustained economic modernization had begun long before the war,
and it continued after 1865. Indeed, almost all the economic development of the United States from 1865 to 1880 occurred in the
North. Northern gross product (in current dollars) was almost $8
billion in 1880, whereas the South's gross product with a quarter to
a third of the nation's population, was only about $1.6 billion. Al-
though the South began to pick up momentum thereafter, the
North had assumed a commanding lead. The North therefore occu-
pies the center of the stage for the U.S. economic historian in the decades leading up to World War I.

This vast area encompassed the Northeast (New England and
Middle Atlantic), East and West North Central, Plains, Southwest,
and Pacific subregions. The "frontier" of significant agricultural
settlement in the North (namely, 24 to 76 persons per square mile)
had approximately reached to the Mississippi River in 1860. This
meant that the latter three subregions were frontier areas after the
Civil War.

In addition, there occurred a vast and rapid indigenous population growth, substantially augmented by foreign immigrants, in
the great North Central subregion during the half century between
the Civil War and World War I. This filling-up process in the older
North Central states was as much a part of the expanding and maturing frontier, now urban, as the growth of population and economic activity (the "mining frontier," the "cattle frontier," etc.)
west of the 100th meridian.[16] As Thornthwaite has pointed out,
there were two distinct forms of migration. One was "the migration
that brought about the agricultural development of the country,"
concluded by about 1910, and the second was "the migration that
followed industrial expansion in all of its manifestations." The regional classification used by Harvey S. Perloff, et al. (Figure 2)
shows that the "Great Lakes" states (East North Central) suffered
a moderate decline in its share of the total U.S. labor force, largely
because of the pull of the West and the closing of the frontier. This
is evident from the figures in Table 10. Yet Easterlin estimates that
it was the great North Central region that raised its per capita per-

Figure 2 Regional classification. Reprinted from Harvey S. Perloff, et al., *Regions, Resources, and Economic Growth*, p. 5. By permission of the Johns Hopkins Press for Resources for the Future, Inc., ©

sonal income from 68 percent of the national average in 1860 to 98 percent twenty years later! Growth there was in this great region, and at a remarkable rate.

The table also reveals the broad outlines of regional labor force shifts in other areas between 1870 and 1910. The impact of the westward movement is clearly seen in the steady relative decline of the three older northern regions east of the Mississippi from 57.5 percent of the national labor force in 1870 to 53.7 percent in 1890 and 50.2 percent in 1910. (This percentage decline did not prevent an *absolute* increase in population and labor force of course.) New England experienced the most drastic relative decline. The Southeast (South Atlantic and East South Central), whose natural white population growth rate was relatively high, dropped behind primarily because of migration to the Southwest, which includes Texas. It is noteworthy that the Great Plains passed its relative peak in 1890 and exhibited a proportionately declining position after the end of the frontier. The Far West, particularly California, showed substantial growth, but its greatest period of labor force growth was not to occur until after World War I. This region, together with the Southwest and the Mountain West, was still a vast,

TABLE 10

DISTRIBUTION OF LABOR FORCE, 1870 - 1910

Region	1870	1890	1910
New England	10.39%	8.82%	7.64%
Middle Atlantic	25.23	24.30	23.56
Great Lakes	21.90	20.61	19.02
Southeast	28.04	24.09	24.51
Plains	9.24	13.14	11.66
Southwest	2.18	3.51	6.20
Mountain West	.57	1.75	2.24
Far West	2.45	3.78	5.19
United States	100.00%	100.00%	100.00%
persons	12,505,923	22,735,661	38,167,336

Source: Harvey S. Perloff, Edgar S. Dunn, Jr., Eric E. Lampard, and Richard F. Muth, *Regions, Resources, and Economic Growth* (Lincoln: University of Nebraska Press, 1960), p. 131, table 31.

sparsely populated land mass on the eve of the Civil War. The westward movement of population continued only until the end of World War I in the case of the Southwest and Mountain West; thereafter, its only manifestation was the great flow into California.

The relatively "rich" and "poor" subregions can be perceived by comparing labor force percentages with percentages of total personal income in 1910. [17] Four regions enjoyed higher shares of total income than labor force: New England, the Middle Atlantic, the Great Lakes, and the Far West. The remaining regions exhibited a reverse order (except for the Mountain West, where the shares were approximately equal). The Southeast showed the greatest discrepancy in 1910, with 24.5 percent of the nation's labor force, but only 13 percent of total personal income. This discrepancy can by no means be attributed primarily to the heavily agrarian character of the Southeast labor force, for the Southwest was about equally agrarian, yet exhibited a much lesser discrepancy.

Regional changes in the pattern of industrialization may be represented by manufacturing. As measured by either labor or value

TABLE 11

DISTRIBUTION OF MANUFACTURING, 1870 - 1910

Region	1870		1890		1910	
	L.F.	V.A.	L.F.	V.A.	L.F.	V.A.
New England	21.65%	23.95%	17.38%	17.48%	13.42%	14.32%
Middle Atlantic	38.35	42.16	35.84	40.05	33.55	36.90
Great Lakes	20.36	18.07	21.23	24.35	22.61	25.59
Southeast	9.94	6.23	10.42	6.83	12.69	10.04
Plains	6.52	6.68	8.88	7.00	8.35	6.42
Southwest	.72	.31	1.31	.68	2.74	1.49
Mountain West	.35	.24	1.44	.68	1.64	1.21
Far West	2.11	2.36	3.50	2.93	5.00	4.03
United States absolute	100.00% 2,643,417	100.00% $1,577,387[1]	100.00% 5,525,692	100.00% $3,453.518[1]	100.00% 10,656,545	100.00% $8,188.527[1]

L.F. = Manufacturing labor force
V.A. = Value added by manufacturing
[1]000s of current dollars

Source: Harvey S. Perloff et al., op. cit., pp. 152-3.

added in current dollars, Table 11 exhibits the salient shifts between 1870 and 1910. In terms of output, the industrial preeminence of the older industrialized areas was clearly shown by the fact that New England and the Middle Atlantic regions accounted for two-thirds of all manufacturing activity at the end of the Civil War decade. But the westward shift of the manufacturing belt into the diversified Great Lakes region during the following forty years was most evident. The latter overtook New England by 1890 to become the second most important industrial region. Thus the relative decline of the two older regions was partly, though not wholly, made up by the expansion in the Great Lakes area. The three regions taken together experienced a decline from about 84 percent to about 77 percent of the U.S. total value added in manufacturing over the forty years. The relatively high level of industrialization per capita is suggested by the fact that the combined population shares of the three were 56 percent in 1870 and 50 percent in 1910. [18]

The beginnings of widespread industrialization in the South are suggested by the notable rise in the Southeast's manufacturing share, especially after 1890. But the comparatively labor-intensive character of Southern manufacturing is indicated by the fact that the region possessed a higher proportion of the country's manufacturing labor force than of its value added. The Great Lakes exhibited the same relationship in 1870, but within twenty years had joined the two older industrial regions with respect to output/labor proportions. In all four of the "Western" regions, manufacturing labor force shares exceeded value added shares, just as in the Southeast. This pattern undoubtedly reflects the heavy weight of first-processing of products of the extractive activities in the manufacturing complexes of these regions. In the great manufacturing belt, on the other hand, advanced levels of fabrication, employing large complements of capital goods, were more typical.

It is evident that these years were accompanied by very great shifts in the relative positions of the different regions within the nation's industrial sector. While the absolute numbers of persons employed in manufacturing rose everywhere, the older regions declined relatively, manufacturing moved noticeably westward, and the South began to industrialize. Equally great shifts were to occur in the next half century. In the early 1960s, for example, manufacturing value added in New England was only 7 percent of the U.S. total! The Middle Atlantic proportion had declined to 23 percent, but the East North Central (Great Lakes) region had *grown* to 29 percent. The Southeast (as defined by Perloff's South Atlantic and East South Central) had expanded to about 16 percent, and the Pacific to almost 12 percent. Hence, the long run pattern of convergence in regional income per capita, owing in large part to migration and the convergence of nonagricultural economic activity, has had no counterpart in the form of a uniform spatial distribution of manufacturing activity. Rather, the pattern is one of ceaseless shifting among the various regions. Perhaps the most striking element of stability in the tenacity with which the Great Lakes region has retained since 1890 such a substantial share of the nation's aggregate industrial activity.

Development of Manufacturing in the North Central Region

In the 1869-1914 period under review the westward movement of manufactures into the North Central region accompanied the westward movement of the population center of the country. This fact by itself suggests that a strong orientation of such activity toward markets was more important than other determinants of location. Between 1849 and 1919 the center of U.S. manufacturing in terms of gross value of products moved westward a distance of 329 miles and southward a net distance of 16 miles, while the center of population moved westward 290 miles. In only two of the decades encompassed by these dates — 1860-1870 and 1870-1880 — did the population center make greater westward advance than manufacturing. [19]

A famous census essay written in 1899 [20] deals with the causes of the location of various manufacturing activities and compares favorably in analytical quality with many more recent treatments of the subject. The essay throws considerable light on the regional distribution of manufactures around the turn of the twentieth century. It lists seven considerations: nearness to materials, nearness to markets, water power, climate, labor supply, capital funds, and the momentum of an early start.

In the case of the westward movement of manufacturing into the East North Central region, nearness to raw materials and to markets were undoubtedly important. "Nearness" is largely a matter of transport costs, and the Great Lakes industries had an advantage in cheap water transport. Proximity to markets is also directly vital to so-called residentiary industries, "markets" including both capital goods and consumers goods markets. Capital funds, on long term as well as short term, for North Central economic development, at least prior to the early twentieth century, according to Lance Davis, came primarily, though by no means exclusively, from within the region rather than from the East. [21]

"Momentum" and local as well as international markets operated to hold manufacturing activity in New England and the Middle Atlantic regions. Water power, always important to New England in the past, of course gradually lost its influence with the spread of steam power after the Civil War.

The cumulative effects of (1) initial activities, when reinforced by (2) associated external economies and linkages, together with (3) local and subregional market-oriented activities, and (4) increasing population, constitute important elements of economic "momentum." In the North Central areas the growth of a diversified agriculture provided an income-elastic market for capital goods produced in the region, a large market for fabricated consumer goods, and foodstuffs for the burgeoning urban populations. A general statement of the cumulative process of industrial interrelatedness has been well formulated by Gunnar Myrdal:

The decision to locate an industry in a particular community . . . gives a spur
to its general development. Opportunities of employment and higher incomes are provided for those unemployed before or employed in a less remu-
nerative way. Local businesses can flourish as the demand for their products
and services increases. Labor, capital and enterprise are attracted from outside to exploit the expanding opportunities. The establishment of a new
business or the enlargement of an old one widens the market for others, as
does generally the increase of incomes and demand. Rising proifts increase
savings but at the same time cause investments to go up still more, which
again pushes up the demand and the level of profits. And the expansion
process creates external economies favorable for sustaining its continuation.[22]

Probably of unique value to the growth of industry was the at-
tractiveness of the North Central region to the iron and steel industry. Walter Isard has pointed to the technological changes that
reduced the relative importance of ore supplies in steelmaking. He
notes that the growth of Cleveland marked the first major shift
away from coal sites, a change connected with the fuel savings associated with both the Bessemer and open-hearth steelmaking techniques. The growth of steel production in Chicago was induced in
part by similar factors, stimulated in particular by the availability
of Lake Superior ores. [23]

The U.S. Steel Corporation erected its gigantic mill at Gary,
Indiana, in 1907. The iron and steel industry was a major industry
in the North Central region in its own right (despite the dominance
of Pittsburgh, technically outside yet just on the edge of the region). [24] But it was also a good example of both the interplay of
several location factors and the role of backward and forward linkages: as pig iron production in the Great Lakes region advanced
from 25 percent of the U.S. total in 1890 to 37 percent in 1910, the
associated steel industry induced the growth of major metal mining
and metal fabricating, from minor steel products to heavy machinery. At the same time the secular shift away from pig iron toward
the use of iron and steel scrap in steelmaking, already evident before the end of this period, presaged another advantage for the Midwest over Pittsburgh. Iron ore output in the North Central region
expanded from 35 percent of the national total in 1879 to 82 percent
in 1909. [25] Perloff et al. show that the Great Lakes' share of iron and
steel products expanded from 19 percent in 1870 to 33 percent in
1910. Of all industries, Albert Hirschman in his *Strategy of Economic Development* assigns the highest linkage score to iron and
steel.

The freedom of movement of the iron and steel industry, however, for many years after 1900 was inhibited and distorted by an administered pricing policy collusively executed by the major steel firms. This "basing point" policy required all steel in the country to be priced at the Pittsburgh mill price plus freight cost calculated from Pittsburgh *regardless of where it was produced or sold!* It took Pittsburgh from 1860 to 1900 to expand its share of iron and steel value added from 7.7 percent to 12.8 percent of the U.S. total, but it took only one more decade, under the basing point arrangement, to expand to a 23.2 percent position. [26] Much, though not all, of this acceleration must have been due to "Pittsburgh plus." One notorious casualty of Pittsburgh plus was Birmingham, Alabama, which had everything in its favor, except local markets, for a steel production center. It seems not to have been a coincidence that most of the facilities in the area were owned and restricted in their growth by the dominant U.S. Steel Corporation, which was a leader in the establishment and perpetuation of the basing point pricing system.

Developments in the Western Regions

The Western regions that we are concerned with make up the bulk of the land mass of the continental United States and embraced the Great Plains, Southwest, Mountain West, and Far West. Clearly there was enormous diversification of economic activity in this vast area. Nevertheless it is possible to say that in general the extractive activities—agriculture (including animal husbandry), mining, fisheries, and forestry—overwhelmingly dominated commodity production in the area during the entire period. Its share of the nation's extractive industries' labor force continued to rise from 1870 to 1910. There was significant manufacturing only in the eastern edge of the Great Plains (especially Minnesota and Missouri), Texas, and the Pacific Coast of the Far West. Over the years 1870 to 1910, however, the relative importance of the manufacturing labor force in each region increased notably; and the relative importance of farming labor declined (although only slightly in the Mountain West and Far West regions).

It was in these Western regions that frontier development rose to a crescendo and then terminated, all in the period from the Civil War to World War I. Actually, historians of the frontier such as

Ray Allen Billington speak of a number of frontiers—the cattle-men's frontier (Texas, the Great Plains, and Mountain regions), the railroad transportation frontier (trans-Mississippi), the miners' frontier (everywhere West except the Great Plains), and the farm-ers' frontier (from the Mississippi to the Rocky Mountains). Fred A. Shannon's term, "livestock frontier," is undoubtedly more ac-curate and comprehensive than "cattleman's frontier" because, as he points out, "before the end of the century, when the cattle indus-try was at its peak, [cattle] were in the minority among the live-stock even of their own section," the 15 million cattle being overwhelmed in 1900 in the "West" by the combined total of 14 million hogs and 38 million sheep. Furthermore, a high proportion of the cattle were not on specialized cattle ranches, but on general farms.

The romanticized cowboy and the glamour of the long drives of Texas longhorns to Kansas and Missouri railroad shipping towns between 1867 and 1885 has given many Americans an oversimpli-fied picture of the livestock frontier. This has concealed or mini-mized the wanton destruction of the buffalo and the more system-atic spread of aminal husbandry in the Western area during these decades. The conflicts between the crop farmer and the animal hus-bandman and the search for water in the West have also provided grist for the cinema studios. But the crop farmer was not a signifi-cant element in the semi-arid and arid regions of the West before 1900. The relatively high income in the West is to be explained by factors other than the crop farmers.

Some mining was done in the "West," the regions being, in order of importance based on labor engaged, the Mountain, Southwest, and Far West. The great bulk of this mining was precious metals mining, with the very important exception of copper. In these areas the heyday of mining employment was over by the turn of the twentieth century. The prominent mining states in the Mountain region were Idaho (lead and silver), Montana (which together with Arizona surpassed Michigan as copper producers in the 1880s), and Wyoming (petroleum). Nevada is most famous for its Comstock Lode (mainly silver, with some gold), originally discovered in 1859, but not fully developed until 1873 and after, just when the coinage of the silver dollar was discontinued by Congress (later called the "Crime of '73"). Nevada contributed enormously to the financial support of the free-silver, cheap-money advocates claiming a good part of the agrarian agitation of the last quarter of the nineteenth century. In the Far West mining was concentrated in California, but here the peak was reached as early as 1880.

Gold and silver were the most valuable nonferrous minerals until about 1900, but copper and lead contributed more directly to the development of industry in the country as a whole. Otherwise, the great mineral out-pourings, so important for industrialization, were from regions other than the West, such as petroleum from Texas, Oklahoma, and Louisiana, and coal from the East and Midwest. Texas and Louisiana also became a world center of sulfur production after 1900. California entered as a significant petroleum producer at the very end of the 1865-1914 period.

Nevertheless, the West was a major farming area throughout the period, and indeed almost doubled its share of the nation's farm labor force between 1870 and 1910. Agriculture in the Great Plains dominated the area's total volume of such activity, and exceeded all three of the other regions combined in its farm labor force until after 1900. But the Great Plains' share of the national farm labor force peaked in 1890, suggesting the coming end of the agricultural frontier in that famed farming region.

In a general way one could say farmers in the Plains produced corn, wheat, hay, and forage, and some livestock. It was in the famous Red River Valley of North Dakota, in the western Plains, that the large "bonanza" farms began producing no. 1 hard spring wheat in the 1870s, a wheat capable of being ground into flour only with the aid of the middlings purifier used in conjunction with the new Hungarian roller grinding process. The eastern Plains states joined with the western Lakes states in the great westward movement of dairying, including manufactured dairy products. Farmers in the Mountain and Southwest regions specialized in livestock.

The Pacific Coast farmers developed a most diversified basket of agricultural products. This was no accident, for the great transport cost barrier represented by the Rocky Mountains, Great Basin, and Sierra Nevada impelled economic diversification in the Pacific region, not only within farming but also in manufacturing and service activities. Thus as early as 1880 the Far West's labor force according to Perloff et al., was distributed as follows:

Agriculture	18.8%
Mining	11.5
Forestry	1.7
Fisheries	1.4
Manufacturing	20.5
Services	36.3

In crude quantitative terms this division has all the earmarks of a modern, advanced economy. Moreover, Easterlin estimates that it had the highest personal income per capita of any region within the United States.

The Western regions as here delineated were initially not a populous area. Together they accounted for only about 15 percent of the total U.S. population in 1870. But they were rapidly growing, and increased their share to over one-fourth in 1910. With their generally high income per head (except for the Southwest) they had accounted for one-fourth of total personal income a decade earlier than that.

Regional Connections with National Development

Each region thus bore a certain more or less individual give-and-take relationship to the general development of the country. There was considerable regional specialization together with uneven growth rates of industries and whole sectors within each region. The South after 1880 moved forward with rapid expansion in lumber products and the coarser cotton textiles. Manufacturing in the South tended to concentrate in the Highland and Piedmont areas near the sources of power sites and raw materials. Cotton production grew but slowly after 1880, and its importance in the total of U.S. exports, although noteworthy, secularly declined. As indicated earlier, the South's growth rate of per capita personal income just about matched the nation's between 1880 and 1900 and then began to exceed it somewhat until 1920.

In the North, New England and the Middle Atlantic forged ahead in a few manufacturing lines and remained highly important parts of the great manufacturing belt. On the eve of the World War I these two regions still accounted for over half the total U.S. employment in manufacturing. But, on the whole, they lost ground relatively to the other regions. Their agriculture declined absolutely, in terms of persons engaged, after 1890, although it was not until twenty years later that the national agricultural labor force reached its peak. The agriculture of these two regions became more capital- and labor-intensive and more diversified in the service of growing local metropolitan markets. But they continued to specialize in marketing and various financial services, both domestic and foreign. It should be realized also that in the economically diversified state of Pennsylvania anthracite coal was always an important, though relatively declining, component of total U.S. mineral fuel production in this period. Pennsylvania also led all other states in the production of bituminous coal. The West Virginia fields rose to prominence only after the turn of the century.

The dynamic Great Lakes region, led by Michigan, Illinois, and Wisconsin, spurred the growth of diversified manufacturing in the nation and added a new dimension to the manufacturing belt. It continued to develop a variegated food basket, contributed an enormous increase in transport services, and dramatically improved its relative income position. Thus, in terms of its increasing weight in the national total and its high rate of per capita income growth it was a powerful stimulus to the national growth rate. Such a convergence pattern is attributable mainly to migration of people, in this case, interregional, interstate, and rural-urban.

Both the Great Lakes and the Great Plains regions owed much to their ability ᴖo tie in with world markets during this entire period. Beyond in the great West the essential national role

was to augment the flow of raw materials into the industrializing Northeast and, in the case of agriculture, to supply international markets as well. The enormous growth in wheat exports is a case in point. Apart from farm produce, the West's most important output was mineral ores, notably copper, lead, zinc, and later, iron. Around the turn of the century the development of oil resources in California (after 1895), in Texas (after 1898), and in Oklahoma (after 1904), represented a major addition to the nation's fuel economy. Following the rapid destruction of the Great Lakes forests in the late nineteenth century, the Pacific Northwest became the new, important source for the nation's lumber supply.[27]

All these innovations and resource shifts spelled more than mere growth in output and population. They involved development in the broadest sense of far-reaching changes in the structure and functioning of the whole economic system and its larger environment. Regional migration, reallocation of resources, and specialization in production was a vital part of the total developmental process. The other vital aspects will be treated in more detail in the chapters that follow. As a first step, it will be pertinent to look briefly at the westward movement of people and economic activity in their aspect as a frontier. An economy with a frontier is rather different from one without a frontier, as Frederick Jackson Turner, Carter Goodrich, and numerous other historians appropriately emphasized.

NOTES

1. Richard A. Easterlin, "Rational Income Trends, 1840-1950," in Seymour E. Harris (ed.), *American Economic History* (New York: McGraw-Hill, 1961), p. 528.
2. Paraphrased by J. N. Bhagwati and S. Chakravarty, "Contributions to Indian Economic Analysis: A Survey," *American Economic Review*, 59 (September 1969), Supplement, p. 31.
3. "Slavery as an Obstacle to Economic Growth in the United States: A Panel Discussion, "*Journal of Economic History*, 27, no. 4 (December 1967), p. 544.
4. J. A. C. Chandler (ed.), *The South in the Building of the Nation*, cited in B. I. Wiley, "Salient Changes in Southern Agriculture since the Civil War," in J. T. Lambie and R. V. Clemence (eds.), *Economic Change in America*, (Harrisburg, Pa.: The Stackpole Co., 1954), p. 379.
5. Harvey S. Perloff et al., *Regions, Resources, and Economic Growth* (Lincoln, Neb.: University of Nebraska Press, 1960), p. 176.
6. Ibid.
7. See Douglas F. Dowd, "A Comparative Analysis of Economic Development in the American West and South," *Journal of Economic History*, 16 (December 1956), pp. 558-74. Numerous criticisms of the Dowd thesis may be found in the Panel Discussion on Slavery in the *Journal of Economic History*, 27, no. 4 (December 1967), pp. 518-60.
8. Before 1910 Southern whites also displayed a remarkable attachment to the South. They were apparently very "patriotic" about their region.
9. T. Lynn Smith, "The Redistribution of the Negro Population of the United States, 1910-1960," *Journal of Negro History*, 51 (July 1966) p. 163.
10. See C. Warren Thornthwaite, *Internal Migration in the United States* (Philadelphia: University of Pennsylvania Press, 1934), p. 12.
11. Paul H. Buck, *The Road to Reunion, 1865-1900* (New York: Vintage Books, 1959), p. 305.
12. Professor William E. Vickery estimates that net migration of nonwhites from the South was:

Years	Nonwhites
1870-1880	62,000
1880-1890	91,000
1890-1900	143,000
1900-1910	160,000
1910-1920	436,000

He notes also that until the decade 1910-1920 most migrants came from the states close to the North. ("The Economics of the Negro Migration," Thesis Seminar presented at a joint meeting of the Thesis Seminar and the Economic History Workshop, University of Chicago, April 8, 1966, p. 8, mimeographed.)
13. It is estimated that boll weevils destroyed an average of over 2 million bales of cotton a year between 1909 and 1921. John Frazer Hart, *The Southeastern United States* (Princeton: D. Van Nostrand, 1967), p.23.
14. See August Meier and Elliott Rudwick, *From Plantation to Ghetto*, revised ed. (New York: Hill and Wang, 1970), pp. 217-8.
15. Cited in Clyde O. Ruggles, "The Economic Basis of the Greenback Movement in Iowa and Wisconsin, "*Proc. Mississippi Valley Historical Assoc. 1912-1913*, VI. Reprinted in L. B. Schmidt and E. D. Ross (eds.), *Readings in the*

Economic History of American Agriculture (New York: Macmillan, 1925), p. 327.

16. The West North Central includes four states — the Dakotas, Nebraska, and Kansas — that are more or less bisected by the 100th meridian.

17. Estimates for the latter are from the work of E. S. Lee, A. R. Miller, C. P. Brainerd, and R. A. Easterlin, *Population Redistribution and Economic Growth, United States, 1870-1950* (Philadelphia: American Philosophical Society, 1957), v. I, p. 753, Table Y-1, and Harvey S. Perloff et al., op. cit., p. 185.

18. These percentages had practically been achieved by 1900. [See U.S. Department of Commerce, Bureau of the Census, *Location of Manufactures 1899-1929* (Washington, D.C.: Government Printing Office, 1933), p. 44.]

19. *Location of Manufactures, 1899-1929*, p. 7.

20. *Twelfth Census of the United States . . . 1900*, v. VII, *Manufactures*. Part I, pp. cxc-ccxiv.

21. See his "Capital Immobilities and Finance Capitalism: A Study of Economic Evolution in the United States 1820-1920," *Explorations in Entrepreneurial History*, second series, 1 (Fall 1963), pp. 88-105 *passim*.

22. From Gunnar Myrdal, *Rich Lands and Poor*, p. 25. By permission of Harper and Row, Publishers, Inc., © 1957.

23. Walter Isard, "Some Locational Factors in the Iron and Steel Industry Since the early Nineteenth Century," in Lambie and Clemence, op. cit., pp.200-1.

24. Pittsburgh-Cleveland is often classified as a major subregion of the manufacturing belt [see S. N. Dicken, *Economic Geography* (Boston: D. C. Heath, 1955), pp. 457-9].

25. Orris C. Herfindahl, "Development of Major Metal Mining Industries in the United States from 1839 to 1909," in NBER, *Output, Employment, and Productivity*, op. cit., p. 334.

26. Allan R. Pred, *The Spatial Dynamics of U.S. Urban-Industrial Growth, 1800-1914: Interpretive and Theoretical Essays* (Cambridge, Mass.: M.I.T. Press, 1966), p. 70.

27. Harvey S. Perloff et al., *Regions, Resources, and Economic Growth*, p. 151. By permission of The John Hopkins Press for Resources for the Future, (c), 1960.

[5]

The rise and decline of the frontier

We are chiefly concerned in this chapter with the economic nature and effect of the agricultural frontier in the North and east of the Rocky Mountains. Reference could also be made to the mining and forestry frontiers. These could be included without fundamentally changing the general analysis of the frontier's role in the economy and society. The extension of rail transport will be viewed chiefly as facilitating frontier expansion from the supply side.

The frontier existed before the Civil War, but it was gone by World War I. We do not have to embrace unqualifiedly Fredrick Jackson Turner's thesis that "the existence of an area of free land, its continuous recession, and the advance of the American settlement westward, explain American development," but we can certainly accept the hypothesis that the rate and pattern of overall development was significantly influenced by the frontier in the whole nineteenth century. The end of what Fred A. Shannon has called "the farmer's last frontier" not long before World War I is one reason for calling the 1865-1914 period an "era" in economic evolution. Furthermore, the rise and decline of the frontier were connected with certain social and political developments that bear upon economic history in ways that will be discussed later in this chapter and elsewhere.

The use of a few simple economic development criteria for the U.S. as a whole will clearly show not only some distinguishing features of the frontier but also the timing of the frontier's end. Such criteria might include the growth rates of the farm labor force, the total number of farms, and the improved land in farms, and the change in the ratio of physical farm capital to improved land in farms. Many others could be employed, such as population density and comparative regional population growth rates. The relevance of each criterion employed here requires certain assumptions. For example, it is assumed that under frontier conditions the rapid growth of farm output is associated with substantial increases in the number of farms and in all the factors of production. The latter is to be expected under a system of *extensive* cultivation such as exists when there is a farm frontier.

Table 12 shows that up to the early twentieth century the farm labor force rose rapidly, although at a declining rate. In this connection it is noteworthy that after 1900 census the farm labor force in all the Great Plains and Great Lakes states except Nebraska experienced absolute declines, showing that migration push factors had replaced pull factors in these former frontier areas. The amount of improved land in farms similarly rose substantially, and in general at higher rates than the labor force increased. Indeed, between 1870 and 1900, labor rose 72 percent and improved land acreage rose 119 percent. The same high rates of addition are found in the case of farm capital, the value of which kept pace with the rise in value of improved land until 1900.

As one would assume, with a frontier, increases in inputs of factors of production, taken together, accounted for the bulk of farm output increases, and technological advance was of lesser importance. For the North as a whole, determinants other than factor inputs accounted for about 44 percent of the rise in farm output over the period 1870 to 1900. But they accounted for 82 percent of the output rise between 1890 and 1910, i.e., as the frontier approached its end. When the frontier ended the relative importance of inputs as compared with other determinants was in the long run dramatically reversed. Without the frontier, only reproducible capital continued to rise substantially, improved land area ceased to increase (or declined) and the number of persons engaged in agriculture fell absolutely. Cultivation became *intensive* as the capital/labor and capital/land ratios rose. The land/labor ratio also rose because of the fall in the labor force.

TABLE 12

MEASURES OF FRONTIER GROWTH, 1870-1920

Census Year	Increase in farm labor force over preceding decade	Increase in number of farms over preceding decade	Increase in improved farmland over preceding decade		Ratio of physical farm capital[1] to value of total improved farmland (1910-1914 prices)
			acres	value	
1870					29
1880	31%	51%	59%	40%	28
1890	12	14	26	20	28
1900	17	26	16	22	27
1910	1	12	15	8	34
1920	- 8	2	5	6	39

[1]Other than land.

Sources: Historical Statistics of the United States; Stanley Lebergott, "Labor Force and Employment, 1800-1960," in National Bureau of Economic Research, Conference on Research in Income and Wealth, *Output, Employment, and Productivity in the United States After 1800,* Studies in Income and Wealth, v. 30 (New York: Columbia University Press, 1966, p. 118; Alvin S. Tostlebe, *Capital in Agriculture* (New York: National Bureau of Economic Research, 1957).

On the basis of these data it may be concluded that in an economic sense the frontier in a general way came to a close no later than the first decade of the twentieth century. Thereafter, a new epoch of intensive cultivation in U.S. farming began.

It is perhaps an informative comment on the role of the Homestead Act that this dating of the frontier's close places over half the final Homestead entries in acreage (and almost half in number) *after* the closure. To be sure, the lands patented later were inferior, economically and in fertility, to those patented earlier. We know that the traditional 160 acres was too small for subhumid homesteading. The popular quip was that the government was betting the settler 160 acres that he would starve in less than five years. It should also be noted that land acquired by purchase was much more important in the frontier period and in the period after the Homestead Act than acquisition free by homesteading.

But aggregates of selected agricultural variables for the nation, while in some cases similar to those for the frontier, conceal some of the distinguishing features of the frontier as compared to the older areas. Table 13 therefore presents similar data for two regions that in different ways may be said to represent the frontier—the Great Plains and the somewhat older Corn Belt—in contrast to the Northeast, which clearly exhibits the characteristics of an old nonfrontier region. The sharpest contrasts are of course found between the Great Plains and the Northeast. In the former region, the farm labor force was still increasing, although at a decreasing rate, through the census of 1910, whereas in the Northeast the farm labor force was stable from the very first decade of the period, and declined absolutely after 1890. The pattern of timing for the number of farms and improved land in farms is roughly similar.

Of particular interest is the relative importance of reproducible capital in the frontier and in the older farm areas of the Northeast. Calculations based on Alvin S. Tostlebe's estimates show that intensity of cultivation as measured in Table 13 by the ratio of the value of reproducible capital to land values was only a third to a half in the West of its value in the Northeast throughout the period 1870 to 1920. The data also show that in the two illustrative frontier regions the degree of intensiveness, as measured, was stable or fell to the low point recorded in the census of 1900 (as in the national figures in Table 13), and thereafter rose as the frontier closed. This supports our dating of the frontier's close after the turn of the twentieth century, more than a decade later than the traditional historians' dating.

Economically a frontier is a condition usually involving the proliferation of activity in an area with substantial natural resources and associated with the accumulative or acquisitive operations of economic and political entities sited in other "older" areas. The latter have experienced, or are expected soon to experience, diminishing rates of returns to factor owners.

Benjamin Higgins once explained the frontier concept as involving possible combinations of an area in which (1) the most advanced known techniques are not yet applied, (2) the productivity of labor or capital is higher than in older areas, and/or (3) the migration of labor and capital into a new area will raise the productivity of these

TABLE 13

REGIONAL MEASURES OF FRONTIER GROWTH, 1870-1920

Census Year	Increase in farm labor force over preceding decade			Increase in number of farms over preceding decade			Increase in improved farm land acreage over preceding decade			Increase in improved farm land value over preceding decade			Ratio of physical farm capital[1] to value of total improved farm land		
	N.E.	C.B.	G.P.	N.E.	C.B.	G.P.	N.E.	C.B.	G.P.	N.E.	C.B.	G.P.	N.E.	C.B.	G.P.
1870													97.15	31.04	42.85
1880	.06%	23.73%	229.6%	15.70%	13.31%	320.3%	12.89%	51.76%	544.4%	10.98%	31.04%	363.53%	96.59	33.43	33.52
1890	.005	-.003	60.33	-5.70	2.94	63.17	-9.69	10.14	182.72	-8.74	9.71	119.30	104.79	35.61	39.71
1900	-.02	11.08	15.81	2.88	11.29	9.66	-8.74	11.60	30.89	-2.37	10.15	42.75	108.53	34.62	33.75
1910	-11.02	-11.28	11.53	-3.09	-3.45	17.04	-6.28	1.63	40.68	-5.32	.08	28.91	119.37	39.44	38.03
1920	-12.51	-11.53	-11.50	-11.30	-4.59	-3.95	-11.93	-1.98	6.51	-10.85	-1.62	12.70	125.89	46.45	39.88

1Other than land.

Note:
N.E. = Northeast
C.B. = Corn Belt
G.P. = Great Plains

Source: Perloff et al., Regions, Resources, and Economic Growth (Baltimore: John Hopkins Press, 1960), p. 624, Appendix Table A-2 (labor force estimates adapted to Tostlebe's regions). Alvin S. Tostlebe, Capital in Agriculture: Its Formation and Financing since 1870 (New York: National Bureau of Economic Research, 1957), Tables 5, 6, 9, pp. 48-69 passim.

factors in the older, more mature areas of out-migration without raising it above the level in the frontier territory.[1] A frontier, therefore, has meaning only in relation to the presence of a metropolitan economy or region to which the frontier is linked in some way. The frontier may be either a domestic one, i.e., one located within the political boundaries of the older sovereignty, or it may be located abroad (or on the Moon). In the middle of the nineteenth century John Stuart Mill argued that secular stagnation from long-run diminishing returns in England could be avoided by foreign trade and investment. *All this implies that a frontier raises the rate of return on investment, and when it is gone, if this rate is to be sustained, it must be by other means.*

The frontier generated a condition the opposite of Ricardo's long-run decreasing returns based on cultivation, *from a given total amount of land*, of the best lands first. In the U.S. case, the western lands were probably at least as fertile as those in the Northeast for the same farm products. Furthermore, technological change, such as mechanization of harvesting, was perhaps more rapid in the West than in the Northeast between the Civil War and the end of the century. It has been shown by William Parker and Judith Klein[2] that this accounted for the great bulk of the rise in the farm output/labor ratio for grains in the frontier regions between 1840-1860 and 1900-1910. In a frontier area technological innovation is less inhibited by the commitment to habit and outmoded fixed capital than it is in older areas. The frontier therefore involved more than dramatic additions of new land for farm purposes; particularly in its later years it was also associated with innovations that marked the beginning of capital-intensive farming.

The fact that the expansion of the frontier in its ascending period made possible the absorption of large increases in the farm force and in farm capital inputs should not blind us to the accompanying fact that both were declining relatively in the economy as a whole. The ascending agricultural frontier slowed the relative decline of farming in the economy as a whole. This was probably the major economic effect of the frontier. Table 13, particularly the first four columns, shows that frontier decline set in sharply after 1880. The eighties were years of sharp acceleration in industrialization and urbanization, i.e., in relative agricultural decline. The nonfarm sector and the urban sectors, *even in those parts of the country embraced by the frontier*, were growing even more rapidly. For example, according to Harvey Perloff et al., in the Great Plains region the farm labor force declined from 62 percent of the regional total in 1870 to 41 percent in 1910, while the regional manufacturing labor force grew from 15 percent to 20 percent and the services labor force from 23 percent to 37 percent. In the North Central region according to Eldridge and Thomas the comparative decennial percentage changes in urban and rural populations were as follows:

Area	1870-1880	1880-1890	1890-1900	1900-1910
Urban	55.4	76.7	37.0	32.7
Rural	28.1	13.9	7.8	1.4

It is difficult not to infer that the urban population of this region was being augmented to a great extent not only by the in-migration from the native East and from abroad but also by the farm population of the region, i.e., by rural-urban migration. In our concern with the expansion of frontier agriculture there may be a danger of overlooking both the more rapid growth of the frontier region's nonfarm sector and the labor force contribution to it made by the expanding farm sector. Indeed, Gustav Ranis and J. C. H. Fei have stated that development consists precisely in the reallocation of surplus agricultural workers whose contribution to output is likely to be very low and certainly less than the contribution of additional workers would be in the nonfarm sector. Other things being equal, this out-migration of labor tended to sustain labor income (e.g., real wages) in agriculture, while depressing it in the nonfarm sector, and stimulate the substitution of capital for labor in agriculture, while retarding such substitution and raising the rate of profit in nonfarming activities.

In the case of the U.S. farm frontier areas, it is to be presumed that rates of return to factor owners were higher there than in the Northeast. Given two typical farms in, say, New York or Pennsylvania and Iowa, the equilibrium average and marginal physical product of all inputs should have been higher in Iowa than in the East. Hence, total factor productivity should have been higher. This should have been translated into higher net value productivity and higher actual rates of return to property. There is evidence to support this. For example, Robert Fogel and Jack Rutner have estimated that even without considering the relatively more favorable incidence of capital gains enjoyed by the frontier farms, the real average annual rate of return on all agricultural capital from current production in 1880 was 9.4 percent in the North Central region and 8.4 percent in the North Atlantic region. In the vast region west of the North Central (Mountain West and Pacific) the average rate was 10.4 percent. The presumption here is that the benefits of higher returns to property (and labor) in the frontier areas accrued to property income receivers excluding the higher transport costs to market (probably borne by farmers) as compared with the East. Otherwise, in fully informed markets capital and labor would not have exhibited the East-to-West mobility that had characterized U.S. experience for generations.

Frontier Farm Sector Influence on Economic Development

The matter of the relationship between the frontier and the overall economic development of the United States is of some significance in view of the great ideological emphasis put on the role of the frontier, and the frontier policy of government, by historians and other social groups. Such an analysis also indicates the interrelation of sectors in the historical process. Furthermore, there are likely analogies and contrasts between U.S. experience and that of other less developed and nondensely populated countries at the present time, wherein slow development of farm output and productivity may jeopardize overall development of the economy. Implicit in the "contributions" arguments that follow are the presumptions that the nonfarm sectors generally were more endowed with the potential for cumulative innovation, external economies, linkage effects, and other developmental processes, than was the frontier farm sector.

We have already indicated that frontier agriculture was by no means unchanging during the period of its rise and termination with respect to technological advance and the relative importance of the factors of production. A number of other important changes within the frontier farm sector were occurring simultaneously— changes that influenced both farming in general and the development of the nonfarm economy and that inaugurated or continued general trends in the structure of the North's farm economy.

As we pointed out earlier, the leading farm commodities produced in the North Central and Plains regions were wheat, corn, fresh beef, and pork from the livestock industry linked with it; hay

and oats for fodder; and dairy products. It may be thought that
these were "growth industries" in the sense that the output of these
commodities in the region rose at rates substantially above total
farm output or even above GNP. But this does not seem to have
been the case. Wheat may be taken as an illustration. Total wheat
output in the United States rose between 1869 and 1899 at an
annual compound rate of rather less than 3 percent. Total farm output increased at rather more than 2.5 percent. The North Central's
share of total U.S. wheat production in 1869 was about 68 percent,
and this proportion remained about constant at subsequent censuses through 1899.[3] It was only with respect to total wheat exports that growth performance was more impressive; for here the
rate, based upon three-year averages centered on 1870 and 1900 was
closer to 5 percent per year. These exports averaged about 21
percent of the crop in the seventies and peaked at 27 percent in the
nineties. (For meat products the export share was much less.)

Clearly, therefore, the moderate secular rise in the demand for
wheat came chiefly from the domestic consumer, and that mainly
from the urban population, which was growing about 3.5 percent a
year over this thirty-year period. The demand for wheat, like that
for cereals in general, and in contrast to the demand for commodities such as dairy products, grew most sluggishly in response to the
rise of population and income per capita. Indeed the consumption of
grain products per head was secularly falling. As we have seen
(Chapter 3), total population and per capita income were rising at
about 2.0 and 2.6 percent per annum respectively between 1869 and
1910. A simple equation will show how unresponsive, or inelastic,
was total domestic demand for wheat as per capita income rose. For
example, take the expression

$$\frac{\Delta Q_w}{Q_w} = \frac{\Delta H}{H} + a\,\frac{\Delta y}{y}$$

where Q_w is the total quantity of wheat *domestically consumed*, H
is population, y is income per person, and a is the average income
elasticity of demand for wheat.[4] Thus we have roughly for 1869-
1909:

$$.020 = .021 + a(.026)$$

$$a = -.04$$

which is negative and very low—more or less representative of the income elasticity in high income countries, where it hovers around zero. In a less developed country today the income elasticity for traditional cereals would probably be positive and two or three times the estimate shown—more like the income elasticity of demand for U.S. wheat and flour exports in this period.

It is hard to believe in the light of these data regarding the expansion of wheat production, a rate approximating the population rate, that public land policy (as represented by the expansion of wheat lands) contributed, in this period, to a too-rapid expansion of cultivation. Fogel and Rutner have argued that the favorable trends of (1) farm real wages in the West relative to manufacturing real wages and (2) comparative rates of return to property are unfavorable to the "too-liberal land policy" thesis. Appraisal of the thesis, however, would have to make allowance, among other things, for the contribution of hypothetical nonfarm domestic alternatives as well as for the total foreign exchange forgone, had there been no exports over the period. Calculations by this writer suggest that on the most extreme possible assumptions (e.g., no farm export increases whatever above the 1870 levels, complete transferability and full employment of resources released in appropriate proportions from producing farm product exports to the nonfarm sectors at existing productivity differentials, and constant returns to scale), GNP in 1900 would have been 10 percent higher than it actually was. Assuming freedom of entry and exit between the farm and nonfarm sectors, together with other competitive assumptions, this result seems inconsistent with the conclusions of Fogel and Rutner. But with more relaxed assumptions the estimated difference between hypothetical and actual GNP would have been much less, thus reducing the degree of inconsistency, yet not eliminating it.

Using wheat as an example, one may conclude that the chief contribution of the farm frontier to overall economic development was to feed the workers in the burgeoning nonfarm economy. Of notable secondary importance was the contribution to the U.S. balance of international payments through the foreign exchange that reverted to the country from wheat exports, and the absence of the necessity to import much in the way of foodstuffs. These exports, together with the high export proportions for meat products, cotton, and tobacco, largely account for the fact that farm exports, though relatively declining, made up on the average about three-fourths of all U.S. exports by value during the 1870-1914 period. Two of these four farm exports—wheat (and flour) and meat—are strongly identified with the expansion of frontier agriculture in these decades.

Since most farm products were processed en route to the domestic or foreign consumer, the extension of agricultural production in the frontier states, as elsewhere, was linked with the proliferation of agricultural processing industries properly considered to be manufacturing, such as meat packing, flour milling, and creameries. Indeed the aggregate price of the output of manufactured foodstuffs rose relatively from 24 percent of the total of all finished commodities in 1869 to 30 percent in 1910. Agricultural expansion in the country as a whole contributed to the growth of numerous nonfood manufactures also, but frontier agriculture in the non-South was overwhelmingly devoted to the production of foodstuffs. In these ways the extension of frontier farming helped to diversify the occupational and product structure of the nonfarm economy even as the export-linked period of frontier agriculture expansion slowed the relative decline of farming in the economy as a whole, especially before 1880.

The changing agricultural sector of the frontier states also contributed to the availability of factors of production in the growing nonfarm activities in those states. It has already been pointed out that the former was providing labor to the latter and therefore kept down nonfarm labor costs. Of course, this argument must be qualified to recognize the associated depressive effects upon consumer spending and the dampening effect on the substitution of capital for labor (due to the relative prices of capital and labor) in nonfarm activities. *Economic development in those days, however, was heavily dependent upon a high ratio of investment to consumption*, whatever adverse value judgments one might make about the constricted level of living. If one accepts this typically capitalistic development pattern, then agriculture's possible net "contribution" to it may be recognized: lower nonfarm wage costs tended to raise profits. So far as we may speculate upon the degree to which somewhat lower wage costs relative to the price of capital dampened the tendency of nonfarm firms to substitute capital for labor, it seems unlikely that the effects were very significant, for in general capital/labor ratios rose.

Beyond this, it seems plausible to say that the frontier farm expansion made only moderate demands upon the capital resources so much needed by the rapidly growing nonfarm sector. This follows from the heavier reliance of frontier farm expansion on additional land rather than on reproducible capital goods, i.e., on extensive forms of cultivation. Simon Kuznets' estimates, which unfortunately are for the entire United States, reveal that agriculture's share of the stock of durable reproducible capital, in his sample of sectors accounting for four-fifths of the U.S. total, fell from 31.9 percent in 1880 to 22.5 percent in 1900. According to Alvin Tostlebe's estimates, the ratio of reproducible farm capital to output in both the Corn Belt and Great Plains was falling from 1870 to 1900, whereas it was rising in manufacturing.

The validity of the point regarding agriculture's contribution by way of being a limited drain on the economy's real capital resources depends on the presumption that capital supply constraints were more severe than demand constraints in the nonfarm sector during those decades. From the demand aspect, the relatively slower growth of demand for reporducible capital in frontier agriculture would have reduced its contribution to capital formation in the economy as a whole. (We cannot have it both ways: if agriculture helped growth from the supply side, it did not help from the demand side.)

Finally, it was pointed out that viewed as a food basket, the expansion of frontier farming made it easy to feed the growing army of nonfarm, primarily urban, consumers. This facilitated capital accumulation in the nonfarm sectors by generating, in all probability, more favorable terms of trade by which the industrial sectors obtained farm products than would have been the case if the latter had had to buy these foods and other farm products from abroad. The empirical plausibility of such a terms of trade proposition can be sustained even though the actual domestic agricultural terms of trade e.g., the ratio of prices received by frontier farmers to prices paid by them, did not change much, or even rose, as claimed by Douglass North and others.

What Made Frontier Expansion Possible: The Supply Side

The spectacular westward shift of farming occurred only because people, income, and property, linked with great innovations in production and the pattern of demand, were mobile enough to respond to the incentives for gain in the West relative to opportunities in Europe and in the East and South. On the supply side white working people expanded cultivation in the Old Northwest and hedge-hopped from farming there to the new lands westward. Some 12 million immigrants and unnumbered millions of native migrants were the human reservoir behind the movement. Of these, about 1.6 million joined the total of persons engaged in agriculture in the Great Plains and Great Lakes states between 1870 and 1900 and contributed to the setting up of over 1 million new farms.[5]

To make this possible the transport cost barriers inhibiting the movement of both people and products were reduced. The provision of transport services and reduction of charges due to railroad construction and innovation were probably the chief means whereby these barriers were overcome, although waterways did contribute something. Railroad mileage in the Western states (excluding the Pacific Coast states) increased from 24,587 in 1870 to 62,394 in 1890. Railroadization in the West was heavily indebted to Federal land grants and various forms of aid from states and local governments. This boost to railroad construction and consequently to agricultural settlement in general and the range cattle industry in particular was conjoined with modest "colonizing" efforts by railroad enterprises in the seventies and eighties.

Robert Fogel has estimated that the absence of railroads in 1890 would have almost doubled the cost of shipping wheat, corn, pork, and beef interregionally. While the proprietory farmers and the growing number of farm tenants, to say nothing of agricultural wage earners, probably reaped only small rewards from the swelling tide of products pouring out from their farms, the railroads moved these products generally eastward at *average* rates that declined. This was true even though the *average* rates west of Chicago were much higher than the *average* Chicago to New York rates, affected as the latter were by strong waterway competition. However monopolistic the price policies of the railroads with respect to both the sale of their lands and freight rates, they did move migrants westward and farm products eastward, thus contributing to the extension of the frontier.

In addition to the availability of land, the migration of people, and the growth of transportation, it was necessary that finance be provided for what was overwhelmingly a commercial type of farming. Farmers needed short term funds for working capital purposes, and intermediate and long term capital funds for financing more durable assets. For short term credit farmers were able to place little reliance on either their own net receipts or the national banks, relatively few of which could even locate in rural areas, and whose directors tended to follow a high-interest, tight-lending policy with respect to loans or farm collateral. Fred Shannon has also argued that farmers wanted loans in the form of scarce greenbacks "to settle Eastern accounts," but that since greenbacks were banks' legal reserves, they did not care to make such reserve-draining loans. Apparently the major sources of short term funds were merchants, commission agents, and farm implement dealers and manufacturers like Cyrus McCormick and J. I. Case, who in turn received credit from city banks in their area and from the East. For longer term funds the mortgage loan association, private loan company, and insurance company were leading factors. Much of this money came from individuals in the East. Interest rates were substantially above those charged other local nonfarm enterprisers and above those prevailing in the East, and were likely to be matched by additional commission charges and handling fees.

It seems apparent that credit and capital funds were a relatively scarce factor in frontier agriculture, but that there was considerable East-to-West flow supplemented by modest provisions from the local area. Even the British made some direct investments in larger farms. The paucity of this resource to working farmers was one of the causes of the growth of tenancy, a development that helped assure the continued flow of output: as noted by Theodore Saloutos, "one could lose his land, farm house, livestock, implements, machinery, and supplies, but still turn around and become a tenant holding from a bank, an insurance company, a mortgage firm, or a farmer, and continue to produce crops for the market as he did when he owned his farm." Sharecroppers and tenants in the North Central region made up 20.5 percent of all farmers in 1880, and this fraction had risen to 27.9 percent to 1900.

The Federal Government's Contribution to Frontier Expansion

Western settlement was stimulated from the supply side by the national government in ways other than through gifts of cash and a gross 125 million acres to railroads between 1862 and 1871. Such settlement involved, among other things, driving the Indians off their ancestral lands, and the history of that influence on the production function for frontier agriculture was written in letters of blood. The advertising slogan that the Winchester was "the gun that won the West" is devastatingly true for this period and for this area that Jack Eblen has called "the second United States empire." It was the Winchester (combined with the genocidal slogan, "the only good Indian is a dead Indian") and the use of U.S. troops that after 1867 largely implemented Congress' reservation system for the western Indian tribes, wiped out the buffalo, and opened 100 million acres of Indian lands for sale subsequent to passage of the Dawes Act of 1887.

The Federal government's public lands policy also emphasized indiscriminate disposition and rapid settlement by and through private individuals and corporations without paying much attention, until the early 1890s at least, to its own timidly professed, belated conservationist principles. Long-run, socially costly externalities such as blighted landscapes, devasted wildernesses, squalid townships, eroded soils, lost soil covers, stranded communities, and subregional distressed areas (all the side effects of growth and technological advance) were ignored because of the veritable worship of economic growth and technological progress that dominated late nineteenth century America. The adverse inheritance left by the frontier was not so much diminishing returns in agriculture, for these could be offset with added effort by technological advance, but rather, as Harold Barnett and Chandler Morse point out, the "social adjustment to a variety of adverse indirect effects of technological change and economic growth." The adjustment required was both social and economic.

In some cases the attempt to deal with external economies and diseconomies was suprisingly unfocused. For example, the Timber Culture Act of 1873 failed to save forest cover on thousands of frontier farms simply because it could not be applied by Plains farmers on their semiarid land. In other cases Federal legislation designed to control the growth process so as to give heed to the externalities connected with growth had just the opposite effect. For example, it is the judgment of Benjamin Hibbard, eminent historian of the public land policies, that the Timber Cutting Act of 1878 "was so framed and so administered that the forest devastation was hastened."

The conservation movement and conservation legislation beginning in the early 1890s (such as the repeal of the Preemption Act of 1841 and of the Timber Cutting Act of 1878, tightening of requirements under the Desert Land Act of 1877, and authorization of the President to set aside forest lands as public reservations) were too weak and too belated to arrest the forces of "growth." Among the repercussions stemming from these clashes of policy we should note again the allegations made by many historians that public policy toward the rate of agricultural settlement was too liberal, too much guided by a desire, in the words of a House bill of 1878, "to place the agricultural interests of the country where they properly belong, and that is above every other branch of the public industries." The question of the empirical validity of these charges will no doubt be debated for a long time.

A point is made elsewhere in this book that laissez faire mainly meant moderate aid to business. Whatever historians may conclude about which business sector was most favored, the general proposition is certainly applicable with respect to the natural resource activities. In addition to the railroad aid and the confiscation and sale of Indian lands to private business, the Desert Land Act, according to John T. Ganoe, chiefly benefited the grazing business interests and immigration companies, engrossing many thousands of acres; the Timber Cutting Act permitted mill owners and lumber companies to cut down trees on the public mineral lands without charge; and the Timber and Stone Act of 1878 expedited the sale for $2.50 an acre of over 13 million acres of public timberlands ("land unsuited for agriculture but valuable for timber") to private corporations and individuals. In the sale at low prices of lands and land scrip given to the states under the Morrill Land Grant College Act of 1862 the states were similarly liberal in subsidizing the growth of the private business sector, in this case at the expense of correspondingly underfunded education in "agriculture and the mechanic arts." That laissez faire was a powerful ideological and practical power on behalf of the business interests engaged in either production or promotion in the extractive activities is well reflected in the statement by the agricultural historian Everett E. Edwards:

> It was practically impossible to have foretold in 1850 that within 30 years a half-billion acres of the public domain would have been disposed of or reserved for governmental purposes. The land was considered valueless unless it was put under cultivation as rapidly as possible and the various land acts did help to people the wilderness. To have opposed unregulated settlement would have been considered either a mad perversion or a reflection of some selfish economic interest endangered by western competition. It was not only the lumber and mining companies and the land speculators that demanded a free hand; the mass of the American people, particularly those who looked westward, kept shouting for land and more land. The

United states in the generation before 1900 was probably not ripe for any
further measures of social control.[6]

The American consensus at the time was to develop overwhelmingly through the private market mechanism, and the laissez faire
partnership of government and business was the decisively chosen
route. It is therefore somewhat ironic to observe the embattled agrarian enterprisers, in precisely this era, as these "rugged individualists" mounted the first great revolt against the private market
mechanism and cried out vociferously for government intervention.

What Made Frontier Expansion Possible: The Demand Side

The most sobering fact about the farm business in U.S. history,
viewed in the aggregate, is that demand has exercised the most
severe constraints on expansion and growth. It has been shown
above that the rate of population growth, which was declining after
the Civil War, was the almost exclusive determinant, other than export demand, of the rate of growth of total farm output, since the
per capita income elasticity of demand hovered in the neighborhood
of zero. This was not true of some specific farm products such as
certain meats and dairy items, but it was true of most products, including wheat, which for a time was even serving a large export demand increase. The Southern cotton producer was favored for the
greater part of the nineteenth century with high annual growth
rates in the foreign demand for his commodity. The frontier producers in the 1865-1914 period were also favored with high annual
rates of increase in both foreign and domestic demand for meat products. These developments mitigated the demand constraints act-
ing upon the farm sector from the domestic market, permitting the
slow growth in domestic demand for cereals to be offset to some extent by the foreign demand for cereals and the more elastic domestic and foreign demand for Western meats.

Nevertheless, frontier agriculture as a whole was inhibited much
more by slowly growing demand than by supply factors. Given
existing conditions determining the money supply, the downward
movement of its price indexes over time, illustrated in Figure 3,
bears witness to this state of affairs. The actual secular decline of
average farm prices from 1872 to 1896, at a rate at least equal to the

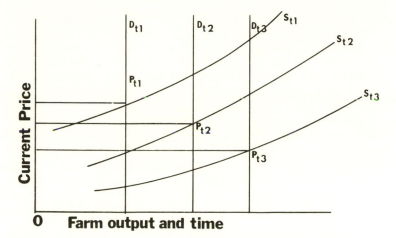

Figure 3 Illustrative supply and demand for frontier farm output. The subscripts t_1, t_2, and t_3 show the historical shifts in time of the short run supply (S) and demand (D) curves.

decline of nonfarm prices, would not have happened, as the chart could easily be used to show, if demand had shifted more rapidly to the right in relation to the rightward-shifting historical supply curves.

Thus what has been said above regarding the determinants of frontier expansion from the supply side must be connected with the well-known fact of easy entry into, and inhibited exit from, the business of farming in order to appreciate the traditional arguments that farmers in this period chronically "overproduced," i.e., generated a secular surplus. Although those arguments have usually assumed a probably exaggerated notion of an adverse trend in the overall agricultural terms of trade, they are, nonetheless, endowed with partially correct insight by virtue of the relatively greater constraints operating from the demand side as compared with the supply side.

The long run increase in total money demand between 1872 and 1896 was constrained by a slow growth in the money stock coupled with a secular decline in the rate of turnover (income velocity) of money. These factors pulled down general prices. But farm and nonfarm prices apparently fell at approximately the same rate, i.e., relative prices for these two sectors—the terms of trade—remained reasonably unchanged. How could this be, if the income elasticity for farm products was high? The answer is probably that the rise of total factor productivity in the nonfarm sector was superior to that for the farm sector. John W. Kendrick has estimated that in the decades before 1899 the average annual rate of increase in total factor productivity in the whole domestic economy was 1.2 percent, whereas in the farm sector it was only .9 percent.[7] Calculation from Kendrick's data of the compound annual growth rate of productivity for the nonfarm sector alone from 1874 to 1899 yields an estimate of 1.8 percent, almost twice the rate of productivity rise in the farm sector. Despite the superior productivity performance of the nonfarm sector, its prices did not fall more than farm products because of upward pressure on that sector's prices from rapidly growing demand: resource growth (supply) barely kept up with demand growth. On the other hand, despite inferior productivity performance in the farm sector, its prices did not fall less than nonfarm prices because of the relatively slow growth of population-linked demand for farm goods, coupled with a chronic tendency toward excess resources (was land policy too liberal?).

Social and Political Impact of the Frontier

The larger effects on society of the frontier and its demise have been debated in elaborate detail by general historians, and need not be examined here in detail. It is nevertheless relevant to economic history to note some of these effects where they may have existed. In particular, brief reference may be made here, prefatory to more elaborate treatment below, to: the emergence of imperialism; the level of living; the impact on labor and labor organization; and the possible connections between the frontier, on the one hand, and the agrarian revolt, the end of laissez faire, and the emergence of the modern "farm problem," on the other. Some of the less certain effects were declining agriculture's contributions to the decreasing importance of small enterprise, and the occupational shift from entrepreneurship and entrepreneurial income to employee status and the service income share. However, these effects are associated with the relative decline in the farm sector in any industrializing economy, whether it has a frontier or not.

Many years ago Chester W. Wright wrote a now famous article on the significance of the disappearance of the frontier,[8] in which he pointed out there was a connection between that event and the appearance of U.S. imperialism on the international scene. The emergence of a new foreign imperial behavior is often dated from the 1890s and the Spanish-American War. Wright stressed the expected increased needs for imported raw material and foods, markets for manufacturers, and opportunities to invest capital. It was the flow of capital abroad, however, that was the new feature of expansionism in our period. Before the Civil War, expansionism mainly meant acquiring contiguous territory, driving out the Indians, and cultivating the acquired resources. U.S. business placement of funds was almost exclusively "domestic," and the country was also importing capital. This was because it had a frontier that attracted funds from both resources. The matter will be discussed in some detail below, but it is no doubt already clear from what has been said about the tendency of the frontier to raise the rate of return on property that when the frontier vanished, a search for other ways to sustain this rate might be sought. Indeed, insofar as international long term creditor status and increasing reliance on raw imports from poor countries may be linked with imperial relationships, the subsequent changes in the U.S. international economic position are consistent with the hypothesis that the frontier, by offering a *domestic* outlet for capital accumulation slowed the acquisition of an *international* imperial stance, and its disappearance stimulated it in the form of a new financial expansionism.

With respect to the impact of the frontier on the level of living, reference will here be made only to the matter of diet. The per capita consumption of farm products was approximately constant during the frontier decades, but the composition of the city dweller's diet changed somewhat from cereals and starches to meat. Some 10 to 13 pounds of meat a week in 1909 were included in an average workingman's family budget, or about 50 percent more than the average for a British working class family. If a customary winter diet in a Midwestern city in the 1890s consisted of steak, roasts, bread, macaroni, Irish potatoes, sweet potatoes, turnips, cole slaw, fried apples, stewed tomatoes, and for dessert Indian pudding, rice, cake, or pie, with no fresh fruit or green vegetables, it may be concluded that frontier animal husbandry and wheat farming were major contributors to the urban dweller's food consumption. At the turn of the century, proportionate expenditures for food by city workers was still historically high, making up 40 to 45 percent of the average total consumption expenditures. The agricultural frontier obviated the need to provide these essentials through more highly priced imports.

Outlays for meat, poultry, and fish (overwhelmingly meat) made up about one-third of total food outlays, and outlays for cereals and bakery products were some 16 percent of total foods. Whereas the per capita consumption of wheat fell, the consumption of meat per head rose. Of course, the distributive shape of these patterns is not revealed in averages.

"Intuition" would lead us to hypothesize that the presence of a frontier with its "safety valve" effect would dampen labor's tendency to organize. At first glance the high level of labor agitation in the seventies and eighties, particularly in the railroads, and the historically large membership of the Knights of Labor, whose ranks totaled 700,000 at the peak in 1886, would seem inconsistent with such an hypothesis. Moreover, the founding of the American Federation of Labor in 1886-1887 would seem to be additional evidence against the hypothesis. Yet the peculiar characteristics of the Knights (e.g., its strong political orientation, its rural-urban composition, its social class heterogeneity) and its rapid collapse after 1887 suggest that it operated in an environment that was inimical to viable organization. But the inimical features of the government were only partly traceable to the frontier's safety valve. Rather they were in major part the bitter and organized opposition of business and laissez faire government to any form of independent unionism. This applied to the AFL as well as to the Knights. The same may be said of the independent railroad unions. Here the violent resistance by the railroads' General Managers' Association and by the national government, particularly in the Pullman strike of 1894, was a powerfully destructive influence against unionization.

The agrarian revolt against the railroads, financial institutions, and industrial and middleman oligopolists was an attempt by commercial family farmers to exert a countervailing power against the superior market power of nonfarm business. It was connected with the frontier only in the limited sense that large numbers of farmers were entering the market system, including the world market, in the frontier states. The agrarian unrest was centered in the Western frontier and the South, more or less bypassing the East. The South had no extensive frontier in this period, and this suggests that the frontier was not a unique determinant of the farmers' unrest. Common elements among farmers engaged in the revolt were (1) production of staple commercial crops for export out of the area of production, (2) vagaries of weather, (3) secularly and cyclically falling farm product prices, and (4) the usual market power problems confronting small farm enterprises operating under conditions of relatively easy entry and difficult exit, and surrounded by oligopoly and oligopsony in the nonfarm sector.

It may be concluded that the emergence of the modern farm problem and the farmers' massive attack on the policy of laissez faire were outgrowths of the special position of staple, small-unit farming in a capitalistic economy becoming dominated by big business in the nonfarm sector.[9] These developments would have occurred even in the absence of a frontier condition. What was required was large numbers of small farmers with weak market power, affected by various particular forms of short run economic adversity.

The decline of the frontier must not be confused with the decline of agriculture in the economy as a whole. The former accelerated the long drawn out process of relative agricultural decline, a process plagued by all the attendant general and special disadvantages that beset a lagging sector. However, the declining frontier did introduce new elements into the mozaic of development. The years of frontier decline from 1880 to 1910 inaugurated the cessation of farm land expansion, the end of railroadization, the absolute fall in the farm labor force, the transformation from extensive to intensive farming that entailed a new emphasis on reproducible capital inputs, the onset of diminishing returns, and the outflow of money capital to foreign lands. By the same token, the potential for further industrialization and urbanization was also to disappear in the very near future. Clearly, there was a new ball game beginning.

NOTES

1. Lloyd A. Metzler (ed.), "Concepts and Criteria of Secular Stagnation," in *Income, Employment and Public Policy: Essays in Honor of Alvin Hansen* (New York: Norton, 1948), pp. 104-5.
2. William N. Parker and Judith L. V. Klein, "Productivity Growth in Grain Production in the United States, 1840-1860 and 1900-1910," in National Bureau of Economic Research, Conference on Research in Income and Wealth, *Output, Employment, and Productivity in the United States After 1800*, Studies in Income and Wealth, v. 30 (New York: Columbia University Press, 1966), pp. 543-4.
3. The share was 55 percent in 1859 and 74 percent in 1909.
4. This latter phrase means the percentage change in per capita quantity of wheat demanded per given percentage change in per capita income:

$$x = \frac{\Delta q_w}{q_w} \bigg/ \frac{\Delta y}{y}$$

where $q_w = Q_w/H$. The low negative elasticity shown for a indicates that increases in the quantity of wheat demanded respond only to population rise, and even not proportionately to that. The rise in income per head has no appreciable effect; rising expenditures are made for other commodities and services.

5. It is difficult to believe that the farm output rise resulting from this great migration of yeoman and tenant farmers could have been achieved in the same time span by a system of black slave plantation agriculture.

6. "American Agriculture—The First 300 Years," in U.S. Department of Agriculture, *Yearbook of Agriculture 1940* (Washington, D.C.: Government Printing Office, 1940), pp. 226-7.

7. *Productivity Trends in the United States*, National Bureau of Economic Research (Princeton: Princeton University Press, 1961), Table 34, pp. 136-7. Data for the immediately following calculation are on pp. 338, 392.

8. "The Disappearance of Free Land in our Economic Development," *American Economic Review*, 16, no. 1, Supplement (March 1926), pp. 265-71, *passim*.

9. As pointed out by William Letwin, the agrarian revolt was not an attack on business as such, but rather an attack on big business (see his "Past and Future of the American Businessman," *Daedalus*, 98, no. 1 (Winter 1969), Warner Modular Reprint #418, 1973, pp. 11-2).

[6]

Industrialization: the growth of manufacturing

The United States became "the leading industrial nation in the world" between the Civil War and World War I. Within the country the relative decline of farming and the relative rise of nonfarm production were perhaps the most striking features among the great structural transformations characterizing the economic development of that half century.

"Industry" in the broadest popular sense means all nonfarm activity, but manufacturing is also widely considered to be the archetype of industrial activity. Both categories will be referred to here and in the next chapter, but manufacturing is more to be recommended for initial emphasis, if only because it is a more homogeneous category, and the more meaningful are analytical statements pertaining to it. Moreover, in the case of the manufacturing sector, there is a greater wealth of data than in the case of any other nonfarm activity. When it was earlier stated in the chapter on performance of the economy that the "industrialization process" had passed its zenith approximately by 1920, it was the manufacturing sector that was referred to.

The two chief concerns here will be first to *describe* the industrialization process in the aggregate, and second to try to unravel the complex question of *why* industrialization took place. These two matters are of course connected in actual experience, but they are analytically separable. Both matters may be of interest to all persons today who are concerned with both the future of the U.S. economy and the developmental problems of other countries.

The Pattern of Industrialization

What has been said earlier about the relative decline in farm production implies at once an enormous rise in nonfarm activity in the period 1865-1914. According to estimates presented by Robert Lipsey, nonfarm gross product as a percentage of GNP, in current dollars, rose as follows:

Year	Nonfarm/GNP
1870	60%
1880	74
1890	78
1900	80
1910	81
1914	82
1920	85

These data show not only the extent of industrialization in the broadest sense, but also the slowing down of the process, particularly after 1890. In the twenty years 1870-1890, an era of falling commodity prices, the proportion rose 18 percentage points, but in the next twenty years 1890-1910, a period of generally rising prices, it rose only 3 percentage points. In the following forty years 1910-1950 it rose 11 percentage points, which is close to what is probably its historic maximum.

Taking manufacturing output as representative of industrialization, we find that its share of GNP based upon census data (in current dollars) increased in the period 1865-1914 from approximately 20 percent to over 25 percent (alternative, lower estimates of GNP suggest as high as 30 percent). Alternatively appraised, Robert Gallman's estimates suggest about a 6 percent annual compound rate of growth of real value added in manufacturing from 1869 to 1899 as compared with an overall growth rate of real GNP approximating 4.75 percent and of total commodity output approximating 4.50 percent. However, Edwin Frickey's index of manufacturing output shows an annual rise for the whole period between 1870 and 1910 of about 5 percent which seems most plausible.

The entire shift toward manufacturing occurs, with respect to output, by 1890, but with respect to persons engaged there is no shift until after 1890 (see Tables 14 and 15 in next chapter). Gall-man's price-deflated estimates show almost a *fourfold* rise in manu-facturing output in the twenty years from 1869 to 1889! This is 7 percent per year, and appears very high compared to Kendrick's estimates yielding only a 5 percent rise per year. In any case, the rise was substantial, and produced a very favorable result for the sector's output/labor ratio for the twenty years. Thereafter the rate of output growth slowed somewhat, approximating that for GNP (e.g., the output rise in the 1890s was only 4 percent per year).

These production data may be supplemented by labor force data which show, according to Stanley Lebergott, the following:

Year	Manufacturing/ total labor force	Manufacturing/ nonfarm labor force
1860	14%	29%
1870	19	40
1880	19	39
1890	19	33
1900	20	34
1910	22	32
1920	27	36

It thus seems clear that in labor force terms manufacturing's dy-namic leadership role prevails with respect to total labor force growth but is diminished once we eliminate agriculture from the total force picture. Manufacturing workers in the aggregate nonfarm sector, ignoring regional differences, show a small relative decline after 1870-1880. Further examination of this matter will be made in the discussion of the connection between industrialization and manufacturing in Chapter 9.

Professor Lebergott has suggested on the basis of his own labor force estimates that there was very little labor force industrializa-tion in terms of total nonfarm labor between 1850 and 1880. How-ever, the national totals are deceptive here. If the South is excluded from the national aggregates (a reasonable procedure in view of the slight contribution of the South to the nation's growth during those three decades), significant labor force industrialization appears, particularly in the important East North Central region and to a lesser extent in the populous Northeast. To be sure, the industrial-ization process shows up sharply only by relating manufacturing to the regional labor force totals, yet this is one perfectly reasonable criterion of industrialization. As an example of what took place, when one disaggregates labor force statistics regionally and applies this criterion to them, it appears that the proportion of the manufacturing labor force to the total in the East North Central region rose from 8 percent to 17 percent between 1850 and 1880, an increase of 113 percent.

Industrialization, similar to a number of other processes, did not occur at a steady rate, but exhibited massive long waves in its rate of growth. If one takes manufacturing output, for example, the decadal increases, based upon Gallman's estimates, were:

Years	Manufacturing increases
1839-1849	157%
1849-1859	76
1859-1869	26
1869-1879	82
1879-1889	112
1889-1899	51

John W. Kendrick's manufacturing output index shows an increase of 59 percent for 1899-1909. It would be hard to find a clearer pattern of long waves in growth rates than that exhibited here: peaks in the 1840s and 1880s, troughs in the decades of the 1860s and the 1890s. Although the output rise in the 1870s was substantial for the longest depression decade in the nineteenth century, clearly the 1880s, a decade of declining prices, was the banner decade of industrialization, on the manufacturing output criterion, for the entire period under review.

The reasons for such long waves in the growth rate during their one hundred year period of prominence ending about World War I remain about as elusive as they were when Simon Kuznets first pointed to the existence of "trend-cycles" in 1930, and Arthur F. Burns reported similar findings for many nonagricultural production series in 1934. In Burns' chronology the years 1875-1885 contained a trend-cycle peak, and Moses Abramovitz has fixed upon the year 1881 (but see Figure 7 in Chapter 10). Some explain these secular swings by hypothesizing that the economy or a major sector needs a period of digestion to absorb the effects of important innovations. Others believe that the heart of the process is to be found in the residential construction and general construction, or railroadization, cycles and their repercussions. But in the mid-1960s Kuznets professed ultimate bewilderment about the origins of long swings when he concluded that there was a "lack of assurance as to what they, their established characteristics, and the factors behind them really are."[1]

The development of the manufacturing sector, which was incidentally almost the sole source of producers' durable equipment for the economy, greatly stimulated the supply of and demand for such tangible capital goods. Within the sector itself both the capital/labor and capital/output ratios rose. The technological changes in the sector were capital-absorbing. This, together with the upward drift of the gross investment ratio (gross capital formation/GNP) in the economy as a whole, tends to support the thesis of W. G. Hoffmann that as the industrialization process reaches more advanced states, the ratio of the net output of the capital goods industries to the consumer goods industries within the manufacturing sector will rise. (Presumably this trend does not necessarily continue after the industrialization process has peaked out.) However, more direct evidence in the form of estimates by Gallman of the value of manufactured producers' durables relative to total value added by manufacture indicates that the ratio of the former to the latter rose from 11.5 in 1839 to a peak of 18.2 in 1869 and thereafter traced a plateau at about 16 until the end of the century. Hence, the rise in the capital/output fraction in the manufacturing sector may not have signified that this sector was producing relatively more producers' durable equipment for itself. It seems more likely, rather, that either the construction industry was contributing to a rising ratio of *plant* to output within the sector of the rising capital/output ratio was due to a relative rise in working capital rather than fixed capital. However, Daniel Creamer has known that both working and fixed capital rose, as compared to output, at least in the short span of years between 1890 and 1904.

In addition to the rapid growth of tangible capital goods in the manufacturing sector, there also occurred investment in the training of the industrial labor force, in "human capital." It is difficult to estimate the amount of this investment, represented by formal schooling, on-the-job training, certain research and development outlays by business, and general communication between people with training in the industrial arts. The allocation of public educational effort and communication to a sector such as manufacturing or the whole nonfarm sector is an equally hazardous task. Similarly, the effects of human training on productivity are very hard to measure.

In recent years economists have placed much emphasis on the role of human training in productivity rise, but analysis has not gone much beyond isolation of the influence of a grab bag residual

on a simple production function, known as the "productivity increment," calculated after trying to remove the influence of most inputs on the growth of output. Application of this technique to
manufacturing suggests that *all* influences other than the growth
of tangible capital or land (of presumed constant quality) accounted for about a third of the growth of total output. This is a historically small weight compared with later times. When it is realized
that investment in human training accounts for only a part, though
perhaps the major part, of this residual influence, it may be noted
that human capital in this period must have been a noteworthy but
modest contributor to the mediocre increase of total factor productivity in the manufacturing sector in this period. It is debatable
how far factory technology in the nineteenth century was complementary to formal schooling above the minimum literacy level.

It seems likely the U.S. "export invasion of Europe" in manufactured goods in the latter part of this period was premised upon the
traditional Heckscher-Olin theorem that the growth of the country's manufactured exports was mainly due to the tangible capital-
intensity of those products, rather than to their human capital-
intensity. This may have changed later in the twentieth century,
however.[2]

Technology, Factor Proportions, and Industrialization

The production techniques of the various nonfarm sectors underwent notable changes in this post-Civil War period, many of the
specifics of which are listed in Chapter 3. But in general these may
be described as "late factory system" techniques. The so-called
"mass production" technology of the manufacturing sector
awaited twentieth century developments, but the late factory system departed significantly from the heavy reliance on manual labor
that characterized the early factory system. The continuous substitution of special-purpose equipment for manual labor decade
after decade was indeed making the term "manufacture"—or fabrication by hand—more and more obsolete. A more appropriate term
for the technology that came to dominate the manufacturing sector after the Civil War would be "machino-facture," but continued
use of the outmoded concept compels use of the Census term.

An important feature of the early factory system that continued
to predominate in the manufacturing sector in this period was the

TABLE 14

DISTRIBUTION OF PRIMARY POWER CAPACITY
IN MANUFACTURING, 1869-1919

Type of Power	1869	1879	1889	1899A	1899B	1909	1919
Steam	51.8%	64.1%	78.4%	81.0%	82.1%	76.7%	47.1%
Water	48.2	35.9	21.5	16.0	14.7	9.8	6.0
Electric (purchased)	0	0	0	1.7	1.8	9.4	31.8
Gas	0	0	.2	1.3	1.4	4.1	4.3
Steam turbines	0	0	0	0	0	0	10.9
Total primary power	100.0	100.0	100.0	100.0	100.0	100.0	100.0

Source: Allen H. Fenichel, "Growth and Diffusion of Power in Manufacturing, 1838-1919," in National Bureau of Economic Research, Conference on Research in Income and Wealth, *Output, Employment, and Productivity in the United States after 1800,* Studies in Income and Wealth, v. 30 (New York: Columbia University Press, 1966), p. 469, Table B-2. 1899A is comparable to earlier years; 1899B is comparable to later years.

system of fixed stations, referred to in Chapter 1. Under that stationary arrangement, either fabrication or assembly took place at points spaced out on the factory floor where machinery and tools were located. Components of a manufactured product were brought to the machine or station at which place workers assembled or processed the product further. Energy was transmitted from steam engines via shafting and belts to the machinery at the stationary point of production. This was in sharp contrast to the forthcoming automatically controlled, continuous flow technology of mass production in the twentieth century, where power was transmitted by electric wires to prime movers (machines that convert natural energy into the energy of motion).

Yet, in this period factory technology changed dramatically in other respects. For example, it shifted from the use of iron, wood power, and water power to steel, coal (including coke) power, and steam power and ended with the beginnings of the revolutionary transformation to steam-generated, purchased electricity. Table 14 shows the decline of water power and the rise of steam, together with the emergence of purchased electric energy in the manufacturing sector, moderate by 1909, important by the end of World War I.

Perhaps more important, the total primary power capacity of the manufacturing sector in the country rose from 2.346 million horse power in 1869 to 18.522 million horsepower in 1909, an eightfold increase that substantially exceeded the sixfold rise in manufacturing output but fell far short of the twelvefold rise in growth in the sector's capital input. These comparisons emphasize how capital-absorbing was the manufacturing technology of the period. Such increases in energy use and tangible capital permitted the 5 percent growth per year in output to proceed with only a 3.25 percent rise per year in labor engaged.

Samuel Rezneck in a most lucid discussion of mass production once referred to the "machine tool" technology of interchangeable parts that came into prominence toward the end of the nineteenth century.[3] Carbon, steel, and petroleum lubricants became indispensable to the steel machinery that went into the new machine tool industry—the strategic, technologically progressive, capital goods industry that served all industry's needs for cutting, planning, grinding, boring, forming, shaping, turning, and drilling metal to accurate dimensions. Because of the vital importance of metal fabrication in a modern economy, the growth of the functionally specialized machine tool industry may be viewed, in spite of its relatively small size, as focal to the industrialization process, both in an engineering sense and an economic sense. Furthermore, it was central to the technological advances made in the industrial sector after 1880. The machine tool industry was a prime example of the connections between the production of sophisticated capital goods, the development of human skills, and the spread of external economies.

For there is an important learning process involved in machinery production, and a . . . highly developed facility in the designing and production of specialized machinery is, perhaps, the most important single characteristic of a well-developed, capital goods industry and constitutes an external economy of enormous importance to other sectors of the economy.[4]

It is significant with respect to timing technological progress that the universal milling machine was invented in 1860, and the Census recognized "machinists tools" for the first time in that year. It was apparently not until the eighties, however, that production became quantitatively notable. Ross Robertson has estimated that the total Cincinnati production of metal working machinery rose from $0.25 million in 1880 to over $1.25 million in 1890 (current dollars), and Duncan McDougall found that shipments of machine tools by the important Rhode Island firm of Brown and Sharpe increased 50 percent between 1879 and 1884, and 376 percent between 1884 and 1889. McDougall reported that of 23,658 machine tools shipped by the firm between 1861 and 1905 over half were shipped between January 1899 and June 1905. But in the first decade of the twentieth century the industry sales (using a 90 percent sample) in current dollars rose 147 percent and physical output must have risen at an annual rate in excess of 8 percent.

As Nathan Rosenberg has emphasized, the machine tool industry was a transmission center for the transfer of new skills and techniques to all the machine-using sectors of the economy. This was accomplished in large part because the machinery and metal-using activities of the growing industrial sector were both creating and enjoying the fruits of "technological convergence," i.e., the development of a changing set of related skills, techniques, and facilities at the 'higher' stages of production serving a wide range of final products.[5] Here was a striking illustration of the essential interrelatedness and cross-fertilization of technology in a diversified, industrial system.

The special-purpose machine tool industry, like the steel industry, was only the most dramatic of several important new or technologically transformed manufacturing industries that improved the technology of that sector and of other sectors of the economy in the period under review. It was the manufacturing sector that contributed: steel, rails, steam locomotives, the refrigerator car and other rolling stock for railroadization, and cars for the street railway; Portland cement (from the 1890s) and structural shapes for the construction industry; steam engines for varied uses; agricultural machinery and equipment; stoves and furnaces for home and industrial use; paper for newsprint, paperboard, and other purposes; the tin can for the newly burgeoning canning industry; and machinery for coal, copper, and lead mining, flour milling, cigarettes, and petroleum extraction and refining. A perusal of this list reveals a surprising amount of the history of technology for the 1860-1913 period; it also indicates many of the rapidly growing industries both inside and outside the manufacturing sector. Furthermore, it suggests the essential interrelatedness of all the parts of the industrialization pattern. Finally, it highlights the fact that industrialization involves not only growing functional specialization but also increasing differentiation in the economy's product mix.

There is more to technological advance and to industrialization than production processes, as we have pointed out earlier. Innovations in organization and administration, such as the corporate form of business, the specialized financial institution, the rise of scientific management, and modern cost accounting were also of considerable import. They will be treated below in connection with developments in the business sector. Sectoral diversification of the nonfarm economy and technological changes within sectors other than manufacturing were also notable features of the period. They will be reviewed in part in the next chapter. Relevant innovations in the larger institutional environment of the economic system, e.g., the rise of organized labor and the emergence of the regulatory governmental commission, contributed to shaping the pattern of industrial development. All these, together with the dramatic and all-important shift to an urban society, made up a new industrial fabric that constituted the world of 1914—a world vastly different and vastly more complex than that which had existed only a half-century earlier.

The Reasons for Industrialization

The explanation of industrialization has been suggested by Robert Fogel and Stanley Engerman as the single most important interest of economic historians. The study of the industrialization tasks of less developed countries has heightened everyone's interest in this matter in contemporary times. What progress has been made on this task in recent years by people like Robert Fogel, Stanley Engerman, Hollis Chenery, and William P. Travis has consisted largely in bringing together the multitude of determinants into a more simplified focus. Before these contributions there was no impressive integrated analysis available—only unweighted lists of "factors," such as the achievement of a high savings ratio, population increase, growing size of markets, transportation improvements, innovations, expansion of education, the rise of capital markets, and the upward shift in tariff rates during the Civil War.

Although one should not exaggerate the recent analytical achievements, they certainly have provided a more lucid classification of the determinants of industrialization and suggested something firmer about relative weights. Furthermore, we can now more easily distinguish a constant from a variable factor, and therefore resist the temptation to employ abiding influences such as high quality entrepreneurship, spatial mobility of the population, and the Protestant ethic to explain the transformation of an agrarian economy into an industrial one. It is counterfactually completely plausible that considerations such as these could have equally well contributed to the continued development and dominance of an agrarian capitalism based upon a nation of family farmers.

Hollis Chenery has presented a simplified classification of the causes of industrialization[6] that can be harmonized with more elaborate mathematical formulations of the Fogel-Engerman variety. Like any economist, Chenery starts with a demand-supply framework. Basic to the analysis in Engel's Law that as per capita income rises the proportion of income spent by people on food falls, i.e., the proportion spent on nonfoods rises. Converted into its implications for economic structure this means that, in the absence of a large, sustained, rapidly growing export demand for an agricultural (or other primary) product, the farm sector will relatively decline secularly and the nonfarm sector will grow, as per capita income rises. (This contrasts with the Southern growth pattern for three-quarters of a century.) Alternatively put and using two broad classes of goods (and implicitly two sectors), it may be said that the per capita income elasticity of demand for farm products is less than one, and for "industrial" goods is greater than one. We have shown in the preceding chapter that in the aggregate the former elasticity was probably close to zero after 1870.

All this clearly highlights the decisive roll of final demand in the explanation for the growth of the nonfarm sector in general and of the manufacturing sector in particular. Although this is not Chenery's emphasis, primarily because his empirical reference is contemporary, less developed countries, in the United States it is by far the predominant determinant of the rise of industry in this period. Supply determinants were of vital, but nonetheless secondary importance compared with the income elasticity of demand. Of course, *both* supply and demand influences were *essential* in the industrialization process, as we indicated in the discussion of technological change in the preceding section.

Chenery classifies demand into two types: final and intermediate. When we interpret and apply this to U.S. manufacturing growth, we are dealing with the demand for manufactured con-

sumer goods by householders and for manufactured or semimanu-
factured capital goods made by firms in the manufacturing sector.
(Of course this latter entails demand for the products of other sectors, including industrial raw materials from the farm sector.) On
the supply side, Chenery refers to (1) the substitution of domestic
production for imports and (2) residual changes such as changes in
relative input prices and the substitution of coal-generated steam
power for food-using human muscle.

Without using Chenery's weights, and with a slight reorganization of his framework, we may say in a summary way that the high
rate of growth of manufacturing output $(\Delta Q_m/Q_m)$ from 1870 to
1910 was a function of the high per capita income elasticity of demand for such output (ϵ_{ym}), and the prices of domestic nonmanu-
factured goods (P_o) and imported manufactured products (P_{im})
relative to the price of domestic manufactured goods (P_m). In other
words, $\Delta Q_m/Q_m = f\left(\epsilon_{ym}, P_o/P_m, P_{im}/P_m\right)$. These variables are
"grab bags" into which all human economic forces are combined,
and their interaction is not represented in the equation. But at least
we have a more clean-cut starting point for study. Furthermore, we
can assign some rough weights and can say that buyers' income
elasticity was by far the most important and P_o/P_m the least
important determinant in the U.S. case.

Demand Influences on Industrialization

Demand, and its income elasticity, need to be classified into final
domestic consumer demand and intermediate enterprise demand
for capital goods—mostly producers' durable equipment made in
the manufacturing sector. Intermediate demand may be broken
down into domestic and export demand. We have intimated in connection with the reference to the Hoffmann thesis that intermediate capital goods demand may have exhibited a greater growth
than manufactured consumer goods. This suggests a possibly
higher income elasticity (relative prices assumed constant) for the
former. In any case, the consumer goods component naturally
carries a much greater weight in the total output of manufactured
products, a consideration that could be expected to swamp the influence of any slightly greater income elasticity enjoyed by manufacturers turning out intermediate products. Two important economic forces behind this twofold breakdown of income elasticity

were, among other things, the community's saving and investment ratios, which we know were secularly rising, and the rate of population growth taken as a partly independent force operating through demand. But the important fact is that for the long run, out of a one percent increase in household consumption per head, people demanded an increase in manufactured products greater than one percent, i.e., its income elasticity of demand for such products was greater than unity.

The foreign demand for U.S. manufactured products is a distinct element on the demand side. This may also be viewed as an elasticity phenomenon, and it is known that foreigners' demand for manufactured exports is highly income-elastic for any given price level, i.e., any given set of relative prices. We do not have satisfactory data on the rate of per capita income growth for all the countries buying U.S. manufactured goods in this period. In any case the level of aggregation would be too high, and the necessary assumptions too strict. However, we can say from Lipsey's and other estimates that U.S. manufactured exports as a percentage of GNP about doubled between 1880 and 1914. Alternatively put, his data show that such exports rose at an annual compound rate of about 6.75 percent over that period — a rate in excess of the growth of total manufacturing output. But the past role of exports should not be exaggerated, for they comprised only a small part of total manufacturing. For example, they amounted to only $124 million in 1889, whereas the total U.S. manufacturing value added, according to Gallman, was $3,727 million. In that year the quantity of manufactured exports was only 22 percent of the quantity of farm products exported, although thereafter manufacturers gained rapidly on the latter, and became of equal importance by 1913.

American exporters were gaining at the expense of foreigners, just as they were gaining in their capicity as producers for the home market. Probably the greatest competitor was the United Kingdom. Lipsey estimates that the U.S. export quantity index in finished manufacturers, which was only 21 percent of the U.K. index in 1879, had risen to equality on the eve of World War I. That the rest of the world was substituting U.S. manufactures for British manufactures was important to Britain, but it was not of great consequence for the total growth of U.S. manufactures. Exports of manufactured products in 1909 were still small at only 5.5 percent of total U.S. gross manufacturing value added.

Supply Influences on Industrialization

On the supply side, the role of the numerous domestic economic forces in the process of industrialization may be appreciated by taking as a starting point the relative prices P_o/P_m. Although we have no satisfactory index for P_m, we are confident that these two sets of prices moved in roughly the same direction and proportion *in the long run* during the years 1870-1910. We have implicit price deflators calculated by Gallman for selected years, 1869-1899, for gross value added by all commodity output and manufacturing output. The ratio of these deflators indicates considerable stability from 1869 through 1889, followed by a modest rise in the 1890s. In other words, the terms of trade in relative prices moved but little for twenty years, then drifted in favor of the substitution of manufactured products for other commodities. This latter movement also may be discerned in other price indexes covering the period from 1900 to 1910. However, the trends were so moderate we can probably ascribe little weight to price substitution effects in explaining the shift to manufactured products.

Most of the traditional treatments of the rise of industry by economic historians unfortunately overstress the supply side. This accounts in large part for the more extensive treatment of the supply than of the demand side here. Historians usually merely list without weights a number of factors without indicating that the net effect on P_o/P_m was negligible until about 1890 and probably quite moderate thereafter. Clearly such forces, for example, as the tariff, or "improved means of internal transport," or "more efficient capital markets," had to operate through relative prices in the market economy of these times if they were to elicit from the supply side a shift in the nation's product mix away from agriculture and toward industry. [Other forces, such as the fact that the United States had the greatest internal free-trade market in the world and the presence of "an area packed with natural resources" (Edward Kirkland), are not specific to either agricultural or industrial production, and therefore should not be cited, without an argument for specific application, as responsible for sectoral shifts from agriculture to industry.]

All other determinants of relative prices, and the list of these is long, are potential candidates for influences on P_o/P_m: the comparative productivity of the two sectors, the comparative prices of labor and capital, the comparative rates of technological advance, the comparative accessibility of scale economies and external economies, Chenery's "residual" influences, etc. All of these cannot be examined here, but the comparative productivity performance of agriculture and manufacturing is worthy of a glance.

Productivity indexes themselves are grab bag variables that contain a multitude of influences. According to Lipsey, the total factor productivity index for agriculture taken as a percentage of the corresponding index for manufacturing was as follows:

Year	Agriculture/Manufacturing
1879	146.2%
1889	126.9
1899	126.1
1909	114.5
1919	108.2

This series may be juxtaposed with the ratio of Gallman's price deflators for farm commodities, P_f, and for manufactured products, P_m:

Year	P_f/P_m
1869	98%
1879	100
1889	94
1899	109

One would presume, other things equal, that the superior productivity performance by the manufacturing sector would be reflected in falling relative prices. But there must have been offsetting factors in the 1880s, for the relative improvement in manufacturing productivity in that decade was accompanied by a mild relative *fall* in the prices of farm goods compared to manufactured goods. In the 1890s Lipsey shows approximate constancy of productivity performance, yet Gallman shows a definite rise in the relative prices of farm products. Either something is wrong with the theoretical presumption about the connection between productivity performance and relative prices, or something is wrong with the data, or something is wrong with the "other things equal" assumption. In any case, it is relative product prices that count in the long-run comparative career of a sector. These could not have counted for much because they were fairly stable into the 1890s, and this fact will have to override considerations involving productivity estimates.

Other considerations involving the determination of relative prices will have to be passed over, with the exception of the question of the contribution of farmers and farm workers to industrialization. This is a high priority topic with economic development theorists and has in one form or another concerned U.S. economic historians for many years.

In dealing with the role of frontier agriculture in the rise of industry in Chapter 5, we pointed out that the farm sector contributed labor and comparatively cheap, domestically produced foodstuffs to the nonfarm sector. It has traditionally been argued, and also implied above, that if the United States had had to import large quantities of foodstuffs during the decades of industrialization, it would have been worse off than it actually was because such imports would have cost more than domestic farm products. "Worse off" is probably to be interpreted to mean that the industrialization process would have been accordingly slowed. As Bruce F. Johnston and John W. Mellor have put it, "if food supplies fail to expand in pace with the growth of demand, the result is likely to be a substantial rise in food prices leading to political discontent and pressure on wage rates with consequent adverse effects on industrial profits, investment, and economic growth."[7]

This generalization might be supported by the argument that (counterfactually) in the absence of cheap domestic foodstuffs and agricultural raw materials, the terms of trade would have moved against the industrial sector vis-a-vis the farm sector and the foreign sector. However, a smaller and more slowly growing farm sector would have flattened the supply schedule of labor to the industrial sector and shifted it to the right (i.e., increased supply). The ultimate effects on the development of the nonfarm sector are hard to estimate, although initially wages would presumably have been lower and profits higher. In the preceding chapter we made the point that if the farm sector had grown more slowly and presumed released resources had moved into industry, the GNP would have grown *faster*. This definitely seems the proper direction to take, even although scores of awkward, empirical assumptions have to be made to implement this argument, just as in the case with the opposite argument.

The alleged virtues of cheap domestic food for U.S. industry are not easy to pin down or evaluate. One day economic historians will have to decide whether the U.S. land policy and farm sector were too expansionist in the late nineteenth century. Perhaps the best tentative conclusion to draw is that an industrializing economy with a large, domestically controlled natural resource base has some advantage over others without such a base, but that this advantage can easily be exaggerated. Indeed, in one sense this is a disadvantage, for as Johnston and Mellor had reminded us, "The relative decline of the agricultural sector will not proceed as rapidly or as far in countries that have a marked comparative advantage in exporting agricultural products."

Any economy can probably acquire the facility to sell the products of skilled labor and superior technique abroad—and the acquisition of this facility will of necessity transform the economy's structure and performance, i.e., will entail industrial development. The fact that the United States did not move even more significantly in this direction during the post-Civil War industrializing decades, but continued to expand its agricultural frontier and to exploit its international comparative advantage in farm products, is consistent with the fact that the internal terms of trade between the prices of farm products P_f and the prices of manufactured products P_m, was fairly stable. The latter was reflected in the fact that the ratio of manufactured exports prices to agricultural exports prices was the same in 1899 as it was in 1879, falling sharply only in the first decade of the twentieth century.[8] This strongly influenced the stability of the ratio P_o/P_m prior to 1899, i.e., kept it from rising until the frontier ended.

In concluding this analysis of supply determinants, we must refer to import substitution as reflected by P_{im}/P_m. Computations by the author suggest[9] that this factor probably accounted for about one-fifth of the absolute growth of the U.S. manufacturing sector during the latter part of the nineteenth century. It was therefore much more important than the substitution effects of relative domestic prices P_o/P_m, and ranked next to, although far below, income elasticity in importance.

Since there is no annual price index for P_m, it is difficult to estimate the trend, if any, in P_{im}/P_m. However, if one makes the reasonable assumption that the trend of prices of exported manufactured products, P_{em} followed a pattern similar to P_m the estimates of Lipsey can be used as a proxy. Calculations based on Lipsey's estimates (including ocean transport costs but excluding tariffs on both sides) revealed that the ratio P_{im}/P_m drifted very slowly and very slightly upwards between 1879 and 1910. Tariff duties collected as a percentage of the value of all dutiable items, did not rise. In the absence of disaggregation, we may tentatively conclude that this factor had little if any effect on the rate of import substitution after the establishment of the high Civil War tariffs. The price trends using P_{em} for P_m are so mild before 1900 that it is hard to believe they alone or in the main could have induced U.S. buyers to substitute domestic for imported manufactured products. What seems more likely is that new production centers developed close to markets. The U.S. manufacturers so located, with factory prices then about equal to the foreigner's because of various economies, had a transport cost advantage that became ever more important as population and markets moved westward away from eastern seaboard ports. Also, by virtue of their proximity to buyers, domestic manufacturers probably had an advantage in the marketing and servicing of durable products implemented by easy face-to-face contact. Machine tools and machinery were no doubt cases in point. This in effect amounted to lower prices (or a preferred product) for home-produced merchandise. Among the important commodities in which growth due to import substitution was large were, according to estimates by M.N. Yahia: iron and steel and their manufactures (including rails), with 44 percent of the growth attributable to import replacement; cotton goods; wool manufactures; sugar and molasses; and manufactured food.

It should be realized that the demand-supply dichotomy employed here suffers from a failure to recognize the interaction of these forces as it actually occurs in the market system. For example, as Schumpeter would have emphasized, import substitution requires demand creation for a differentiated product (domestic as distinguished from foreign). The demand schedule is not "given" in this case; it is elicited by the innovative and sales promotive activities of private enterprisers and "entrepreneurs" in government service. Another example of the way in which demand and supply forces are intercorrelated is illustrated by Keynes' belief that about half of investment demand (whether viewed as "final" or "intermediate") in the two generations preceding World War I was attributable to increasing population (implying "income" and therefore "induced investment") and the other half to technological change (implying "supply factors" or "autonomous investment" involving the substitution of capital for labor). Although Keynes was thinking of the entire economy, the same kind of interpretive theorizing could be applied to either the growth of producers' durable equipment made in the manufacturing sector, or the growth of nonfarm structures.

Nevertheless, it is helpful to allocate the sets of economic influences as has been done here, and the overwhelming influence of considerations properly classified under demand cannot be doubted. Chenery concludes that for the less developed countries in the contemporary world, supply influences are predominant, but this stems from his emphasis upon import substitution in the industrialization of such countries. This component in the case of the U.S. experience between 1870 and 1914 could not have been responsible for more than 20 percent of manufacturing growth, especially since the U.S. is a country whose foreign trade has long accounted for a contrastingly small proportion of its GNP.

NOTES

1. Simon Kuznets, *Economic Growth and Structure* (New York: W. W. Norton, 1965), p. 353. The analysis of aggregate data on long swings in the United States in this period is complicated by the drastic demographic impact of the Civil War. See Allen C. Kelley, "Demographic Cycles and Economic Growth: The Long Swing Reconsidered," *Journal of Economic History*, 29, no. 4 (December 1969), p. 654.
2. See Peter B. Kenen, "Skills, Human Capital, and Comparative Advantage," in W. Lee Hansen (ed.), *Education, Income, and Human Capital*, National Bureau of Economic Research, Studies in Income and Wealth, no. 35 (New York: Columbia University Press, 1970), pp. 195-205.
3. Samuel Rezneck, "Mass Production and the Use of Energy," in Harold Williamson (ed.), *Growth of the American Economy*, second ed. (Englewood Cliffs, N.J.: Prentice-Hall, 1964), p. 722.
4. Nathan Rosenberg, "Technological Change in the Machine Tool Industry, 1840-1910," *Journal of Economic History*, 23, no. 4 (December 1963), p. 425.
5. Nathan Rosenberg, loc. cit., pp. 423-4, *passim*.
6. Hollis Chenery, "Patterns of Industrial Growth," *American Economic Review*, 50, no. 4 (September 1960), pp. 624-54, *passim*.
7. "The Role of Agriculture in Economic Development," *American Economic Review*, 51, no. 4 (September 1961), p. 573.
8. Robert E. Kipsey, *Price and Quantity Trends in the Foreign Trade of the United States*, National Bureau of Economic Research (Princeton: Princeton University Press, 1963), p. 451, Table H-9.
9. See Harold G. Vatter, "An Estimate of Import Substitution for Manufactured Products in the U.S. Economy, 1859-1899," *Economic Development and Cultural Change*, v. 18 (October 1969), pp. 40-3.

[7]

Industrialization: other nonfarm sectors

Industrialization in the broader sense involves the relative growth of the whole nonfarm sector—a vast, heterogeneous aggregate that demands a more detailed look if the process is to be even minimally understood. Probably the chief initial task in this connection is to look at the anatomy of the nonfarm economy. In the preceding chapter the rise of the vitally important manufacturing sector was examined. Here the main concern will be with the changing relative status of other nonfarm sectors.

There are several possible measures of structural change within the nonfarm sector, but sector output, or "income originating," is probably the best single criterion. Available output data may be organized around several different sets of sector classification, however, and it is advisable to look at two or three different sets. Those employed here do not pretend to be exhaustive for describing the structural changes accompanying industrialization, but when taken in conjunction with the related discussions elsewhere in this work they should give a good view of the process.

Probably the most widely employed sectoral format is that shown for output and labor force in Tables 15 and 16 respectively. It has already been used extensively in preceding chapters in connection with the discussions of agriculture and industrialization as represented by manufacturing.

The major features of structural change shown in the tables are:

1. the implicit relative decline in farm employment and output;
2. the relative rise in manufacturing employment and output, with the latter occurring entirely in the one decade of the 1880s;
3. the substantial relative rise in "all other" employment compared with the very moderate rise in "all other" relative output;
4. the relative increase in service sector employment but the absence of a trend, after 1879, in that sector's relative share of output as measured in current prices.

Isolation of the "all other" category of economic activity produces a somewhat surprising result when the criterion of production is used: it shows that *if manufacturing is excluded from total nonfarm output the aggregate of everything else reveals no rising relative output trend as the economy industrialized* after 1879 [Table 15, col. (7)]. Alternatively put, in the relative output sense the entire industrialization process appears to be embodied in the relative rise of manufacturing production occurring in the 1880s [Table 15, col. (6)]. Such a conclusion should of course give us pause, for we rightly suspect that important shifts in the comparative significance of other nonfarm sectors must have been occurring. The answer to this puzzle is that, while in a brute quantitative sense manufacturing output growth in the eighties did overshadow everything else, and while the approximate constancy of the output of the "all other" group of activities after 1879 nicely reveals this, the group nevertheless represents too high a level of aggregation. This can be appreciated by more detailed reference to construction, mining, the service sector, and certain subcategories of the service sector.

Construction was a rather large activity with a value added of over $500 million in 1869, and about three times that total in the later years of the 1890s. The sector accounted for about 12 percent of commodity output during the last quarter of the century and from three-fourths (1869) to two-thirds (1899) of the total production of capital goods. But again, the share of construction in total commodity output was roughly constant, and in GNP only slightly falling. Hence, as a component of "all other" activity it contributed to relative constancy on the output criterion. We must therefore look elsewhere within the "all other" aggregate for shifts in the comparative importance of economic activities that may be associated with industrialization.

TABLE 15

SELECTED SECTOR OUTPUTS, 1869-1909 (billions of dollars)

Year	Gross national product (1)	Gross farm product (2)	Gross manufacturing product (3)	All other sectors (1)-[(2)+(3)] (4)	Gross service sector product (5)	Manufacturing/GNP (6)	All other/GNP (7)	Service/GNP[1] (8)
1869	7.64	2.42	1.63	3.59	2.93	21.0%	47.0%	38.4% (37%)
1879	9.64	2.60	1.96	5.08	4.34	20.3	52.7	45.0 (42%)
1889	13.67	2.77	3.73	7.18	5.80	27.2	52.4	42.3 (46%)
1899	18.34	3.40	5.04	9.90	8.14	27.5	54.1	44.5 (47%)
1909	30.40	5.46	8.16	16.78		27.0	55.2	

[1]Figures in parentheses are independent estimates from R. E. Gallman and Thomas J. Weiss, "The Service Industries in the Nineteenth Century," in NBER, *Production and Productivity in the Service Industries*, Studies in Income and Wealth, v. 34 (New York: Columbia University Press, 1969), Table 2, p. 291. There is no available estimate for GNP in 1869 with which to compare the estimate derived here. Estimates available for 1879 are particularly shaky. The selection of the components making up GNP for these two years was arbitrary, and was done with a view to making the annual compound rate of growth of real GNP roughly comparable with various estimates elsewhere that lend plausibility to the apparently good growth record for the decade. Thus, deflation of the estimates here for 1869 and 1879 by Lipsey's GNP deflator (1913 dollars, *op. cit.*, pp. 422-3) yields estimates of $6.00 billion and $11.14 billion respectively. These show a growth rate of about 6.5 percent a year, which may be compared with Kendrick's real gross product estimates (*op. cit.*, Table A-IV, p. 303) which yield a growth rate of about 7 percent. The estimates here are *minimal* ones for components for 1869, maximum ones for components of GNP for 1879.

Sources: Col. (1) (sum of cols. (2), (3), (5) plus sum of estimates for value added by construction and mining) in Gallman, NBER, *Trends*, Table A-1, p. 43, except for 1909, which is from Kuznets, *Capital, etc.*, op. cit., Table R-25, p. 561.
Col. (2), 1869 and 1909 from Lipsey, *Price and Quantity Trends*, op. cit., Table G-9, p. 425, remaining years from Gallman, ibid.
Col. (3), Richard Easterlin, "Comment," in NBER, v. 30, p. 81.
Col. (5), R. E. Gallman and Thomas J. Weiss, op. cit., Tables 1 and A-1, pp. 288 and 306.

TABLE 16

SELECTED SECTOR LABOR FORCES,
1870-1910
(millions)

Year	Total	Agriculture	Manufacturing	All other sectors (1)-[(2)+(3)]	Service sector[1]	Manufacturing, fraction (3)/(1)	All other, fraction (4)/(1)	Service, fraction (5)/(1)
	(1)	(2)	(3)	(4)	(5)	(6)	(7)	(8)
1870	12.93	6.79	2.47	3.67	3.23	19.1%	28.4%	24.9%
1880	17.39	8.92	3.29	5.18	4.38	18.9%	29.9%	25.2%
1890	23.32	9.96	4.39	8.97	7.27	18.8%	38.5%	31.2%
1900	29.07	11.68	5.90	11.49	9.62	20.3%	39.5%	33.1%
1910	37.48	11.77	8.33	17.38	12.67[1]	22.2%	46.4%	33.8%[1]

[1] The service sector labor force for 1910 is an employment estimate calculated by applying the percentage figure in Victor R. Fuchs, *The Service Economy* (NBER, New York: Columbia University Press, 1968), p. 24, Table 4, variant 2, to the total labor force for 1910 shown in col. (1).

Source: Cols. (1)-(3) from Stanley Lebergott, "Labor Force and Employment, 1800-1960," in National Bureau of Economic Research, Conference on Income and Wealth, *Output, Employment, and Productivity in the United States After 1800,* Studies in Income and Wealth, v. 30 (New York: Columbia University Press, 1966), pp. 118-9, Tables 1 and 2. Col. (5) from Gallman and Weiss, loc. cit., in sources for Table 15 col. (5), p. 299.

A modest contribution to these shifts may be found in mining, which rose from 2 percent of all commodity output in 1869 to 5 percent in 1899, according to Gallman. Thus, as proportion of GNP, mining approximately doubled its position over the period. But its weight in the totals was small. All this should not obscure the vital *qualitative* contribution of the products of the mining sector to the industrialization of the economy, however.

On quantitative grounds it is the production of the service sector that, along with the manufacturing sector, chiefly compensates for the relative decline of agriculture. Yet, taking this sector in the aggregate (and including in its definition transport, communications, and public utilities), its compensatory influence after 1879 involved an output rise, measured in current dollars, no more than equal to the secular rise in GNP. Hence, its income elasticity of demand in that period was, unlike that for manufacturing production, surprisingly enough no more than unity. This finding agrees with that of Victor R. Fuchs[1] in his study of the service sector, defined to exclude transportation, communication, and public utilities, covering the period 1929-1965. Although Fuchs found that the demand for services is positively correlated with the growth of urbanization, education, and goods-producing industries (intermediate demand with elasticity slightly above unity), he suggested that the substitution effect of a relative rise in the price of services offset these positive correlations. Fuchs also found that service *employment* rose relatively between 1929 and 1965, just as it did from 1880 to 1900, as shown in col. 8 of Table 16. The conclusion must therefore be that output per person in the service sector rose less rapidly than in the goods sector, and this productivity lag was the chief reason for the relatively rapid growth of the service sector labor force after 1880.

How buyers distributed their outlays among the various products of the service sector is perhaps more revealing, and is shown in the disaggregation of that sector in Table 17. The table shows that in the U.S. case at least the process of industrialization from the output aspect entailed a relative decline in trade and housing outlays, and a distinct rise in the comparative importance of transportation, public utilities, and financial and professional services. Gallman and Weiss comment in part on these trends as follows: [2]

> In constant prices, the share of transportation and public utilities would surely rise, and the share of housing (including imputed rents) fall much more prominently. . . . The share of distribution would fall somewhat and the share of professional services perhaps remain constant, perhaps fall. Without much doubt, a table produced from constant price magnitudes would show that the output of industries producing chiefly intermediate services grew very much faster than the output of the entire sector.

Since constant price estimates approximate output changes better than current prices, we know that the growth of finance, transport and public utilities must have accounted for a noteworthy portion of the relative growth of the service labor force after 1880, shown in Table 16. Indeed, the railway transport labor force increased from 416,000 in 1880 to over 1 million by 1900, and again to 1.7 million by 1910, according to Albert Fishlow. This absorption of labor occurred not because of a poor relative productivity record but in spite of substantial accompanying increases in output per worker exceeding, on the basis of Fishlow's indexes, 2 percent per year! And Gallman and Weiss indicate that the labor force in finance, transport, and public utilities accounted for 17 percent of the total persons engaged in the service sector in 1870, but that this had grown to 23

TABLE 17

DISTRIBUTION OF SERVICE INDUSTRIES,[1]
1859-1899 (percent)

		1859	1869	1879	1889	1899
(1)	Distribution (trade)	38	33	34	30	30
(2)	Transportation and public utilities	15	17	18	20	20
(3)	Finance	3	4	5	6	6
	Intermediate products subtotal (1)-(3)	56	54	57	56	56
(4)	Housing (shelter)	23	24	18	17	16
(5)	Professional	6	7	11	11	13
(6)	Personal	5	5	6	7	6
(7)	Government	4	2	2	3	3
(8)	Education	2	3	3	3	3
(9)	Repair hand trades	5	4	4	4	5
	Final products subtotal (4)-(9)	45	45	44	45	46

[1]Current prices.

Source: Adapted from Gallman and Weiss (see Table 16, Sources), Table 4, p. 296.

percent in 1899, a 35 percent rise in the proportion. Thus the shifts toward these activities with respect to labor absorbed were even more dramatic than the shift toward manufacturing, although of course their size was much less than the size of manufacturing employment. What all this means is that the high income elasticity of demand for transport and utility services induced an output growth so great that relative labor released through superior productivity performance was more than offset by relative labor absorbed through rapid output growth.[3]

By virtue of what has been said about the transport and utility sector, it would seem that the other service sectors taken together must have had comparatively poor output per worker performances because their output grew more slowly than service sector output as a whole. For example, Gallman and Weiss estimate that distribution's important share of service output fell, but its share of the service labor force rose. However, the enormous difficulties of estimating output in the case of the employment-important personal services sector, and the absence of any definable employment in the output-important housing sector (where "output" is mainly imputed property income) make useful generalizations about productivity next to impossible. Further research may show, however, that a major reason for the failure of output per worker in the nonfarm sector to grow a great deal faster per year than the farm sector (about 2 percent compared with 1.5 percent, respectively) was the poor performance of the service sector, defined to exclude transportation and public utilities.

Other service sectors also grew significantly in this period, and their economic importance with respect to the character of their output may well have outweighed their minor quantitative weight. For example, according to Gallman and Weiss the number of persons engaged in education rose from 170,000 in 1869 to 446,000 in 1899, and government employment rose from 121,000 to 504,000 over the same period.

In general, the *level* of the ratio of output to labor engaged, Q/L, in the commodity producing sector was notably below that for the service sector, as appropriate comparison of proportions in Tables 16 and 17 will suggest. Gallman and Weiss estimate (variant 2, excluding housing services) the Q/L in 1859 for the former was 88 percent of the national average, while that for the service sector was 1.36 percent. The respective relatives in 1899 were 85 percent and 1.31 percent of the national average. Hence the comparative growth of the service sector, as a whole, had a favorable impact on Q/L ratios for the economy as a whole prior to 1890. But within the service sector the big activities with greater than average Q/L ratios were trade, transportation, and public utilities. In the latter group at least, this may be attributed in considerable part to a relatively high capital/labor (K/L) ratio. The great period of growth in the real net capital stock of the railroads, especially the investment in road, a period during which the stock sometimes doubled in one decade, had come to a close by 1890, however, and for the whole period the change in the railroad K/L was negative (see Chapter 13, Table 25, col. (4)). All this indicates that much bewilderment can come from including transportation and public utilities with the service sector.

Railroadization

Economic historians have long treated the expansion of the rail-roads in the second half of the nineteenth century as in some sense strategic to the entire development process. This emphasis, together with its dramatic growth and large size, warrants special attention to the railroads. With Joseph Schumpeter the railroad was the major innovation and prime mover of an era. In the present work the importance of this industry will be examined from two aspects: (1) its quantitative importance and impact on employment, income, investment, etc., and (2) what Alfred Chandler has termed its influence on the "patterns of economic and business action and new institutional forms." Chandler argued that the railroad promoters and managers "were the first American business to work out the modern ways of finance, management, labor relations, competition, and government regulation." In this chapter the general concern will be with the first aspect of the railroad industry's importance. In the next chapter on changes in the business sector the second aspect will be treated.

Probably the most sophisticated recent examinations of the railroad are the works of Robert Fogel[14] and Albert Fishlow.[5] Both with quantitative matters: Fishlow with the development record and productivity, Fogel with the railroad's quantitative impact. Fishlow's estimates will be heavily relied on here.

Railroad employment as estimated by Fishlow consistently accounted for somewhat over half the total employment in the transportation and public utilities sector as reported by Gallman and Weiss, and grew between 1870 and 1910 at an annual rate of about 5 percent a year. Output grew at a remarkable 7.3 percent per year! Both these rates exceeded the record in manufacturing, (3.25 percent and 5 percent respectively) and the productivity record for the whole forty years in railroading was also better. But of course railroad employment in sheer numbers carried much less weight than *all* manufacturing (not necessarily a good sectoral comparison), rising from about one-eleventh to one-fifth of manufacturing employment over the four decades. The railroad sector compared more favorably with respect to output increase, however, value added in steam railroads rising from 20 percent of manufacturing value added (current prices) to about 25 percent in 1899. Certainly this rapid output rise, taken in conjunction with the industry's large size, would make the railroads a likely candidate for a "leading sector." Steam railroad value added accounted for about 5 percent of GNP in 1880. Railroad operating expenses in 1890 equaled about 6 percent of GNP. The derived demand for the products of the steel, coal, transport equipment, and construction materials industries consequent upon the growth of both railroad capital and operations was notable. Also, Douglass North has reminded us that the railroad influenced the location and relocation of numerous economic activities, such as the shifts of cotton textiles from New England to the South beginning in the 1880s, the establishment of some resource-oriented industries, and the growth of agricultural production in the West.[6] P. H. Cootner and Perloff et al. have suggested it was largely burgeoning railroad construction that revealed the critical limits to the industrial raw material potential of the Northeast at the end of the Civil War. No one has ever provided an acceptable statement on how "large" a leading sector needs to be. It is doubtful, however, whether any other industry ("reasonably" defined) in the nineteenth century accounted for at least 5 percent of GNP and also expanded at a rate 60 percent above that for GNP.

Many writers have also emphasized that railroads' gross capital formation was a substantial proportion of total gross investment, peaking at 20 percent in the 1870s. But this proportion falls to about 16 percent in the eighties and to between 7 and 8 percent during the next two decades. Robert Fogel has approached the matter from the aspect of total income, and estimated by way of one test that the railroad "social saving" (hypothetical income associated with resources presumably released by the railroad, taken as a percentage of total income) in 1890, for example was about 5 percent of GNP. He concluded from this that the railroads were probably not indispensable to U.S. economic growth, but he never questioned their importance. The thrust of Fogel's research results nevertheless seems to be clearly adverse to the notion that railroads were a leading sector. However, Robert P. Thomas and Douglas D. Shetler have noted that Fogel's 5 percent social savings very greatly exceeds the roughly comparable estimates by others in the cases of the expansion into the Canadian prairies made possible by the chilled steel plow and red fife wheat, the steam powered ocean vessel, hybrid seed corn, and general agricultural research for the years 1940-1950. Thomas and Shetler tentatively conclude that "the traditional view of the iron horse was, perhaps fairly close to facts."[7]

As previously mentioned, one of the striking features of the railroad sector was its high utilization of capital, its high capital/output ratio, and its high and falling capital/labor ratio. Railroad capital formation, proceeding in massive long waves, and the capital-absorbing character of railroad technology are held by Davis and Gallman to have been importantly responsible for the rise in the investment ratio to about 28 percent of GNP in the 1890s. This capital, so far as its fixed component was concerned, consisted of tracks, equipment, and structures. The net track mileage (in 1909 track mileage equivalents) rose from over 40,000 in 1869 to 219,000 in 1909. Fishlow ascribes the largest share of railroad output growth in our period to geographic extension. As with frontier agriculture, the railroads thus exhibited a striking pattern of "extensive cultivation," mileage in use increasing about twice as rapidly as "intensive cultivation," i.e., the increase in traffic density. A glance at Figure 4 showing the great transcontinental roads, the first of which was the transcontinental Central Pacific-Union Pacific, united at Promontory Point, Utah in 1869, will suggest in large part the vast extent of this geographical widening. Almost one-third of the total mileage in 1890 was west of Missouri, compared with one-tenth in 1870. Of course, in addition to such new trunk lines there was substantial construction of feeder lines and linkage of fragmented shorter roads. As a result of such construction and linkages, associated with the adoption of the standard gauge, standard time belts, and through bills of lading, what George R. Taylor and Irene D. Neu have called a pre-Civil War "uncoordinated railroad patchwork" was converted into an integrated network by about 1890. As they further point out, these changes contributed importantly to the conversion of the economy from local-regional to national. After the period of rapid roadbed construction, the railroads, similar to the farm sector after the end of the frontier, experienced their era of "intensive cultivation" in the form of increasing traffic density associated with the cessation of increases in first main track mileage in 1916.

The regional pattern of railroad extension reveals that the Western regions experienced the greatest relative increase in mileage operated from 1870 to 1890, and their combined absolute mileage increase approximated that for the Great Plains. In the West and the Great Plains the rate and pattern of penetration, as would be expected, followed fairly closely that for agricultural settlement and the development of mining. The greatest decadal growth in the

Figure 4 Early transcontinental railroads. Reprinted from Nelson Klose, *A Concise Study Guide to the American Frontier* (Lincoln: University of Nebraska Press, 1964), p. 124.

Great Lakes came in the 1870s, and in the rapidly expanding Southeast in the 1880s. The increase in the latter region during that decade from 16,000 to 32,000 miles of track no doubt significantly influenced the new character of Southern economic development in the last two decades of the nineteenth century. In general, however, as one looked eastward the rate at which new mileage was put into operation declined—a reverse frontier phenomenon again resembling the development contours of the farm sector.

It is clear from Fishlow's estimates that road investment, despite the vast rise in mileage, grew less rapidly than equipment in our whole period, and that total capital, the sum of road and equipment, while rising substantially at 4.5 percent a year along with labor's 5 percent over the whole period, grew much less rapidly between 1890 and 1910 than it did in the preceding twenty years. Thus 1890 is a sort of watershed in the rate of railroadization. As this suggests, there was overcapacity due to indivisibilities and perhaps some building ahead of demand before about 1890, leaving the increase in traffic density (output) to catch up over the whole period. Hence the capital/output ratio secularly fell and this contributed to the startling rise in railroad total factor productivity. By 1910 the capital/output ratio had fallen from its 1870 level of 10 to approximately 4, which latter ratio may be viewed as a sort of protracted equilibrium.

The railroads were remarkable in that their output/labor ratio rose in the face of both this declining capital/output proportion and a slightly falling capital/labor ratio (see Chapter 8).

The dramatic rise in total factor productivity was also probably due partly to economies of scale and, more importantly, to external economies of specialization, whereby production at first carried on by railroad firms or not at all was later handled by separate and largely backward-linked specialized suppliers. Beyond these influences on productivity, there were improvements in the flow of communication, together with certain outstanding production innovations, notably the telegraph, block signaling, steel rails, more powerful locomotives, larger and sturdier cars with greater hauling capacity per dead weight, and automatic couplers.

Fishlow notes that the air brake and automatic coupler innovations—which probably had more to do with saving lives than saving operating expenses—were widely adopted only at the turn of the century, and then only after Congressional legislation. This is consistent with the absence of any organized safety movement and the sway throughout industry of the "fellow servant" legal doctrine, according to which a worker who suffered an injury on the job through the alleged negligence of some fellow worker could not obtain compensation from the employer. There were 2,660 railroad employees killed and 26,140 injured on the job in 1891. It is some credit to the industry, however, that it was the Chicago and Northwestern Railroad that helped lead the national movement for job safety after 1907, a movement that eventuated in workmen's compensation laws placing responsibility on the employer after 1911.

The railroad came to dominate domestic interurban freight and passenger transportation in this period. In the case of freight traffic, according to Harold Barger, steam railroads hauled 76 billion ton-miles in 1890 compared with 36 billion ton-miles hauled in 1889 by coastwise, intercoastal, Great Lakes, and inland waterways combined. This dominant proportion of over two to one in terms of ton-miles had risen in 1920 to three to one. Thereafter, with the coming of the motor truck, the railroads entered a period of relative decline. The ascendency of the railroad over waterborne alternatives in this period, which was even greater in terms of gross revenues, cannot be attributed importantly to a differential fall in rates. Indeed, in the case of domestic Great Lakes shipping, the increase in ton-miles, strongly influenced by the movement of Mesabi iron ore after 1893, almost kept pace with U.S. total rail freight hauled from 1890 to 1920.

Average freight rates from the end of the Civil War to the turn of the century fell from about 2 cents per ton-mile to .75 cents per ton-mile. Rail freight charges, while declining much more rapidly than general prices, especially before 1880, remained above inland water rates, such as canal rates. The reasons for the shift in demand toward rail services were to be found in the superiority of rail freight services, i.e., in the quality of the service not represented in the trend of price per ton-mile. This superiority resided in such factors as lower costs of transshipment, a closer approach to all-season service, and a great reduction of time in transit. No rival with similar service advantages for intercity hauling of general merchandise existed until the coming of the motor truck after World War I.

Changes in "All Other" Subsectors

With respect to productivity change, broadly conceived, in the "all other" sector, there are a number of subsectors other than the railroads about which, unfortunately, little can be said. Within the service sector the quantitatively important subsectors were transportation, communications, and other public utilities, personal services (hardly a category in any way connected with industrialization), trade, and housing. In addition, the "all other" category includes mining and construction.

We are fortunately able again to draw upon the productivity analysis of John W. Kendrick[8] for some historical information on all these sectors, except personal services. On the basis of the comparison of partial productivities represented by the output/manhour ratio, it appears that our previous inferences about the superior technological advances and associated productivity performances of communications and public utilities, and possibly finance, were correct. In the former sector the compound annual rate of increase of the output/manhour ratio was 2.6 percent, and in finance it was a remarkable 3.1 percent (1889-1909 only). These compare with Kendrick's estimate of 1.7 percent for the national economy for the whole forty-year period, 1869-1909. It is impossible to break down the relative contributions of capital input and the technological residual in the important case of communications and public utilities, but we do know that the capital/labor ratio rose substantially in this subsector, as did the output/capital ratio. Intuitively, the estimate for finance seems on the high side, but the absence of capital input data makes it difficult to evaluate. Contract construction also did very well, with a 2.5 percent per year rise for the forty years. The laggard sectors were trade with 1.3 percent, and mining with 1.4 percent per annum (1879-1909). The important trade sector must have had a low rate of investment and only minor technological improvements. The poor performance for mining is apparently attributable to Pennsylvania antracite, for in ore, bituminous coal, and other subsectors the performances were above that of the national economy, as was their record for the rate of increase of total factor productivity.

Regional Patterns in the "All Other" Sector

Chapter 4 treated briefly the regional fabric of the economy with particular reference to agriculture and manufacturing. The relative importance of other activities, such as mining and forestry, was indicated for the Western regions and the South, and the diversified sectoral division of the Far West's labor force in 1880 was also shown. Reference was made to the considerable relative importance of finance and distribution in New England and the Middle Atlantic regions.

It is now appropriate to take a brief, closer look at the sectoral pattern among the different regions. In the interest of brevity only the labor force distributions will be referred to. Table 18 reveals the main features of the pattern for four great regions, unfortunately only for a twenty year span, but that span does happily fall in the heart of the period under consideration. This table will reward careful study.

It was previously argued that the West was the most economically dynamic part of the country in this period, and that because of its greater concentration of population, economic activity, and manufacturing growth the North Central region in particular was the heart of the development process in the country as a whole. At this juncture, in an examination of the industrialization patterns in the larger sense, using the North Central region as a focus, we are chiefly concerned with those sectors that fall within the "all other" category, i.e., everything but agriculture and manufacturing. Changes in the relative status of these sectors were fundamental to the development process.

The sectoral shifts in the North Central's occupational pattern as

TABLE 18

LABOR FORCE BY INDUSTRIES, 1880 AND 1900

Industry	Northeast		South		North Central		West	
	1880	1900	1880	1900	1880	1900	1880	1900
Agriculture	23.3%	14.4%	75.4%	65.5%	54.5%	40.2%	28.8%	29.6%
Forestry & fisheries	0.4	0.3	0.3	0.6	0.1	0.1	0.9	0.5
Mining	2.2	2.9	0.3	1.2	1.1	2.2	16.2	9.3
Construction	8.1	8.5	2.3	2.9	5.6	6.4	7.5	6.8
Manufacturing	25.7	25.9	4.0	6.3	10.5	12.0	9.5	10.1
Transportation, etc.	6.6	8.1	2.3	4.0	4.7	6.9	7.3	9.7
Trade, finance, etc.	13.8	17.1	4.4	6.4	9.1	14.1	12.6	14.7
Services & pub. adm.	19.7	20.5	11.1	12.7	14.3	16.9	17.0	18.6
Private household	8.7	7.9	6.5	6.7	5.5	6.0	6.0	5.8
All other	11.0	12.6	4.6	6.0	8.8	10.9	11.0	12.8
Not reported	0.1	2.3	0.0	0.4	0.1	1.2	0.1	0.8
United States	100.0%	100.0%	100.0%	100.0%	100.0%	100.0%	100.0%	100.0%

Source: Simon Kuznets, Ann Ratner Miller, and Richard A. Easterlin, *Population Redistribution and Economic Growth, United States, 1870-1950,* v. II, "Analyses of Economic Change" (Philadelphia: American Philosophical Society, 1960), p. 70. Table 2.16.

indicated in Table 18 are reasonably close to being a classic illustration of modern economic development. In addition to the dramatic decline in agriculture's relative share (despite the ascending frontier), and the 14 percent rise in manufacturing's share, simple addition shows that "all other" activities rose strikingly in relative importance from 35 percent to 59.8 percent. The corresponding changes for the Northeast were from 50.9 percent to 59.7 percent, and for the South were from 20.7 percent to 28.2 percent. Aside from the light these ratios throw upon the national aggregates contained in Table 16, they suggest, with the aid of a little addition, a few interpretive generalizations about regional economic development, *viz.*:

1. The North Central is less industrialized in "all other" terms than the Northeast at the beginning of the twenty-year period, but it industrializes rapidly to catch up with the more industrially mature Northeast by the end of the period.

2. The South is industrially backward in "all other" terms at the beginning of the period, and although it industrializes rapidly (a 36 percent rise in the ratio) it remains quite backward in 1900. Comparison with Table 17 shows the South in 1900 at the level of the nation in 1870.

3. It is clearly the South that pulls down the national ratios in Table 17, col. (7), giving as usual a very deceptive view of the level of industrialization of the country.

4. Corollary to (3), the North Central begins the period above the national average in "all other" activities. Also, in the course of the twenty years it increases its superiority over the national average and gains relatively on the older, more industrialized Northeast. This is the regional meaning of "dynamic."

Deletion from these calculations of the commodity-producing activities within the "all other" category—forestry, fisheries, mining, and construction—would leave the above generalizations intact, except that the North Central would not catch up with the Northeast, but rather would achieve a 1900 proportion close to the latter's 1880 proportion of persons engaged in such "tertiary" activities. If one were to argue that private household services were not very "developmental," it is only in this regard that the North Central's pattern of change in the tertiary sector would look unfavorable as compared with the Northeast, although this is a comparatively stable proportion in all regions.

The North Central region has a particularly favorable development record in the case of the "social overhead" activities contained in the transportation, trade, and finance categories of Table 19, for the sum of the proportions for these increased twice as fast as the Northeast's. It is also noteworthy that the South's percentage of social overhead labor *rose* as rapidly as the North Central's, although its *level* was only half that of the North Central at the turn of the century. Unfortunately, "trade" is included in these figures, but is not usually classified as social overhead. In this connection Perloff et al. estimate that the proportion of persons engaged in the highly productive overhead, transport, and communications sector in the Great Lakes and Plains regions taken together rose over 100 percent, from .071 to .154, between 1870 and 1910, a growth rate distinctly above that for either New England or the Middle Atlantic.[9]

But commodity production within the "all other" sector is not to be ignored. Aside from the special case of mining, whose employment doubling in the North Central region was nonetheless of minor weight in the region's total, construction clearly played a notable role. This region's construction employment somewhat exceeded the national average proportion at both dates, and also rose at a somewhat faster rate.

This review of relative sectoral growth associated with industrialization shows that in labor force terms the typical pattern is a relative expansion of the "all other" sector and the service sector, and that this pattern held for all the great regions shown in Table 18, just as it did for the entire economy. Employment in construction also increased relatively in the economy, in the dynamic North Central region, and even slightly in the more mature Northeast. Only in the West did construction employment experience a relative decline. The relative position of private household services does not seem to have been developmentally sensitive. But in all four great regions the proportion of persons engaged in "all other services and public administration" increased, suggesting a clear positive correlation, from the viewpoint of employment, with the process of industrialization. It is important to note, however, that the relative increase in this broad category is not a phenomenon unique to industrialization, for its rise continued long after the end of the era of industrialization. This was chiefly because of the continued poor Q/L performance of the service sector, and because it encompassed government employment, a category that from 1879 to 1899 increased its relative importance by only one percentage point (4 percent to 5 percent of the service sector), according to Gallman and Weiss. It must be remembered that industrialization in the United States took place under conditions of laissez faire. The relative increase in trade and finance also continued after the termination of the economy's industrialization phase, but for different reasons from those that underlie the rise of government employment.

NOTES

1. Victor R. Fuchs, *The Service Economy* (New York: National Bureau of Economic Research, Columbia University Press, 1968).
2. Op. cit., p. 297. The authors note that the product of the housing sector (which is of course not housing construction, but the "services" of the stock of housing) is almost exclusively represented in property income (ibid., p. 301). Parentheses in quotation added by this writer.
3. The difference in the employment growth rate in any sector and the rest of the economy is of course equal to the difference in output growth rates minus the difference in growth rates of output per worker.
4. Robert Fogel, *Railroads and American Economic Growth* (Baltimore: The Johns Hopkins Press, 1964).
5. Albert Fishlow, "Productivity and Technological Change in the Railroad Sector, 1840-1910," in NBER, *Output, Employment and Productivity*, op, cit., pp. 583-646.

6. See his *Growth and Welfare in the American Past* (Englewood Cliffs, N.J.: Prentice-Hall, 1966), pp. 116-7.
7. See their "Railroad Social Saving: Comment," *American Economic Review*, 58, no. 1 (March 1968), pp. 187-8.
8. *Productivity Trends in the United States*, National Bureau of Economic Research (Princeton: Princeton University Press, 1961).
9. Harvey S. Perloff et al., *Regions, Resources, and Economic Growth* (Lincoln, Neb.: University of Nebraska Press, 1960), p. 167, Table 55.

[8]

Changes in the business sector

Enormous changes in the structure and operation of markets, the internal structure and administration of enterprise, business behavior, and the relations of business to the larger community took place in the half-century following the Civil War. Some of these developments were touched on in Chapter 1; for example, the transformation from agrarian-based to industrial-based economic fluctuations, the proliferation of the specialized, nonagrarian entrepreneur in trade and finance, the transformation from the economic dominance of the individual proprietor to that of the corporate manager facing a nation of employees, the rise in importance of fixed capital and overhead costs, and the emergence of the multiplant, multiproduct firm. But this enumeration merely suggests some of the important changes, and a more complete, detailed review is now called for.

Such a review will show that most of the features of twentieth century business, at least until the immediate post-New Deal era, were already shaped in this period and revealed themselves in their crude youthful form at that time. Many of the important developments may be seen in the evolution of the railroad industry; the railroads chalked up many "firsts" in the inauguration of the abiding patterns typifying business in general. Alfred Chandler has characterized them as the prototype of the nation's first big business. Nevertheless, the railroad industry, characterized by a "natural" tendency toward monopoly (and therefore a "public utility"), is not sufficiently typical to provide the most appropriate framework for examination of the rise of big business in all its major ramifications. An oligopoly model (industry with a few firms), or even better a dominant group industry (one with an oligopoly core and a small-firm fringe) is more representative of events. Hence, while the railroads will contribute heavily to the examination that follows, the manufacturing sector, wherein the dominant-group industry became typical by 1919, provides the best single empirical reference for the evolution of the business sector and its relationships to the economy and society at large.

Changes in the Structure and Operation of Markets

The spread of railroad transport with its dramatically declining through rates, the accompanying fall in domestic waterway and ocean freight charges, and the development of telegraphic communication opened national and international markets to the U.S. business firm. While agricultural technology and the family farm enterprise kept the producing units small in that sector, such limitations did not constrain the growth in size of the business firm in many parts of the nonfarm sector. There the national extension of the market was the occasion for the widespread competitive destruction of much of the old local and regional market segmentation, with its peculiar forms of product differentiation and heavy reliance upon the independent merchant. The large-volume plant and firm and the multiplant firm could sell or buy in several regions, in the entire national economy, and in the rest of the world. Large production of commodities of uniform quality brought lower unit costs than was possible when the scale and techniques of production were constrained by more limited sales areas. This development worked in favor of bigness.

"Bigness" is a relative term. What is here meant is bigness relative to plants and firms in the pre-Civil War decades. The giant firm as it evolved in the period under study was not necessarily bigger, *in terms of its market share in a market defined in terms of a single product*, than its predecessor who operated in a much smaller local or regional market segregated by a high transport cost barrier. The issues implied in this comparison regarding the extent of enterprise concentration and monopoly in the long run have not yet been resolved.

The oncoming giant firm, with certain notable exceptions such as the great transitory "trusts" in sugar, tobacco, whiskey, petroleum, steel, harvesting equipment, and shoe machinery, was likely to share the bulk of the market with a few large rivals, i.e., to be an oligopolist. The giant product-diversified conglomerate corporation of the later twentieth century does not emerge significantly before World War I. With respect to size, our period is marked more prominently by the development of the large *plant*, the vertically integrated *plant*, and the multiplant incorporated *firm*. This firm usually produced either one product or at the most a narrow line of very close substitutes. In a 1924 study by Willard Thorp of central-office firms based on census data for 1919 it was revealed that, of 4,813 firms operating two or more plants out of a common central office, 63 percent were firms that were active in only one industry (product).

Although the large single-product, multiplant firm of this period thus lacked the protection against the risks of market fluctuations provided by extensive product diversification, it was able to achieve some protection in the form of regional diversification by virtue of its geographical plant dispersion—an advantage not possessed by its single-plant, small-firm rival.

Multiplant organization was also one important way in which the differentiation in market power between the large and the small firm developed and thus gave rise in great part to the modern "problem of small business," the conflict between the "leaders" and the "independents."

The size of manufacturing plant rose substantially in this period, but estimation is difficult because the census stopped including the very small "hand and neighborhood industries" after 1899. These inadequate figures suggest that average real capital invested per manufacturing establishment almost doubled between 1879 and 1899 and then more than doubled between 1899 and 1919. This indicates the increasing difficulty involved in mobilizing the funds necessary to engage in manufacturing production in many lines. Moreover, average capital per plant is particularly deceptive because there were many "small business industries" dominating the universe of establishments and usually having lower capital/labor ratios than others, such as lumber and lumber products, wherein plants remained at roughly constant size between 1899 and 1919. These industries were all too easy to enter (and to leave).

The degree of concentration of production on the basis of plant size was of course much less than that based on firm size. This is suggested by the fact that in 1914 the group of establishments with an annual product value in excess of $1 million accounted for only 2.2 percent of all establishments, but employed 35 percent of all manufacturing wage earners and produced 49 percent of the total value of products in the country! A. D. H. Kaplan has estimated that in 1909 about one-fourth of the total assets of all industrial corporations were owned by the 100 largest, and the 10 largest in 1904 held 46 percent of the assets of these 100 corporations. In the small-enterprise markets, in contrast to the dominant-group oligopolies that accounted by World War I for the overwhelming bulk of total manufacturing value added, capital requirements for new entry remained relatively easy, and the associated business turnover rates remained comparatively high. Thus within the manufacturing sector there developed market bifurcation in two senses: there were concentrated industries and small-business industries, and also bifurcation of size and market power in concentrated (dominant-group) industries. In any case, a remarkable growth of plant size was a distinguishing feature of the whole period under review, but after 1919 the rate of growth of plant size declined notably.

An increase in the number of plants per firm was the second major means whereby the expansion of the firm's assets or net worth proceeded. In Thorp's previously mentioned pathbreaking study of the integration of industrial operation, an analysis was made of all cases in which two or more plants in more than one locality or industry were operated from a single central office. Thorp estimated that as of 1919 approximately 7.8 percent of all manufacturing establishments operated out of central offices, but that these employed more than one-third of all manufacturing wage earners. If this were the case, then such multiplant firms probably sold almost one-half of all manufacturing output.

The multiplant firm was, by the time of World War I, no longer restricted to the domestic market. For example, the Hershey Chocolate Company then had two sugar mills and 69 square miles of sugar plantations together with necessary railroad facilities in Cuba. International Harvester Company also operated 3,000 acres of fiber plantations in Cuba twenty years after the victorious conclusion of the Spanish-American War. Its controlled firms also owned plants in Canada, France, Germany, Russia, and Sweden, and marketing enterprises in nine other nations. The United States Rubber Company owned 93,000 acres of rubber trees in Sumatra, Anaconda Copper had extensive operations in Brazil, as did Standard Oil in Mexico, International Paper had forest reserves in Canada, and the Singer Sewing Machine Company operated plants in Quebec, Scotland, Prussia, and Russia. U.S. large-scale enterprise had thus inaugurated a historic policy of expanding beyond the domestic borders even as the domestic frontier came to an end.

Of course, in terms of sheer numbers in the nonfarm sector as a whole, the large enterprise was in a distinct minority. Thomas C. Cochran, time-honored and scholarly business historian, reminds us that business firms were increasing in number twice as fast as population (and therefore about as fast as GNP). There were about 750,000 nonfarm firms in 1880 and over 1,100,000 in 1890, and "the typical American businessman in every major field of activity except public utilities and railroads operated a small shop with no more than a handful of employees."[1] What is at least equally significant, however, is that the emerging pattern was one in which a very small proportion of all nonfarm firms came to account for a very large proportion of all nonfarm assets, sales, and employment at one end of the array of business firms. Seymour Friedland has shown that the 50 largest manufacturing corporations in 1906 accounted for 74.2 percent of total manufacturing sales.[2] The multitude of little proprietorships continued to be *socially* important, but they were in the aggregate not nearly so important *economically*. Even in retail trade, haven for the small enterprise, the mail-order houses and the chain store had begun to make inroads.

The growth in firm size and the geographical dispersions of the fabricating operations of large firms wrought significant changes in the structure of commodity marketing. Patrick G. Porter emphasizes that accompanying the emergence of the giant, oligopolistic firm there was a shift in the nature of manufactured products as the nineteenth century changed from the relatively simple, unspecific, and undifferentiated to the more and more technologically complex, specific, and differentiated commodity. These changes in firm size, market structure, and product characteristics made it possible for large manufacturers to make profits more secure and for wholesale merchants to sell more cheaply than independent merchants. One reason was that sales of commodities such as capital goods were increasingly made in oligopsonistic markets (markets with only a few large buyers), in which orders were large and buyers no longer anonymous; another was that in many consumer goods lines, markets became ever more urban and therefore dense enough to offer high-volume sales that would justify the cost of the creation of a permanent sales force for what came to be called mass distribution. As many durable products high in unit price became more technically complex and were sold in considerable quantities, such as machine tools and consumer durables, it became economically appropriate for manufacturers to link servicing, repair, and customer consultation with a factory controlled marketing network. This system came to be called direct distribution. This penetration into marketing, against the protests of established middlemen, was part of a general pattern of growing vertical integration in U.S. manufacturing. Harold C. Livesay and Patrick G. Porter have estimated that by 1909, of a sample of the 100 largest manufacturing firms, 51 percent were engaged in the extraction or production of needed raw materials, 31 percent in wholesaling, and 17 percent in retailing their own products.[3]

Porter points out that where markets remained spatially diffuse and products undifferentiated and low in unit price, the old marketing structure, with its general or specialized independent middleman, survived, and such markets were likely to be populated in their manufacturing segment by the small fabricator. The latter also tended to remain dependent upon the middleman for "trade credit," whereas the larger manufacturing concern could rely on either retained profits or the proliferating financial intermediaries, some of them interlocked in personnel with manufacturing firms, a development that distinguished the later years of this period. This writer[4] has brought into focus a bifurcation in marketing arrangement, implied in all this, between the small and the large manufacturer with respect to particular industries. For example, in the case of flour milling on the eve of World War I the Federal Trade Commission reported that:

> Several of the larger mills have established branch houses for the distribution of their product and sell from 30 to 60 percent of their output in this way, the remainder going to jobbers and wholesale grocers. The smaller mills, on the other hand, distribute most of their output, exclusive of local sales, through brokers and jobbers, and make very small use of the branch house method.[5]

The extension of marketing organizations controlled by large manufacturing firms was closely linked with the growth of their advertising that attempted to differentiate their products in the mind of the buyer. Almost heroic feats were performed in distinguishing by brand commodities with practically identical physical and chemical characteristics.

In the markets for products, then, if the "grey areas" are ignored, the emerging large manufacturer, particularly after the end of the era of the monopoly "trusts" (1890-1910), competed and/or colluded with other large "rivals" as well as with much smaller firms in the same industry. In its marketing sphere, this emerging oligopolist confronted either oligopsony or numerous small buyers, a confrontation increasingly mediated by his own sales organization in the whole or part of his markets. In the case of complex capital goods with substantial unit prices, there was likely to develop person-to-person exchange in the ever more frequent case of bilateral oligopoly (oligopolists confronting oligopsonists). In the case of consumer goods with mass markets the large manufacturer increasingly came to employ the new mass media to differentiate his products from those of his rivals. But in none of these structural juxtapositions could it be said that there obtained the neoclassical economist's requirements for strictly competitive structural features *on both sides* of such product markets. This was increasingly the case not only with respect to the number and size distribution of firms, but also with respect to the differentiated character of the product. Perhaps a bilateral monopoly or bilateral oligopoly model, or some model dealing with oligopoly in confrontation with small-firm constellations, had become the appropriate, realistic model for the analysis of twentieth century industrial markets. Unfortunately, it took four decades from the passage of the Sherman Antitrust law in 1890 before orthodox economic theory projected formal positive models designed to treat the market phenomena long known to historians, businessman, and the people at large.

Capital Markets and Financial Intermediaries

The development of the giant firm also restructured the markets for factors of production, particularly capital (funds), labor, and entrepreneurship. In the development of institutions for the provision of money capital the spread of the corporate form of business was, as in the case of the spread of the giant firm itself, an enormously powerful facilitating instrumentality. In addition to perpetual life for the firm and the advantage of limited liability for stockholder owners, the corporation, now operating under *general* state incorporation laws rather than specific charters, could mobilize through its various types of securities substantial sums from both large and small savers.

Savers as holders of money who desire to convert their funds into less liquid, income-yielding assets have varying investment psychologies and attitudes toward risk. The large corporation was able to adapt well to this spectrum of investors by developing a variety of securities that appealed to both creditor and owner types of investors and numerous subtypes within each of those. At the same time the large borrowing enterprise was enabled to command funds for varying periods of time (or uses for the funds) and varying kinds of commitment to the lenders. The best-known broad classification of lenders (or their security perferences) embraces bondholders, preferred stockholders, and common stockholders.

Although reinvested corporate income continued to be a major source of funds, the large expanding enterprise also had to turn to external sources, particularly in cyclical upswings such as 1878-1882, 1888-1893, and 1904-1907. In general, external financing was the more important where industry growth was rapid and fixed capital needs greater. Hence the volume and variety of securities proliferated (in the case of manufacturing enterprises only by the turn of the century) with the general growth of the economy and the large nonfarm enterprise.

If business enterprise in the nonfarm sector had remained small and used but little fixed, or durable, capital goods in production, its major needs for funds would have been confined to working capital. Such short term and intermediate credit could have been provided for by the state and national commercial banks. According to the classical or "real bills" theory of commercial banking it is the unique function of the commercial bank to create money by making such *short term loans* for working capital purposes, accepting fairly *liquid* "commercial paper," such as warehouse receipts extended by middlemen or bills of lading by common carriers, as collateral against the new loan-created money that would thenceforth function as capital in the hands of the borrowing firm.

The large manufacturing enterprise also reached outside for sources, and had its own uses for working capital. Its chief sources of working capital were (1) the funds generated "internally" from receipts and (2) the loans of state and national banks. Out of the latter market nexus there slowly emerged the increasingly important "prime rate" of interest—the rate paid by the large corporate borrower for short term loans from commercial banks. Middleman or trade credit for the large firm, which in turn had to come ultimately from commercial banks, was to experience a secular decline.

The chief uses of working capital funds were outlays for labor and raw materials. The latter came from markets in which the sellers were either (1) large or small firms in mining or semifabricated materials manufacture or (2) farm product middlemen of varying sizes. Working capital funds were also expended on transport services, and here the large buyer confronted a large seller. Working capital outlays continued to be extremely important, a fact attested to by the farmers' protest over their allegedly adverse terms of trade in farm product markets and the workers' protest over the large firms' policy of minimizing their wage bill.

But with the newly extended use of fixed capital goods, it became necessary for expanding industrial firms, just as with the smaller agricultural enterprises operating with much land and buildings, to submit those types of *illiquid* collateral in exchange for funds to be tied up for a *long period* of time. We know from Simon Kuznets that the combined total absolute amount of reproducible fixed capital stock (structures and producers' durable equipment) in mining, manufacturing, and the public utilities doubled between 1880 and 1900. Furthermore, Raymond Goldsmith has estimated that the "real value" of the fixed capital stock in the economy, when calculated by Gallman on an 1879 price base, was 3.1 times the total commodity output in 1879 and 3.9 times the commodity output in 1899. These developments with respect to fixed capital were of course consistent with the secular rise in the ratio of net investment to GNP, because the telegraph and the railroad had made possible a reduction in businesses' inventory/sales ratios, thus cutting the relative inventory component, a working capital element, in total capital formation. M. L. Daly has estimated that at a much later date (1939) overhead costs (including noncapital overhead costs) were more important than variable costs in nearly 90 percent of the nation's industries.

In general, then, the growth of the giant firm was associated with the secular expansion of fixed capital and the spread of the corporate form. The functionally connected growth in enterprise demand for long term funds produced a spectacular increase in bonds, mortgages, and corporate stocks, called "primary" securities. In a trailbreaking study of this phenomenon, John G. Gurley and E. S. Shaw estimated that the total outstanding volume of primary securities (including government), valued at issue-date prices, rose from $14,500 million in 1870 to $101,600 million in 1912.[6] There was a 100 percent rise between 1900 and 1912! As might be expected, the volume of primary securities rose more rapidly than total money income in the economy, e.g., from 2.13 times income in 1870 to 3.10 times in 1890 and again to a more secularly stable 3.29 times in 1912.

With so many millions of private securities (debt) offered to lenders, who could now increasingly turn to these instruments as more or less close substitutes for holding money in their ever more diversified asset folios, there arose a demand in this 1870-1912 period for business firms that could deal and/or invest in such securities. This demand was met by the expansion of the older types of financial intermediaries, such as commercial banks, mutual savings banks, fire and marine insurance companies, savings and loan associations, and mortgage companies.

The savings and loan "associations," unlike the savings banks, did not accept deposits, but rather sold shares to savers who legally became rather tenuous "owners" of the association. These associations also specialized in financing residential construction by innovating the low down payment and long term, monthly-amortized, home mortgage. As pointed out by Edward C. Ettin, toward the end of this period these associations began seriously to join the commercial banks in usurping the savings depository function of the old mutual savings banks. [7]

The private life insurance companies became significant mobilizers of savings (out of premiums) only after the Civil War. Life insurance in force grew from about $2 billion in 1870 to $8 billion at the turn of the century and $20 billion on the eve of the World War I. Negative laissez faire attitudes toward government protection of the public (including the bribing of state legislators by insurance companies) resulted in little government protection for policyholders (savers) before the 1890s, despite the dedicated reform efforts of people like Elizur Wright. The "big sell" by agents working for commissions was associated with many failures to pay on policies, high rates of cancellation on the burgeoning "industrial" life insurance sold to blue-collar workers, and ruthless treatment of defaulting policyholders. One of the "good deals" whereby savings were mobilized, often by virtual expropriation of the low income policyholder, was the application of the "tontine" principle. According to the tontine, the insurance policy deprived the policyholder of either extra dividends on his particular policy or (often) any dividends until the term of the policy (usually five or fifteen years) elapsed. Then heirs received only the face value of the policy, lapsed policyholders got little or nothing, and the more financially intrepid survivors among the policyholders divided the accumulated dividends among themselves.

In this particular "capital market," as in the markets for labor, farm products, and many consumer goods, the individual did not confront the large concern with either equivalent knowledge or equal market power. One group of writers cites the case of a disgruntled policyholder who, after being denied redress from the state insurance commission, was told "he could not quote from the proceedings of the commission because the entire minutes had been copyrighted by the insurance company in question"![8] The important insurance state of New York in 1906, during the heyday of the progressive era of popular clamor for control of business abuses, inaugurated a nationwide reform movement, following the exposé and recommendations of the famous investigating Commission under attorney Charles Evans Hughes, instituting regulation of insurance companies somewhat more in the policyholder's interest. Other states widely copied the New York example.

The disposition of "other people's money" by the insurance companies required making policyholders' savings available to productive enterprises issuing primary securities so that the latter could purchase capital goods. State laws restricted insurance companies to nonspeculative issues, such as government and railroad (!) bonds, but beginning in the 1890s and largely at the initiative of trust companies, according to the venerable student of business consolidation John Moody, the life insurance companies started placing substantial amounts of their funds in the stocks of trust companies (state chartered semibanks supposedly devoted chiefly to handling individual and corporate financial affairs as trustees). Note that these stocks fell in the category of *indirect* financial paper, rather than *primary* securities; they were the securities issued by nonmonetary *financial* institutions, rather than productive, nonfinancial enterprises. Thus the rise of financial intermediaries added an additional layer of securities to the growing volume of primary securities. Hence the opportunities for financial investment as distinguished from real investment were vastly multiplied. Also, the possible volume of economic activity that would be controlled by an individual, a corporation, or a small group through the power linked with financial claims was enormously extended. Furthermore, the inducement to engage in highly speculative and promotional financial transactions was greatly intensified.

In this same period (the 1890s) the trust companies began to subordinate their fiduciary activities and to stress the financing of productive enterprises and the marketing of their securities, after the manner of an investment bank. Trust companies burgeoned, and their stock prices soared. This attracted more insurance company money and personnel to them and their boards of directors. Interlocking directorates became widespread and brought together into interest groups the practitioners of high finance in industry, banking, insurance, and other nonmonetary financial intermediaries. According to Gurley and Shaw the "indirect" financial assets of private nonmonetary financial intermediaries such mutual savings deposits, savings and loan shares, policyholders' "equities" in life and other insurance companies, and trust companies' funds rose from $890 million in 1870 to $2.78 billion in 1900 and $9.42 billion in 1912—a growth rate considerably in excess of that for primary securities. Raymond Goldsmith's estimate for the latter year is $10.51 billion. If investment banks and dealers in securities were added, the total would be a billion higher in 1912. But the fact remains that underneath this mountain of financial claims funds were in fact also channeled from savers to production enterprises acquiring physical capital goods.

Another important institution in the markets for funds after 1870 was the investment "bank." A handful of noncommercial banks, associated with such famous names as J.P. Morgan and Company, Kuhn, Loeb and Company, Kidder, Peabody and Company, and Lee Higginson and Company, worked closely with a small group of large commercial banks to market, or "underwrite," important industrial, railroad, and utility securities nationally.

The investment bankers and their cohorts were a fairly close-knit oligopoly that by the late 1880s performed not only the middleman underwriting function in linking savings with investment, but was also extremely aggressive in promoting business consolidation and monopoly and in creating "communities of interest" on a spectacular scale. This group formed the heart of what was unpopularly known as the "money trust." The Pujo Committee Report of 1913[9] named the four investment banking houses just mentioned plus the First National and National City banks of New York as the "most active agents in forwarding and bringing about the concentration of control of money and credit." But the interlocks of this group, together with seven other banks and trust companies, went far beyond the world of financial institutions. The Committee found that

firm members or directors of these thirteen firms plus the directors
of the Morgan-controlled Equitable Life Assurance Society, held:

118 directorships in 34 banks and trust companies having
total resources of $2.679 billion and total deposits of $1.983
billion.

30 directorships in 10 insurance companies having total
assets of $2.293 billion.

105 directorships in 32 transportation systems having a total
capitalization of $11.784 billion and a total mileage (exclud-
ing express companies and steamship lines) of 150,200.

63 directorships in 24 producing and trading corporations
having a total capitalization of $3.339 billion.

25 directorships in 12 public utility corporations having a
total capitalization of $2.150 billion.

In all, 341 directorships in 112 corporations having
aggregate resources or capitalization of $22.245 billion.

The fusion of interest groups linking finance and industry, as
illustrated by this report, became an abiding feature of the business sector in the twentieth century and elicited the appellation
"finance capitalism" to describe the era following about 1890.
Robert Sobel has paid doubtful tribute to the leading clique in the
unfolding of this process in his characterization of it as "the
Morganization of America." Sobel notes that in Wall Street the
Morgan group was known as "Jesus Christ and his Twelve Apos-
tles." Unfortunately, the interest group, while vital to the structure
of industrial markets and to business behavior in the twentieth century, never achieved a respectable place in the body of neoclassical
economics, but performed a more important role in the hands of
such maverick institutional economists as Thorstein Veblen and
John R. Commons.

The growing flood of primary and indirect securities was absorbed in the portfolios of a world of financial "asset holders" who no
longer, as in earlier times, bought securities as a lifetime investment, but possessed only an absentee, transitory, or speculative
interest in them for either their yield or their appreciation prospects. That is to say, there had to be a market for these securities
after they got old, and financial investors wanted to speculate in
them and/or shift the composition of their portfolios. This was the

function of the stock exchanges—primarily to accommodate the purchase and sale of old shares, most of which were stocks, in contradistinction to the investment markets in which bonds predominated.

As industrial firms and financial intermediaries added their supply, particularly after the 1890s, to the long existing government's and railroads', the stock markets, and particularly the New York Stock Exchange founded in 1792, handled an increasing volume of business. Behind the Exchange, organized as a partnership, was an elite club of stockbrokers, who had bought "seats" entitling them to access to the market as agents for buyers and sellers of securities. To paraphrase Robert Sobel's cool expression, the coming oneness of the world was made evident in the Exchange's financial appraisal of events all over the globe. In a more seamy sense, however, the unregulated Exchange also became an arena for making speculative profits between bulls and bears, such as Daniel Drew (of "watered stock" fame) and Jim Fisk and Jay Gould (both notorious for the failure of their attempt to corner the gold market that led to the financial ruin of hundreds of speculators on "Black Friday," September 24, 1869). In addition, on the more mundane speculative side, the Exchange brokers created a national center for the financially dangerous seasonal centralization of interior "country" bank reserves, in the form of call money loans at high rates from commercial banks to stockbrokers using securities as collateral and trading on a frequently small margin. This deposit pyramiding exacerbated monetary stringency across the country during panics under the National Banking system.

Other corporations also lent surplus funds on the call market, competing with the commercial banks and adding more cancerous cells to the financial connecting tissues of disaster when cyclical "panics" struck. The rich and well-to-do financial investors in 1903 (there was no stockholding proletariat then any more than now) managed to engineer for themselves a major "rich man's panic" in the context of a mild, minor general business "downswing" lasting from September 1902 to August 1904 during which on an annual basis the GNP deflater *rose* and real GNP hardly quivered. The inherently destabilizing role of the financial institution was not new, but it operated with added power in the "panics" of 1873, 1893, 1907, and the speculative boom of the 1920s.

All this financial hustle and bustle was thus a particularly essential attribute of a developed security capitalism once the corporate form of business and the corporate security became widespread. The volume of securities traded on the Big Board rose from 54 million shares in 1875 to an average of 85 million annually during 1885-1893, 139 million in 1900, and 212 million in 1909, as the stocks of manufacturing corporations came increasingly to be added to the list of rails, coal companies, mines, and utilities. According to Margaret Myers in her scholarly study of the New York money market, the number of industrial issues listed by the Exchange was only 15 in 1867 but had risen to 191 by 1913. The trend was similar on other exchanges across the country.

Yet financial investment is not real investment, as the great founder of institutional economics in the United States, Thorstein Veblen, was always prone to emphasize. Making money is not necessarily an accompaniment of making goods, and Veblen pointed out that the two may well conflict. John Maynard Keynes mounted a similar attack upon *capital as acquisition* at a much later time, arguing that the stock market siphoned off funds that could not be competed for by employment-creating enterprise, particularly in the late phases of cyclical prosperity. Thus the development of the capital markets after the Civil War was not at all a simple one whereby the flow of savings was smoothly channeled into real investment. When speculative financial investment, promoter's profits through corporate reorganization, and the achievement of monopoly power through business consolidation and communities of interest also emerged in connection with the institutionalization of these markets, the restriction of output rather than its expansion was often the result. Financial investment had become a major competing substitute for real investment.

Changes in the Labor Markets

The growth of the giant nonfarm enterprise, particularly in manufacturing, public utilities and finance, also changed the structure of factor markets in which labor services were sold and bought. The emerging labor markets were unlike the markets for capital goods and for money capital, in which, with the notable exception of the decreasingly significant petty proprietor, large organizations were ever more likely to confront one another on more or less equal footing. The unorganized worker, like the family farmer, increasingly after the 1880s confronted a large monopsonistic or oligopsonistic buyer, just as the unorganized urban or farm consumer came to confront a monopolist or an oligopolist. The new market was a metropolitan area whose labor force possessed either a variety of closely substitutable skills, or was largely unskilled. Moreover, except in the tight labor markets characterizing the late boom phase of the business cycle, there was likely to be an unemployed reserve for most occupations. These supply determinants made the market supply schedule for labor quite elastic at the going wage, and left the individual worker with a very low reservation price (i.e., wage below which he would withdraw the offer of labor services). From the standpoint of the business corporate buyer with many employees, his preference for the labor power of any one worker, except in the case of unusual skill requirements, was negligible.

As C. H. Salmon, a leader of the Brotherhood of Locomotive Engineers on the CB&Q put it, "one man alone counts nothing before a powerful company; one day's work bears a poor proportion to the thousands of millions of capital invested in railroads." The growing size and complexity of urban labor markets also put the worker at a disadvantage with respect to job information, which fact in turn adversely affected his bargaining skill and alternative job opportunities. Furthermore, the employer's great size and production for national markets, together with the secrecy of accounts, then considered an inalienable right of private property, meant that the worker was uninformed regarding the firm's ability or willingness to make wage or other job concessions to him. But the worker was acutely aware of the superior resources and market power of the employer as well as the latter's determination that *he* would run the business. Thus in the coming industrial labor markets, with atomism on the selling side and oligopsony on the buying side, a structural condition existed out of which a money wage rate below a "fair" or competitive level was likely, and job conditions tended to be unilaterally determined by the employer.

With an "organizational revolution" occurring on the buying side as an accompaniment of industrialization, there was a classic case of the emergence of John Kenneth Galbraith's "original power" (the giant enterprise and the antilabor employers' association) that was certain sooner or later to elicit from the sellers (labor) a "countervailing power" center in the form of labor organization around the job and job conditions. The analogy with the family farmer is striking. Clearly in these changing structural features of the markets for labor as well as for farm products, we have the differentiation in market power that holds the clue to the behavioral response in the form of countervailing organization on the part of the atomistic seller. As the *Report on the Chicago Strike of June-July, 1894* by the U.S. Strike Commission put it, "the rapid concentration of railroad capital and management demands a like union of their employees for the purpose of mutual protection."

However, Thomas H. Wickes, second vice-president of the Pullman Company, expressed the employer's failure to acknowledge any structural changes in labor markets or in market power associated therewith when he testified:

> Question: Don't you think that the tendency . . . of the concentration of capital in large corporations has a tendency to make the strict application of the rule of supply and demand somewhat unjust and harsh upon the laborer?
>
> Wickes: No, I do not see that it does. I should sell my labor for the highest price I could get for it if I were a mechanic. I think every man has the same right.

What ensued was a long, bitter, and bloody guerilla war. The employers strove to impose a new, exacting, industrial discipline upon labor, insisted upon the exercise of arbitrary supervisory power, and violently resisted with the aid of the police, the military, and the courts, labor's efforts to secure collective bargaining for wages and working conditions through independent labor unions. Most, although of course not all, employers subscribed to Arthur Young's dictum that "everyone but an idiot knows that the lower classes must be kept poor or they will never be industrious." Parity for unskilled labor's terms of trade with employers was long delayed, for the approaching end of the frontier was flooding the cities with migrants. Mechanization of the work process was breaking down occupational barriers and diluting skills. Women were leaving the household. Blacks were migrating from the South. Southern and eastern Europe between 1900 and 1914 was flooding the Northern states with 13 million "new" and largely unskilled immigrants, and the American Federation of Labor was confining its membership largely to the skilled workers in the small enterprise activities of the economy.

The decline of the individual proprietor began to destroy the older, face-to-face relationships between employer and employee. Despite the frequent paternalism and the deprivation of the worker's personal privacy associated with the older relationships, it had some human advantages over the new ones, which were impersonal and alienated. The laborer now had no control over the rhythm of his work, lacked ownership of his tools and equipment, and, as Thorstein Veblen emphasized, lost his sense of pride in his personal workmanship. Routinization and alienation from the product of his labor were overriding aspects of the new job as corporate blue-collar employee. If Adam Smith had linked "laborers and laboring cattle" into one category, the new corporate leaders hired labor as another "input," distinguished from inanimate fixed capital inputs chiefly by virtue of its being, similar to agricultural raw material pruchases, working or "circulating" capital.

With the large firms that early typified the railroad industry, the abiding structural features of industrial labor markets with their characteristic pattern of differential market power, "corrected" more or less by labor organization, can best be detected in that sector. Alfred Chandler explains the fact that the railroad brotherhoods were the most powerful and effective national craft unions prior to the twentieth century by pointing to the early conjuncture of oligopsony and the high skills and job responsibilities associated with railroad work that endowed these workers with greater bargaining power than was possessed by their fellow workers in manufacturing. In the case of the railroads, the organized worker was also dealing with professional corporate managers at a time when the worker in manufacturing still bargained alone or dealt with a "robber baron," or active industrialist-owner.

Changes in Enterprise Administration and Behavior

The rise of the giant enterprise, together with the increasing role of fixed charges and the corporate form, all worked together to produce new kinds of business policies and behavior in the "Gilded Age." That age ushered in the separation of business ownership from control over operations, although until nearly the end of this period the active "captain" of industry and finance, or all-purpose entrepreneur, was more prominent than the upcoming professional manager. Accordingly, the corporate administrative bureaucracy of the twentieth century "megacrop" was in its infancy. The entrepreneurial functions of risk-taking, organizing, promoting, supervising, capital-raising, and innovating were widely performed by single persons rather than being split up among owners, boards of directors, division managers, and production engineers, as they were in the late twentieth century corporate conglomerates. Hence the period is replete with the names of "robber barons" and "industrial statesmen" such as J. P. Morgan, John D. Rockefeller, Charles E. Perkins, Andrew Carnegie, Jay Gould, D. George Westinghouse, Cyrus McCormick, Jim Fisk, Solomon Guggenheim, Edward H. Harriman, James J. Hill, and those whom Stewart Holbrook has called the "'Big Four' of authentically western exploitation," Collis Huntington, Charles Crocker, Leland Stanford, and Mark Hopkins. As Joseph Schumpeter perspicaciously emphasized, it was possible to glamorize the capitalist system by endowing these entrepreneurs with a certain swashbuckling romanticism, a buttress for the system that disappeared with the subsequent emergence of the unheralded corporate manager coming out of the Harvard graduate school of business administration. Thereafter people knew brand names but not people.

The growth of the giant enterprise brought into prominence not only the abiding problem of corporate bureaucracy, but the theoretical and practical question of the optimal size firm. George Stigler has persuasively argued that the giant enterprise of the twentieth century became much larger than optimal from the standpoint of productive efficiency in any engineering sense. And most economists accepted the empirical postulate that it was diseconomies of management that made the long run cost curve of the large firm turn upward—hopefully long before that firm accounted for a noncompetitive share of the typical industrial market. In this way, among others, orthodox economics was able to find a determinate equilibrium for the large firm and, more important, to cling to the notion that its purely competitive model was a reasonably good first approximation to the actual economy. Unfortunately for that doctrine, big business soon saw the desirability from a profit standpoint of decentralizing high-level decision making in the large enterprise, and it has been extremely difficult for economic theorists to demonstrate that the long-run cost curve turns up in the controversial ranges of large volume production. In the regulated public utilities it came to be accepted that the long-run cost curve continued to slope down at output rates so large that the expansion of the enterprise eventuated in a "natural" monopoly of the market for several publicly essential services.

As this period drew to a close, the common stockholder was already becoming a transient, absentee risk-taker, reduced to the status of the corporate creditor without a controlling voice in management. As Thomas Cochran has succinctly put this evolution, "from the eighteenth to the twentieth century, the migration of effective control in large-scale corporate business has been from operating owners to wealthy directors to professional managers," [10] or, as Mabel Newcomer has called them, "career men." There was an age of the robber baron ("industrial statesman"?); it dawned and died between the Civil War and World War I. The logic of the giant corporation was legally expedited under the leadership of the state of New Jersey with its general incorporation law. New Jersey lowered the requirements for incorporation, permitted corporations to own stock in other corporations, and allowed its corporations to do business anywhere. This assured the transitory role of personal entrepreneurship. Some of the business leaders of the times often stood out for a particular personal activity or trait (e.g., Charles E. Perkins of the CB&Q for administrative talent, J. P. Morgan, Sr., for corporate consolidation linking financial and industrial institutions, John D. Rockefeller for building the national Standard Oil monopoly, George Westinghouse for combining invention with business objectives, and Collis Huntington of the Central-Southern Pacific for demonstrating the importance of political lobbying to successful "railroading"). But most of them were active in all types of business manipulation, promotion, organization, and even, in many cases, of operation.

The construction of monopoly positions, with exquisite neutrality included by Schumpeter and others as a form of innovation, absorbed much of the attention of the industrial statesmen. The reaction of these leaders to the new industrial and financial context was, among other things, to abjure price competition. As Joe S. Bain has pointed out, free-moving and uncontrolled market prices were becoming rare, and price rivalry was becoming deliberate rather than automatic, sporadic rather than persistent. [11] The rate wars of the railroads in the 1870s and 1880s had instructed an entire generation of business leaders in the discipline of fixed costs, and this was no accident, for fixed charges were a particularly prominent feature of the railroad industry. The reaction throughout industry against the acute threat of price competition in the new setting of heavy overhead costs took many forms. For example, entrepreneurs attempted suppression of such competition through nonprice competition (especially advertising), "gentlemen's agreements," pools, use of the trustee device (for the centralization of voting control over active corporations through the exchange of their voting shares for trust certificates, a device requiring no state charter and from whence the (un)popular word "trust"), holding companies, interlocking directorates, acquisitions and mergers, cooperation through industrywide trade associations of firms, "Gary dinners," various forms of tacit collusion, and the appeal to government for regulatory intervention.

It will be observed that many of these techniques relied specifically upon the corporate form of organization. None of these penetrated the thick ideological veil of formal neoclassical economic theory, but they contributed heavily to the theory of the caustic genius Thorstein Veblen and his disciples in the critical institutionalist school of economic thought. Out of this turmoil grew Veblen's distinction between business, which meant making money, and industry, which meant making goods, with the two in frequent conflict. In his famous *Theory of the Leisure Class* Veblen also attacked the conspicuous consumption of the robber barons and financiers, falling back on the time-honored classical distinction between productive and unproductive consumption to lambast these capitalists for generating a form of consumerism that diverted resorces from productive investment to growth-inhibiting consumption of luxury goods and services.

The discipline of fixed costs soon taught entrepreneurs that price wars would readily cut average revenue below average total cost, down toward the level of average variable cost. Although a firm would not shut down in the short run under such conditions—*assuming it knew its cost breakdown*—it would approach insolvency in a longer period as uncovered fixed charges mounted. In that case it faced losses if it continued, and failure to cover fixed costs if it shut down. How long was the short run? Entrepreneurs did not know the answer in precise terms. But they did know that in the long run if prices failed to cover average total costs, some of them would be dead as enterprisers. It would be better to exert heroic efforts to eliminate this most deadly of all forms of market uncertainty. The discerning Andrew Carnegie saw clearly the significance for price policy and the time problem stemming from the historical shift in the structure of business costs when he wrote in 1889 that

> Political economy says that ... goods will not be produced at less than cost. This was true when Adam Smith wrote, but it is not quite true today. When an article was produced by a small manufacturer, employing probably at his own home, two or three journeymen and an apprentice or two, it was an easy

matter for him to limit or even stop production. As manufacturing is carried on today, in enormous establishments with five or ten million dollars of capital invested . . . twenty sources of expense are *fixed charges*, many of which stoppage would only increase. Therefore the article is produced for months and, in some cases I have known, for years, not only without profit or without interest on capital, but to the impairment of the capital invested . . . . While continuing to produce may be costly, the manufacturer knows too well that stoppage would be ruin. His brother manufacturers [sic!] are of course in the same situation. . . . It is in the soil thus prepared that anything promising relief is gladly welcomed . . . . Combinations—syndicates— trusts—they are willing to try anything. . . . Such is the genesis of "Trusts" in manufactured articles.[12]

The connections between fixed costs, price policy, and attempted monopolization were more sharply registered in the minds of business leaders partly because of the economy's performance in the thirty years between 1865 and 1897. This was a period of secularly falling commodity prices and four severe cyclical contractions: October 1873 to March 1879 (the so-called "great depression" of the nineteenth century), March 1882 to May 1885, January 1893 to June 1894, and December 1895 to June 1897. With secularly falling prices, the service charges on fixed assets, priced at earlier higher levels, exerted a continuing price-cost squeeze on both farm and nonfarm enterprises, exacerbating their disadvantages in their capacity as debtors. In partial consequence, the farmers mounted the agrarian revolt and big nonfarm firms monopolized markets. The great merger movement of 1897-1903, a period of prosperity, was the lagged culmination of the whole trend, and greatly overshadowed the twelve major combinations spasmodically formed during 1879-1896, a period that Henry Seager and Charles Gulick have called the period of the trust proper.

Organizational developments would have been essentially the same with secularly constant prices and dampened cycles, but they were no doubt accentuated by the actual performance of the economy. It never dawned on a business community enamored of laissez faire and Social Darwinism that a Keynesian type government fiscal policy could have dampened the cycles and alleviated capacity underutilization, although, as Robert Sharkey has emphasized, businessmen in their entrepreneurial capacities, as with the farmers, were aware that the prevailing tight monetary policy perpetuated by creditor interests, and especially the bankers, was maintaining an unacceptable price environment.

The rise to prominence of fixed assets also created the conditions and the imperative for the development of modern cost accounting, as well as its handmaiden, full-cost administered pricing. The link between the two was firmly established by the railroads' experience with price wars and the necessity to set both freight and passenger rates in the context of large overhead allocation. The analysis of the composition of a commodity's total cost between overhead and out-of-pocket outlays was therefore, so far as we know, first undertaken in a systematic way by railroad managers. Cost accounting in general, and depreciation accounting in particular, were perhaps the most important innovation in accounting since the invention of double entry bookkeeping in the thirteenth century, and clearly delineated accounting from bookkeeping. Elementary cost accounting spread gradually through the nonfarm business sector in the last quarter of the nineteenth century, and was facilitated by the emergence of scientific management under the inspiration of Frederick W. Taylor and by the inauguration of higher education in accountancy in the Wharton School of Finance and Economy of the University of Pennsylvania in 1881.

We are fortunate to have available a fine discussion of the subject of cost accounting and rate setting by Albert Fink, president of the Louisville and Nashville Railroad, in the corporation's Annual Report for 1874. Fink refers to expenses "not affected by the amount of business transacted" that do not "vary with the amount of business," as contrasted to the portion of expenses that do so vary. He even recognized that a portion of the wage bill consisted of fixed costs, i.e., that for "a certain number of agents [who] have to be employed, whether there is more or less work to be done." He emphasized that the "fixed or inevitable" expenditures "which are entirely independent of the amount of work performed, such as interest on capital invested, form a "large proportion" of total operating expenses. In an incisive passage on rate setting, Fink reveals a recognition of the modern concepts of joint products, fixed costs, variable costs, marginal prime coats, and average total unit costs, together with some of the relationships among them as those relationships impinge upon price administration and price discrimination:

> In order to estimate the cost of transportation under the various conditions that occur it is necessary to classify the expenditures, and to separate those that increase with the amount of work done from those that are fixed and independent of it; and to ascertain the ratio of increase of cost with the increase of work. Without such an analysis of the cost it is impossible to solve the question of cost of transportation that arises in the daily practice of rail-

road operation. A mere knowledge of the average cost per ton-mile of all the expenditures during a whole year's operation is of no value whatever in determining the cost of transporting any particular class of freight, as no freight is ever transported under the average condition under which the whole year's business is transacted. We can therefore not make the average cost per ton-mile the basis for a tariff, if it is to be based upon cost; but we must classify the freight according to the conditions affecting cost of transportation, and ascertain the cost of each class separately.[13]

In a famous study of railroad rate wars published in the very midst of those wars, Arthur T. Hadley pointed out that

> Where a railroad . . . comes into competition with a water-route, or with another railroad, its charges are brought down to the lowest possible figure. The points where there is no competition are made to pay the fixed charges, while the rates for competitive business will little more than pay train and station expenses. It is better to have business on those terms than to have it go by a rival route. In a railroad war this competition is carried beyond the bounds of reason. There was a time when cattle were carried from Chicago to New York at one dollar a carload. These low rates develop the competitive point rapidly, while the higher rates retard the growth of the places where there is no such competition.[14]

It may be presumed that the "lowest possible figure" was per unit variable costs. This assumes the railroad knew its variable costs on particular portions of its business. Hadley indicates that an uncontrolled price war could carry prices for a time below the level necessary to cover such direct costs, as in his example above.

The postulate that all costs must be covered in the long run was more operationally meaningful in the case of the one-product firm in manufacturing than in that of the multiproduct railroad, in which many particular "products" (shipments) shared the fixed costs in common with the other goods in the firm's family of products. Latter day cost accountants attempted to allocate these "common costs" among the numerous products of the multiproduct firm with varying degrees of success. In this way it was hoped that each item in the firm's product mix would bear its aliquot share of the "burden" of overhead costs. But in the days of the rate wars among the railroads such price administration techniques were not well developed. On the basis of rough distinctions between fixed and variable costs, the roads "charged what the traffic would bear" in the case of one market or one shipper, and charged less than current costs, directly or through rebates, etc., to others. They anticipated that by such price discrimination they could come out on balance with long run total receipts sufficiently greater than long run total costs to return a profit to the equity interests. But the difficulty of common cost allocation led the railroads in the rate-war era into a pricing morass. This problem arose historically with the emergence of multiple nonjoint products in firms having heavy fixed charges emanating from a *large and varied* complement of durable capital inputs.

In the absence of effective market control as represented by the unstable cartel, competition between the roads, as well as between them and the waterways earlier, eventuated in rates no doubt frequently approximating average variable cost. Attempts to retrieve the lost overhead in the long haul market by charging more than full cost plus a moderate markup, i.e., charging what the traffic would bear, may have been more successful in short haul markets in arousing farmers and other shippers and "retarding the growth" at noncompetitive points than in achieving the desired overall profit targets. Many farmers clearly believed they were the victims of monopolistic price discrimination that resulted in excessive rates to them. For example, the farmers' price complaints against the railroads were aired in a speech by Congressman Lewis B. Gunckel in the House of Representatives on March 25, 1874:

At the recent meeting of the National Grange the following facts, among many of like character, were stated: An Illinois farmer sent his corn to New York City, and received for it fifty-six and one-half cents per bushel; the railroad charges were forty-eight and one-half cents per bushel, leaving him eight cents per bushel for his corn. An Iowa farmer sent his to Springfield, Massachusetts, and sold it for sixty-eight cents; the freight charges were sixty-seven cents, leaving him one cent per bushel for his corn. Another sent his corn to some interior village in Maine, and got ninety cents per bushel, the railroad and commission charges were more, and he fell in debt by an attempt to supply his old neighbors with cheap corn. Is it a wonder that the western farmer complains that he does not get a living price for his grain? It is reliably stated that three hundred and fifty million bushels of grain raised in the Mississippi Valley, and transported by railroad to the Eastern States, paid an average freight charge of fifty cents per bushel; and yet the corn so transported did not average to the farmer more than sixteen cents per bushel. . . . It is known that grain can be carried over this very distance for from fifteen to twenty cents per bushel, and afford a very liberal profit to the capital really invested in the railroad. But how can reasonable rates be established and enforced and the producer and consumer brought closer together?[15]

Fortunately, farmer pressure and group actions led to the establishment of the Interstate Commerce Commission in 1887, which then broke down the previous segregation between the long and short haul markets, without which price discrimination would have been impossible, and in consequence short haul rates initially fell approximately 15 to 30 percent while competitive long haul rates rose slightly. [16]

The whole downward pressure on rates and railroad profits in the 1870s and 1880s emanating from the enumerated causes was accelerated by the accompanying cost savings. These resulted partly from decreases in factor prices and partly from the technological improvements made in that period. Among the latter were: the adoption of the steel rail; larger, heavier, and more durable rolling stock, including locomotives; the air brake; the adoption of standard gauge track (4'8½''); the refrigerator car; longer trains; improvements in switching facilities; etc. Thus, while many shippers and areas, particularly local ones where specific railroads had an area monopoly, suffered under the burden of excessive and inflexible rates, i.e., rate discrimination, the "economy as a whole" benefited from the technological improvements and the cutthroat competition, two forces that mutually induced each other to bring down the long run freight and passenger rates by spectacular percentages.

The further development of cost accounting and industrywide, as distinguished from individual enterprise, price administration was stimulated by the spread of the trade association movement. One of the earliest trade associations was the northern railroads' Joint Traffic Association, a cartel declared in violation of the Sherman Antitrust Act in 1898. Although the origin of the trade association movement was in considerable part due to antiunion efforts by employers, it was also regarded, according to the U.S. Department of Commerce, as a substitute for the "trust," particularly in many small business industries in which there were obstacles to the growth of concentrated production. After the passage of the Sherman Antitrust law in 1890 several trade associations were charged with unlawful attempts to control the market. But when a promonopoly book appeared in 1912 entitled *The New Competition* by A. J. Eddy, legal counsel for a number of trade associations, many of these associations followed his advice. They also emulated the pioneering work of the Bridge Builders Society and the Yellow Pine Association in establishing "open-price" policies for whole industries, based upon an accepted system of uniform cost accounting designed to facilitate noncompetitive price administration. Eddy's influence perhaps contributed to the odd practice by latter-day economists of classifying monopoly and oligopoly as a type of competition.

Changes in the Business-Community Relationship

In general the great changes wrought by the spread of the giant corporation did not appear to the business leadership of the times to be the occasion for reconstituting the social and political prerogatives in the community that traditionally had been enjoyed by people of property. Jay Gould of the notorious Erie Ring testified in 1883 that "a corporation is only another name for the means which we have discovered of allowing a poor man to invest his income in a great enterprise." The banker Henry Clews expressed the widespread conviction among the business elite that God in his infinite wisdom had endowed the propertied interests uniquely with the inalienable obligation to further the material and spiritual interests of all mankind. And when Andrew Carnegie proclaimed that "upon the sacredness of property civilization itself depends," he meant "Individualism, Private Property, the Law of Accumulation of Wealth, and the Law of Competition"—without interference from government. In this laissez faire view, government subsidies, franchises, tariffs, land grants, general incorporation laws, and the like were not considered interference, however. Laissez faire always meant, among other things, piecemeal aid to industrial enterprise, just as mercantilism had meant piecemeal aid to mercantile enterprise.

But what was widely overlooked at the time was the fact that the corporate form of business in the new context of giant trusts and later oligopolies was itself producing an organizational and managerial revolution that was significantly altering the system of business property rights as traditionally constituted. In this period the separation of ownership from management was in its infancy, and the active participation of many business leaders in the affairs of their respective enterprises contributed to a postponement of the recognition of the full implications of Veblen's attack on absentee ownership. Enterprisers of the time cavalierly appointed themselves to be the trustees of the public interest as they busied themselves with the substitution of administrative decisions for the former presumably blindly working forces of supply and demand. Any interference with their assumption of this trusteeship "burden" was viewed with amazement and alarm as arbitrary encroachment upon the inviolable right of (business) property.

But it was increasingly otherwise with the public. That "public" was of course itself comprised of differentiated interest groups—

farmers, small businessmen, urban workers, immigrants, urban middle class, professionals, inarticulate consumers, and the various levels and organs of government through which the great conflicts of the period operated to express their group interests as they viewed them. Although as a whole the overwhelming consensus was proprivate property and probusiness, the state was increasingly invoked (hopefully) as a countervailing power against what the giant business enterprise had seemingly done to make the private market mechanism malfunction. The malfunctionings appeared to be effects other than those that would have obtained under atomistic competition, which was still a sacred cow in the normative sense and was presumed to prevail in fact.

To countervail against the public's attacks on the new oligopolistic private market mechanism, the growing corporate power, while at first fighting tenaciously to defend its laissez faire bastions, had by World War I found itself even more frequently invoking piecemeal government intervention. The era of laissez faire had both its heyday and the beginning of its demise between the Civil War and World War I. Indeed, as is well known, the era of laissez faire ended in the United States about a decade after Versailles.

An example of business's wavering strategy toward laissez faire is found in the evolution of public utility regulation as it affected the railroad industry. The farmers and other small shippers mounted a vigorous attack upon railroad price discrimination between persons, places, commodities, and particular descriptions of traffic. As one phase of the agrarian revolt, farmers in the Midwest beginning in the 1870s succeeded in passing "Granger Laws" in a number of states that established commissions to set maximum rates, prohibit rate discrimination, and otherwise regulate common carriers. The railroads' legal attack on the state laws was based on the grounds that (1) rate regulation deprived them of property without due process (invoking the Fourteenth Amendment, passed to protect the freedmen after the Civil War!) and, of more interest for present purposes, (2) since most rail traffic was interstate, the *Federal government should perform the regulatory function* if necessary. While the railroad leaders hoped for no such Federal regulation, their strategy appeared to boomerang after the railroad's final legal victory before the Supreme Court in the Wabash case in 1886. One year, later, abiding agrarian pressure secured passage of the Interstate Commerce Act. A protracted period of railroad hostility to the new law was nevertheless marked by the general absence of rate wars except during the downswing after 1893. According to Robert M. Spann and Edward W. Erickson, between 1887 and 1893 "the trunk line cartel fixed long-haul rates and the ICC ratified and enforced them." [17] Eventually there was railroad acceptance of Federal rate setting. The death of "destructive" price competition was the payoff for government intervention. The railroads were now a public utility, providing an essential service, and therefore "affected with a public interest." Thus a vast and, with the inclusion of other public utilities, growing area of the economy became legally exempted from the competitive norm and subject to public commission regulation.

Railroads and the Development of the Regulatory Commission

The history of the Interstate Commerce Commission from 1887 to the end of this period provides a tortuous, frustrating, and controversial record of a popular effort to deal with private business monopoly in the context of widespread faith in laissez faire, in competition, and in the Constitutional concept that government is composed only of legislative, executive, and judicial departments. The checkered childhood of the ICC during its first quarter-century represented the country's first lasting Federal effort to regulate a public utility through the "independent" commission. As a product of the popular protest movement dating from the agrarians through the well-meaning reformist Progressives, this first commission was purportedly directed toward the correction of abuses perpetuated by common carriers rather than overall industrial planning in the public interest.

The sphere of abuse regulation was largely confined to "unjust and unreasonable" rates. Moreover, the original Interstate Commerce Act dealt only with rates already in effect (which were required to be published), rather than with proposed rates. Furthermore, it empowered the Commission to initiate proceedings in a rate case only when a shipper made a formal complaint. The Commission for the first ten years assumed the authority to fix maximum charges when, in response to a complaint, it found existing rates unreasonable. But a jealous railroad-approved, Federal Supreme Court, as part of a general judicial emasculation of the Commission's power, deprived the agency of the rate proscribing authority in two decisions in 1896 and 1897. Hence the Commission asserted plaintively in its 1904 Annual Report that it could "condemn the wrong but could not prescribe the remedy."

It was not until 1906 in the Hepburn Act that the agency was empowered, as a result of pressures from the shippers' lobby, to proscribe maximum rates. The railroads had sponsored and supported the Elkins Act of 1903 because it had outlawed rebates and concessions representing competitive departures from published rates that were seriously cutting into revenues. [18] But they bitterly opposed the setting of maximum charges by the Commission, as embodied in the Hepburn Act. [19] In the Mann-Elkins Act of 1910, the original Act's prohibition against long and short haul discrimination, which had so angered farmers and which had lain practically dormant since the destructive Supreme Court decision in the Alabama Midland case (1897), was revitalized. The Commission was additionally authorized (not required) to suspend *proposed* rate changes for a period up to ten months, and to initiate rate changes without a formal complaint from a shipper. Finally, an additional interventionist step was taken when the Commission was granted by the Valuation Act of 1913 the power to estimate the "fair valuation" of railroad property in order to make it possible to determine rates that would yield a "fair return." In the sphere of rate determination, but in that sphere alone, public utility regulation had come quite a long way despite its hostile coexistence with the Supreme Court. But the ICC in this period "failed to develop techniques required for administering novel, experimental, and complex regulatory policies. It regarded itself as a tribunal for the adjudication of disputes between private parties, rather than an aggressive promoter of the public interest in railroad transportation." [20] Furthermore, as Bernstein points out, the influence of the idealistic Progressives between 1906 and 1917 was to inject more firmly into the concept of regulation the mistaken notion that regulatory commissions could be independent of politics and could make impartial decisions on the basis of "expert knowledge." [21] It must be admitted, however, that these problems have not been by any means resolved to this day. In truth, the perennial problem of commission regulation, as in any agency of government, either under laissez faire or our contemporary mixed economy, is that "experts" (if such they be) typically expressed some vested interest. A "public" composed of countervailing power groups produces few if any impartial minds. Moreover, specific decisions in particular cases are usually subject to immediate pressures by conflicting interests. This is the nature of the governmental process in a parochial society. The people making up the ICC, for example, could not easily rise above this sordid situation. Appraisals differ as to who was most favored by the Commission's activities, weakened as they were by judicial constraints. Locklin claims that in general the railroads endeavored to conform to the provisions of the Act (which were not, as we have seen very harsh), and "exhibited a disposition to obey the Commission's orders."[22] The Minnesota Home Rule League, a group partial to municipal regulation, found in 1913 the state public utility commissions were often loaded in favor of the regulated enterprises. It asserted that with few exceptions the men occupying positions on state (public utility) commissions "had no technical or special qualifications for the work, and in most cases were selected for services past or prospective to the appointing power, and in other cases were men with public utility or allied affiliations, or men known to have a strong corporation or property bias."[23] In his influential Promise of American Life (1909), the eminent Progressive Herbert Croly claimed that the state railroad commissions were captives (mere "clerks") of the railroads. But in the judgment of historian Samuel P. Hays, shipper influence was predominant in the record of the ICC prior to World War I, most complaints brought were decided on the side of shippers, and as of 1916 the shippers had "often" succeeded in getting men partial to them appointed to the Commission and its staff.[24] The importance of this question of partiality, and even corruption, goes far beyond the sphere of the regulated industries, of course. It is a general problem of public administration and bureaucracy with which every generation has to deal.

Business and Laissez Faire

Business, both within and without the public utility sector, hated to accept the idea that laissez faire might no longer be the optimal arrangement for protecting and furthering its material interests. But gradually and reluctantly as this period waned business left behind the partnership-in-subsidy characterizing laissez faire and began to embrace certain more advanced forms of government intervention in order to try to secure its position in the existing economy: (1) government participation on its behalf in the welter of conflicts with other economic interest groups, (2) Federal government regulation of private markets wherein the reduction of competitive "excesses" could not be satisfactorily achieved by self-policing, and (3) government underwriting of aggregate income (business sales) and profits. [25] The third type of intervention was to wait upon the crisis inaugurated in the second quarter of the twentieth century. The first and second types were well on their way to acceptance by World War I.

With respect to the related question of antitrust regulation, the position business took reflected the schism between large and small business, the latter generally, but not always, favoring antitrust. Large business, on the other hand, wrestled with the problem of self-policing among fellow oligopolists, but generally rejected the European policy of the regulated cartel. Also, it preferred to leave the right to monopolize unfettered, and hence opposed antitrust. The ambiguity emanating from the fear that privately applied methods to achieve market "stability" (uncertainty reduction) might be inadequate in oligopolistic markets was reflected in two famous sets of Congressional hearings in 1911 and 1912. In the hearings before the Committee on Investigation of the U.S. Steel Corporation (Sixty-second Congress, second session, 1912), Judge Elbert H. Gary, Chairman of the Board of the Corporation, testified:

Mr. Gary: I realize as fully, I think, as this committee that it is very important to consider how the people shall be protected against imposition or oppression as the possible result of great aggregations of capital, whether in the possession of corporations or individuals. I believe that is a very important question, and personally I believe that the Sherman Act does not meet and will never fully prevent that. I believe we must come to enforced publicity and governmental control.

Mr. Young: You mean governmental control of prices?

Mr. Gary: I do; even as to prices, and so far as I am concerned, speaking for our company, so far as I have the right, I would be very glad if we knew exactly where we stand, if we could be freed from danger, trouble and criticism by the public, and if we had some place where we could go to, to a responsible governmental authority, and say to them, "Here are our facts and figures, here is our property, here our cost of production; now you tell us what we have the right to do and what prices we have the right to charge.

Mr. Littleton: Is it your position that cooperation is bound to take the place of competition?

Mr. Gary:	It is my position.
Mr. Littleton:	And that cooperation therefore requires strict governmental supervision?
Mr. Gary:	That is a very good statement of the case. I believe that thoroughly.

Before the same Committee, the great "individualist" Andrew Carnegie replied "certainly" to the question, "your present idea, Mr. Carnegie, is that, for the present at least, we should travel in the direction of the recognition, by Government control over large units, such as the same direction which we have taken with regard to railroad corporations?"

A year before, at hearings before the Senate Committee on Inter-State Commerce, George W. Perkins, partner of J.P. Morgan and a director of International Harvester and U.S. Steel, testified in part:

> My own belief is that we have got to come to national incorporation of large interstate business enterprises . . . expand the Bureau of Corporations by giving it power enough to license these large combinations. . . . Mr. Chairman, immediate relief is most desirable—I mean relief from the uncertainty in which every businessman who is doing anything that approaches a large business finds himself. . . . We have got to have here in Washington a controlling commission, composed largely of business men, to which a business enterprise could come and say, "Now we want to do thus and so; here is our capitalization, here are the methods we are going to employ; here is the manner in which we propose to treat labor; here is the manner in which we are going to treat our competitors, and here is the method of treating our consumers. Is this in keeping with good public policy?" And find out whether or not they can do it.

These statements of representative, experienced business leaders of the largest corporations at the end of the first decade of the twentieth century show how fearful was big business of unfettered competition, how far business had come from laissez faire thinking, how willing it was to embrace the European monopoly policy of the regulated cartel, how clearly it recognized the new public character of giant enterprise as well as the inevitable encroachments on traditional private property rights emanating from that new public character, and how cavalierly it presumed that any public regulatory agencies would be "composed largely of businessmen." Gabriel Kolko has argued persuasively that large corporations tended to prefer national legislation rather than state, believing they could shape legislation and administration more effectively at the central government level. Men like Gary, Carnegie, and Perkins recognized with uncanny foresight that, in the face of competitive adversity and the threat of the exercise of a constraining governmental power at the behest of other interest groups, the empire of business could keep its basic positions intact while accepting interventionist reforms similar to those represented in public utility regulation. This was essentially the position on antitrust taken by President Theodore Roosevelt.

Yet U.S. trust policy was not to go the route of the publicly regulated cartel. Big business's opponents, as represented preeminently by merchants and farmers who had antimonopoly laws passed in many states before 1890, had too much failth in the continued de facto virility of market competition, too little understanding of how oligopoly worked, too much hostility to big government, and too much confidence in the joint exercise of private countervailing power with piecemeal government regulation. Consequently, these reformers had passed what critics of laissez faire consider an archaic sop, the Snerman Antitrust Act of 1890, the basic antimonopoly statute of the United States, with overwhelming bipartisan support in both Houses of Congress. Many Republicans traded votes on this act for the high McKinley tariff.

The Act declared illegal "every contract, combination in the form of trust or otherwise, or conspiracy, in restraint of trade or commerce among the several States, or with foreign nations" and declared persons engaged in such transactions guilty of a misdemeanor subject to fine and imprisonment. Students of the antitrust law as amended and applied by the courts still disagree on whether it has inhibited the growth of monopolistic market results. Since the Sherman Act was based on behavioral criteria, notably "conspiracy," it could not easily attack tacit collusion. Also, for the same reason, it placed a premium upon the discovery by business of new forms of combination that had not yet been ruled as monopolistic. Thus the subsequent history of amendment is largely a history of plugging up behavioral loopholes.

From 1891 through 1905 the Act was almost inoperative. Attorney-General Richard Olney, who was happy when the Supreme Court in the inaugural E. C. Knight case (1895) declared manufacturing (sugar) was not "commerce," declared that the law was "no good" and that he had no desire to enforce it. He and his followers got help from niggardly Congressional appropriations, protracted litigation, and perplexed and baffled courts. A change occurred, however, in 1903, which became a year of some signifi-

cance for antitrust history. Hans B. Thorelli has pointed out that
this year marked the "institutionalization" of antitrust and was the
year in which the nation became conscious for the first time of a
President taking a personal interest in the application of the law.

Joe S. Bain argues that "moderately active enforcement" began
only in 1906 with the "Progressive" Theodore Roosevelt's "trust-
busting" of 37 cases, followed by 43 under Taft and 53 under Wilson
(in his first administration). This period brought forth the famous
merger-dissolution cases — the Standard Oil and American Tobacco
decisions in 1911 — where the criterion of *intent to monopolize* was
employed and the "rule of reason" was also iterated, i.e., the notion
originally projected in a disserting opinion by Justice Edward D.
White in the Trans-Missouri case, that only contracts *unreason-
ably restraining trade* were illegal. The tortuous legal first quarter
century of corporate oligopoly under the Sherman act is appraised
by Bain as follows:

> The total effects of these prosecutions on the structure of American indus-
> try and on the character of competition was not very great [.The Act's] pro-
> hibition of monopolization was not directed at the phenomenon of indus-
> trial concentration or market control or at its implicit effect on competition,
> but rather at specific actions designed to exclude competitors or to restrain
> their ability to compete . . . .
>   The courts showed no disposition, therefore to apply the penalties of the
> Sherman Act to the already typical American case of a highly concentrated
> industry, the ruthless tactics of whose member firms were in the past, their
> purpose having been accomplished, and the market behavior of whose mem-
> bers evidence some limited degree of rivalry. Concentration was accepted as
> a *fait accompli* . . . The Sherman Act had lain idle when it might have been
> employed to prevent concentration; it now appeared that it could not be
> used to dissolve most well-established combinations.[26]

Judge Gary must have been incisively correct in his agreement with
a member of a Congressional Committee that the Sherman Act as
interpreted had endowed the country with "an archaic law to deal
with the modern situation." If big business had deliberately set out
to construct a legal sop to the militant farmers and merchants that
would replace state antimonopoly laws and satisfy their clamor for
monopoly control without doing anything substantive on the Federal level, perhaps it could scarcely have contrived a better foil than
the Sherman Act together with the subsequent Court interpretation in our period.

It seems proper to conclude that the U.S. variant in modern antitrust policy had a negligible effect on the rate and pattern of either
industrialization or overall economic development. It is conceiv-

able, however, that in the very long run antitrust was contributing to the "crumbling walls" surrounding the still intact "capitalist engine." But this Schumpeterian notion of an increasingly hostile environment encompassing the business system does not fit well into Galbraith's countervailing power "equilibrium." Other economic interest groups lived in intense conflict with the big business group, and it would be difficult to argue that as producers labor (or the farmer) was not an intrinsic part of the capitalist engine. On the other hand, Schumpeter may have been right in his implication that in the long run there is no countervailing power equilibrium—that business enterprise either dominates or it is driven out of its dominant position in society—even though he was wrong in thinking that western European capitalism would collapse after World War II.

In its relation to the system of Federal tariff protection the business community after the rise of large corporate enterprise continued to enjoy the insulation against foreign competition that had existed in an earlier era of small firms and "infant" industries. Indeed, when the infant became a giant, instead of tariff reduction to let the modern manufacturing enterprise stand on its own feet and give domestic consumers the benefits of foreign price and quality competition, the general trend in this period, certainly until 1909, was to sustain and even raise the level of protection! At a time when the iron and steel industry, for example, had become a formidable competitor in world markets, it continued to receive overgenerous protectionist support. The tariff record in summary form for this period was as follows:

1883: Slight reductions on some items, increases on others—"a bending of the top of the branches to the wind of public opinion to save the trunk of the protective system," according to Tariff Commission chairman John Hayes. Said Professor F. W. Taussig, tariff historian, "it retained, substantially unchanged, the high level of duties reached during and after the Civil War."

1890: The McKinley tariff act. A marked increase in duties from an average rate of 44 to 48 percent, pushed through on a Republican political groundswell. Taussig called it "a radical extension of the protective system." The "billion dollar Congress" found that Federal taxes exceeded expenditures, so it raised tariff *rates* to try to reduce tariff *receipts!*

1894: A tariff of minor reductions that would have been larger if a coalition of Republican and Democratic Senators had not prevailed over popular protest. Says Taussig of the Wilson-Gorman tariff, "A slice was taken off here, a shaving there; but the essentially protective character remained." This Act provided for a moderate income tax (later declared unconstitutional—and "anarchistic") to assure revenue offsets to the modest reductions.

1897: A Republican Congress together with several years of deficit in the Federal budget yielded the Dingley tariff with the highest general level of duties in U.S. history, averaging 57 percent.

1909: The Payne-Aldrich tariff. Moderate reduction, mostly of only nominal significance. Says Taussig, "The act of 1909 brought no essential change in our tariff system. It still left an extremely high scheme of rates." This tariff provided for a small tax on corporate net income to meet the need for growing federal expenditures. It failed to embody the Republican-Democrat-Progressive "scientific", "competitive", or "true principle" of protection, i.e., the notion that the tariff should impose such duties as would equalize the difference between the cost of production at home and abroad, together with a reasonable profit to U.S. industry!

1913: The Underwood tariff, under the influence of the Wilsonian victory in 1912, brought a temporary swing to the most moderate protection since the 1857 tariff. Moreover, a federal income tax was passed that the courts could no longer declare unconstitutional (because of the Sixteenth Amendment, 1913).

All the while dust had been thrown in the farmers' eyes to get tariff supporters through merely nominal imposts on wheat, corn, and meat products—foods produced more cheaply in the United States and exported in large volume.

If Federal antitrust policy had had even the slightest adverse effect upon the business environment and therefore upon business growth and innovation decisions, tariff policy would have been at least a partial offset. Few believe any more that "the tariff is the mother of the trusts," but certainly on two counts—as protection against foreign competition and as a means of taxation adverse to consumption and favorable to saving and investment—the tariff record was proindustry and held an honored place in a laissez faire world. The "special interests" that were protected were manufacturing interests, and it would be hard to show that the incidence of the tariff as it entered the costs of other, unprotected industries was upon those industries. This is attested to by the absence of significant organized protest emanating from the latter groups as contrasted with "the constant shouting about safeguarding American industries against pauper labor" (Taussig). The trouble is that freer trade helps the unprotected merchant and importing community, labor, agriculture, and the consumer on a smaller scale than the manufacturers, and that its benefit is diffused through the whole economy.

The relations of U.S. nonfarm business with the rest of the world were marked not only by strong special interest tariff protection but also by the spreading conquest of foreign markets for manufactured products, the considerable replacement of imported manufactured commodities in the domestic market, the beginning of significant U.S. capital exports, adherence to the gold standard, the continuation of massive immigration to swell the domestic labor supply, and close working relationships between business and government with respect to other aspects of foreign economic policy. The latter relationships involved mainly big business since it was primarily the larger enterprises that had an interest in foreign trade and investment.

In every respect except the promotion of the merchant marine engaged in foreign trade, the Federal government pursued the time-honored policy of promoting the commercial and financial interests of domestic enterprise. Here was a policy continuity that reached back to mercantilism and forward to the era of the mixed economy in the later twentieth century.

In the case of the merchant marine, U.S. ships were given a monopoly of a coasting trade whose ship tonnage expanded from 2.6 million in 1860 to 6.7 million in 1910. In the oceangoing shipping trade, however, absorption with the domestic frontier and western Europe's low-cost advantages in building iron and steel steamships led to U.S. ship tonnage dropping from 2.4 million in 1860 to only .782 million in 1910. World War I brought about an enormous increase to 11.1 million tons, however.

In other aspects of foreign economic policy, business had every reason to bask in the sunlight of Federal encouragement. Indeed the State Department, Congress, and the Presidential office frequently anticipated business's needs and inaugurated policies consonant with business's economic interests abroad. Federal activity was prominent in: the pursuit of the Open Door policy in areas such as China where foreign business interests had "gotten there first," and the Closed Door policy in areas such as the Philippines where U.S. business had the inside track; the pursuit of special concessions for U.S. exports; tariff bargaining; the development of Pan-Americanism as a vehicle for trade promotion in both exports and raw materials imports; efforts to secure the removal of discriminations against U.S. exports; the replacement of foreign, especially European, with U.S. capital investments as in Haiti, Cuba, and Panama — to say nothing of European portfolio investment in the United States; and "dollar diplomacy" in multitudinous ways. Certainly there was no more favorable element in the larger environment surrounding business decision making than the foreign economic policy of the U.S. government.

The record of the judiciary at all levels was an equally emphatic probusiness factor in the environment of enterprise. If Edward Kirkland is at least partially correct in hypothesizing that "the character of American institutions, many of them outside the economy, explained the nation's industrial triumph,"[27] perhaps the judiciary is a prime candidate for this role. With regard to business-labor relationships particularly, the courts at all levels were hostile to labor's struggle for union recognition, better wages and working conditions, the right to bargain collectively, and the right to strike, picket, and boycott. Although unions had been given the legal right to exist in *Commonwealth v. Hunt* (1842), the judiciary vigorously restricted their behavior. As Abraham Gitlow has aptly put it, "collective bargaining does not take place in a vacuum." (One exception to judicial antilabor action was the upholding by the state courts of child labor laws in the early part of the twentieth century. Another exception was the U.S. Supreme Court's approval in 1908 of state laws limiting the maximum number of working hours for women. By 1917, 39 states had enacted such statutes.)

The Sherman Act was applied frequently against labor, notably in six cases connected with the great railroad strikes of 1894 and the famous Danbury Hatters' boycott case (*Loewe v. Lawler*, 1908). A major judicial instrument used by employers against labor activity was the injunction or court order requiring a person or group to cease performing certain acts within a specific time period. Most injunctions were issued by lower courts to restrain labor action. Harry A. Millis and Royal E. Montgomery in their massive study of organized labor comment that, "from the 1890s to the early 1930s...the power of the courts was invoked to assist in defeating most of the important strikes." Injunctions were often issued in support of "yellow-dog contracts," i.e., promises exacted by employers, as a condition of employment, that workers would not join a union during their period of employment. Labor came to speak of "government by injunction," and John Mitchell of the United Mine Workers said, "no weapon has been used with such disastrous effect against trade unions as has the injunction in labor disputes." According to E. E. Witte, injunctions issued upon the application of employers in industrial disputes, allegedly to prevent labor violence and threats to property, increased from 28 during 1880-1889 to 122 during 1890-1899, 328 during 1900-1909, and 446 during 1910-1919. However, the percentage rise was no faster than that for trade union membership.

In the era of laissez faire the judicial machinery acted generally in the service of business to implement the latter's violent determination to keep labor unorganized. The "potency of mental prepossessions" that the workers still confronted a small entrepreneur in the labor market was reflected in the Supreme Court's decision in the yellow-dog case of *Coppage v. Kansas* (1915), in which the majority opinion declared,

> To ask a man to agree, in advance, to refrain from affiliation with the union while retaining a certain position of employment, is not to ask him to give up any part of his constitutional freedom. He is free to decline the employment on those terms, just as the employer may decline to offer employment upon any other; for "It takes two to make a bargain."

From the business viewpoint a free worker was an unorganized worker, and the betterment of labors' condition was to be secured by the fruits of the secular rise in total factor productivity to be generated mainly by greater saving and capital formation.

Progressivism and Laissez Faire

In the sphere of social welfare legislation, business held a firm, constraining, upper hand throughout most of this period, but had begun to yield some ground as World War I approached. In a perceptive reflection on the history of the recent past, the Progressive Theodore Roosevelt pointed out in the presidential campaign of 1912 that his "new nationalism" demanded that "the judiciary. . . shall be interested primarily in human welfare rather than in property." The conflict between labor, the farmers, and the Progressives on the one hand and the new corporate power on the other hand was frequently expressed as a conflict between human rights and property rights.

Labor, and particularly organized labor, was persistently pressing for the eight-hour day, and especially after 1900 for industrial accident protection through employers' liability and compensation, restriction of child labor, votes for women, the restriction of immigration, statutory recognition of the right to organize, constraints on the injunction, exemption from the Sherman Antitrust Act, and creation of a department of labor. Although the Progressives were (to some observers) a heterogeneous, paradoxial aggregation of confused critics of corporate capitalism, their demands coincided in part with those of organized labor. Progressives such as Robert LaFollette invoked the aid of government during the prosperous years between the late 1890s and World War I in a multitude of economic areas wherein the underprivileged seemed victimized. Various persons usually considered to reflect the Progressive currents advocated on the monopoly issue either regulatory supervision (Theodore Roosevelt) or dissolution (Woodrow Wilson). Other Progressive proposals involved: government regulations to "preserve" (or "restore") competition and small enterprise; the conservation of natural resources against what they viewed as depredations of profit-making that ignored general social and replacement costs, such as those of sustained yield forestry; an income tax with progressive rates; municipal ownership of public utilities; and various other reforms. As was a frequent pattern with U.S. reform legislation, many of the progressive laws were first passed on the state level.

Economic legislation on the various government levels that might reasonably be allotted to the Progressive hopper, almost all of which encroached or was thought by most business elements to encroach on business prerogatives and the "free atmosphere of laissez faire," included the following measures: compulsory school attendance laws; the first eight-hour law for children in Illinois (1903); the Federal Keating-Owen Child Labor Act of 1916 (subsequently ruled unconstitutional); the Adamson Act providing the eight-hour day for railroad operating workers (1916); laws for the protection of the economic rights of seamen; railroad and other workmen's compensation laws such as the New York law of 1910; the New York State safety and sanitation laws of 1912-1913; Wisconsin's progressive social legislation to protect women and children; and the Massachusetts minimum wage law of 1912 affecting women, children, and public employees. Other Progressive legislation embraced such varied statutes as: Federal meat inspection laws; the Pure Food and Drug Act of 1906; New York State laws restricting insurance company investment, forbidding political campaign contributions, and requiring that an insurance policy in effect for at least three years have a surrender value; the Federal farm loan act of 1916; the beginning of the Federal forest conservation program under the Pettigrew Amendment of 1897, ten years after the establishment of the Division of Forestry and six years after the passage of the Forest Reserve Act; the purported exemption of trade unions and farm marketing cooperatives from the antitrust laws under the Clayton Act amendment to the Sherman Act in 1914; and tariff reduction together with the establishment of a permanent graduated income tax in the Underwood-Simmons Tariff Act of 1913.

Peter G. Filene may be correct in asserting that all this (and more) does not add up to a "Progressive movement." But despite the mildness of these measures, their undermining or nullification by the courts and by direct business counter-strategy, labor leaders' opposition to some of them as unwarranted government "interference," and the subsequent long fallow period in many areas, such as conservation, that followed the Progressive years, the laissez faire method of handling the relations between government and business was thereby subjected to a great wave of public encroachment. That wave went farther and deeper than the agrarian revolt of the seventies and eighties, and set the stage for the death of laissez faire to come with the Great Depression of the 1930s. Business, in a surge of prosperity-induced anti-interventionism, was to effectively hold off further significant encroachment during the 1920s, but as it turned out, the Progressive years made a much greater contribution to the subsequent emergence of the mixed economy, for all the contrasts between the two periods, than is often recognized.

Of course, all that had happened constituted an attack merely upon the *uncontrolled* operation of the private market mechanism. Unless the reform had been revolution, it was not, despite the misguided fears of business, an attack upon that market mechanism itself. And on the level of intent, all the Progressives' encroachments were designed to make the business system function more competitively and more palatably to the critical strata of the public—to attempt to redress a countervailing power disequilibrium that would leave private capitalism as an economic system essentially intact. Admittedly, such an effort was beset with paradoxes. For example, the conservationists typically worshipped business competition (small enterprise variety), but the wanton and precipitous misuse of natural resources was an embarrassing phenomenon of private (and interstate government) *competition* at least as much as it was of private *monopoly*. Indeed, as Samuel

Hays has emphasized, big companies were frequently more in favor of conservation than small timber firms or the states.

With respect to making the private market system function more palatably, we shall recall that perhaps the greatest achievement of the Progressive years was the final victory in the long fight of the little people, with some allies in the "establishment," for the progressive income tax. Yet a contemporary inheritor of the Progressive tradition, John Kenneth Galbraith, has said of that tax, "It is doubtful . . . if any single device has done so much to secure the future of capitalism."[28] Progressivism may have seen much more clearly than hostile big enterprise what was in its long-run best interests.

The rise of big business in the nonfarm sector confronted atomistic farming with superior market power in the markets for funds, capital goods, transportation services, farm consumer goods, and farm products. The farreaching changes in the nonfarm business sector had passed over the farm business, leaving that nonurban, land-intensive business overwhelmingly competitive in structure, organized under the proprietorship or tenancy form of enterprise, employing much family labor, and partially combining the economic functions of the firm with the household. Of the total farm employment of 13.6 million people in 1910, about 10.2 million were family workers, i.e., farm operators and members of their families doing farm work without wages. This fact no doubt tended to make human considerations and "human rights" a prominent feature of the exchange relationships in all markets in which farmers participated. Hence the continued sharp juxtaposition of human rights versus property rights in the agrarian tradition of revolt against corporate industrialism.

The exercise of augmented market power by large nonfarm firms may have lifted their rate of profit somewhat above the level it would have achieved had there been competition on both sides of the market, but it also elicited great hostility and militancy among the family farm population. The agrarian revolt will be treated in detail later, but here it is relevant to note that nonfarm corporate business had to deal with a generally hostile and constraining small-enterprise group in the case of the farmers. It was the "individualistic" farmers and their merchant allies who organized and mounted the first great wave of attacks after the Civil War on the prerogatives of big business, on laissez faire, on private business monopoly and oligopoly in marketing, transportation, and finance.

The farmers and the merchants with their state antimonopoly laws and their Sherman Antitrust Act were the main source of the revitalized antimonopoly tradition after the Civil War. On the other hand, labor's leadership was much more willing to live not only with laissez faire, but also with the giant industrial corporation. As Samuel Gompers, President of the American Federation of Labor, testified, the "State is not capable of preventing development or natural concentration of industry." It was rather the refusal of big business to negotiate with independent unions that elicited the hostility of labor. The farmers' demand for cheap money and low interest rates was generally pro-entrepreneur and anticreditor, so it had a different significance for two groups within the business sector, and it was hostile to big business largely although not entirely in its capacity as a "money trust."

It may be concluded that the bastions of laissez faire and the traditional prerogatives and prerequisites of private enterprise remained substantially intact on the eve of World War I despite the rise of the large industrial corporation and the attendant changes in market structure and performance. Yet there was a gathering storm of reform that was to be unleashed two decades later. The emerging business leadership throughout the period enjoyed generally sympathetic Federal government policies in the areas of immigration and other foreign economic relations, fiscal affairs, antitrust, public utility regulation, and judicial rulings with respect to social legislation and industrial strife. In its relations with other socioeconomic groups or strata, however, big business encountered much hostility. This was true of its relations with the family farmers, labor, nonfarm small enterprise, and that motley and inconstant group known as Progressives. These hostile strata accepted a private enterprise system but fought a vacillating guerilla war with the giant corporation. By the end of the period they had in the economic sphere racked up some very modest legislative victories, inaugurated a Federal policy for the conservation of natural resources, made a public issue of the social and economic responsibility of big business, founded an abiding labor movement, laid the ground work for the subsequent demise of laissez faire, and partially prepared the American people for a future national commitment to underwrite the welfare of the disadvantaged.

Yet throughout the period itself it is doubtful that these changes altered in any detectable way either the rate and pattern of industrialization or economic development. Schumpeter was in all probability absolutely correct in characterizing the period as the era of "intact capitalism." How very intact it was could be plainly perceived in the roaring business dominated 1920s. Yet that decade too was a "seedtime of reform," to use Clarke Chamber's phrase, and an inheritance that was still buried beneath the surface would appear with shocking suddenness when long-run economic changes made things ripe for it. How paradoxical that so many believers in economic individualism were working to verify John D. Rockefeller's assertion in the 1890s that "the age of individualism is gone, never to return"!

NOTES

1. Thomas C. Cochran, *Basic History of American Business* (Princeton, N.J.: D. Van Nostrand, 1959), p. 71.
2. Seymour Friedland, "Turnover and Growth of the Largest Industrial Firms," *Review of Economics and Statistics*, 39, no. 1 (February 1957), pp. 70-80.
3. Harold C. Livesay and Patrick G. Porter, "Vertical Integration in American Manufacturing, 1899-1948," *Journal of Economic History*, 29, no. 3 (September 1969), p. 497, Table 2.
4. Harold G. Vatter, *Small Enterprise and Oligopoly* (Corvallis, Ore.: Oregon State University Press, 1955), p. 47.
5. *Report on Flour Milling and Jobbing* (Washington, D.C.: Government Printing Office, April 4, 1918), p. 8.
6. John G. Gurley and E. S. Shaw, "The Growth of Debt and Money in the United States, 1800-1950: A Suggested Interpretation," *Review of Economics and Statistics*, 39, no. 3 (August 1957), p. 256, Table 3.
7. Edward C. Ettin, "The Development of American Financial Intermediaries," *Quarterly Review of Economics and Business* (University of Illinois, Summer 1963), p. 56.
8. Lance E. Davis, Jonathan R. T. Hughes, and Duncan M. McDougall, *American Economic History*, third ed. (Homewood, Ill.: Richard D. Irwin, 1969), p. 205
9. *Report of the Committee Appointed Pursuant to House Resolutions 429 and 504 to Investigate the Concentration of Control of Money and Credit* (House Report No. 1593, 62nd Congress, Third Session, 1913).
10. Thomas Cochran, *Basic History of American Business* (Princeton, N.J.: Van Nostrand, 1959), p. 46.
11. Joe S. Bain, "Industrial Concentration and Anti-Trust Policy," in Harold Williamson (ed.), *Growth of the American Economy*, second ed. (Englewood Cliffs, N.J.: Prentice-Hall, 1964), p. 623.
12. Quoted in Thomas Cochran, *Basic History*, op, cit., pp. 139-40.
13. These excerpts are from Alfred D. Chandler, Jr., (ed.), *The Railroads, The Nation's First Big Business* (New York: Harcourt, Brace, and World, 1965), pp. 108-15.
14. Arthur T. Hadley, *Railroad Transportation* (New York: G. P. Putman's Sons, 1885), p. 114.
15. Cited in David M. Potter, E. David Cronon, and Howard R. Lamar (eds.), *The Railroads* (New York: Henry Holt, 1960), pp. 32-3.

16. Cf. Robert M. Spann and Edward W. Erickson, "The Economics of Railroading: The Beginning of Cartelization and Regulation," *The Bell Journal of Economics and Management Science*, 1, no. 2 (Autumn 1970), p. 237.

17. Loc. cit., p. 238, no. 32.

18. See D. Philip Locklin, *Economics of Transportation*, third ed. (Chicago: Irwin, 1949), p. 221.

19. Ibid., p. 223. Note that the actual rates resulting from the web of countervailing power were administered prices. No one knows what the rates would have been under market competition, or therefore, whether the administered "fair" rates approximated competitive ones.

20. Marver H. Bernstein, *Regulating Business by Independent Commission* (Princeton: Princeton University Press, 1955), p. 29.

21. Ibid., p. 36.

22. Op. cit., p. 219.

23. Cited in Bernstein, op. cit., p. 40.

24. Samuel P. Hays, *The Response to Industrialism, 1885-1914* (Chicago: University of Chicago Press, 1957), p. 57.

25. The viewpoint expressed here regarding the business-government relationship after the turn of the century is the third of William Letwin's four interpretive schools of thought on the matter. But this is an emphasis, and does not preclude overlap with other interpretations.

26. "Industrial Concentration and Anti-Trust Policy," loc. cit., pp. 627-8.

27. Edward Kirkland, *Industry Comes of Age* (New York: Holt, Rinehart and Winston, 1961), p. 194.

28. John Kenneth Galbraith, *American Capitalism* (Boston: Houghton Mifflin, Sentry ed., 1962), p. 182.

[9]

The growth
of urban economy

Modern economic development in the nineteenth century brought with it a differentially high growth of city population and the spatial clustering of economic activity, just as it required a relative growth of the nonfarm sector. "Urban economy growth" meant two things in the period under study: the United States became predominantly nonrural as well as nonagricultural (urbanization), and the growing cities (metropolitanization) developed their own distinct economic characteristics.

There is perhaps no sharper contrast between agrarian and industrial society than is found in the contrast between the spatial dispersion and spatial convergency of population and economic activity in the two cases. The phenomenon does not seem to be unique to modern capitalism, either, for Soviet industrialization was also accompanied by the differential growth of urban population, the growth and transformation of older cities, and the dispersion of such cities geographically. The development of modern cheap internal waterway and railroad transport in both countries, as elsewhere, facilitated this striking economic pattern of coagulation and dispersion.

Urbanization and metropolitanization in this period were due to the growth of farm productivity that released increasingly large percentages of the labor force from agriculture, the consequent rural-urban migration, the growth of nonfarm output, and the propensity to cluster nonfarm economic activities. Hence urbanization was inextricably linked with industrialization in the broader of the two senses in which the term is employed in this work. The high income elasticity of demand for nonfarm products was therefore the major single factor inducing urbanization, although strictly speaking urban production was a function of the growth of total demand rather than merely nonfarm demand, as Richard Easterlin has pointed out.

The urban labor force (and population) between 1870 and 1910 grew at about 3.5 percent a year, compared with a rural population growth rate of slightly over 1.25 percent per year. The former was roughly equal to the growth rate of nonfarm output of slightly less than 5.5 percent a year, minus the rise of nonfarm output (income) per worker of rather less than 2 percent a year. On the factor supply side, the absolute growth in labor and entrepreneurship in each city came from indigenous city population increases, immigration, and most important, rural to city migration. Of course, the *relative* growth of the total urban labor force was entirely due to migration since urban places have lower natural rates of population growth than rural areas. Money capital for each city was imported and generated or transferred by local financial institutions; physical capital equipment and materials were largely imported from elsewhere within the country.

The Clustering of People and Production

The small quantity of land requisite for almost all nonfarm economic activity was not sufficient to explain the spatial agglomeration, or clustering, of such activity. Urbanization (or perhaps more properly, metropolitanization) means population concentration in two senses, as Hope Tisdale Eldrige has pointed out—that is, the multiplication of concentrated population centers and the increase in population of particular centers. Viewed from the standpoint of the supply side, agglomeration in towns and later cities was greatly facilitated by input lumpiness, external economies of large-volume technology, and the savings from reduction in transport costs accompanying distance.

Input lumpiness, or factor indivisibility (usually capital), became prominent wherever the minimum scale of capacity production (least average unit cost output level) became "large." The classic example was, of course, the railroad, but many of the social overhead industries, wherein the unit of capital equipment and/or minimally efficient plant was also large, had the same characteristics. Such a supplier's long-run average and marginal costs were high when the quantity produced and demanded was small, but these costs (and consequently competitive prices) fell as capacity output was approached through time. A single municipal water works could typically deliver water cheaply if and only if users were numerous enough to approach minimum production costs and there were numerous users close enough also to minimize delivery costs. To get cheap water transported short distances, both firms and their workers' households had to cluster their establishments. Therefore, input lumpiness and the transport cost barriers associated with weight and distance were positive inducements to firms and households to cluster, both *into* cities and *within* cities.

Workers' households had overriding inducements to cluster within cities near job locations and, later, metropolitan areas in order to minimize both the costs of burgeoning municipal services and the costs of commutation to and from work. Commutation costs were in inverse proportion to intracenter traffic density. In this period these inducements, among others, produced the densely populated "central city" that lingers on today, even through manufacturing plants now have generally moved out of the central city and been replaced by and large with various commercial, trading, and other service activities. The pattern of the main arterial streets radiating out from the core of the central city has remained almost unchanged since the early nineteenth century, despite the superimposition of a freeway network in recent times.

With the advent of the electric streetcar in the 1890s commutation costs were kept within the reach of worker's budgets, and thus the central city was permitted to expand spatially. At the same time, however, the periphery began to explode into a metropolitan area, increasing commutation time as well as generating urban blight. Charles N. Glaab and A. Theodore Brown cite Sam B. Warner, Jr., to the effect that in 1850 Boston was still a "walking city," but by 1887 the "horsecar" had pushed settlement outward by two miles (about four miles from city hall), and by the early 1890s the electric streetcar had pushed the area of "convenient transportation" outward by six miles.[1] In Milwaukee in 1880 only 17.4 percent of the population lived over three miles from the central city, but twenty years later almost 31 percent resided more than three miles out.[2]

The increase in commutation time was an important disutility entering into the worker's level of living as the nation urbanized. The advent of the space-conquering automobile at the end of this period made it possible to increase commutation distance without necessarily increasing time in transit, but it did raise the share of commutation costs in workers' budgets while at the same time it tended to hold down working class rentals in the central city. These commutation costs are treated today in the national income accounts and by the income tax law as household "consumption" rather than employee business expense!

The electric streetcar and interurban electric trolley gave a minor boost to the economy and to the shift of economic activity from the satellite small town to the larger urban center. John B. Rae has asserted that if the automobile had developed a bit earlier, the slow-moving electric street railroad would never have existed. But this was not anticipated by investors, and between about 1895 and World War I this short-lived, minimally air polluting industry completely replaced the even less efficient horse-drawn tram and grew at a simply enormous rate, only to die an untimely death at the hands of the pre-freeway passenger car and motorbus by the end of the twenties.

External economies of large-volume technology, as they operated to induce urban clustering, resulted from the proliferation of economic activities that were either "locally oriented" or "export oriented." This proliferation raised both the quantity demanded of the output of supplying activities and the volume of products sold through common marketing facilities.

Hence such supplying and marketing activities were able to adopt cost-savings technologies that were feasible for them only when sales volume was relatively large and when they were able to pass on such cost savings as technical and pecuniary external economies to buyers or sellers who were thus in turn able to "internalize" the savings. Firms using these services thus avoided, by clustering, costly do-it-yourself alternatives. Examples were improved warehousing of stocks, better loading and docking facilities, cheaper energy supplies, and more efficient rail terminals. The great Chicago stockyards opened in 1865, and the similar stockyards in Omaha and Sioux City were major innovations made possible not only by the development of rail transport, which increased the volume of livestock transportation by rail on the hoof, but also because of the proliferation of the economic base activities, which was slaughtering in those particular cities. The reduced private costs of assembling livestock, due to the establishment of stockyards, was an external economy to the meat-packing industry attributable to the clustering and expansion of the latter. Indeed, what was initially an external economy to the infant meat-packing industry in Chicago when that city was still only a serious challenge to Cincinnati's comparable industry became a partial cause for further concentration in Chicago as both Swift and Armour were consequently induced to locate large slaughtering plants in the Windy City.

Viewed from the demand aspect, cities that grew to be large did so because their "economic base" in the usual case, though not in every case, expanded in this period beyond the mere servicing of their own agricultural hinterland to include at some point production for "export" (not necessarily manufacturing production; services can also be exported). "Export" meant selling beyond the city's own hinterland market. Falling transport costs and production for export pried loose an increasing number of nonresidentiary activities from their earlier location at specific natural resource or raw material sites, although a latter continued to be important in many cases. The railroads, by reducing transport costs, also destroyed the expansion potential of some towns by raising the competitive advantages of other towns, a process much expedited, particularly in the frontier regions after 1860, by municipal promotors' scramble for railroad location.

The towns whose growth into cities was facilitated by railroadization were of two kinds: hinterland market centers on railroad lines, and towns that were both hinterland market centers and railroad terminal centers. The fall in transport costs increased the size of the favored towns' hinterland economy (from both the buying and the selling sides). This in turn raised the opportunities for division of labor and the exploitation of lumpiness within the cities that enjoyed, for topographical or other reasons, an initial advantage in the competition to serve the hinterland. The export base of a city may have been a nearby natural or agricultural resource (e.g., copper for Butte, Montana, wool and mining for Denver, wheat (flour) for Minneapolis-St. Paul and Kansas City, or the development of specialized services (e.g., insurance in Hartford, government services in Albany, Sacramento, and other state capitals), or a transportation center (e.g., Chicago, the port of New York), or specialized manufacturing (e.g., steel in Pittsburgh, heavy machinery in Cleveland, motor vehicles in Detroit), or a mixture of these. Indeed, such a mixture was typical of the larger cities.

Because of common elements in their technology and for other common supplying or marketing needs, different manufacturing products (industries) often clustered in one city to produce diversified manufacturing centers with surrounding satellite towns. In many cases this diversification came about not only through complementary linkages, but also because of the emergence of quite new activities springing from innovations, such as the manufacture of refrigerator cars. The economic base of growing cities was not necessarily limited to one export product, and as a city grew it usually acquired several bases serving the export market. Certainly a city such as Chicago, while it became "hog butcher for the world," also diversified its base to become "tool maker," "stacker of wheat," steel producer, and the world's greatest railroad center. The economic base often changed radically and caused the earlier base to practically disappear because of outside competition. The economy of Lexington, Kentucky, for example, was based on the hemp industry in the early 1800s, but turned to burley tobacco and thoroughbred racehorses after the Civil War. Although Cleveland initially relied heavily on petroleum refining, it subsequently shifted toward iron and steel products especially heavy machinery. Finally, as Robert Higgs[3] has pointed out, in some cities in the western prairie region in the 1870-1900 period, the economic base may have been the production of goods and services in response to the hinterland demand of an expanding farm population. It so happened that in the Great Plains region total real per capita income grew relatively fast, and output per worker in farming greatly exceeded the national average between 1800 and 1900. The subsequent fate of the region was, however, another matter.

The clustering of economic activities serving export markets as the national economy grew induced the accompanying labor force and population agglomeration with the fall of transport costs in this period. This agglomeration in turn attracted, often at approximately the same time, residentiary, or local market-oriented, activities in manufacturing, trade, public utilities, finance, printing, eating places and other private service lines, thus creating new economic bases. Local government services also expanded. A growing pool of both specialized and unskilled labor usually emerged. The larger this local consumer market, the greater the likelihood that it would attract even residentiary fabricating activities, some of which would substitute for or forestall fabricated imports. And of course, such growth stimulated private residential, commercial, industrial, and public construction. Because of the differential growth rates of these sectors, it is difficult to find a close correlation in time between the surges of growth in the manufacturing sector alone and the rate of urbanization.

From what has been said it may be appreciated that there is perhaps no better illustration of cumulative economic change than the growth of urban clusters. Although the unfolding pattern did not fit a rigid scheme, each development of one kind of activity usually induced development of linked types of activities, especially after some minimum *threshold* of population and diversification of economic activities had been achieved. On the basis of input lumpiness, external technological economies, transport savings, and the effects of supplying and/or marketing activities on the economic base, those industries that were export-oriented elicited expansion of activities complementary to the basic economy. Both sectors in turn stimulated more or less simultaneously the growth of a local market-oriented sector whose growth in turn induced more residentiary employment as people with rising incomes "took in one another's washing."

Thus there was cumulation along with spatial agglomeration. Figure 5 illustrates the process, based upon Gunnar Myrdal's "process of cumulative causation." This process, once in motion, produces a "ratchet effect" inducing further expansion, and probably prompted Wilbur R. Thompson to argue that, once a certain *size threshold* is passed, a city's continued growth is almost inevitable in a growing economy.

Cumulative change in each city's economy was probably facilitated by the increasing communications flow, as emphasized by Richard L. Meier.[4] Meier points out that information concerning opportunities for many external economies becomes available first to "neighbors." This seems plausible for this period since cities were not as large as they later became, and communications media had not yet developed to the degree that people more distant had access to information on an almost equal basis with local persons. Hence these decades probably conformed to Meier's hypothesis that "change encourages change in the vicinity of a communications focus, and activity is piled upon activity within a small

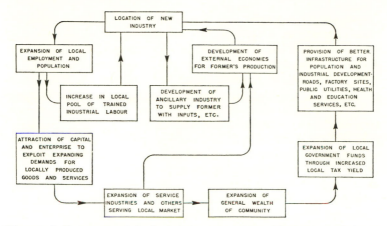

Figure 5 Process of industrial expansion. Reproduced from Richard J. Chorley and Peter Haggett (eds.), *Models in Geography* (London: Methuen and Company, Ltd., 1967), p. 258.

amount of space, subject only to diseconomies associated with intense land use."[5]

In the normal case the urban clusters exploited the advantages derived from their previous development, growing along with the overall economy, and particularly its most rapidly developing, dominant sector, the whole nonfarm economy. The growth of demand for the output of each metropolis was composed of distant export demand, immediate hinterland demand, and "domestic" demand. For each city, however, exports and imports were large relative to "gross city product." This proportionately large balance of payments attested to the fact that the proliferation of cities had created as an end product by the turn of the century a *national network of specialized urban agglomerations*. This was the urban content of the creation of regional and national markets in our period. There would be subsequent shifts and innovations in this pattern of urban specialization, but the essential contours were shaped by 1900.

Each cluster competed with varying success for its share of the expanding total in the context of nationally rising per capita incomes. But on the level of the particular enterprise, the exporting firm had no overriding loyalty to its original urban home, and its long-term expansion was likely sooner or later to contribute to the growth of another "competing city" as that expansion took the form of multiplant operation. However, locally patriotic political entrepreneurs in each city administration attempted always to off-set this "depressing" effect by trying to attract other activities. In-deed, the city promoter and booster made the decades 1870-1890 in particular a speculative and almost glamorous era of intercity com-petition for railroad and business location. Perhaps the most famous of such struggles in the era was that between Chicago and St. Louis for western business, a grim war that left St. Louis in-creasingly far behind the victor after 1880. But just as in interna-tional trade, there were transport costs barriers that at some point gave the advantage to competing cities. Thus there were limits to the extension of the export markets of any particular urban cluster. These barriers therefore placed a ceiling on the rate, and also shaped the pattern, of a city's growth. Eugene Smolensky and Donald Ratajczak have called this relationship "the equilibrating interaction of transport costs and specialization economies."[6]

The General Pattern of Urbanization

Because of the superior productivity of the nonfarm population, nonfarm production substantially exceeded farm output on the eve of the Civil War, even though the nonfarm population (and labor force) were still notably smaller. Nevertheless, the relative growth of the urban population had already been considerable, for by 1860 it accounted for one-fifth of the total population of the country. "Urban" was defined by the Census as places having a population of 2,500 or more, and thus by excluding the nonfarm population residing in smaller places, it understated the extent of the shift out of agriculture. The relative importance of these three population categories may be seen from the following estimates for 1860:

Farm population	20.1 million
Urban population	6.2
Rural nonfarm population	5.2

Evidently the rural nonfarm population was large relative to the urban population (by 1900 it was less than one-half) and probably accounted for a considerable portion of nonfarm, i.e., "urban," economic activity in 1860. As this period unfolded, the farm population lost relative to the rural nonfarm, and the urban population gained on both the farm and the rural nonfarm. Clearly these changes were intrinsic to the phenomenon of clustering discussed in the preceding section.

The pace of urban population growth for the country as a whole is viewed from four perspectives in Table 19. In the sixty years shown the urban population grew from one-fifth to one-half of the total. Moreover, beginning in 1870, the rate of increase in the urban proportion of the population, as shown in col. (4), was positive for every *region* with the country. [7] The dynamic Great Lakes region more than doubled its urbanization proportion, from 22 to 52 percent, between 1870 and 1910, bringing the region from a position below the national average to one well above it. The Southeast however, despite a bias due to a number of cities in its northern border regions, barely doubled its urban proportion, from 9.5 to 19.4 percent, a share well below the national rate for 1870. Glaab and Brown point out that before convergence set in after 1900, the South's urbanization about paralleled the national process with a fifty-year lag.

The rate of urbanization for the country as a whole was uneven, as may be seen in the last two columns of Table 19, with long wave peaks in the decades 1860-1870 and 1880-1890. Perhaps the long wave trough in the rate of urbanization in the 1870s can be partly explained by the unusually great decadel rise of between 4 and 4.5 percent per year in farm output. Since farm output therefore almost held its own in the race with GNP, it tended to retain population in agriculture. Also, the long depression of the seventies, although shallow, dissuaded people from coming to the cities.

A cyclical pattern was also evinced on the regional level, though with different timing in some cases. The 40 percent increase in urban population between 1900 and 1910 is suggestive of another long swing peak, but it is essentially washed out by the secular decline in the rate of urbanization, shown most clearly in the last column to have set in at the national level after the decade of the eighties. Urbanization could never again perform the dynamic developmental role that it did in this period, although substantial urbanization lingered on through the decade of the 1920s.

The phenomenon of clustering was also evinced in the relative growth rates of cities (defined not as metropolitan areas, but in terms of their legal municipal boundaries) of different sizes. The larger city group falling between 25,000 and 250,000 population in

TABLE 19

GROWTH OF URBAN POPULATION,
1860-1920

Year	Urban population (millions) (1)	Urban/total population (2)	Decennial increase in urban population (3)	Decennial increase in urban/total population (4)
1860	6.2	20%		
1870	9.9	25	60%	25%
1880	14.1	28	42	12
1890	22.1	35	57	25
1900	30.2	40	37	14
1910	42.0	46	40	15
1920	54.2	51	30	11

Source: Historical Statistics of the United States, Colonial Times to 1957,
Series A 34-50, p. 9.

1870 grew by far the fastest—400 percent by 1910, compared with only 230 percent population growth for the group falling between 2,500 and 25,000 as of 1870. The handful of very large cities having over 250,000 population in 1870 grew even more slowly. The implication seems to be that urban economic activities, such as manufacturing, were widely dispersed through urban territory at the beginning of this period but clustered more and more as time passed. A wide dispersal of manufacturing activity in the early part of the period is consistent with a number of characteristics of the economic landscape that have been pointed out earlier, i.e., (1) the first-processing of agricultural and mineral products accounted for a historically high proportion of all manufacturing activity at that time, (2) railroadization had not yet fully accomplished its work of enlarging markets and contributing to the demise of many lcoal manufactories and "hand and neighborhood industries," and (3) the heavy reliance of manufacturing on local water power sites (see Chapter 6, Table 14) that obstructed the freedom to cluster in space permitted by steam power.

This apparent initial spatial ubiquity of manufacturing probably explains the fact that Figure 6 shows the manufacturing labor force in 1860 and 1870 to account for as high as 25 percent of the urban population, even though Allen R. Pred estimates that in a group of ten very large cities in 1860 only Philadelphia and Pittsburgh approached the percentages shown in Figure 6 for 1910.[8] The 1860 proportions for St. Louis and Cleveland, for example, were only 5.8 and 8.0 percent, respectively; for Buffalo it was 6.9 percent, for New Orleans 3.0 percent; and Chicago, with a population of 109,000 that year, had only 5,360 persons employed in manufacturing! Yet only thirty years later most of these cities had at least 19 percent (compare Figure 6) of their population engaged in manufacturing pursuits.

Urbanization therefore was loosely associated with industrialization, defined narrowly as the growth of manufacturing activity. If industrialization induced urbanization, it was equally true that urbanization was necessary for industrialization. This association was evidently true despite the sharp drop in the manufacturing labor force curve in Figure 6 for the decade of the eighties. That decade is full of remarkable developmental changes (if the data are roughly accurate) of interest to the economic historian. It was shown in Chapter 6 that the manufacturing labor force, while rising absolutely from 3.29 million to 4.39 million, *fell* as a fraction of the *nonfarm* labor force, from 39 to 33 percent during that decade. This was apparently associated with a remarkable productivity spurt, for the decadal manufacturing output increase was 112 percent! No other decadal manufacturing output increase in our period even approached such a figure. The remarkable spurt in manufacturing productivity was no doubt due in considerable part to the great increase in manufacturing capital with which the average employee worked—according to Daniel Creamer, the greatest increase in any decade beginning with 1880. In Richard Easterlin's judgment the share of manufactured producers' durables in total capital formation also experienced its greatest decennial rise in the 1880s. Industrialization meant industrial output as well as industrial employment. A very rapid rise in manufacturing output was bound to stimulate output and employment in other nonfarm sectors and thus accelerate, through "multipliers," "linkages," and "induced investment," the urbanization of economic activity through those sectors.

Thus the 1880s, embracing a number of important long-wave peaks, witnessed the second highest rate of increase in urban population in the entire period 1860-1920, and almost equaled the 1860s

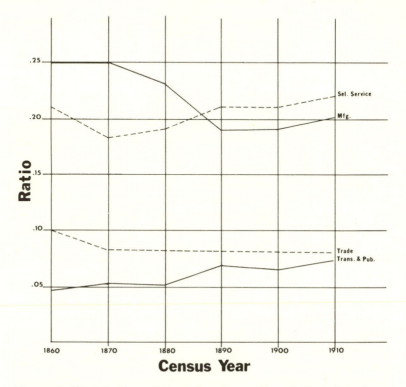

Figure 6 Distribution of the labor force. Population data from *Historical Statistics*; manufacturing from Stanley Lebergott's labor force estimates; remaining categories from Richard A. Easterlin, "Discussion," in Gallman and Weiss, op. cit., p. 358, Table 1. Selected services means all services minus personal services and hand trades.

in the rise of the urban/total ratio (Table 19). The 1880s was also notable for great advances in other concomitants of urbanization, e.g., the highest decennial increase in the output of the manufacturing sector, in minerals output as a percentage of GNP, in the output of fixed capital, in the output of the vital construction industry, and also in the number of workers engaged in construction during the whole period from the Civil War to World War I. Small wonder that this decade attracted the largest number of immigrants—5.25 million—in the whole nineteenth century! Although the immigrants were overwhelmingly of peasant background, the famous Dillingham Commission estimated that between two-thirds and three-fourths settled in urban places. (Note from Table 19 that this far exceeded the distribution of the indigenous population between urban and nonurban.)

Industrialization in the broadest sense used in this work is equivalent to the relative growth of all nonfarm activity. Figure 6 shows certain other nonfarm sectors entering into industrialization in this broader sense. The trend of employment in these sectors relative to the growing urban population reflects the weighted influence of the sector's participation rate (proportion of the population in the labor force), its proportionate share of urban output per head, and, as was pointed out with respect to manufacturing, its productivity performance (in the sense of output per worker). This interpretation can be simplified by the bold assumption that the known upward drift of the participation rate, which would tend to incline the curves upward, was approximately the same for all the sectors represented in the chart. Then, in the case of the curve for selected services for example, we could conclude that, compared with the perfectly flat curve for trade, those services, whose productivity performance was probably no poorer than trade, must have increased their comparative share of urban output per head after 1870. A glance back at the percentages in Table 17 in Chapter 7 will indicate the plausibility of this interpretation. Similarly for transportation and public utilities: a superior productivity performance, which tended to expel workers from the sector, was more than offset by the 33 percent rise in importance of the sector from 15 percent of all services to 20 percent in 1889.

It follows from these interpretations of Figure 6 and from the discussion of nonmanufacturing sector growth in Chapter 7 that, while manufacturing growth was important to urban growth, it by no means had a sectoral monopoly, nor was it a "leading sector," at least in this period. A number of important sectors contributed to the urbanization of the United States, and, at least in the period under review, one cannot say that manufacturing "led" and that the so-called "tertiary" (service) sectors only subsequently "took over" the urbanization process. It can readily be seen, for example, from evidence put together by Harvey S. Perloff et al., that between 1870 and 1910, as would be expected, the group of states experiencing important net upward shifts in their service labor force was largely the same as the group experiencing important net upward shifts in urban population, and vice versa.[9] Since the urbanization process was essentially terminated by the 1920s, it makes no sense to seek for the role of the service sector in urbanization thereafter. (The relatively growing component in the long run after the 1920s was government.)

The Effects of Urbanization

The economic impact of urbanization was too ramified and far-reaching for us to examine here in detail. Since the country was fast becoming predominantly urban, almost everything that happened was connected with that transformation. However, there are certain effects that almost cry out for some attention.

One effect is still only a hypothesis, but because of its combined plausibility and importance it is worthy of some treatment. This is the proposition that urban communities greatly facilitated the interchange of economically productive knowledge, particularly among technically trained people. The notion is an important corollary to the drift of the argument in Meier's work on communications in urban society, referred to above. Every technically qualified person knows the inestimable worth of dialog with professional fellows, and the rising density of the specialized technical population in the larger cities in all probability contributed to the advance of both purely scientific and applied technical knowledge. As Simon Kuznets has expressed it:

> creative effort flourishes in a dense intellectual atmosphere, and it is hardly an accident that the locus of intellectual progress (including that of the arts) has been preponderantly in the larger cities, not in the thinly settled countryside. The existence of adequate numerous groups in all fields of creative work is one prerequisite, and the possibility of more intensive intellectual contact, as well as of specialization, afforded by greater numbers may be an important factor in stepping up the rate of additions to useful knowledge.[10]

Since in the long run the growth in total factor productivity is entirely a function of the growth of (applied) knowledge, the improved communication among specialists in every field encouraged by the spreading urban environment must have made its impression upon the rate of technological progress in the long run.

The growth of knowledge in the cities was further facilitated by educational policy. City public education was generally better than rural public education, and not only because the city had a superior cultural environment. Adna Ferrin Weber reminds us in his classic study of city growth that in the United States by 1890 the urban schools had 190 class days per year, but the rural schools averaged only 115, and that average daily attendance in the cities was 70 percent, while in the country schools it was 62 percent. [11]

But population density had other side effects. When people are dispersed spatially as in an overwhelmingly agricultural society, many of their actions have little or no discernible effects upon others. Examples are noise making, methods of sewage and trash disposal, air pollution through burning, the personal appearance of the individual and of his or her premises. But in the densely populated city the effects of such things on others are likely to become important environmental "externalities." Their importance stems not so much from the "quality" or "size" of the individual's action as from the fact that (1) many other individuals may be affected by the single act of a person and (2) many persons may act similarly (e.g., several thousand decisions by a few hundred slum landlords to build tenements without running water, toilets, or heat) so as to produce large aggregations of environmental externalities. Sewage disposal methods on the extensively cultivated farm probably create no discernible externalities; in the city they inevitably do. The history of the Chicago river is a case in point. So if cities accelerated technical advance (a production externality), they also enormously accelerated the production of environmental externalities, some of them amenities and economies, some of them disutilities and diseconomies. Until very recently this ecological aspect of economic development was practically ignored by theorists and economic historians, despite the enormous effort devoted to dealing with some of them, and the heroic indifference to others of them, at the time. Dedicated reformers like Jacob Riis in the 1890s vividly and with profound sympathy portrayed both the negative externalities grinding down the New York slum tenant, and the calloused indifference of maximizing landlords, with a clarity of insight that compares most favorably with the writings of late twentieth century urban reformers. It is nothing if not depressing to realize that the contemporary urban black ghetto resembles all too closely many of the conditions that gave rise to the New York Tenement Law of 1901.

We now understand that we should at a minimum try to "net out" the external utilities and disutilities connected with the annual growth of the GNP as traditionally calculated in order to get a decent estimate of the actual GNP in those days. We do not know what the GNP would have been in 1900, etc., if we did net them out! So we do not actually know how fast the U.S. economy grew—if at all. It will not do to assume that positive and negative externalities simply cancel out; indeed, the subject of externalities is today a frontier in the field of economic history.

It is difficult to segregate analytically the effects of urbanization from the effects of industrialization. Indeed there is no point in it, for in the discussion of the effects of urbanization our broader concept of industrialization is the appropriate one. With respect to the impact of urbanization on the working classes in particular, such segregation is neither necessary nor desirable. In any case, this matter will be treated below in some detail, but here it may be noted that in one respect the urban workers were in a very different position from the family farmers or even farm tenants. That difference resided in the character and extent of employment insecurity. Farmers experienced most of the insecurities of the ordinary small business proprietor, accentuated by the vagaries of the weather. But these insecurities were largely related to the fate of the business. The new millions of city workers also had to "make ends meet," but for them there was added the menace of recurrent, total, undisguised unemployment. Without reserves of food or cash, and living as tenants, full- or part-time unemployment struck them immediately, depriving them of shelter and food.

Unemployment was of course only one prominent concomitant of the transformation of the working population involved in the development of the economy from agricultural capitalism to industrial, i.e., urban, capitalism. That development required the conversion of the labor force from one largely composed of proprietors, tenants, and farm laborers to one largely made up of employees of nonfarm employers.

The occupational distribution of the labor force, shown in Table 20, in the first two decades of the twentieth century suggests the extent to which urbanization and industrialization had generated a nation of employees as early as the end of the period under study. Even if *all* persons in the three categories "professional, technical, and kindred," "managers, officials, and proprietors," and "farmers and farm managers" could be considered employers or self-employed—an obviously unlikely case—almost three-fourths of the economically active population were employees. It may also be seen that farmers and farm managers made up over half of the three categories of nonemployees in 1920. This group was rapidly declin-ing relatively and absolutely. Stanley Lebergott's estimates show that all nonfarm self-employed persons increased only 13 percent between 1900 and 1920 while the whole labor force rose 43 percent. Densely congregated wage workers provided the precondition for the rise of a modern labor movement and a concomitant socio-economic reform movement, spurred on by the great growth in the size and consequent power of the individual business employer in the labor market and on the job. All this helped lay the groundwork for the decline of laissez faire.

Urbanization and industrialization also inaugurated a protracted period of economic and social history that was ultimately to eman-

TABLE 20

DISTRIBUTION OF OCCUPATIONS[1]
1900-1920 (percent of total)

Major Occupation group	1920	1910	1900
White-collar, except farm	24.9	21.3	17.6
Professional, technical, and kindred	5.4	4.7	4.3
Managers, officials and proprietors	6.6	6.6	5.8
Clerical and kindred	8.0	5.3	3.0
Sales workers	4.9	4.7	4.5
Blue-collar	40.2	38.2	35.8
Craftsmen, foremen, and kindred	13.0	11.6	10.5
Operatives and kindred	15.6	14.6	12.8
Laborers, except farm and mine	11.6	12.0	12.5
Service	7.8	9.6	9.0
Private household	3.3	5.0	5.4
Service, except private household	4.5	4.6	3.6
Farm	27.0	30.9	37.5
Farmers and farm managers	15.3	16.5	19.9
Farm laborers and foremen	11.7	14.4	17.7

[1]The universe consists of gainful civilian workers age ten and older. No attempt was made to revise the figures to a labor force base.

This table updates the material in the 1940 Population Census report, prepared by Alba M. Edwards, entitled *Comparative Occupation Statistics in the United States: 1870-1940*, published in 1943. The figures were adjusted to conform to the definitions of the 1950 occupational classification system. The early data are approximations only, particularly the figures for 1900.

More details about these estimates appear in the original source *Occupational Trends in the United States, 1900 to 1950*, Bureau of the Census, Working Paper No. 5, 1958.

Source: Bureau of the Census, *Economic Almanac*, 1967-1968, p. 40.

cipate women from confinement to household work and dependence of many kinds upon men. In the agrarian societies of the historical past and in the era of predominantly agrarian capitalism, women worked long hard hours in both the household and the fields. Thus they were always very much "in the labor force."

But as capitalism became industrialized, as it did in nineteenth century United States, household work and "production" (in the orthodox sense of production for the market by business firms) became separate activities, even as that production also came to be an overwhelmingly urban activity. This new urban capitalism then proceeded, in a general way, to exclude women from their time-honored practice of engaging in productive labor outside the household and to try to confine women to productive labor in the household. At the same time, the ideological counterpart of a business-dominated society had the audacity to adjudge household labor "unproductive" since it involved almost entirely nonmarket production. It consequently proceeded to exclude it from the calculation of the annual net product, to assert nevertheless that home management and rearing the nation's growing population and labor force was a heaven-blessed, benevolent, chivalrous, "efficient," and biologically determined form of the eternal division of labor, and all the while to bemoan the alleged "scarcity of labor" in the market economy! Since the emergence of certain new twentieth century capitalist and noncapitalist societies, and the United States' own experience during World War II, has shown there are eminently feasible [12] alternatives to the division of labor between the sexes adopted in our period, we now know that it was the weight of two or three millennia of male-dominant institutions and traditions that primarily account for what happened.

Indeed, urbanization, industrialization, and economic growth themselves, even as they fostered a subjugating division of labor upon women, also inaugurated the ultimate demise of that division by drawing women in ever larger numbers and proportions into nonhousehold, market production. The change was most clearly marked in the predominantly urban, clerical occupations. These occupations employed only 8,301 women in 1870, but over 584,000 women by 1910.[13] In the latter year women clerks and kindred jobs accounted for 7.2 percent of all "gainfully occupied" women, and women already accounted for 28.4 percent of all gainfully occupied persons in clerical occupations.[14] This phenomenal growth reflected both the process whereby the allocation of women to the household was being undermined and the ideological and institutional weight of that allocation as it operated to sustain a system of inadequate market preparation for women as well as employer market discrimination.

The rise of urban economy appears in the available statistics to be the great source of market employment of women. This seems to be essentially correct, although the standard concept of gainful labor deceptively excluded much of the productive labor of farm women. The data as constructed show that in 1890 about 25 percent of urban women 14 years or older (18 percent for whites and 37 percent for nonwhites) were in the labor force, whereas only 12 percent of rural women were gainfully occupied.[15] Hence the shift effect of urbanization was to raise the participation of women in the labor force and to sever them from material dependence upon the household economy and its subculture.

But the traditional confinement of women to housewifery, home management, and child care was apparently the continuing barrier to labor force participation, even in the burgeoning urban economy. For example, according to estimates by Clarence D. Long, the fractions of various classifications of women age sixteen and older in the labor force of the rapidly urbanizing nation of 1890 were:[16]

	1890	1950
Single	40.4%	57.8%
Widowed and divorced	41.4	59.7
Married	4.5	24.0
Without children under 10	7.7	33.8
With children under 10	2.1	7.6

The 1950 estimates are included for historical comparison. These figures suggest that an urban business economy that could employ almost 60 percent of all single, widowed, and divorced women could also employ 60 percent (or more) of all women. It is true that all was not well on the demand side. There was strong employer and societal resistance to the employment of women. Also, occupational, racial, and price discrimination in the labor market, combined with low skill levels, had long kept the wages of women, particularly black women, below those of men. For example, data for a selected group of manufacturing industries from the First Annual Report of the Commissioner of Labor for 1885 and from the Dewey Report on the Census of 1890 show that the average wages of adult women were rather less than 60 percent of the adult male average. [17] And the ratio of female to male earnings did not begin to rise secularly, according to Long, until after World War I. However, the Aldrich Report indicated that where women were nominally doing the same work as men in the same establishments in the textile industry their wages were only moderately below men's. [18]

But it is to supply, and more pointedly to *the determinants of supply*, that we must look for an explanation of both the secular rise in female participation rates and the failure of those rates to equal the greater than 95 percent rates for males. This conclusion is underscored not only by the classification of female participation in the labor force by marital and child status, but also by Long's inability to find any evidence that the lower earnings of women compared to men had anything to do with the ratio of women to men in the labor force. [19] Policy requirements directed toward equalization of women's status, then and later on, clearly belonged primarily in the sphere of supply determinants. The well-intentioned progressive legislation to protect women as such on the job ironically provided employers with new excuses not to hire women. Meanwhile, the concentration of women on the suffrage movement, while essential to political equality, was associated with a neglect of economic endeavors directed toward restructuring the vital supply determinants.

Urbanization also slowed the "natural" rate of population growth. If we ignore net immigration, the natural rate of population change is the birth rate minus the death rate. Urbanization reduced the role of children as an investment in labor by the parents, a most significant role in an agricultural economy. Instead of being an expected future source of an income stream, the child in the city economy, particularly the male child, as contrasted with the child in the farm economy, tended to become a burden whose consumption requirements represented an outlay by the parents for upbringing that would only prepare the youth for future employment ordinarily by some business firm. As a result of the undermining of the common economic stake in a joint business venture possessed by parents and children in the former farm economy, this new urban family was more alienated within itself. Hence the traditional "generation gap" widened, a widening accentuated by the later age of marrying that came to characterize city behavior.

As a consequence of these and related changes, the birth rate in the city was lower than on the farm, and family size was smaller.

The birth rate in the country as a whole declined from about 44 per thousand of the population in 1860 to 30 per thoushand in 1910. Since improvement in sanitation and health, and especially the substantial reduction in infant mortality among whites, cut the death rate from about 21 per thousand to 15 per thousand over the same half-century, the rate of natural increase fell dramatically from 23 to 15 per thousand. Clearly the achievements in death rate reduction were somewhat outpaced by birth rate reduction, and consequently the long secular decline in the natural population rate that had begun early in the nineteenth century continued throughout the period under study. With the end of urbanization soon after the closing of this period, the population rate continued to decline in the secular long run. This fact suggests that other new factors must have replaced urbanization as the primary determinant of the decline.

If we assume somewhat boldly that the growth rate of GNP was largely independent of the population rate, then the declining population rate sustained economic growth, defined as growth in GNP per capita. This is simple arithmetic, since income per head is a fraction, and with the growth rate of the numerator given, holding down the growth rate of the denominator raises the value of the fraction. As a result, although the growth rate of GNP alone in the very long run showed retardation (despite the "shift effect" of resource movement from lower productivity agriculture to higher productivity urban industry) the growth rate of GNP per capita held roughly constant in this period. This yielded a rather favorable comparison between the United States and the other countries of the North Atlantic world.

There are numerous other important effects that resulted from urbanization, some of them well supported by evidence, others hypotheses still to be tested. Among these honorable mention should go to: (1) the tendency for urbanization to "justify itself" economically by creating a whole new gamut of almost uniquely urban demands, e.g., the demand for processing, transporting, and marketing of foods, and the demand for a whole new layer of highly labor-intensive municipal government, including education; (2) the tendency for private consumption as a proportion of disposable income to be constant in the long run, despite rising incomes, as a result not only of what Simon Kuznets has called "extra cost of urban life," but also of rising consumption aspirations connected with the quickly communicated "demonstration effects" of upper class consumption patterns on middle and lower income consumers (in recent times institutionalized into what is called "consumerism"); and (3) the enormous stimulation given the construction industry with its associated rise in investment relative to total output, and fixed investment relative to total investment. Other urbanization effects include: (1) the opening up of a vast urban job market that ultimately pulled millions of Southern rural blacks, blocked from entry into a secularly contracting Northern agriculture, out of their semifeudal economic condition into Northern cities that did not yet, as they did to many immigrant groups, herd them into ghettos; (2) the acceleration of the absolute and relative growth of deposit money as distinguished from currency, owing to the improved interpersonal communication and the easier development of institutions for check clearing in densely populated centers—a phenomenon exhibited long before this period in the larger Eastern seaboard cities; (3) the undermining of the property tax, more appropriate to an agrarian society of taxable income linked to obvious tangible wealth than to an urban society of employees and business firms whose income bore only a loose relationship to tangible property owned; and (4) the decline in the spatial specialization of agricultural production as many thousands of farmers in the hinterland of each great city adjusted their crop and livestock mix to the local urban market—"milk sheds," "truck crops," poultry raising, etc.

Although this list and the points reviewed in somewhat more detail in this discussion of the effects of urbanization by no means exhaust the topic, it will perhaps convey something of the vast economic changes wrought by the rise of urban economy and society. In a sense, these matters are only among the more obvious and direct effects. Other aspects, perhaps more subtly and indirectly related to urbanization, have already come up for discussion in ostensibly other connections. Still others will be treated in the chapters that follow.

NOTES

1. Charles N. Glaab and A. Theodore Brown, *A History of Urban America* (New York: Macmillan, 1967), p. 155.
2. Ibid., p. 158.
3. See, e.g., his "Growth of Cities in a Midwestern Region 1870-1900," *Journal of Regional Science*, 9, no. 3 (1969), pp. 369-75.

4. Richard L. Meier, *A Communications Theory of Urban Growth* (Cambridge, Mass.: M.I.T. Press, 1962).

5. Ibid., p. 43.

6. Eugene Smolensky and Donald Ratajczak, "The Conception of Cities," *Explorations in Entrepreneurial History*, Second Series, 2 (Winter 1965), p. 91.

7. See Harvey S. Perloff, et. al., *Regions, Resources, and Economic Growth* (Lincoln: University of Nebraska Press, 1960), pp. 15-21 *passim*.

8. Allan R. Pred, *The Spatial Dynamics of U.S. Urban-Industrial Growth, 1800-1914* (Cambridge, Mass.: M.I.T. Press, 1966), p. 20, Table 2.2. Another exception was Cincinnati with 18 percent of its population engaged in manufacturing.

9. Op. cit., pp. 128 and 163, Tables 29 and 52.

10. Simon Kuznets, *Economic Growth and Structure* (New York: W. W. Norton, 1965), p. 128.

11. Adna Ferrin Weber, *The Growth of Cities in the Nineteenth Century* (Ithaca: Cornell University Press, 1963), p. 397. This work was originally published in 1899.

12. "Feasible" here means the ratio of social costs to social benefits. In our period the dominant consensus asserted that the social costs of a Soviet or Israeli approach would have exceeded the social benefits, or, to use the language of those times, would have been "inefficient."

13. See H. Dewey Anderson and Percy E. Davidson, *Occupational Trends in the United States* (Stanford: Stanford University Press, 1940), p. 19, Table 6.

14. See Clarence D. Long, *The Labor Force under Changing Income and Employment*, National Bureau of Economic Research (Princeton, N.J.: Princeton University Press, 1958), p. 139, Table 27.

15. Ibid., pp. 127-8, Table 23.

16. Ibid., p. 115, Table 16. The 1890 proportions are standardized for age.

17. Clarence D. Long, *Wages and Earnings in the United States, 1860-1890*, National Bureau of Economic Research (Princeton: Princeton University Press, 1960), pp. 104-6 *passim*.

18. Ibid., p. 107, Table 50.

19. Clarence D. Long, *The Labor Force under Changing Conditions of Employment*, op. cit., p. 134.

[10]

Money, prices, income, and productivity

In this age of price inflation it is hard for many of us to believe that there was ever a protracted period, not only in the United States, but in the whole Atlantic trading economy, in which the prices of goods and services fell. Yet that is exactly what happened over a secular period of 33 years in the United States from the Civil War peak in 1864 to 1896-1897. Thereafter the general price index began a long rise, with occasional reversals, that was only further buttressed after the emergence of the mixed capitalist economy during the decade of the Great Depression of the 1930s. Hence the era under review encompasses a period with a most thought-provoking secular price pattern. The long price decline was apparently not harmful to the growth of output and the rise of industrialism, but it did contribute to striking social and political upheavals. Moreover, the price decline itself was the expression of massive shifts in the social consensus. The forces inducing increases in productivity of different sectors vied with bankers, the U.S. Treasury, and the community's preferences regarding the rate of growth of the money stock and the amount of their money holdings. The net decision was to determine the ultimate impact of money and its velocity on price behavior. As always, changing general prices were both an arena and a determinant of group conflict. These matters of human decision making and behavior will be treated in the chapter that follows. Here the emphasis will be on the economic patterns.

The real GNP for the whole period seemed to proceed upwards almost independently of longer period changes in the money stock, the price level, and the rate of turnover of the money stock (velocity). To be sure, the growth rate of GNP, along with other phenomena such as construction and immigration, exhibited cyclical "long waves" of 15 to 20 years duration, but aside from ordinary business cycle slowdowns it never fell below 3.5 percent a year for any extended period. There was some retardation early in the twentieth century, but those were largely years of *rising* prices.

Cyclical Patterns

Growth and development were marked by great cyclical disturbances and attendant employment until after the turn of the century. Immigration and domestic rural-urban migration were stimulated during periods of prosperity, but when downswings subsequently hit the burgeoning urban economy, many of these migrants found themselves unable to find jobs. It has been shown by Brinley Thomas and others that the immigrant waves, which generally accounted for about one-fifth of population and labor force growth, were largely, from the standpoint of the "pull" influence on migration, the lagged effect of tighter U.S. labor markets in the expansion phases of the aforementioned long waves. Sometimes these long swing expansions more or less coincided with the expansion phase of the ordinary popularly-known business cycle, or "Juglar" cycle, named after the nineteenth century French economist Clement Juglar. He was among the first to treat the well-known economic cycles as a total interconnected system rather than as "crises" or, to use the American term, "panics." Sometimes the Juglars and the long wave turning points did not coincide.

As Figure 7 shows, there were seven Juglars in overall economic activity and three long swings in the growth rate of gross output — measured from trough to trough — between 1870 and 1914. The Juglars selected here were those featuring most prominently in the social controversy of our period, and averaged 6.3 years in duration. Two of the long wave peaks in this schematic graph, which indicates cycle duration but not amplitude, are shown as zones because there is a dispute about the dating.

It is ordinarily assumed that long wave upswings and peaks lend strength to Juglar expansions, while restraining Juglar contrac-

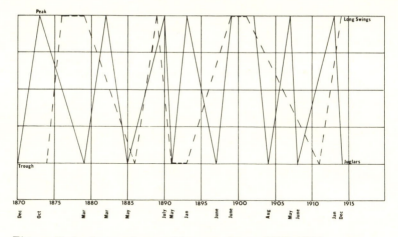

Figure 7 Juglar cycles and long swings, 1870-1914.

tions, and conversely for long wave downswings. This may solve some of the riddle of the long Juglar downswing of the 1870s, with its inordinate duration alongside a truly remarkable growth performance of at least 5 percent per year in real GNP for the decade: it was interwoven with a construction cycle that had peaked in 1871-1872 and troughed in a long wave upswing in the GNP growth rate having a peak zone extending over the last years of the Juglar "depression." Also, a third type of economic cycle, the building or construction cycle, was interwoven with this Juglar, but in such a way as to aggravate the Juglar, for the construction cycle peaked in 1871 and troughed in 1877-1878.

Why this Juglar depression-with-growth could also have had substantial unemployment extending into the years 1876-1879 may possibly be explained in part by Brinley Thomas's hypothesis. This postulated an immigrant influx ending in 1874 that occurred as a response to the long wave expansion in construction peaking in the early seventies, reinforced by the Juglar expansion from December 1870 to October 1873.

It will be seen that the 1880s, years of remarkable urbanization and industrialization, were characterized by both a Juglar downswing and a long wave downswing terminating about mid-decade. The Juglar downswing from March 1882 to May 1885 should therefore have been severe. Yet Rendigs Fels emphasizes that "like the depression of the seventies, it was severe primarily in financial series like outside clearings and wholesale prices rather than in indexes of production."[1] One reason for buoyancy in all probability, according to Moses Abramovitz, was the fact that the cycle of gross new construction was in a long upsweep extending in most departments over about a decade from the late 1870s to the end of the 1880s.[2]

We have already emphasized that both capital formation and its major component, construction, called the tune much of the time in the growth and cycle dynamics of the latter nineteenth century. This was particularly true of residential and railroad construction. Still, average annual unemployment in the eighties was estimated by U.S. Labor Commissioner Carroll D. Wright at about 7 percent. Nevertheless, immigrants continued to enter in ever larger numbers *after* the long wave peak years of 1876-1879 (Figure 7), from an annual average of 157,000 in those years to 640,000 per year during 1880-1883. Perhaps the Juglar cycle recovery phase from March 1879 to March 1882 also explains in part this inflow from Europe. Hence it is not surprising that Terence V. Powderly, "Grand Master Workman" on the Knights of Labor, as a spokesman for the already established American workers, was inspired to write in 1885 in the *North American Review* on "The Army of the Discontented."

One reason for the difficulty of interpreting effects of the connections between long waves and Juglars is now apparent: the important construction cycle, similar to the investment cycle for regulated industries (including railroads), seemed to have its own *modus operandi* to a great extent, and its timing consequently failed to coordinate with either of the other types of cycle. Look, for example, at the annual turning points for gross new construction in current prices:

Peak	1873
Trough	1878
Peak	1892
Trough	1896
Peak	1913

These turning points on an annual basis agree with those for the investment of regulated industries (transportation and other public utilities) in only one case, the year 1896.[3] Although there is some closeness in the timing of the upper turning points with Juglars (see Figure 7), the construction cycle upswings were long (15 and 17 years), and these upswings essentially bypass downward movements in both of the other types of cycle in those years. But one should also observe that the construction cycle upswings spanned all of the 1880s and almost the whole period embracing three Juglars and the secularly rising prices from 1896-1897 to the eve of World War I.

Although there was a protracted long wave downswing, from 1901 to 1911 in this period, the Juglar downswings were mild, a fact inconsistent, for this period at least, with the Marxian thesis that as industrial capitalism developed, cycles would get more severe. The weak Juglar downswings may be attributable in substantial part to the long construction cycle upswing, However, the rate of economic growth from 1898 to 1914 (and to 1929 for that matter) was a mediocre 3.5 percent a year. This no doubt reflected the pattern of the long wave in GNP as well as, in all probability the forces of secular retardation in output growth.

The "Great Depression" Hypothesis

While there seems to be no doubt about secular retardation in the output growth rate after the turn of the twentieth century, many economic historians believe they have also found the period from the late sixties or early seventies to 1897 to be one of continuous secular contraction, and have called it the "great depression" of the nineteenth century. The original impetus for the notion was the long downward drift of prices. More recently attention has been called to the behavior of real magnitudes, particularly to data that seem to suggest a continuous downward trend in productivity over this period.[4]

However, the notion of a steady, thirty-year slowdown in real growth rates during the postwar era of industrialization has appeared implausible to many other interpreters, and their view of the data is quite different. For one thing, the seventies, as already noted, racked up a remarkable decadal GNP growth rate, despite the longest Juglar downswing of the century, of at least 5 percent per year. This of course provides a historically high base for comparing what happened in the next two decades. But even such a comparison yields performances in the eighties that in many important economic statistical series are equal to or higher than the record for the seventies, e.g. commodity output per worker, including output per worker in manufacturing, mining, and railroads, total commodity output growth, industrial production, net capital stock growth, output of fixed capital, horsepower of all prime movers, urban population, railroad output, and total construction. If the eighties was as good as or better than the seventies, then growth rates were not continuously declining over the thirty-year period, a phenomenon essential to the great depression hypothesis. The implausibility of the hypothesis is underscored by the likely buoyant influences of sectors with long wave peaks in the late eighties or early nineties (e.g., see the above gross construction peak in 1892 and Ulmer's regulated industries investment in 1893). These influences no doubt also contributed to poorer records for the nineties than for either the seventies or eighties in most important economic series. The Juglar downswing of the nineties (Jan. 1893-June 1897) was reinforced by a longswing contraction. In any case, the issue of the existence of a "great depression" remains an unresolved challenge to historians. But the concern in this chapter with the long price decline should not be interpreted to imply a secular slowdown in real terms. Indeed the point featured here is the dramatic economic growth and development record accompanied by secularly falling prices in the thirty years 1867-1897.

The Checkered Pattern of Price Change

Economic growth and development thus occurred in the context of ordinary business cycles, construction cycles, and long waves. It also took place with cyclically falling prices in Juglar downswings and rising prices in Juglar upswings, together with secularly falling general prices and somewhat faster growth, followed by secularly rising general prices and somewhat slower growth, after the 1896-1897 secular price nadir.

During the long price decline of 1864 to 1897 all prices fell, but not by any means always in equal proportion, i.e., there were some shifts in *relative* prices. For example, while farm and nonfarm prices fell at more or less the same rate over the long run, the prices of both all manufactured products and producers' durable goods fell more than the former. Average rail freight rates fell more than any of these. Prices of construction materials, however, declined only moderately as compared to most commodities. House rent showed scarcely any trend, although all consumer prices together followed the general downward movement. Long-term interest rates also declined moderately, and as therefore would be expected, so did the rate of return on capital (defined as total property income divided by the value of the total capital stock excluding consumer durables and land). The latter fell from over 8 percent in 1869-1878 to rather more than 5 percent in 1890. Money wages, defined as annual earnings of nonfarm employees when employed, also declined, according to Stanley Lebergott, from their high of $512 in 1865 to a low of $474 in the cyclical trough 1879, after which they drifted upward. This made it possible for labor to receive after 1880, through the money wage rise, coupled with the decline of consumer prices, some of the fruits of the economy's productivity growth.

The shifting pattern of relative prices among different economic sectors revealed the well-known condition that on a falling price trend some groups gain and others lose "pricewise" precisely because relative prices typically do move differently in the context of such a trend. Of course, the people in a sector whose prices fall compared to others may not lose with respect to their relative material position if their productivity performance exceeds that of the others. In that case their *net* income is a function of *costs* together with receipts, and, other things equal, productivity improvement can cut costs to keep pace with any adverse effects of relatively declining prices on receipts.

Just as relative prices shifted in the long downward movement of general prices, so did they in the long upward movement that was inaugurated in 1898. For example, farm prices on a basis of 100 in 1926 were 42.5 in 1897, and all prices were 46.6. On the rising price trend farm prices increased the more rapidly, overtaking all prices in 1909. This massive relative shift upward seems to have contributed importantly to the notable reduction in the farmers' militancy that had characterized the preceeding quarter century. Indeed, the price ratios of farm to nonfarm prices were so satisfactory to farmers from 1910 to 1914 that those closing years of this period came to be known as the "golden age" for agriculture. When the New Deal sought a parity concept for agriculture's price terms of trade with the nonfarm sector twenty years later, it found that norm in the average of the 1910-1914 ratios.

Other important shifts in relative sector prices also took place on this rising general price trend. For example, manufactured products' wholesale prices rose more slowly than all prices. Yet it seems, unfortunately for that sector, that its productivity performance, while much better than agriculture's mediocre record, was poorer than the record for the entire nonfarm economy. However, between 1897 and 1913 average annual earnings of wage earners in manufacturing, although not the best indicator, rose by 42 percent, about the same proportion that the prices of manufactured commodities rose. Hence, on that crude measure the total factor productivity increment that the sector could boast of may well have accrued overwhelmingly to the sector's property income claimants and/or salaried staff. This tentative conclusion is consistent with the more rapid increase in manufacturing value added than that in the total manufacturing wage bill over this period, especially from 1899 to 1909.

Rising prices after the turn of the century were accompanied by continued long-term stability of the short-term loan rate (secularly stable after the late 1870s), a gentle upward drift in long-term interest rates (e.g., in railroad bonds and stock yields), and a rise in the rate of return on property to its secular long-run approximation to 8 percent. Average annual earnings of workers in all industries except farming rose from $462 in 1897 to $682 in 1914, an increase of 48 percent that may fruitfully be compared with a roughly equivalent wholesale price index rise.

The question of the comparative rise in money wages and prices has been a matter of some controversy. Certain of the possibly relevant price indexes increased as follows between 1897 and 1914:

Index	Increase
W. Randolph Burgess cost of living index	60%
Bureau of Labor Statistics Food at Home index	56
Bureau of Labor Statistics Wholesale price index	46
Robert E. Lipsey GNP price deflator	41
John W. Kendrick price deflator for personal consumption expenditures	40
Albert Rees cost of living index	21

Clearly the differences are due to different bases, assumptions, and methods of estimation. However, this writer's judgment is that the Burgess and Rees indexes are probably less reliable than the other indexes. Most scholars have reasonable confidence in the BLS wholesale price index; and if the Rees index, for example, were anywhere near correct, it would represent a deviation from such wholesale price trend that could not be remotely approached at any other time in the annals of price history. Furthermore, as shall be seen below, the Rees and Burgess price rate increases are far out of line with Kuznets' and with Friedman and Schwartz's estimates of changes in the money stock, velocity of money, and total output during this period.

Since we assume that the Kendrick-Lipsey estimates are approximately correct, the rise in nonfarm annual money wages somewhat outpaced the upward movement of general prices. As total factor productivity rose by only a sluggish 10 percent, wage earners' share of the productivity increment may have approximated the rise in property's share.

Money, Prices, and Income, Civil War to 1879

It is no doubt evident already that this whole era revealed sharp contrasts among its various subperiods. It is definitely desirable in a discussion of money and prices to contrast the period after 1896-1897 with what occurred before, and this will be elaborated below. Yet it is also desirable to break down the years from the Civil War to 1896-1897 into at least two subperiods, and the reasons for this will now be made clear.

Our first subperiod covers the years from the end of the Civil War decade to the end of the second great Juglar depression of the nineteenth century in 1879. Happily we can rely upon the Censuses of 1869 and 1879 to clarify much that happened in that dramatic decade. It also fortunately (for the economic historian) happens that the country returned to a specie standard in 1879 in accordance with the stipulations of the Resumption Act of 1875. Prior to the early 1870s the high *market* price of silver compared with the U.S. *mint* purchasing price had prevented actual operation of the nominal official bimetallic standard, but this became a monetary policy issue when the market price of silver began to fall as the seventies drew to a close. The years from 1862 to 1879, when the Union and then the Federal government suspended the domestic convertibility of money into specie, and specie was used only for foreign transactions (except in California), are usually known as "the greenback period." The long struggle over the volume of U.S. notes (greenbacks) to be permitted to circulate ended with their stabilization of $347 million in 1878.

The seventies also makes a convenient unit of analytical time because by 1879 about 84 percent of the secular wholesale price index decline of 50 percentage points from the Civil War peak of 75 in 1864 had been achieved. Prices during that 15 years had returned to their pre-Civil War level, making possible the return to specie payments and prewar foreign exchange rates. In the 17 years of secular decline following 1879 the wholesale price index fell only 24 percent, from 33 to 25 (1957-1959 basis of 100). The only comparably protracted period of declining prices was the 50 percent fall in the 16 years from 1814 to 1830, and that experience was also attended with substantial economic growth (including a long wave upswing), but probably rather less social and political upheaval.

The 1870s was further notable for the fact that in fiscal policy the Federal government completed its work of refunding the national debt to take advantage of falling interest rates. Thereafter until 1892 debt policy was marked by substantial debt retirement, thus resuming a controversial strategy that had obtained from the end of the War until the cycle peak year of 1873. The lapse in retirements during the depression from 1873 to 1879, although of minor influence because of the relatively small size of such operations when they did occur, could only have further contributed to continued deflation in the economy's financial overlay. The reason is that debt retirement is in general a mild stimulant similar to open market purchase operations under the Federal Reserve today: the "public" exchanges its bonds for cash.[5]

Thus the first subperiod ends in 1879-1880. We have a simple framework for analysis of the financial overlay in that subperiod in the equation of exchange, mentioned in Chapter 1: $MV = PQ$, where M is the stock or "supply" of money (currency plus demand and time deposits) in the economy, V is its velocity or rate of turnover in any given time, P is the product price level, and Q is total physical output. PQ is therefore GNP or NNP. When these magnitudes are viewed as changing from year to year, they are usually expressed as percentage changes, and the annual percentage changes on the left side must equal the sum of the percentage changes on the right hand side. Thus.

$$\frac{\Delta M}{M} + \frac{\Delta V}{V} = \frac{\Delta P}{P} + \frac{\Delta Q}{Q}$$

If percentage changes on the two sides of the equation must always maintain the equality of the two sides, then these changes must be additive. For example, to take the right side of the equation, the percentage rise in GNP over time is the sum of the percentage rise in prices *plus* the percentage rise in physical output.

The annual compound percentage rates of change in these four magnitudes during the years 1869-1879 presents a startling picture. They were, roughly,

$$.01 + 0 = -.04 + .05$$

We know that during the whole period of secularly declining prices there was a great political struggle between the "sound" or "hard" money advocates (bankers, creditors, foreign traders, some other business elements, and regionally speaking, the East) and the "easy" money pro-inflation groups (farmers, debtors, some labor spokesmen, some largely nonfinancial business elements, and regionally speaking, the West). Clearly, those who wanted to infuse more purchasing power into the cheap Civil War greenbacks, to raise the value of greenbacks in terms of gold, to get prices down, to thus lay the basis for resumption of the full domestic gold standard at prewar parity with the English pound by 1879, scored a smashing victory. They succeeded in holding down the rise in the money stock during 1864-1879 to less than 1 percent a year.[6] It should be noted, however, that the failure of the money stock to grow much was partly due to a massive velocity-raising shift by the people from currency and commercial bank deposits (money) to mutual savings bank deposits, which are not defined as money here. The accompanying drop in prices was phenomenal and should have put to shame all those who defended the tradition that an inconvertible "fiat" currency would inevitably fan the fires of inflation. It was clearly the amount of money that counted, not the absence of "gold backing."

Friedman and Schwartz in their famous *Monetary History* conclude that "the primary factor producing the decline in prices that made resumption possible was, therefore, the rapid growth in real income — the economy grew up to its money stock" (p. 31). This is a surprising emphasis that seems to divert attention from the fact that the hard money groups in a period of power struggle and extended "depression" were able to *hold the line on the money stock increase.*

While averring that no "positive" policy of deflation was pursued generally by "the government" from 1865 to 1879, James K. Kindahl acknowledges that there was a "negative" policy of "refraining from expanding the money supply," which was a "noteworthy accomplishment" that under deflationary conditions was "tantamount, in its effect, to the pursuit of deflationary measures during a period of price stability."[7] Clearly, the positive-negative dichotomy, while descriptively useful, need not conceal or confuse the substance of policy, which was, as we would say today, tight money.

Nonfinancial business's decisions to invest and expand output at a fast rate of over 5 percent a year got little encouragement from either the tight policy regarding the money stock or the "community's" velocity consensus. Those decisions exhibited a remarkable buoyancy that could conceivably have been in part a response to only one "monetary determinant": falling interest rates.[8] It seems much preferable to conclude, as contrastd with the Friedman-Schwartz interpretation, that an almost constant money supply shared with a rapidly rising physical output the explanation for the rapid price decline. Both the supply of money ($\Delta M/M$) and the demand for money to hold as an asset or reserve and for transactions purposes ($\Delta V/V + \Delta Q/Q$) must be considered in determining what happens to prices. With constant velocity there is a close link between the money stock and money income. Thus money income rose extremely slowly in this decade.

The constancy of the income velocity of money was indeed striking. This will be seen when the secularly *falling* velocity is examined for the period after 1880. This velocity is simply defined by the following equation:

$$V = \frac{PQ}{M}$$

It is called the income velocity of money because it relates money to income—PQ, or GNP. From the subsequent behavior of velocity we know that something was inducing the community as a whole to hold more money relative to its total income, i.e., bringing about a *decline* in income velocity. Yet during the seventies, according to Friedman and Schwartz, velocity was 4.6 in 1869 and 4.7 in 1879 (op. cit., p. 774), and alternative calculations based on Lipsey indicate only a modest decline. Hence, during the seventies the community did not or could not conform to its long term behavior pattern any more than it did from 1914 to 1929, when there was also no trend in velocity.

Two prominent hypotheses have been advanced to explain the long secular decline in velocity for the whole period from the Civil War to World War I (and after). The first is represented by Friedman and Schwartz: money is a "luxury good;" so when income rises the amount of money demanded rises proportionately more. If this were correct, then we must conclude that the community was either frustrated or confused in the seventies, for income, both total and per capita rose—at least *real* income did, and Friedman and Schwartz indicate that they mean real income whey they say that "the rise in per capita real income tended independently to produce a more than proportional rise in the real amount that wealth holders demanded of both currency plus demand deposits adjusted and the broader total we term money."[9]

Possibly rapidly falling prices created the mistaken belief that the value of money assets was not only rising, but rising relative to real income. However, this cuts two ways—there should have been a "flight to money" because of its rising purchasing power, a flight accelerated by falling interest rates. Perhaps in the seventies the "sound money" consensus favoring resumption through a nearly constant money stock overrode the tendency to hold more money relative to income (i.e., for V to fall). At any rate, the secular fall in velocity did not set in until after 1880.

The second hypothesis regarding this fall is represented by George Garvy and Martin R. Blyn,[10] and argues that money is not a luxury good, that the secular fall in velocity from 1880 to 1914 may properly be attributed to economic development and attendant institutional changes. In their view the study of velocity is an excellent focus for the study of institutional changes. That is one important reason for devoting attention to it here. Such changes after 1880 included the great spread of commercial banks and their deposit money (at the relative expense of currency); a sharp relative shift of time deposits after 1880 from mutual savings banks, located overwhelmingly in the East, to commercial banks, where they would be included in the money stock; a rapid growth in money-creating consumer loans; and the relative decline of farming (and later the frontier), which had a high velocity pattern. One might add that other structural changes may have on balance tended to lower velocity by raising the relative importance of sectors found by Richard T. Selden to have, in contemporary times at least, comparatively low velocities, e.g., large businesses, the public utility sector, and the state and local government sector. With regard to the velocity effects of the spread of financial assets, it would be necessary to test the hypothesis that the use of money for *financial transactions*, which are not included on the right-hand side of $MV = PQ$ although the M is included on the left-hand side, must have risen more rapidly than the rise in holdings of *nonmonetary financial assets* of those intermediaries, assets that are close substitutes for holding money. If such were the trends, they would have reduced velocity on balance.

Assuming these institutional factors were significant in their impact on velocity, they did not operate in the seventies to reduce velocity. Some possible reasons for this can be discerned. For example, agriculture, which is a sector with a high income velocity, almost held its ground in its share of growth in the economy during the seventies, but lost ground rapidly thereafter. And the shift in time deposits to commercial banks did not yet occur in the seventies. Indeed if anything, it moved slightly the other way. But more research on the relation of institutional and developmental changes to velocity is clearly called for, a recommendation that may also be applied to the Friedman-Schwartz hypothesis.

Money, Prices, and Income, 1880-1897

If the greenback period is full of dramatic and puzzling experiences in the economy's financial overlay, the subperiod thereafter, ending with the trough of the secular price decline in 1896-1897, is more intelligible to a twentieth century interpreter. Yet, it is marked by several challenging contrasts with respect to the preceding period. A glance at our equation of exchange expressed as percentage changes, $\Delta M/M + \Delta V/V = \Delta P/P + \Delta Q/Q$, will reveal some of these contrasts at once. The annual compound percentage changes from 1880 to 1897 were approximately as follows:

$$.050 - .035 = -.020 + .035$$

Compared with 1869-1879, there are notable changes here in all respects. The policy of severe restriction in the money stock had ended. The pendulum swung moderately in favor of the soft money forces. Velocity had begun its long secular decline which was to last until 1914, and to resume again from 1929 until 1946. The rate of price decline had been halved, and the rate of GNP growth, according to Kuznets and Gallman, had significantly slowed to slightly over 3.5 percent a year.

The eighties and early nineties were also years of emotion-laden controversy over monetary and price policy. The Pulitzer prize his-

torian Irwin Unger has commented that financial questions have
often been the distinctive form that social conflict has taken in the
United States.[11] Although Unger's specific reference is to the
greenback era, his interpretation is at least as applicable to the period that followed. In those years what Marx called the "fetishism of
money" was much in evidence. Generally the same social groups
continued to favor an antibanker policy of cheap money and rising
prices.

These groups characteristically concentrated on the currency
supply, and tended to neglect the less obvious but increasingly
dominant role of deposit money in the money supply and the attendant fall in the ratio of currency to money. They had lost the struggle to increase the quantity of United States notes in 1878 when the
$347 million then outstanding was made the permanent legal per-
missable amount. The issue of the other major component of the
currency supply, national bank notes, was restricted by what Friedman and Schwartz have called a "puzzling" tight issue policy, far
below the maximum permitted by either bank capital or the volume
of government bond "backing," and the quantity of such notes did
not rise during the seventies. It may not be so puzzling, however, if
we recognize that note issues were probably not very profitable
after government bond prices began to rise in the late seventies [12]
and if we further allow for overreaction by bankers to the cheap
money pressures of the "inflation fanatics." On the other hand,
nonbank financial intermediaries had a rising demand for government bonds, thus limiting the amount available to the national
banks and contributing to their rise in price. In the next decade and
a half, national bank notes declined in amount from a peak of $352
million in 1882 to $226 million in 1897.

These facts regarding restriction of the paper money issues show
in part the importance to the soft money groups of the addition to
their ranks of the silver money advocates. The latter include
spokesmen for the silver producing states and some persons who
had been "gold men" until the increasing production and falling
price of silver (due to falling demand as numerous countries went
off the silver standard), made feasible its monetization at the old
mint ratio of 16 to 1 with gold. As it turned out, Congress at a most
inopportune time had discontinued the minting of more silver dollars in 1873 and demonetized silver a year later. The former act
subsequently became the "Crime of '73" to the silver advocates and
their easy money allies who fired the first shot in the war for silver

in 1876 in the form of a letter by Republican George M. Weston in the *Boston Globe*. Although there were some conservative, bimetallist silverites who opposed a cheap dollar, most were in the anticreditor, anti- "Money Trust" group who wanted "free silver" coinage. If it is appropriate to call 1865-1879 the "greenback period," 1880-1897 should be called the "silver era." As the latter subperiod waned the silver advocates were able to add to the silver currency supply to compensate for the restricted supply of greenbacks and the declining volume of national bank notes. Under the Bland-Allison Act, in operation from its passage in 1878 over President Hayes's veto until 1890, the Treasury Secretary was instructed to purchase between $2 and $4 million of silver bullion a month. The silver advocates overcame only in 1886 the Act's limitation on silver certificates to denominations of $10 or more. However, domestic bankers and even some Treasury secretaries continued their opposition to silver money because of their fear that it would undermine their precious gold standard, and foreign bankers pressured domestic bankers and others similarly to resist the threatened official monetization of silver because it made them reluctant to hold dollar exchange (payable in gold).

In consequence of these forces, together with the Treasury's release of sliver money and smaller silver certificate denominations after 1886, the quantity of silver money in public hands rose from about $75 million in 1880 to about $408 million in 1890 and over $500 million in 1898.[13] Meanwhile, the free silver forces had secured the passage in 1890 of the Silver Purchase Act under the sponsorship of the eminent Senator from Ohio, John Sherman (who had also earlier promoted passage of the Resumption Act!). Under this Act the Treasury was directed to purchase monthly 4.5 million ounces of sliver, almost the entire domestic supply, in exchange for "Treasury Notes of 1890," which were redeemable in either silver *or gold*! If these Notes are counted in the supply of silver money in public hands in 1898, the total becomes about $600 million.

But gold money in the public's hands was also making a contribution to the money supply after resumption, rising from $90 million in 1879 to about $450 million in 1890, then leveling off. Thus the total nondeposit money outside the Treasury rose from $974 million to $1,839 million, or at an annual rate of about 3.5 percent between 1880 and 1898. This money is sometimes called high powered money because as it moved into and out of the banks in response to the nonbank public's desires, it added to or reduced bank reserves (vault cash) required by law and practice to be held against deposits. The banks were committed to convert deposits into currency at par. Since there was a legal fractional reserves arrangement (no 100 percent reserve), deposit creation by the banks was some multiple of vault cash. The deposit/reserve ratio was about twice as high for state banks as for national banks. Also, there was a distinct secular rise in the deposit/vault cash ratio in this subperiod for the more "liberal" nonnational banks while the ratio for national banks was constant. Other things equal, therefore, the entire rise in the deposit/reserve ratio was attributable to the more liberal policies of the state and other nonnational banks. Treasury cash, including gold currency, also moved into and out of the hands of the public and might well be included in high powered money. In this subperiod the deposit/currency ratio rose even more than the deposit/reserve ratio.

The relations among all these ratios and the institutions or groups whose policies were the immediate determinants of the ratio has been neatly, although admittedly simplistically, stated in a review of the Friedman-Schwartz book by James Tobin: "The stock of high-powered money is determined by the government, the deposit-currency ratio by the public, and the deposit-reserve ratio by the banks."[14] In general, the Treasury and the bankers in the national banks followed a somewhat more conservative monetary policy, partly by choice and partly because of legal constraints, than the bankers in the state commercial banks. Paul B. Trescott has summarized it well:

> It was the non-national, non-note issuing banks that clearly dominated the half century following the Civil War. National banks were subject to onerous restrictions on capital and assets at a time when geographic and economic expansion created unprecedented profitable opportunities for bank credit. Non-national banks mushroomed in numbers and deposit volume and were the chief vehicles for financial innovations, particularly in such matters as investment banking and industrial finance.
>
> Non-national banks other than mutual savings banks increased their deposits 170 percent between 1880 and 1896, while national banks increased their deposit contributions to the money supply by only 100 percent. In the former year such non-national bank deposits were 35 per cent of the money stock; but by 1896 they were 43 per cent.[15]

It will be noted that velocity declined by a significant 3.7 percent a year in this subperiod. It is hard to understand why the community's preference for money to hold as a "luxury good" experienced such a massive change during 1880-1897 when there is practically no evidence of such preference during 1869-1879 or 1914-1929. We are inclined to rely on the institutional and development-al changes occuring during this subperiod to explain such a dramatic velocity drop. The eighties were the years of enormous sectoral shifts with, for example, only a 20 percent rise in farm out-put, a contrasting decadal peak of 112 percent for manufacturing production, and decadal peak for urbanization. These shifts, in all likelihood, tended to reduce velocity as consumers and business in-creasingly accustomed themselves to the use of check money but had not yet learned to conserve on the amount of deposits they held.

With respect to velocity, holding money competed, then as now, with the holding of other financial assets. In that period of Federal government debt retirement the asset-holding community ex-changed its holdings of government securities for money, yet it put some of that money into other financial assets, such as railroad bonds and corporate securities, according to estimates by John G. Gurley and E. S. Shaw. On balance, however, householders and firms between 1880 and 1890, for example, increased the proportion of their income that they preferred to hold as money much more than they increased the proportion of their income that they prefer-red to hold as other financial assets — 54 percent for the former com-pared with 24 percent for the latter. So income velocity still fell. Al-though statements about the interest rate influence on these matters are risky, we can suggest that given the fall of product prices, this pattern was consistent with the continued downward drift of interest rates.

The Federal government's "classical" debt retirement policy, al-though deflationary in the context of the bond-restricted currency of the National Banking system, was antideflationary in that it met some of the community's secularly rising demand for money to hold as cash balances, i.e., for nontransactions purposes. But, that was not enough. We should remember the government's deflationary budget surpluses were financed out of taxes imposed largely on con-sumption. All but 1.5 percentage points of the 5 percent annual in-crease in money was dissipated by velocity decline. With physical output rising at 3.5 percent, this velocity drop had to pull down the price level. Consequently, the rise in the real value of the money stock was at a rate of 7 percent a year — 5 percent nominal money stock rise plus 2 percent price fall. This was twice the annual rate of increase in real income.

It is hard to believe that the gradual secular price fall of 2 percent a year could itself have had much reciprocal effect on the decision patterns represented in the other variables in the equation of exchange. Effects of the price fall on social and political behavior were assuredly more significant by far. This is particularly true if we change outlook from the secular to the cyclical setting, wherein the price declines were concentrated, for example, between 1882 and 1886.

The long-run growth of output was also probably but little affected by the behavior of money, velocity, or prices. One of the most comfortable ways to underpin this interpretation is probably to contrast it with either the preceding subperiod or, perhaps more fruitfully, the later subperiod, 1898 to 1914, when output also rose at about 3.5 percent a year while prices *rose* rather more than 2 percent a year—even though money increased and velocity decreased, as it did between 1880 and 1897.

If we can assume the output rise to have been practically autonomous, then the community's velocity behavior had a deflationary effect on prices similar to that which would have obtained under a tight money stock policy. In other words, although the soft money forces, insofar as they desired inflation, scored when it came to the money supply, they lost by virtue of offsetting changes on the velocity front. Their achievement in partially influencing the growth of the money stock was far from satisfactory—given the pattern of velocity change. A cheaper dollar, the nightmare of the gold people, thus continued to be an empty dream for the silver people. An inexorable law? Apparently not in the very long run, as history would show, and paradoxically it was *gold* that seemingly had much to do with the ultimate victory, of the inflation goals at least, of the soft money groups in the next period!

Money, Prices, and Income, 1898-1914

"You shall not press down upon the brow of labor this crown of thorns, you shall not crucify mankind upon a cross of gold" roared free silverite leader, William Jennings Bryan, to the Democratic national convention in 1896. Less well timed words were never spoken. Not only was Bryan defeated by McKinley in the 1896 election, more fundamentally, the North Atlantic trading community was on the threshhold of a reversal in the long downward price trend that in the United States had contributed so much to the demand for cheap money for over a quarter century. That reversal drew its sustenance in the sphere of monetary policy largely from the great increase in world gold production stimulated in large part precisely by the long price decline. This is not to say that in the absence of larger gold stocks the money supply could not have been increased faster. It only means that, given gold standard banking rules for restraining the money supply, larger monetary gold stocks permitted faster increases in the money supply — and therefore in the price level. The monetary effects partially resulting from the new golden flood soon destroyed the power of the soft money forces in the United States by giving them the rising price level they had so long demanded. Furthermore, the Gold Standard Act of 1900 made legally certain the exclusive sway of gold convertibility, assuring the final defeat of silver bimetallism. The paradox was completed: the price goals of the free silver movement were achieved under the regime of the free coinage of gold!

Let us look at the record of annual percentage changes as revealed by our equation of exchange, $\Delta M/M + \Delta V/V = \Delta P/P + \Delta Q/Q$. In approximations for 1898-1914:

$$.075 - .02 = .02 + .035$$

The real GNP rise of 3.5 percent progressed "as usual," despite, in comparison with 1880-1897, a sharper increase in the growth rate of the money stock, a sharp fall in the rate of velocity decline, a consequent dramatic rise in the sum $\Delta M/M + \Delta V/V$ from 1.5 percent to 5.5 percent per year, and a switch from 2.0 percent fall in the price level to a 2.0 percent rise. We seem to have here a clear case of inflation induced by a rapid rise in the money supply. Almost two-thirds of the price rise in the whole period took place during the first five years after the cyclical trough of June 1897 (see Figure 7). What could have been better designed (although it was fortuitous) to appease quickly the cheap money groups? Of course, these are aggregates and do not tell us how the agrarian and industrial debtor interest, the heart of the cheap money movement, fared under the new state of affairs. But their monetary demands were partly met, as can be observed both in the aggregative monetary changes and the price changes.

For the three subperiods, we can now draw upon the annual rates of change in the components of the equation of exchange to explain in a simple way the course of prices. The average annual percentage increase in the supply of money is $\Delta M/M$. With the annual average percentage increase in the demand for money for income transactions purposes, at constant prices, being $\Delta Q/Q$, and the percentage increase in the demand for money to hold as a cash asset being $\Delta V/V$, the total annual percentage increase in the demand for money is $\Delta Q/Q - \Delta V/V$. [16] Then the average annual percentage increase in prices, $\Delta P/P$, is the resultant discrepancy, $\Delta M/M - (\Delta Q/Q - \Delta V/V)$, in the supply of and demand for money. Table 21 presents this in summary form for the three subperiods. The table shows that during the first two subperiods the annual average price decline was equal to the excess of money demand over money supply. During the last subperiod the annual average price rise was equal to the excess of money supply over money demand.

Soft money advocates from 1898 to 1914 could hardly have asked for a more liberal rise in the rate of money supply growth—over twice the growth rate of physical output (although they might have desired a greater rise in prices—for the whole period). Even allowing for a massive relative transfer of deposits away from mutual savings banks, the rate was about twice that for real GNP.

The nonnational commercial banks, whose deposits of $2,041 million about equaled those of the national banks in 1898, again proved more liberal in their deposit creation policies than the banks in the National Banking system: 9 percent increase as against 7.5 percent for both National bank deposits and for notes over the years 1898-1914. The notes, totaling $738 million were of course high powered money that along with a U.S. monetary gold stock increase of about 5.5 percent a year accounted for the total rise in such money.

The considerable rise in National Bank notes, and the accompanying rise in National Bank holdings of the Federal interest-bearing debt, along with a reduction in legal bank entry barriers, may be attributable in part to the liberalizing provisions of the Currency or Gold Standard Act of 1900. [17] Credit should also go to the liberal note issue policies of the Treasury secretaries under President Theodore Roosevelt, particularly Leslie M. Shaw of Iowa, Secretary from 1902 to 1907.

Friedman and Schwartz call this subperiod the era of gold inflation. They emphasize the great rise in the monetary gold stock from $591 million in 1897 to $1.891 billion in 1914, a rise that increased the U.S. share of the world's gold stock from 14 percent to almost 25 percent. Yet, only about a fifth of this rise was from net gold imports as the United States cashed in on its persistently positive

TABLE 21

	1869-1879	1880-1897	1898-1914
Money supply			
$\Delta M/M$	1.0%	5.0%	7.5%
Money demand			
$\Delta Q/Q$	5.0%	3.5%	3.5%
$\Delta V/V$	0%	-3.5%	-2.0%
$\Delta Q/Q + \Delta V/V$	5.0%	7.0%	5.5%
Price change			
$\Delta P/P = \Delta M/M - (\Delta Q/Q + \Delta V/V)$ - 4.0%		-2.0%	+2.0%

foreign trade balance. The remainder came out of the total domestic gold production of almost $1.5 billion over the period. Still, it is clear to us in retrospect that the abiding U.S. export balance on its current account was beginning to absorb an inordinate share (inordinate from the standpoint of the future health of the gold standard) of the world's gold stock. This threatened in the long run the very international gold standard that was so highly prized in this period.

The decline in velocity, distinctly less than the rate during 1880-1897, may plausibly be explained by the same previously discussed institutional and developmental changes, and the leveling off of the pace of those changes. The influence of Federal fiscal policy with respect to both the money supply and its velocity was inconsequential. The end of an era is thus demarcated, as velocity ceased to decline between 1914 and 1929. (The resumption of velocity decline in the 1930s and 1940s requires its own specific analysis, just as the apparent rise after World War II.)

Both data and analysis are confusing with respect to the pattern and significance of nominal interest rates for monetary velocity changes between 1897 and 1914. The average annual rate on prime commercial loans (four to six months) jumped around, but exhibited no trend; indeed it revealed no trend from the early 1880s to 1929. Long term corporate bond yields, however, experienced the same reversal in trend that characterized the secular pattern of product prices. It is therefore hard to see that "the" interest rate had much of anything to do with the velocity of money.

The reversal of the downward secular price trend coincided with a Juglar upswing that overlapped a long swing peak-plateau and that, in terms of real GNP, itself revealed a peak-plateau (see Figure 7). All this, together with the rapid price rise, dramatizes for us the massive and decisive character of the change that was occurring in the economy. According to Robert Lipsey, [18] real GNP in 1913 dollars experienced a sustained seven-year rise as follows:

1896	$17,700 million
1897	19,300
1898	19,600
1899	21,500
1900	22,200
1901	24,800
1902	25,000
1903	26,300

The original recovery from the long Juglar downswing of 1893-1897 was facilitated by expansive changes in the foreign balance: a spurt in exports, especially wheat and wheat flour, a sluggish import response to that recovery, and a jump in gold imports that no doubt aided the substantial expansion of the money stock.

The rise in real GNP during this entire subperiod through 1913 was remarkable for its generally sustained character, there having been only one short, significant drop in the slump year 1908 (Figure 7). However, as has been noted, the secular rise of slightly over 3.5 percent a year was very modest. But it was apparently representative of twentieth century laissez faire growth rates, for the annual rate for the much longer period 1898-1929 was also no more than 3.5 percent.

The secular price reversal practically brought to an end the great monetary controversies of the years from the end of the Civil War to Bryan's "cross of gold" speech. Aside from banking reform agitation that led to the establishment of the Federal Reserve System in 1914, the economic, social, and political issues that occupied the "progressive era" after passage of the Gold Standard Act—the last subperiod to be considered here—were but little concerned with monetary matters. People turned particularly to social conditions, urban environmental externalities, conservation of natural resources, foreign policy and naval expansion, the income tax, and monopoly problems (including the "money trust"). Many of these issues had been initially brought into the limelight as part of the farmer's protest movement in the years before 1897. People also continued to press for the betterment of labor's material conditions.

Background of the Federal Reserve System

In the pre-World War I world laymen widely believed that "panics" were largely due to monetary maladjustment and the few business cycle theorists overwhelmingly subscribed to monetary explanations of one sort or another. Hence, it is not surprising that monetary and banking reform occupied a prominent place in the reform movements of the progressive years, years marked appropriately by the inconsequential "rich man's panic" of 1903-1904 and the brief but sharp "bankers' panic" of 1907-1908. Most historians agree that these "panics" helped bring to fruition the efforts to correct the alleged long standing defects of the banking system, of the Independent Treasury system established by the Democrats in the administration of President James K. Polk in 1846, and of the relations between the two. While the Federal Reserve System is relevant to a later period in economic history, the events and ideas behind the passage of the Federal Reserve Act in December 1913 mark the culmination of the financial and fiscal controversies of our period. At the same time they also emphasize a certain continuity in the historical process.

Alleged defects of the banking system and the Treasury's relation to it included the arguments that the currency was too "inelastic," that bank reserves were inadequate, excessively concentrated, and too much used for financial speculation, that banks should create and destroy money (credit) in accordance with the needs of trade. It was also widely asserted that the national banks discriminated against farming and the small town, and that the stricter requirements and regulations of the national banks put them at a disadvantage as compared with nonnational banks. Viewed from an international perspective, there was no central bank such as European countries with large international trade interests had enjoyed for a long time, just as there was no central bank which viewed from a domestic standpoint could provide immediate acceptance of payment anywhere in the country. There was no central bank to be "lender of last resort" and to coordinate bank monetary policy with the monetary actions of the Treasury. Many argued that private control of the money supply was exploitative and should be replaced by government ownership of the banking system. Finally, there was the claim that the banks as they actually functioned were largely responsible for "panics." Apparently the final victory of the gold standard advocates in the Currency Act of 1900 had not brought monetary nirvana.

The currency inelasticity argument was in the center of the stage. One reason for this was that farmers and other people west of the Alleghenies and south of the Potomac continued to feel that monetary policy discriminated against them in order to make profits for the Eastern "money trust." This became the subject of a famous investigation by a committee under Congressman Pujo beginning in 1912. It was true that, as Friedman and Schwartz put it, there was no "effective interconvertibility between currency and deposits." This in a practical sense meant deposits could not readily be converted into currency. In the short run the volume of currency was quite rigidly limited. What was needed was an arrangement whereby in noncrisis periods currency could be issued as readily as demand deposits could be created—against commercial paper collateral or borrowings by a member bank from a central bank (the lender of last resort). In other words, the system of vault cash reserves was too fixed. For crisis periods, runs on the banks for currency could have been prevented, as they later were, by deposit insurance, together with the power of a central bank to create more currency against rediscounted commercial paper or just the IOUs of members of the system. But such a socialized insurance system was incompatible with the laissez faire atmosphere prevalent before 1914.

Furthermore, under the then existing banking institutions much of the vault cash reserves of country banks were put on deposit for interest in large city banks and particularly in New York City, the center of the nation's money market. These funds were then substantially tied up by the New York City banks as reserves against loans, even loans for stock market transactions. This geographic and institutional concentration of vault cash greatly aggravated the shortage of cash demanded by farmers, urban working people, and small businessmen in the most inopportune periods of cyclical crisis, and generated annual seasonal shortages of currency facing farmers every fall when crops had to be sold and farm harvest wages and other costs paid. (International gold flows, of modest size, clearly had little if any systematic connection with this pattern of currency needs.) Country banks could not readily get the currency they needed from their city correspondents, and the fact that the reserves of the former were committed in part to speculative uses was a cause for anger in the outlying parts of the country.

There were strict limits on what the Treasury could do about the problem, not only because its cash balances were relatively small, but also because the use by the Treasury of selected national banks as depositories was considered by many as contrary to the independent treasury principle and a temptation to favoritism. The selective depository arrangement was also viewed as unfair to the banks when deposits were withdrawn and inequitable in the sense of granting these banks the free use of Treasury funds while at the same time paying them interest on government bonds used as security against their bank notes. Perhaps the most impertinent criticism was that which claimed "interference with business" whenever the Treasury reduced its total deposits. [19] These problems of fiscal relationships were abiding ones despite frequent, almost heroic, efforts by Treasury secretaries to relieve particular currency shortages.

The essentially ineffectual efforts of the Treasury to provide a sort of central currency reserve available for emergency distribution were supplemented in the Aldrich-Vreeland Act of 1908. This Act anticipated the Federal Reserve in that, among other things, it legalized the establishment of National Currency Associations to issue currency to member national banks in an emergency, subject to an aggregate limitation of $500 million, in amounts up to 75 percent of the value of commercial paper they deposited with the association, and up to 90 percent of the market price of approved state and local government bonds.

The Aldrich-Vreeland Act not only anticipated the Federal Reserve, but provided for the establishment of a Republican dominated National Monetary Commission in both houses of the Congress to study the presumed monetary and banking morass and make appropriate correction recommendations. It presented its Report in 1912, and the reforms proposed in that Report, drawing heavily upon the experience of the Bank of England, provided the basis for the Federal Reserve Act. Under that Act, bank reserves were freed from their ultimate complete dependence on gold, as had been the case in the period under study here. Also, the "real bills" advocates, rather to their subsequent regret, got their system of deposit creation—which had existed under the arrangements obtaining in this period—through the discounting of commercial paper according to the "needs of trade." However, as Gurley and Shaw point out, "It was contemplated in the Federal Reserve Act that the monetary system would remain 'on gold' and that the bank reserves and money would fluctuate independently of gold only as the 'needs of trade' led to rediscounting." [20]

And the farmers? Their commercial bank needs for nine months' intermediate term credit based on farm products as collateral, and for loans on real estate, had not been met by the National Banking System, and had been poorly met by the nonnational banks. But credit unavailability and high interest charges for agriculture were not overcome by the conservative Federal Reserve either. It consequently became necessary for the Federal government, under pressure from the agrarians' long standing demands for "subtreasurys," to set up a system of Federal Land Banks in 1916 to make loans on first mortgages, and Federal Intermediate Credit Banks in 1923 to try to fill that gap in the provision of credit to farmers. In these actions the U.S. government was only following a pattern adopted in most other industrialized countries, where farm loans, as with small urban business loans, tended to be too risky in the view of conservative bankers formally committed to the acceptance of only short term liquid collateral.

Was all this pointing to the beginning of the end of laissez faire, as some have suggested? One can safely say that it would be difficult to operate the monetary policy of a contemporary mixed economy with the banking system and Independent Treasury as constituted in our period. Nevertheless, a central bank, such as the English example, proved quite congenial to generations of laissez faire capitalism. It would seem safer to say that the agitation and controversy antedating the Federal Reserve had the result of bringing a somewhat atavistic banking system into line with the requirements of an industrial urban economy with large national markets. Furthermore, the new institution was better equipped to accommodate a growing volume of international transactions that strongly influenced the state of affairs in a number of nations whose foreign trade vitally affected their internal economic health. It was therefore also a more effective vehicle for the implementation of the nation's foreign economic policy in the forthcoming era of guided capitalism.

NOTES

1. Rendigs Fels, *American Business Cycles, 1865-1897* (Chapel Hill, N.C.: University of North Carolina Press, 1959), p. 128.

2. Moses Abramovitz, *Evidences of Long Swings in Aggregate Construction Since the Civil War* (New York: Columbia University Press, for the National Bureau of Economic Research, 1964), p. 31, Table 4, line 1. The immediately following data on peaks and troughs in the gross new construction cycle are from the same source, p. 31.

3. Ibid., p. 33. Data, which are from Ulmer, are the same for both current and 1929 prices.

4. See Jeffrey G. Williamson, "Late Nineteenth-Century Retardation: A Neoclassical Analysis," *Journal of Economic History*, 33, no. 3 (September 1973), pp. 581-607.

5. This assumes practically unlimited private investment opportunities regardless of what is happening to the rate of consumer spending. Otherwise, debt retirement could have been an economic depressant for it required a surplus in the government's budget, which in turn required that taxes be greater than expenditures.

6. Milton Friedman and Anna Jacobson Schwartz, *A Monetary History of the United States, 1867-1960*, National Bureau of Economic Research (Princeton, N.J.: Princeton University Press, 1963), pp. 28-9. Their *M* estimates probably err toward understatement in the early years of 1867-1879, which would tend to exaggerate the rate of increase of the money stock.

7. See his "Economic Factors in Specie Resumption: The United States, 1865-1879," *Journal of Political Economy*, 59, no. 1 (February 1961), p. 47.

8. According to a famous economist of the early twentieth century, Irving Fisher, falling product prices raise the purchasing power of both the principal and interest on bonds. Hence bond prices would rise, and bond marginal interest rates fall, on a falling product price trend. This hypothesis seems consistent with the trends in these from the Civil War to 1879.

9. Op. cit., p. 654.

10. George Garvy and Martin R. Blyn, *The Velocity of Money* (New York: Federal Reserve Bank of New York, October 1969). See esp. pp. 79-83 *passim*.

11. Irwin Unger, *The Greenback Era* (Princeton, N.J.: Princeton University Press, 1964), p. 3.

12. See Richard Sylla, "Federal Policy, Banking Market Structure, and Capital Mobilization in the United States, 1863-1913," *Journal of Economic History*, 29, no. 4 (December 1969), p. 663.

13. These and the immediately following estimates of money in circulation are estimated from Paul Studenski and Herman E. Krooss, *Financial History of the United States*, second ed. (New York: McGraw-Hill, 1963), pp. 189, 239; and Friedman and Schwartz, op. cit., pp. 130, 179.

14. James Tobin, "The Monetary Interpretation of History," *American Economic Review*, 55, no. 3 (June 1965), p. 468.

15. Paul B. Trescott, "An Old Look at American Monetary History," *Explorations in Entrepreneurial History*, second series, 6, no. 3 (Spring/Summer 1969), p. 258. This view undermines the thesis that the National Banking System was a great boon to capitalist development.

16. $\Delta V/V$ being subtracted algebraically, of course.

17. See Richard Sylla, loc. cit., pp. 663-4.

18. Robert E. Lipsey, *Price and Quantity Trends in the Foreign Trade of the United States* (New York: National Bureau of Economic Research, 1963), p. 423.

19. See D. R. Dewey, *Financial History of the United States* (New York: Longmans, Green, 1939), p. 418.

20. "Money" in Seymour Harris (ed.), *American Economic History* (New York: McGraw-Hill, 1961), p. 117.

[II]

The social response
to economic change

The great developmental changes in the economy during this half-century caused equally deep social and political upheavals. Those upheavals in turn influenced, although to a surprisingly minor extent in the period under review at least, the pattern and pace of economic development. In general, the urban entrepreneur and the creditor were in the saddle, and it was they who largely determined the course of events. Other socioeconomic groups therefore found themselves in the position of adapting to and modifying the impact of the developmental process on their lives. This adaptive and modifying response seemed intense and dramatic to a degree all out of proportion to its effects upon the functioning of the market system at the time. Nevertheless it is probable that in the very long run the effects were significant and far reaching. To test such a hypothesis requires an interpretation of the connections between social and political action in this period and the later emergence and evolution of the mixed economy in the twentieth century. But the analysis is complicated by the undoubted additional connections between the more or less strictly economic changes in this period and the economic changes characterizing the evolution of the mixed economy after 1932.

The nineteenth century confronts us with a society of conflicting economic interest groups. This is an interpretive proposition which is essential to the understanding of U.S. economic history. In a discussion of group response it is necessary to delineate a small number of groups and to assume that they are internally quite homogeneous, at least for some significant period of time. If a particular group is chronically split, however, this must also be considered. Furthermore, the delineation of interest groups must allow for "overlaps at the boundaries." This refers to the phenomenon of cooperation, at times and on certain controversial issues, between a given interest group and "defecting" elements of varying size that ordinarily adhere to other groups. An illustration is the identification of some merchant enterprisers, and of small and even big businessmen, with agrarian and other reform groups. Finally, one must be primarily concerned with the articulate groups, for they are the only ones that exercised sufficient leverage to change anything.

Here we shall build the discussion chiefly around three groups: family farmers, urban workers in transport and certain commodity-producing activities, and for the years after 1870 and especially after 1897, urban middle class "Progressives." It has already been indicated how heroic the assumption of internal homogeneity is with respect to the Progressives. Hence in this case it will be particularly necessary to follow the guideline "by their actions you shall know them." From the standpoint of these groups, they had opponents, as well as allies, among other groups. Therefore, the behavior of opponents and allies is also relevant to this review of social response.

The Agrarian Revolt

Economic historians have used this term to describe the response of the numerically important family farmers, in the West and South especially, to industrialization in the broad meaning of the term. It should be recalled that the farm population as late as the 1890 census accounted for 47 percent of the total population of the country. Of course, a notable proportion of that population was made up of inarticulate unorganized farm wage earners and family members who did not participate in the agrarian protest movement. The farmers' revolt waxed and waned through the "greenback era" and the period of the free silver movement until rapidly and relatively rising farm prices took the steam out of it after 1897. However, even after the ending of the revolt about that time, farm groups continued to provide mass support for the progressive reform movement.

As a massive group attack upon the operation of the private industrial market system, and the laissez faire policy of the Federal government by a class of "rugged individualists," the farmers' revolt is enormously significant. Hindsight shows us why: the private market mechanism was under the almost exclusive power of the urban industrial business and banker groups. It produced ever more organized and articulate centers of countervailing power which in the very long run would undermine that position of exclusive power and force an accommodation to broad public participation. The agrarian (and to some degree mercantile) revolt was the first interventionist wave to reveal in ultimately irreversible fashion that the private market system was no more "automatic" than the gold standard. The system was a socially contrived institution to be operated and altered according to the wishes of the dominant social consensus at any particular time.

The evidence of an agrarian crusade against certain aspects of the private market system and the probusiness, procreditor, laissez faire policies of the government was manifest, dramatic, and in one form or another, continuous from the late sixties to the 1896 presidential campaign. Indeed it lingered on in the vitiated form of cooperation with the Progressive movement. The agrarian crusade was an uprising of commercial family farmers located primarily in the South and the states west of the Ohio river, particularly the area now called the Middle West together with the prairie states.[1] Northeastern farmers were not prominent in the movement because their problems were different and less acute, as will readily be inferred after a review of the agrarian crusade.

The commercial farmer's hostile response across the whole North Atlantic world to industrialization, urbanization, and the corporate revolution in the late nineteenth century was in the U.S. case encouraged by the tradition of the Jacksonian agrarian dislike of the urban rich who held wealth largely in the intangible form of money and securities. More immediately, it was propelled by the growing differentiation in market power of the atomistic agricultural entrepreneur in confrontation with the large monopolistic and oligopolistic firm on both the selling and buying sides of his domestic and international market. Other impelling forces were the onset of serious decline in the social and political importance of the farm population in the nation, by what Irwin Unger has referred to as the resentment against the growing economic gap between the city and the country,[2] and by the apparent partiality of laissez faire government policy toward big nonfarm business in this power confrontation. The farmers' response did not in general attack labor. Indeed, in a loose way it treated urban labor as another oppressed industrial class with whom during these years it maintained a somewhat tenuous collaborative relationship.

Most of the farmers' demands, advanced on specific controversial economic issues, may be viewed as dealing with the particular forms assumed under the contemporary historical conditions by the aforementioned emerging differentiation in market power. In its own peculiar way agrarian discontent was a part of the whole modern multifaceted problem of small business in the giant corporate age—excessively easy entry, tight credit, unstable prices, weak bargaining power, failure to reap "normal profits," etc. Because of the abiding nature of agriculture's problems, the termination of the revolt at the end of the nineteenth century was merely an interlude of somewhat lessened activity. Following agriculture's "golden age" from 1900 to 1914, the 1920s and 1930s saw another protracted crisis period attended by much activity on the part of the "farm bloc."

Although the economic and political grievances of the farmers seemed to be much the same throughout the thirty years after the Civil War, there was a change in emphasis in the late 1870s. This change, together with the decline of farmers' cooperatives, spelled the doom of the Granger organization which had stressed cooperatives and action against railroad abuses and monopoly. Its replacement in the 1880s by the more vehement Farmers' Alliances and related organizations culminated in the establishment of the Populist party in 1891. The National Grange of the Patrons of Husbandry was originally founded by a Federal government clerk named Oliver Kelley, as a social and educational organization in 1867, but it became a vehicle of agrarian protest, and by 1872 was under farmer leadership. Its brief period of prominence as a protest organization spanned the years 1871-1877. Grange membership included many thousands in the South, and even in the Northeast, as well as in its Midwestern centers of strength. In late 1875, out of a national membership of 760,000 according to Solon J. Buck, some 276,000 were in the South but only 64,000 in the Northeast.

The Grangers reflected, in their attack upon private business monopoly, the small firm's loss of market power. This attack was focused on the railroads and the middlemen, and, among the latter group in particular, the railroad subsidiary grain dealers and the warehouse firms. It also fought the market power of supplying enterprises, especially of the new direct-selling agents of manufacturers and the manufacturers themselves. This gave rise to complaints resembling later protests of urban small business firms against alleged exploitative pricing based on patent rights and their abuse. Apparently the Grangers' bargaining organizations gave a good account of themselves as one party in a dynamic bilateral monopoly situation, for the record of price decline in farm machinery after 1870, for example, left little if anything to be desired.

Alleged railroad monopsony (the Grangers had not studied elementary economics!) prevailed outside the great urban terminals. As Irwin Unger so well put it, when "agriculture moved farther away from the population centers of the East, a growing portion of the agricultural community became entangled in a web of intermediaries between itself and the consumer of its product."[3] The farmer had to store and ship with one grain dealer, warehouse, or tough-minded railroad whose economic resources vastly exceeded his own and whose business with him was a miniscule portion of the latter's total business. Solon J. Buck, leading historian of the movement, describes the plight of the choiceless, unorganized farmer:

> A farmer was afraid that, if he angered the railroad, misfortunes would befall him: his grain might be delivered to the wrong elevators or left to stand and spoil in damp freight cars; there might be no cars available for grain just when his shipment was ready; and machinery destined for him might be delayed at a time when lack of it would mean the loss of his crops.[4]

As for the controversial railroad rates, particularly freight rates, it is not elucidating to refer to the general drop in rates for the whole period from the Civil War to the 1890s. It is true that the railroads east of Chicago, such as the Pennsylvania, lowered average rates *pari passu* with the decline in farm prices for the whole period.[5] Average rates, however, obscure monopsonistic rate discrimination. Equally important, the rate pattern over time for the "Granger railroads" was very different. Between Chicago and the Missouri River, for example, if one takes a three-year average of annual average rates, while farm product prices were falling 39 percent between 1864-1866 and 1875-1877, freight rates for the Illinois Central fell only 7 percent, for the Rock Island 15 percent, and for the Chicago and Northwestern 31 percent. It was only *after* the late seventies that rates changed by these railroads fell more rapidly than farm product prices, that is after the Grange's success in the Granger cases (1876-1877) in getting the U.S. Supreme Court to validate state regulation of railroad and grain elevator rates. Indeed the decline occurred after the Grange had gone out of existence as a significant farm protest organization and been replaced by other more militant organizations with different programmatic emphases.

The complaints against the railroads were not limited to average rates and rate discrimination, however. This is no doubt why anti-railroad protest and the demand for government ownership lingered on as part of the agrarian and mercantile movement's program. Other criticisms revolved around allegations that still command research effort, such as discriminatory state and local taxation partial to railroad property, losses by farmers and local governments on watered or bogus railroad securities purchased with the proceeds of farm mortgages and public bond issues, waste and corruption in construction, and the holding by railroads of lands in excess of need for transport use.

These criticisms tended to ignore the many contributions of the railroads, including their more solid growth-promoting and "colonizing" work. But protest movements address themselves to defects or alleged defects.

One important outcome of the Grangers' and merchants' antagonism to shipping monopoly was the state Granger laws beginning in Illinois in 1871 that set up railroad and warehouse commissions to fix maximum freight and passenger rates and to regulate grain elevators. These laws inaugurated public utility regulation in the United States, provided the ground work for their replacement with the Interstate Commerce Act in 1887, and contributed to the antimonopoly cause that eventuated in the passage of the Sherman Antitrust Act in 1890. It is noteworthy that a considerable, and some historians say leading, contribution to the Granger rail-regulation movement was made by Western and Midwestern merchants. Also, Chicago commodity dealers were in the leadership of the drive to regulate grain elevators.

The second major concern of the Grange was to try to combat monopoly market power by establishing producer, purchasing, insurance, and marketing cooperatives. Cooperation as an alternative to "wage slavery" was being unsuccessfully advanced contemporaneously by the National Labor Union under William H. Sylvis and the Knights of Labor under Uriah S. Stephens. With the Grange, however, cooperation was viewed primarily from a business standpoint as a way of achieving a greater degree of economic independence and superior bargaining power. It was part of its attack upon the market power of middlemen, manufacturers, and bankers. But cooperation in its aspect as a profitable business venture was in general a failure in the United States in the nineteenth century, and the Grangers' efforts were no exception. The decline of Granger cooperatives in the mid-seventies contributed much to the defection of members and the consequent decline of the organization. However, as Buck points out, even their short-lived threatening cooperative experiments had a sobering influence on middlemen's price and credit policies, taught the farmers that marketing actually involved substantial legitimate costs, and spurred the emergence of the mail order business.

The Farmers' Alliances, which replaced the Grange as leading farm organizations beginning about 1880, also endeavored to promote cooperatives. But these groups made less of cooperation than the Grange and their efforts were similarly unsuccessful.

It was with the decline of the Grange in the mid-seventies that greenbackism and soft money generally came into the ascendency in the agrarian protest movement. Greenbackism in the form of the Greenback and Greenback-Labor Party (1874-1880) provided a transition from the anticreditor protest of the late sixties to the establishment of the currency conscious Northwest and Southern (white) Alliances and the "separate but equal" Southern Colored Farmers' National Alliance and Cooperative Union. Yet, the money question in the eighties and early nineties by no means squeezed out antirailroad antimonopoly agitation, the demand for government relief for mortgage indebtedness, hostility for "the accursed foreclosure system" (farm tenancy was rising), and criticism of the payment of interest on government bonds. Nor did it displace protest against discrimination allegedly favorable to railroads and urban owners of intangible wealth in property tax assessment, the demand for deduction of the amount of mortgage debt from assessment of all mortgaged property, pleas for the reduction of the tariff to a "revenue basis," and advocacy of a graduated income tax. The agrarians continued their insistence upon regulation of public utilities, their pressure for the elimination of "speculative" dealing in futures of "all agricultural and mechanical productions," and their call for revision of the patent law insofar as it unduly sheltered monopolies. The elaborate program was rounded out with a demand for prohibition of alien land ownership, and, parallel with labor's independently advanced program, for restriction of immigration and the eight-hour day for urban labor, and numerous political proposals such as the direct election of senators, the initiative and referendum, the secret ballot, and "economy in government." These were the main issues that, along with money and banking reforms, lay behind the famous call by Populist leader Mary Elizabeth Lease to the farmers to "raise less corn and more hell."

Clearly the agrarians had a full-bodied program of reform, and many of their proposals contemporaneously or later came to be enacted into law. Although accused of being everything from crackpots and fanatics to communists, the agrarians and their allies within the urban debtor business group were solidly in favor of a capitalist economy.

Monetary, Banking, and Fiscal Reform

The monetary and banking reformist demands themselves made up a complex packet that featured prominently in the agitation of the eighties and dominated the Populist Party platform when it became a full-fledged third party political arm of the agrarian protest movement under the name of the People's Party in 1892. As the money and banking reform packet evolved from the Civil War years to the birth of the Populist Party it was definitely more than a demand for higher prices. But there can be no doubt that the lag between some farm costs, particularly fixed costs, and falling farm product prices exerted a price-cost squeeze that generated partiality toward a reversal of the secular price decline. Also, in the short run on a rising price level, farm prices were likely to gain relative to nonfarm prices. Farmers may not have remembered the failure of this to happen during 1861-1864, or the inconsequentially favorable differential in the upswing of 1871-1872, but in the eighties they had fresh memories of the cyclical price rise between 1879 and 1882, when on an annual basis nonfarm prices rose 20 percent and farm prices rose 38 percent. And at least equally to the point, in the Juglar cycle price fall from 1882 to a temporary trough in 1886, farm prices declined 31 percent while nonfarm prices declined only 24 percent. In the case of such disparate movements, if the farm product prices could be separated from the nonfarm price indexes, the disparity in the percentage changes would of course be even greater. And although economic historians live largely in the long run, the farmers in this period no doubt lived mainly in the short run. Farmers did not look favorably on falling general prices.

Yet the agrarian cheap money movement was basically a monetary, banking, and fiscal policy reform movement hostile to private bankers and the whole creditor stratum, together with their predominantly Republican cohorts. Strong elements within the Democratic Party, especially in the West and South, tended to join the agrarians during most of the protest years. But as the eighties waned, it became evident that the divided Democratic Party, traditionally hostile to paper money and big government, hesitated to become the standard bearer of either agricultural reform in general or of soft money in particular. The ensuing resentment of the farmers led to their pro-third party, populist consensus. Hence from 1892 to 1896, the last dramatic years of full agrarian protest, the movement was centered in the activities of the Populist Party that had been founded largely by Southern and Western Alliance members in 1891. However, even in the 1892 presidential election the influence of white supremacy leaders in the South held the Southern movement in the "white man's" Democratic Party camp, contributing much to holding down Populist candidate James B. Weaver's popular vote to about 1 million. And again in 1896, William Jennings Bryan was the reluctant Democratic Party's free silver candidate, the Populists joining forces with the Democrats in an unsuccessful attempt to elect him.

The complex packet of monetary and banking demands advanced over the years culminating in populism in the nineties was advanced by classes, groups, and organizations that were changing over time and that overlapped with others who sometimes temporarily defected from the ranks. Such spillover at the boundaries of different interest groups was particularly widespread in the months immediately following the downswing of 1873 when almost everybody was apprehensive about the price collapse and the business contraction. At the same time, the inflationist sentiment was not solidified into a power force until the 1873 downswing.

But the Western and Southern farmers were by far the most

stable component of the easy money camp—after they had definitively given up their "sound money" advocacy in the early 1870s. (One quip had it that the farmers wanted "sound money and more of it.") It is revealing for the interpretation of their overall reform program that the agrarians' money and banking demands were essentially the same both when they were sound money advocates and when they later became inflationists. The easy money camp may be loosely described as including, at one time or another, in addition to the core of Western and Southern farmers, most of the Western and Southern Democrats, some Western Republicans, some industrialists, some Western merchants, most labor spokesmen, businessmen interested in Western real estate and transport, agrarian debtors, and the silver interests. Their somewhat ambiguously delineated and overlapping opponents at one time or another included the creditor interests, most bankers, especially in the East, debtors on international account, foreign traders, Eastern merchants, most manufacturers, especially the New England textile enterprisers, leading spokesmen for the churches, most Republicans (again excepting just after the panic of 1873), both major political parties in New England, New York, and New Jersey, conservative businessmen, and most Western merchants. The large number of people involved and their high emotional pitch at various times shows that neither the private market system nor the environment in which it functioned were automatic or constant. Alternatively expressed, what was "private" was also "public," i.e., affected with a public interest. However, it must be noted that the focus was on only limited monetary and fiscal aspects of the market and its environment, although the total agrarian program was more far reaching on the level of regulatory intervention.

The programs of the easy money forces with respect to monetary and banking reform were varied. Their partiality for paper money included at one time the demand for full legal tender status for greenbacks so that the greenbacks would have the same position in the country's money stock as gold. At other times they were for the abolition of the bond-linked national bank notes and their replacement with Treasury paper money in an amount equal to $50 per capita, together with geographical redistribution of currency more favorable to the West and South. Finally, they came out for the free coinage of silver into coin and currency. There is no doubt that Western silvermine owners, many of them millionaires, played an important role in getting the Populists to focus on the free silver issue and thereby led them into the Democratic party. Some Populist leaders and agricultural editors tried to preserve a broad reform Third party, but the politicians favorable to free silver won out.

The paper money movement linked its demands for more paper not only with bimetallism and hostility to gold and the resumption of specie payment in 1879, but with an attack upon the private creditor interests as represented by Federal bondholders. Demanding equal treatment for plowholder and bondholder, it variously called for total repudiation, repudiation of the obligation to pay principal and interest in gold only, and interconvertibility of government bonds with greenbacks. Other proposals were the elimination of the bond-connected arrangement for restriction of national bank note issues, and reduction or elimination of interest on the government debt. Certainly the Treasury's refunding at lower interest during the seventies was partly a response to this attack upon the transfer burden represented by the Federal bond interest cost averaging over $100 million a year—over one-third of all Federal government expenditures during that decade.

The antagonism to bondholder creditors was extended to an antagonism to private bankers as a group. The focus here was on the National Banking system, however. Both of the white Farmers' Alliances in 1889, for example, demanded the abolition of the national banks. The agrarians were bridling under the high cost and unavailability of credit to farmers associated with a private banking system and thought public banks would be preferable. They asked for a postal savings system, the elimination of the government depository banks and the substitution of subtreasuries. The white Southern Alliance proposed the famous subtreasury plan to make one-year loans to farmers at 1 percent on nonperishable products as collateral, and the Northwestern Alliance advocated a Federal bureau to make loans at 2 percent on agricultural land as collateral. Thus the proposed monetary and banking reforms of the agrarians rounded out their extensive set of demands for intervention in many other spheres.

The Income Tax

Meanwhile the clamor for an income tax, first imposed on the Federal level during the Civil War, and usually associated with the graduated progressive rate feature, was also given strong leadership, along with labor, by the agrarian revolt. The Federal wartime tax had been preceded, it is significant to note, by the introduction of income taxes in six states in the 1840s.[6] The battle for a Federal income tax was waged with varying intensity from the time of the termination of the Civil War tax in 1872 until final acceptance by constitutional amendment on February 25, 1913, and subsequent legislation in the same year. Just prior to passage of the income tax amendment there had been a wave of state corporation and personal income taxes passed. Wisconsin adopted the first effective state progressive income tax in 1911.

The graduated income tax was the most important single reform in public revenue systems in modern times. Excises, the real estate tax, and custom duties had completely dominated the systems of regularized taxation since antiquity, and they dominated in the main the U.S. state, local, and Federal system taken as a whole until the end of this period, i.e., until several decades after the industrial and urban transformation of the economy had made the introduction of a more equitable tax a democratic imperative. It should be noted, however, that the income tax was a major *addition* to a predominantly regressive tax system (slightly ameliorated by government spending for the poor). It did not replace, and indeed has not yet by any means completely replaced, taking the U.S. tax system as a whole, the regressive system inherited from the distant past.

The struggle for tax progressivity was thus not by any means fully successful in this period, but it made giant strides forward. The forces on the income tax side were spearheaded by the farmers' organizations, the Greenback-Labor Party, and, as usual, Congressmen from the West and South beginning in the late seventies. They were aided by the small surpluses in the Federal budget from 1873 to 1879. The forces against the income tax were made up of the usual hard core antiagrarian, antilabor "malefactors of great wealth" as Theodore Roosevelt once called them. In the eighties the movement smoldered under the avalanche of large Federal budget surpluses that induced controversy to center on tariff revision and how to dispose of the surpluses. But there was some activity. The Knights of Labor, the most powerful labor organization in U.S. history up to that time, came out for a graduated income tax in 1886. A great deal of intense, cooperative political activity between farmers and workers in favor of the income tax during 1886 and 1887 had only an insignificant impact, partly because of the considerable adverse influence of Henry George's atavistic alternative proposal for a single tax on the capital gains accruing to landowners through general economic development.

The nineties were a more fateful decade. The reiteration of farmers' demands for a graduated income tax by the Northwest Alliance in 1889 inaugurated a new upsurge that was soon picked up and vigorously advanced by the Populists and liberal Democrats. In time even a group of insurgent Republicans joined their ranks. So successful was the new upsurge that, with the aid of public dissatisfaction with the McKinley Tariff and declining Federal surpluses, turning into deficits beginning in the last six months of fiscal 1893, the Congress passed a trailbreaking income tax bill as part of the Wilson-Gorman Tariff in July 1894, and Cleveland allowed it to become law without his signature the next month. It was, however, a nongraduated, proportional tax of only 2 percent on all personal and corporate incomes over $4,000, and was to expire in 1900. But even this was too "communistic" a violation of the sacred rights of private property for the Supreme Court, which declared all the income tax provisions of the law unconstitutional in May 1895.

From the date of the infamous reactionary decision frustrating the will of the majority of the people as represented by the Congress, the battle was joined between farmers, labor, small businessmen, Progressives, and latterly, insurgent Republicans and substantial elements, even among the wealthy, on the one hand, and a distinctly hardcore minority, on the other hand, at the center of the Establishment. Ultimate success in the long battle was not to be prevented by passage in 1909 of a diversionary 1 percent "excise" tax on corporate net income over $5,000, and in July of that same year Congress passed overwhelmingly the constitutional amendment for an income tax that was, to the chagrin of Rhode Island's Senator Aldrich and his plutocratic followers, speedily ratified by the necessary number of states.

We have suggested earlier in this work that, while the graduated income tax was a great victory for equity and the submerged socioeconomic strata, it was less of a victory than those low-income groups believed it to be, and also not nearly as radical as many among the vested property interests believed it to be. With respect to the latter it is noteworthy that many wealthy conservatives, led politically by the insurgent Republicans and conservative Democrats, came around to support the tax during the Progressive era. The tip-off should have come when Andrew Carnegie came out in 1890 for a Federal progressive inheritance tax. And again, James C. Carter, leader of the American bar, had argued before the Supreme Court in 1895 on the 1894 income tax case that the best way to preserve private property was to relieve the masses of the people from excessive and inequitable tax burdens. [7]

Theodore Roosevelt, who was an ardent defender of capitalism, but could distinguish fearsome socialism from reformist populism, called for a Federal income tax and inheritance tax in June 1907. [8] The conservative Democrat Joseph W. Bailey had also favored an income tax as early as 1897, and he joined ranks with the conservative but independent Republican Senator William E. Borah in the crucial debates in 1909. [9] The progressive tax reform, as with such reform, was always a two-edged weapon. It not only left intact the system of private property rights but also made its own peculiar, modest, and equalitarian contribution to the stability of the long-run distribution of income between property and labor and the stability in the very long run of the after tax rate of return on property at approximately 8 percent.

When the agrarian's monetary and banking program is combined with their fiscal program and all the other demands of the farmers, mentioned above, it is clear that the movement did represent one effort to modify in important ways, not the growth rate, but the distribution of income as it impinged on the agricultural sector. The economic result in the intermediate period was, however, merely to contribute to securing some modifying regulatory legislation in the fields of public utilities and monopoly, some mitigation of the secular price decline, some modernization of the banking system, some improvement in agricultural credit-creating institutions, and the graduated income tax. In the longer run the late nineteenth century agrarian protest contributed significantly, along with the more important influence of labor and the Progressives, to the demise of laissez faire and the emergence of the mixed economy. However, it is doubtful that if affected the distribution of income much if at all.

At best the agrarian movement helped to protect a small enterprise sector from a more serious deterioration of its disadvantaged status in a now big enterprise system. Small farm enterprise labored under all the difficulties of urban small business plus the vagaries of the weather and exceptionally great barriers to exit. [10]

With easy entry and difficult exit, the atomistic farm firm suffered rates of return probably far below the norm for even petty urban enterprise. Indeed, the structure of the terms of trade is such that it is doubtful family farmers *as enterpreneurs* received any income above what they would have received as farm laborers. This is likely the case generally for peasant agriculture throughout the world. In more recent times in the United States, however, agriculture has fortified its power position by influencing government policy and by virtue of the structural changes within the sector that have gradually destroyed the family farm and made farming big business.

Labor's Response to Industrial Capitalism

Farmers confronted the new corporate power centers in the product markets, employees in the factor markets for their personal services. The factor markets for labor involved much more than bargains over the prices of commodities or services. Unlike the farmers' product markets, in the labor markets in 1865, workers sold and employers bought between 10 and 11 hours of a person's daily time, on the employers' premises, at the disposition and under the surveillance of the employers, and subject to a highly structured system of "labor discipline." In such situations, "market" relationships persisted throughout the six-day workweek, which made up much the greater part of the employees' waking life. As business proprietors the small farmers did not experience any such direct, intimate, and continuous interweaving of human and pecuniary influences. Hence the daily clash of human and property rights between labor and business in the industrial sector exhibited in this period a bitter and bloody pattern whose intensity was not to subside until big business came to terms with the institution of collective bargaining, and the government became an established third party in industrial disputes, some years after the inauguration of the mixed economy, i.e., from about the end of World War II.

Whereas no important social group seriously questioned the legitimacy of organization by farmers to agitate for economic and political redress for their alleged grievances, labor's efforts to build a countervailing power center to cope with the original power of large enterprise in the nonfarm sector were often met with a savage suppressive exercise of naked power by business to protect the rate of return on property. The eminent historians Samuel Eliot Morison and Henry Steel Commager once referred to the nineteenth century's "double standard of morality," one for business and another for labor, by which they meant that business organization was eminently respectable, but labor organization to further its interests was considered conspiratorial and a menace to society. Although the Massachussets Supreme Court as early as 1842 in the case of *Commonwealth v. Hunt* had upheld the right of workers to organize, collective bargaining between business and labor in the post-Civil War decades was still deemed by many to be a revolutionary threat to private property.

In good classical fashion, employers believed that wages and profits were inversely related and, more generally and statically, maximizing profits required minimizing wage costs, i.e., labor's livelihood. In the climate of the times, business was able to mobilize quite easily in most cases of overt conflict the overwhelming military power of the state and Federal governments, state legislatures, the judiciary, and private bands of mercenary toughs, deputized with legal police authority although responsible only to private corporations, to break strikes and to counter workers' violence or alleged threats of violence. [11] These early decades of labor's efforts to maximize wages and better its job conditions through organization were marked by inordinate violence and bloodshed, with the odds in most cases very much against labor.

Labor had many decisions to make about its program and organizational strategy. The quarter century from 1860 to the late eighties was noteworthy for such experimentation in both areas. But in the strategic 1880s, which added to the labor force for a brief period almost as many organizationally "eligible" workers in manufacturing, mining, and construction as had been added in the *two* preceding decades together, labor's major lines of attack and defense were set, and the trade union movement began to assume the patterns of organization and activity that were to dominate until the 1930s.

From the 1850s through those experimental years, a number of crafts set up regional or national organizations and also came together in the larger cities to form city federations, or "trades assemblies," composed of the various local trade unions. But as the national market developed, the national trade union became the dominant organizational form. It is notable that the *craft* formed the basis of viable labor organization then, as it had even earlier, and that the semiskilled and unskilled, like farm wage earners, women, and black workers, were generally excluded from the main stream of organization except when the Knights of Labor flourished between 1879 and 1886. Prominent exceptions were the brewery workers' and the powerful coal miners' unions. Important craft unions in the sixties and seventies were to be found in the printing and building trades, and among the shoemakers, cigarmakers, coopers, iron puddlers and molders, machinists and blacksmiths, and the prominent locomotive engineers.

Thus labor made an early decision not to organize unions on industrial lines, a decision that, given the long run advance of technology with its accompanying dilution of skills, was to exclude from the unions an ever rising number of the eligible labor force. The semiskilled and unskilled made up over one-third of the total labor force in 1910.

The experimental years from the Civil War to 1886 resolved not only the question of craft versus industrial unionism, but also determined that organized labor, unlike British labor, would not form its own permanent political party, would concentrate on issues around the job such as wages, hours, and working conditions and would resort to strikes and boycotts only in extreme cases. Moreover, it would rely overwhelmingly upon its own class resources and reject abiding alliances with other, possibly sympathetic, social strata, and would remain all-white segregationist. Also, while it did exert itself to some extent to influence both the law and judicial policy, a long record of administrative sabotage of eight-hour legislation (among other things) induced organized labor to emphasize direct confrontation with employers in its efforts to better its conditions.

These were the outstanding features of the mainstream of organized labor's program after the experimental period. During the experimental years from the Civil War until the late 1880s some of these abiding orientations had already emerged, but others provided areas of policy conflict within the labor movement. For example, the so-called "National Labor Union" that was prominent from 1866 to 1872 attempted to bring about nationalization of a labor movement built chiefly around the demand for an eight-hour day based on the conviction of Boston machinist Ira Steward and his wife that "whether you work by the piece or the day, decreasing the hours increases the pay" and raises the worker from the subhuman to the morally, intellectually, and socially human level of existence. [12]

The National Labor Union advocated this lasting and wide-spread proposal of labor for allocating the productivity increment between work and leisure, together with other frequent demands for larger social measures such as employment of women and Negroes in industry, a mechanic's lien law, and an increase in green-back currency (1867). Additional measures it supported included the disposition of the public domain only to actual settlers, estab-lishment of cooperative stores and workshops, elimination of tene-ment house pauperism, and the early formation of a national inde-pendent labor party. Nevertheless, the National Labor Union foundered on the central task of organizing trade unions. It was almost exclusively, and through time increasingly, oriented toward *legislation*, economic and otherwise. It gave only sentimental support to the local union, and it was very hostile to the use of the strike as a union weapon. Consequently, out of some twenty national unions in existence throughout the years of its life, not more than four sent delegates to any of the NLU conventions. [13]

Failure to base its organization on the existing trade unions was also the chief reason the NLU never had sufficient revenues to func-tion as an organization.

William H. Sylvis, president of the NLU, was an idealist like Terence V. Powderly, Grand Master of the Knights of Labor, from 1879 to 1893. They both believed in producers' cooperation rather than in the capitalistic wage system:

> Powderly bore unmistakably the stamp of . . . idealism throughout all the time he was the foremost labor leader in the country. Unlike Samuel Gompers, who came to supplant him about 1890, he was foreign to the spirit of combative unionism which accepts the wage system but concentrates on a struggle to wrest concessions from the employers. Even when circum-stances which were largely beyond his control made Powderly a strike leader on a huge scale, his heart lay elsewhere—in circumventing the wage sys-tem by opening to the worker an escape into self-employment through cooperation. [14]

The search for alternatives to the wage system, along with green-backism, independent political party organization, belief in the harmony of all "producing class" interests, abhorrence of strikes and strike reserve funds, and failure to vigorously organize workers around the job characterized the dominant tone of the labor move-ment throughout the experimental years, culminating with the "great upheaval" of railroad strikes under the leadership of the Knights during 1885-1887. The influence of the agrarian traditions of the past, of the continued importance of agriculture in the economy, and the large members of recent rural-urban migrants in the industrial labor force all contributed to the slow pace at which "pure and simple trade unionism" took hold.

Yet it was pure and simple trade unionism that was to become dominant, indeed that already dominated labor organization in the railroad industry—the sector of the country's first big business. Although it was not then recognized, the wave of the future was marked by the founding of the Brotherhood of Locomotive Engineers in 1863. Other Brotherhoods were subsequently established among the firemen, conductors, and brakemen (switchmen), all devoted primarily to the negotiation of very concrete economic matters pertaining to the job.

Meanwhile the Noble and Holy Order of the Knights of Labor was founded by Uriah H. Stephens and a group of Philadelphia garment workers in 1869. But the time was not propitious, for no sooner had it gotten under way than it was struck, like the membership of nearly all the loose-knit, decentralized, national trade unions then existing, by the depression and the accompanying employers' antiunion attacks of 1873-1878. During the depression years 1873-1879, wage cuts were met with bitterly fought strikes by a number of trade unions, particularly in cigarmaking, textiles, and coal mining. The year 1877 was marked by a nationwide railroad strike during the month of July set off by a wage cut on the Baltimore and Ohio Railroad system. The struggle was violent, many persons were killed and wounded, and Federal troops intervened for the first time in a national industrial conflict. Many state legislatures re-enacted conspiracy laws. Labor reacted by turning to politics, some workers temporarily to radical movements, e.g., socialism. Meanwhile trade union membership had fallen drastically from about 300,000 in 1869 to perhaps 50,000 in 1878.

With the return of prosperity in 1880 the stage was set for another upsurge in "pure and simple" trade union membership and organization, and also for the growth of the Knights of Labor, the organization that was to dominate the labor history of the eighties. The Knights was to enroll the largest number of workers in U.S. labor history up to that time, and yet to go out of effective existence with the closing years of that decade. Thus the eighties again stands out as a special period in economic history, for it marks the heyday and the end of labor's grand experiments with certain types of organization it believed could best represent its interests. As this "great upheaval" came to an end, straight job-conscious business unionism was fastened upon the labor movement as the dominant organizational vehicle for decades to come.

The Knights, unlike the AFL, was not a national federation of trade unions. Neither was it a political party. In form it resembled a national union of workers of all types of skill. Organized into local and district assemblies, most of them mixed in crafts and skills, the Knights were a highly centralized group, with the assembly directly responsible to the general executive board and the Grand Master Workman.

Its moderate central goals, while including the eight-hour day, the substitution of arbitration for strikes, job safety laws, a "national circulating medium," and the reservaiton of all land for actual settlers, emphasized production and market cooperatives, "education" of the masses, and the unity of all "producers" — workers, farmers, and small proprietors — regardless of craft or skill, race or sex, or political belief. But it did not lay out or execute a program of action to implement these broad goals. Moreover, the leadership was hostile to what it considered the narrow orientation of craft-unionism. When the leadership of the Knights did find itself reluctantly but actively supporting big strikes and boycotts during the first half of the eighties and in 1886, it was due to the overwhelming pressure of the rank and file.

The Knights was initially a secret organization that, like the terrorist "Molly Maguires" in the anthracite coalfields and others that were not terrorist, attracted many organized workers in the seventies whose open unions were falling apart under the depression blows of unemployment, wage cuts, and employers' attacks on the right to organize. But under pressure from the Catholic Church, which was hostile to any secret order, the new Grand Master Powderly in 1878 led the Knights into the open, just in time to make the most of the Juglar upswing beginning 1879. Thus membership in the organization grew from only 9,000 in 1878 to about 43,000 in the Juglar cyclical peak year 1882.[15]

However, the membership of the Knights was responding thereafter to powerful forces that were much too strong to be dominated by the mere cyclical determinants of labor union membership, for in the Juglar downswing from 1882 to 1885 membership increased to over 100,000. And the membership record thereafter was practically independent of business cycle influences (compare Figure 7, page 240):

1885	104,000
1886	703,000
1887	501,000
1888	260,000
1889	221,000
1890	100,000

How do labor historians explain this phenomenal rise and fall? The rise was brought about by a swing toward small producers co-operatives and a militant, sometimes socialistic, upsurge of the un-skilled and semiskilled elements among the workers; particularly among the predominantly foreign-born in the larger cities. The Knights' trade assemblies were allowed to strike without prior ap-proval of the organization's top officials. Often the workers joined the Order after they had already gone on strike.[16] The Knights were involved in several railroad strikes in 1883 and 1884. The ca-pitulation of one of the leading capitalists in th United States, Jay Gould, in a combined strike-lockout-boycott war in 1885 involving the Knights on labor's side, encouraged labor everywhere and pro-duced almost a stampede to join the burgeoning Order.

The craft unions, many of whose members carried two cards, also doubled their membership in 1886, but not because of the Knights. Rather was it due to a successful national eight-hour day strike in May 1886 that had been planned for two years as a growth-stimu-lating campaign by the AFL's forerunner, the craft-based Federation of Organized Trades and Labor Unions (FOTLU). The eight-hour day argument had now become a "spread-the-work" argument in response to the unemployment problem. Powderly had issued a secret circular in March 1886 advising the Knights against rushing into the eight-hour day movement. To Powderly, "talk of reducing the hours of labor without reducing the power of mach-inery to oppress instead of to benefit, is a waste of energy." But the rank and file of both the FOTLU and the Order felt differently, and between 300,000 and 400,000 working people took part in the strike.

The equally rapid decline of the Knights after 1886 was not pri-marily due to public smear attempts to identify it with the Hay-market bombing in Chicago on May 4 during the eight-hour strike. Nor was it because of aggressive attacks upon it by the craft unions with which it was locked in ever more bitter conflict. (Selig Perlman argues to the contrary that the Knights were the aggressors against the craft organizations.) Rather it was due to a number of other factors among the most important of which were the short cycle of ascendency and failure of the Knights' producers' cooperatives (a movement inimical to simple trade unionism), and the failure of the Knights either to further the direct job interests of the unskilled or to support vigorously through the accumulation of reserve funds and continuous on-the-job contact the strike, the boycott, and general organization and resistance actions of the skilled workers. The indifferent pursuit of its own reform program and a systematic drive by newly formed employers' associations, beginning in 1886, to destroy the Order and eradicate labor organization generally were additional factors in the debacle.

The fate of the unskilled and unemployed already enrolled in the ranks of the Knights was particularly tragic, for they, like the black workers, were ruthlessly excluded from the leading trade union organizations that succeeded the Knights—the AFL and the Railroad Brotherhoods. The latter also failed to undertake vigorously the task, but weakly undertaken by the Knights, of overcoming employer resistance to the hiring of women. In many cases the rank and file, as in the cigarmakers, frustrated a liberal official policy toward female membership.

It was in the large cities particularly where the Knights had mushroomed in 1886 that their following was wiped out. Perlman notes that the great upheaval of the urban unskilled and semiskilled had ended and that the Knights had lost their hold forever on the wage-conscious, largely foreign, city population. Henceforth, during its few remaining years the Order would be an organization chiefly of rural and small town people, mechanics and self-employed small merchants and farmers with a middle-class philosophy. This group accounted in the main for the Knights' support of the Populists. [17]

This situation left the field open to the FOTLU, which had been formed in 1881 and became the AFL in a sharp break from the Knights in the fateful year 1886. Although the craft trades assemblies within the Knights did not openly attack the Order, their departure under duress in 1886 hastened the death of the Knights. Most of the Knights' local or district assemblies in the larger cities had been either craft or industrial unions, the former being frequently affiliated with national craft unions whose members carried two cards. These differed from the large minority of "mixed" assemblies made up of more than one craft and also having farmers, unskilled workers, and middle-class persons. It was in the industrial union and mixed assemblies in the cities that the unskilled and un-employed were concentrated. However, the middle-class elements were to be found mainly in the mixed assemblies in the small cities and towns, especially in the Middle West. The craft union trade assemblies in the larger cities were the heart of the group that broke away in 1886 to form the AFL.

The FOTLU, predecessor of the AFL, had included among others the Cigarmakers Union under Adolph Strasser (which had been for some time running a collision course with a socialist-led rival "Progressive Union" latterly backed by the Knights), the Amalgamated Association of Iron and Steel Workers, the important International Typographical Union, and the Lake Seamen's Union. Other crafts involved were the carpenters, coal miners, boiler makers, iron molders, coopers, granite cutters, and the cotton and wool spinners. There were also a number of city central trades and labor assemblies. The leading "international" (i.e., including Canadian) unions among the twelve AFL founders at the December 1886 convention were the cigarmakers, typographers, miners, carpenters, iron molders, and journeymen tailors. Samuel Gompers of the Cigarmakers Union was elected and remained president, except for one year, until 1924. Gompers, like his new organization, was a wage-and-hours business unionist, opposed, he confusedly thought, as much to theory as to socialism, and determined to keep unionism and politics divorced.

After the end of the experimental years, the dominating American Federation of Labor and the Railroad Brotherhoods embraced the prevailing laissez faire political climate by concentrating on building nationwide craft monopolies on the supply side of the market. With certain exceptions, this entailed until 1906 opposition to government intervention, both hostile and helpful, to the farmers' interventionist program, to the Progressives' prolabor endeavors, and of course to socialist and other radical groups.

The exceptions to noninterventionism were in general peculiarly connected with securing craft monopolies of the labor supply in order to improve working conditions. Prominent among the exceptions, both during the experimental years and afterwards, were organized labor's agitation for restricted immigration, Chinese exclusion, a protective tariff, limitations on the employment of child and convict labor, and curbs on the sale of convict labor products. Labor also engaged in "trade union political action" for securing of the eight-hour day standard, job safety legislation and accident compensation, abolition of state conspiracy laws as applied to labor unions, and exemption of labor from the application of the Sherman Antitrust Act of 1890. Above all after the late 1880s it strove for strict limitations on the devastating use of the injunction against labor in industrial disputes. These demands also brought the trade unions with reluctance into the arena of narrow party politics, their nonpartisan ballot policy of merely "rewarding friends and punishing enemies" was still designed primarily to better labor's position on the job or implement its power to bargain collectively about wages, hours, and working conditions. Only in an ancillary manner did organized labor, after the experimental years, indicate support for larger social goals such as public schools with free textbooks (in the pre-Civil War period also unions had agitated for public schools), old-age pensions, and woman suffrage.

So strong was conservative labor's anti-interventionism that it opposed even health and unemployment insurance! As Lloyd Ulman has acutely observed, the business unionists in the leadership of the AFL rejected measures "that would be regarded as competing with collective bargaining by providing the same types of benefits to wage earners through the alternative channels" as well as help from "do-gooders" in other social groups, help that might undermine labor's ability to help itself.[18] AFL president Samuel Gompers wrote in the *American Federationist* in 1915:

> Where there is unwillingness to accept responsibility for ones' life and for making the most of it, there is a loss of strong, red-blooded, rugged independence and will power ... we do not want to place more power in the hands of the government to investigate and regulate the lives, the conduct and the freedom of America's workers.[19]

This pro-laissez faire statement of the basic philosophy of the leading labor organizations from the end of the eighties through and past the end of the period under study was in sharp contrast with the interventionist thrust of the struggling Progressives during the years after the turn of the century.

The unionism of the new Federation and the four Railroad Brotherhoods (engineers, firemen, trainmen, and conductors) was challenged between 1887 and 1914 by small radical or industrial unions such as the industrial American Railway Union (1893-1897) under Eugene V. Debs, the militant independent Western Federation of Miners (1893-1911), with its offshoot, the socialist American Labor Union (1898-1905), and most important, the industrial syndicalist-socialist Industrial Workers of the World (1905-1918), or "Wobblies," under "Big Bill" Haywood. These challenges often exposed the dominant union organizations for their lack of militancy, their narrow craft orientation, their indeterminate policy toward political action, and their organizational neglect of the semi-skilled, unskilled, blacks, women, and other unorganized workers. In a vociferous but essentially ineffective way these maverick and revolutionary unions also questioned the acceptance of the wage system itself by the leading trade unions. But basically they failed to make a dent in the solid wall of white, wage-and-hour craft unionism.

While the AFL membership marked time with a near-constant total of about 275,000 from its inception until the cyclical and secular price trough year of 1897, the industrial sector entered a period of hardening class alignments and a violence-packed struggle by labor for the right to organize, to bargain collectively, and to strike about working conditions at the local and national level. It was also a period of powerful and successful antiunion action by large corporations in railroading, mining, and manufacturing, and of overwhelming judicial antiunionism exercised through the labor injunction and the application of the Federal interstate commerce and antitrust laws to labor unions. It was remarkable that labor unions held their own in absolute terms. But of course with approximately constant membership, their numbers failed to keep pace relatively with the growth, for example, of the total labor force in manufacturing, mining, transport, and construction of 2.3 million between 1890 and 1900. Total membership in all unions in 1900, after a sharp jump accompanying the Juglar and longswing upturns, was about 870,000 — only 9 percent of the 9.3 million workers in the four sectors referred to in Table 22.

One additional inhibiting influence on the growth of trade union membership was the cultural and linguistic heterogeneity of the urban working classes because of the very large proportion of immigrants from many lands. Despite the existence of pockets of union-minded and socialist workers, for example among the Germans, on balance national differences, ignorance of circumstances, and language barriers made it easier for employers to play one group off against another. Nor were the AFL and the Railroad Brotherhoods by any means bulwarks of solidarity with workers of differing national origin. Indeed, the AFL stand against open immigration and its support for more vigorous enforcement of the Chinese Exclusion

TABLE 22

TRADE UNION MEMBERSHIP, 1897-1914

Year	Average annual total trade union membership (millions) (1)	Average annual AFL membership (millions) (2)	AFL total trade union membership (percent) (3)	Total trade union membership/ all workers in manufacturing, mining, transportation, and construction (percent) (4)
1897	.45	.27	60	
1900	.87	.55	63	9.3
1902	1.38	1.02	75	
1904	2.07	1.68	80	20.0
1910	2.14	1.56	75	16.0
1914	2.69	2.02	75	18.0

Sources: Cols. (1) and (2) from U.S. Department of Commerce, *Historical Statistics of the United States* (Washington: GPO, 1960), p. 97, Series D 735-40. Persons engaged in the four sectors in col. (4) are from Lebergott in NBER, v. 30, p. 118, for 1900, 1910, and 1920, and by linear interpolation for 1904 and 1914.

Acts was underscored by its increasing national as well as racial chauvinism in the early twentieth century. Its attack on immigrants impeded several major organizing drives. For example, during the organizing campaign in the steel industry in 1909 and 1910, slavic workers were called "foreign intruders" by AFL official John Mitchell of the mine workers. [20] The building of craft monopolies in the labor market was historically associated with exclusionism, elitism, and chauvinism.

The policy of excluding blacks, or where necessary of organizing them into separate Federal locals, parallel locals, or segregated city central bodies, represented a hardening of white attitudes in the early twentieth century compared with the late nineteenth. Gompers, for example, was initially committed to inclusion of all workers in a given craft, regardless of race. But he gradually changed under pressure from other AFL leaders and the white rank and file. The upsurge of white reaction in the South in the late nineteenth and early twentieth centuries and the segregationist doctrine perpetuated by the Supreme Court in the notorious separate-but-equal *Plessy v. Ferguson* decision in 1896, contributed to the subsequently growing white exclusionism of the trade union movement. In the period under study, of course, trade union organization in the South was particularly weak, and the phenomenon of exclusionism and segregation in the Northern unions was less important quantitatively than later because of the relatively small black labor force in the non-South. As late as 1910, only 11 percent of the black population of about 10.25 million lived beyond the Mason-Dixon line. It was, however, heavily concentrated in a handful of Northern cities, and in those cities the blacks were systematically driven by the unions as well as by almost all forces in society into unskilled and menial work.

The great period of total trade union membership growth was during the long cyclical upswing 1897-1903, a growth based mainly on the organization of new craft unions. Thereafter, membership was approximately constant for seven years as another employers' direct antiunion drive gathered momentum, the judicial attack on labor intensified, and the white unskilled continued to be excluded. Then from 1910 through 1914 there was a "catching up" increase, mainly in the number of skilled workers brought into the existing trade unions, e.g., in coal mining, the railroads, and the building trades. Table 22 shows, however, that the proportion of organized to highly organizable workers in 1914 was no better than it had been ten years earlier.

Strikes

The emerging trade unions in this period, like the large corporation, typically used the method of direct confrontation in industrial disputes. Disagreement, usually over wages, hours, and the assertions by labor of a right to organize and bargain collectively, in many cases resulted in either the discharge or lockout of workers by the employers, or the strike of employees, or some combination of the two. Such confrontations were immediately wrought with potential violence because the two parties then became locked in a battle over whether the struck enterprise would continue to operate with nonstriking black or immigrant workers. Hence the history of labor organization under laissez faire, unlike the agrarian revolt, was often marked by violent and bloody industrial conflict.

With certain notable exceptions such as the demand of the Progressive Democratic Illinois governor John Peter Altgeld, for the withdrawal of Federal troops sent to Chicago during the Pullman strike of 1894, and some of the states' social legislation, e.g. protecting child labor, the power of government was strongly committed to the support of business. This alliance frequently if not usually had the active assistance of important groups within the urban public, ranging from respectable elements such as small businessmen, professionals and especially the press, to thugs and toughs. In the post-Civil War period, the judiciary was usually in the forefront of the business-government alliance, especially after the late 1880s. The state courts repeatedly nullified state legislation designed to protect labor's right to organize, and to restrain various types of employer antiunion activities, especially employers' use of the antiunion contract such as the peculiar "yellow-dog" contract, whereby a worker as a condition of employment agreed not to join a union. The lower federal courts had brought unions within the purview of the Sherman Antitrust Act long before the Supreme Court added its ultimate sanction in 1908 in the famous Danbury Hatters secondary boycott case (*Loewe v. Lawlor*, 208 U.S. 274). Just as the Federal judiciary had blocked the earlier efforts of agrarians to regulate private monopoly at the state level, and later of the ICC at the Federal level, so the judiciary at all levels was now blocking the efforts of labor to bargain collectively and independently with large private enterprises.

Most of the big strikes and mass discharges ended in defeat, in the immediate sense, for the workers between 1886 and 1914. Nevertheless, in the long run the labor movement received through those actions the gradual recognition that labor unions were here to stay, that they had the right not only to exist but to exert some collective control over wages, hours, and job conditions. For many years over 400,000 workers per year were involved in strikes, i.e., in 1894, 1897, and every year from 1899 through 1904. Unfortunately, there are no aggregate statistics on work stoppages covering the years from 1906 through 1913, but it is unlikely that figure was exceeded in any of those years.

A complete review of strike actions would not be appropriate here. However, some of the major conflicts that were significant in some way for the history of the labor movement may be noted. The next to the last serious railroad strike in this period was the strike against the Burlington and related railroad systems in 1888-1889.

The action involved wages and was led by the Brotherhood of Locomotive Engineers and the Locomotive Firemen. The workers were defeated, an outcome that in general provided a fitting preface to the history of the ensuing two decades of strike history. This strike sharply posed the question (unanswered in our period) of what was to be done about stoppages in "industries affected with a public interest."

The prosperity year 1892 was notable for a famous and violent strike in the gold, lead, and silver mines in the Coeur d'Alene area of Idaho, conducted spontaneously by a miners' union that eventually won a partial victory for the union. But an even more important action was the Homestead, Pennsylvania, strike of the powerful Amalgamated Association of Iron, Steel and Tin workers against the more powerful Carnegie Steel Company. A small army of Pinkerton police and the militia defeated the steel workers in the whole Pittsburgh region and broke the back of what was then the strongest craft union in U.S. history up to that time. According to Perlman's interpretation, the Homestead strike "forcibly demonstrated the unconquerable fighting strength of the modern large corporation . . . and the . . . far-reaching control which the employing class exercised over government, both state and national." [21] One important side result of the strike was the lesson for the workers that a tariff was no sure support for the wage level in a protected industry.

Over 660,000 workers (Perlman claims 750,000), were involved in defensive work stoppages in 1894, the greatest by far in the whole decade. Two strikes stood out, both involving wages, both defeated: that of the United Mine Workers in the Ohio area, and more important by far, the Pullman Strike. This latter action was initially directed by the spontaneous, Debs-led American Railway Union against the Pullman Palace Car Company, but soon spread as a sympathetic strike to the railroads, since the movement of Pullman cars on the roads was a closely related issue. Many Brotherhood members allied themselves with the strikes even though the Brotherhoods were officially opposed to the strike. The powerful General Managers Association smashed the strike and the union with the help of the federal courts and U.S. troops brought in despite the protest of Governor Altgeld.

The march of Jacob Coxey's "Army" of unemployed on Washington in the depression spring of the same year, a year in which 18 percent of the labor force was unemployed, was not a strike. Nevertheless, it and other less dramatic unemployed marches added up to significant workers' demonstrations reflecting the historically growing rejection of cyclical unemployment, another aspect of the private market system, by the urban laboring classes. In any age that generally accepted depressions as a necessary price for economic "progress," the demands of Coxey's Army of the Commonwealth of Christ anticipated the kind of overwhelming insistence of the unemployed for relief and public works that was to help topple the laissez faire approach to mass unemployment 39 years later.

The nineteenth century closed with a massive conflict in Chicago between the Building Trades Council and the Building Contracts' Council, the largest strike in the industry up to that time. The action involved between 50,000 and 60,000 construction workers. It was fraught with violence and lasted from February 1899 to February 1901, ending with the capitulation of the unions.

Direct employer aggression against collective bargaining by powerful and militant independent unions assumed two forms in the early years of the twentieth century. The first was the ferocious open shop drive to protect the alleged rights of nonunion and antiunion workers led by particular giant industrial corporations and such employer organizations as the National Association of Manufacturers. The second "enlightened" form was not to prevail until the latter half of the twentieth century and was represented preeminently by the short-lived National Civic Federation (1900-1905). The NCF was an association of large corporate representatives, some representatives of the "public" like Grover Cleveland, and participants from the AFL such as Gompers and John Mitchell of the United Mine Workers. The ruthless and brutal antiunionism of the times made the NCF a strange conception before World War I. Nevertheless, its belief that "organized labor cannot be destroyed without debasement of the masses" and that corporate oligopoly could gain from the market stability expected to accompany collective agreements and the absence of strikes embodied a comparatively clear vision of the long-run future of industrial relations. The NCF's conviction that "the twin foes of industrial peace are the antiunion employers and the socialists," was ineffective at the time against the first-named foe. But it helped to make the AFL more conservative, to isolate from the public the main centers of labor militancy, and to aid Gompers' drive to defeat the AFL's socialist-centered opposition within the trade unions.

In the raw-boned West in 1903 and 1904 the pattern of industrial violence reached its grimmest point of development in the strike of nonferrous metal miners organized by the militant Western Federation of Miners. Centered in the areas around Cripple Creek, Independence, Victor, Trinidad, Idaho Springs, and the Telluride district, the Colorado Mine Owners' Association entered upon a war to the death against the independent Western Federation that in the course of the strike received no help from the AFL. Although the mine owners were forced in the end to grant the eight-hour day, the union was crushed by the combined power of the mine owners, state militia, strike breakers, local vigilantes formed into the familiar "citizens" alliance, and deputized private police, who taken collectively represented almost the whole gamut of industrial warfare techniques. As revealed in that one industrial dispute alone, those techniques included illegal arrests, wholesale deportation of strikers, vagrancy orders against idle workers, defiance of *habeas corpus*, blacklists, martial law, suppression of freedom of the local press, the forced resignation of local civil authorities who exhibited either partiality or neutrality toward the strikers, and the rigged election of procorporation replacements for such civil authorities. But that was not all. The weapons employed against labor also included the institution of the "rustling card" (a grim sort of ID card), issue of warrants for the arrest of the national union officers in Denver, mob invasions of miners' homes, wrecking of union stores, offices, and apprentice-training equipment, seizure of relief orders for families of deported union men, and various armed attacks and killings. This was the kind of arsenal drawn upon to suppress union organization and strikes during this period, and it was understandably associated on frequent occasions with counterviolence by desperate union workers.

During the years 1902-1903 the United Mine Workers in the anthracite fields of eastern Pennsylvania waged a bitter and violence-ridden strike action for improved conditions and union recognition against a most intransigent coalition of mine owners. The intervention at various times during the strike of President Roosevelt, J. P. Morgan (!), the U.S. Attorney General, and the entire national guard of Pennsylvania ended with a binding commission report granting wage and working conditions concessions, but there was no recognition of the union as collective bargaining agent for the workers.

From the end of the Cripple Creek strike in 1904 until 1910 the union membership record shows that the employer offensive bore fruit. There was no growth during those "Progressive Years." The victory for business's antiunion policy was underscored by the defeat of a major steel strike in 1909-1910 conducted by the Amalgamated Association of Iron, Steel and Tin Workers with the help of the AFL against the U.S. Steel Corporation and the Bethlehem Steel Company. The Amalgamated was practically smashed as a result of three things: the inauguration of a policy of "welfare capitalism," anticipating the 1920s, by the Corporation beginning in 1902, including profit-sharing, a job-safety program, an old-age pension system, an employee home building program, and a number of other vocational, social, and health measures;[22] a parallel direct attack, employing the usual violent techniques, on Amalgamated workers at the time of the strike; and the failure of the Union during the preceding decade to bring in the mass of semiskilled and unskilled workers in the steel industry. There was no clearer demonstration of the crying need for industrial unions and the weakness of the craft union form in most of the heavy manufacturing industries by the time of World War I.

The AFL and Political Action

The economism of the AFL leadership and philosophy was antithetical to its participation in the political arena, as noted above. However, as a loose Federation of autonomous craft organizations it was under continual pressure from Progressives as well as the more militant class-conscious elements in the rank and file, particularly the socialist workers and their opposition unions. This pressure was exerted to try to get the unions to enter politics and exert an ameliorating influence as an organization on the oppressive legislative and judicial framework generally characterizing the laissez faire era. As a result, the Federation followed at times an erratic and wavering policy that broke out of its professed and overriding affinity for merely "rewarding labor's friends and punishing its enemies" through such actions as individual members' votes at the polls or letters to legislators. In the 1890s, the organization had come out for free silver, and was forced to mobilize political resistance to "government by injunction."

Under strong opposition the Federation in its 1894 convention had come out against both a socialist commonwealth and independent political action. But in 1895 — the year in which Gompers was reinstated as president after having been unseated by a socialist for one year — it merely recommended "more independent voting outside of party line" to union workers. In the Bryan campaign of 1896 AFL organizers participated, although the Federation as such refrained from committing itself. In 1906 there was a need to mount a counterattack against the employers' offensive and to combat the indiscriminate use of the blanket antilabor injunction. This induced a special conference of the heads of the leading international unions to submit a "Bill of Grievances" to the President of the United States and both houses of Congress. The Bill was in effect a collection of economic and political demands of long standing. But the important aspect of it was that the demands were introduced into the political arena at the highest level. The Bill also contained a threat that if its demands were ignored, the Federation would "appeal to the conscience and support of our fellow citizens." The indifferent response to the Bill in Washington prompted the Federation leadership to call upon its membership actively to push for prolabor candidates of the two major parties and where candidates were unresponsive to labor's demands, *to advance a straight labor ticket.* What was significant about this move was not its failure in the 1906 elections, but rather the fact that the Federation leadership had been compelled by events to deviate somewhat from both its pure and simple trade unionism and its politically pure and simple "reward friends and punish enemies" position.

Meanwhile the Federation had also been active on the state and local level, but its strong immigrant membership tended to tie the organization on the local level to the old line parties. Nationally however, Gompers, although not the Federation executive council, in 1908 again departed from his politically isolationist stand and for the first time entered a presidential campaign, supporting the Democratic candidate, William Jennings Bryan, because the Democratic platform was strongly prolabor. But a retreat to nonpartisanship began in the Congressional elections of 1910 when it again for the most part rewarded prolabor Republican and Democratic candidates and opposed antilabor ones. When the Progressive-Democratic Wilson was elected in 1912, and the Federation's belief in his Party's prolabor views was underscored two years later by the passage of the Clayton Antitrust Act — quite erroneously labeled labor's "magna charta" by Gompers—the retreat from advocacy of an independent political (labor party) organization to nonpartisanship was completed. Yet this type of nonpartisanship was not quite the same. The continuing war of big business against organized labor and the pressure from labor's ranks itself had involved the Federation's leadership in politics to a much greater extent than it had wished in the earlier laissez faire years. It even pointed with hesitant pride to a senator and a few Congressmen who carried union cards.

Wages and Hours

Because of its general interest and because labor's struggle for the right to organize and better its job conditions focused so much on the matter of wage and hours, it is worthwhile to take at least a quick glance at the record. Only the crudest aggregates can be treated here. It must be recognized that there were great sectoral variations. Also, we are mainly concerned with the nonfarm economy, since this was the area of labor's organizational response to industrialization and urbanization. Reference was made in Chapter 3 to the poor progress of real farm labor wage rates.

Table 23 shows the outlines of the wage and hour pattern, including by implication nonfarm labor's terms of trade. Adequate interpretation of these data would require an elaborate analysis, including extensive comparison with much other related data. Still we know enough to make some first approximations, particularly if we supplement the data in the table with other information. It is clear that when annual money wages are deflated, as here, by a consumer price index, the trend suggests that labor had reason to complain. It was not until the prosperity year 1883, when annual earnings of all employed nonfarm workers reached $459, that the pre-Civil War level was again achieved—almost a quarter of a century without a secular rise in real annual wages! We do not know the mixture of real and money wage rates in determining the effect of one or the other upon the motivations of workers. But in terms of money wages, a postwar peak was reached in 1868, at an average of $499 per year. This level was not exceeded in the remainder of the nineteenth century. But if we know how prices were falling, it makes good sense for understanding the long run at least to emphasize real annual wages. Moreover, such real earnings were closely related to

TABLE 23

NONFARM WAGES AND HOURS
1860-1914

| Year | Annual earnings | | Average prevailing hours worked | | Annual manhours per employee | Total economy: annual manhours per employee |
	Money (when employed) (1)	Real (1914 dollars) (2)	Per week	Per day (3)	(4)	(5)
1860	$363	$457		11.0		
1869	496	380	62.7	10.6	3,259	
1874	439	403		10.5		2,762[2]
1879	373	391	61.3	10.3	3,187	
1884	441	478		10.3		2,777[3]
1889	471	510	60.4	10.0	3,140	2,781
1899	470	563	59.1		3,073	2,776
1900	490	568	59.0[1]			
1902	519	583	58.3[1]			
1904	540	592	57.7[1]			
1909	594	586	56.8[1]		2,893	2,704
1914	682	620	55.2[1]			

[1]All manufacturing industries
[2]Decade average, 1869-1878.
[3]Decade average, 1879-1888.

Sources: Cols. (1) and (2), 1860-1899, from Stanley Lebergott, *Manpower in Economic Growth*, p. 528. Col. (1), 1900-1914, from *Historical Statistics of the United States*, p. 91, Series D 603-17, col. 604. Col. (2), 1900-1914, calculated from deflator estimated by linking Kendrick's price deflator for personal consumption expenditures (see U.S. Dept. of Commerce, *Long Term Economic Growth* (Washington: GPO, Oct. 1966), p. 200) with Lebergott's for col. (2), 1890s—the conversion coefficient being 1.727.
Col. (3), 1860-1899: weekly, from John W. Kendrick, *Productivity Trends in the United States*, NBER (Princeton: Princeton University Press, 1961), p. 310. Table A-IX; daily, from *Historical Statistics*, p. 90, Series D 573-7. Col. (3), 1900-1914, from ibid., p. 91, Series D 589-602.
Col. (4) calculated from Kendrick, *op. cit.*, p. 314, Table A-XI and p. 308, Table A-VII.
Col. (5) from *Long Term Economic Growth*, p. 192 (from Kendrick).

long-run changes in the living levels. And it is clear that the secular trend of real annual earnings was upward after the post-Civil War trough of $322 in 1866.

In the short run, labor as we know, often faced hourly or weekly money wage rate cuts to which it on occasion responded with vigor. Annual money wages fell, for example, in every year from a cyclical peak of $486 in 1872 to the 1879 trough of $373. Thus, both money and real wages fell in the seventies: the latter from $416 in 1872 to $391 in 1879. The eighties looked better in both aspects, with both money and real annual earnings increasing steadily. In the first decade of the twentieth century, after a moderate rise between 1899 and 1902, it appears that real annual earnings were approximately constant until 1909 (unless one were to use Rees's remarkable price index). But in the next half-decade, when union membership surged upwards, real wages also rose noticeably.

On the other hand, labor's increasing concern with the long hours of work in the eighties may perhaps be best comprehended in view of the fact that average daily standard hours, after an earlier decline, remained at 10.3 for the entire decade 1875-1885. Apparently some slight advance toward shorter standard hours took place in the late eighties, however. But *actual* as distinguished from *standard* full-time annual hours in the whole economy (including the shorter year and shorter workweek farmers) did not fall until after the turn of the century.

Labor in general in this period looked upon shorter hours as not only a way of securing more "leisure," and reducing work fatigue, but also, and perhaps mainly, of increasing wages and reducing unemployment by spreading work. Labor stuck quite consistently to its belief (and demands based on that belief) that "whether you work by the piece or by the day, reducing the hours increases the pay." Manufacturing labor cut the workweek an hour each decade until the turn of the century, and it took over a quarter century to cut the average workday from 11 hours to 10 hours. Inded the eight-hour day goal was not achieved in this period—even after the more rapid decline in weekly hours between 1900 and 1914.

Lionel Robbins, noted English economist, has argued that the connection between the wage rate and the demand for "leisure" is indeterminate in the twentieth century. But in the period under study, according to John Kendrick, the long hours of work in 1879 averaged 35 percent higher in the nonfarm sector than in farming. This fact undoubtedly endowed an additional hour off the job with a high degree of satisfaction—probably much more than the dissatisfaction associated with the wages foregone. Only as the workday became shortened did labor approach a long-run equilibrium point at which the satisfaction associated with an hour more of "leisure" began to appear about equal to the dissatisfaction from an hour's real wages foregone. But this equilibrium was certainly not closely approached in this period. Of course, to make use of what is somewhat naively called leisure time, it was necessary to spend more of one's income. The secularly rising real wage, by bringing recreational and other discretionary spending more within the reach of some workers, further inclined the more highly paid skilled workers, particularly, to agitate for more leisure (more reduction in hours of work). As economists put it, labor's shorter hours movement demonstrated that the income effect of secularly rising real wages was stronger than the tendency of such wage increases to induce workers to substitute secularly higher paying work for leisure.

A further question, although one extremely hard to treat properly, is to what extent the data in Table 22 provide an answer to how well nonfarm labor fared *relative* to the rest of the nonfarm economy. Again, a first approximation suggests that labor had reason to complain and to try to organize its countervailing power to that of big business. For example, from 1869 to 1899 real wages in the nonfarm sector rose about 1.25 percent per year. But private domestic nonfarm gross product per person engaged (including nonwage earners) rose at a rate of approximately 2.25 percent between 1874 and 1899, according to Kendrick's estimates.[23] This leaves an annual shortfall for labor of about 1 percentage point per year, a very substantial amount of output. It should be acknowledged in this connection that, other things being equal, unless real average hourly wages rise proportionately as fast as output per manhour, the share of wages in total product will fall. The relative share of nonfarm labor in nonfarm product in current dollars was, of course, the annual average wage when employed multiplied by the number of nonfarm workers and then divided by the total nonfarm product. Rough estimates of this quotient show the share may have fallen slightly between 1869 and 1899. With all of labor's wage raising activity in the years from the Civil War to the end of the century, it may not have assured the maintenance of its relative position in the nonfarm economy.[24] Referring to the years 1860-1890, Clarence Long once cautiously commented "despite the quickening in the 1880s, the pace of real wages and earnings during these three decades of almost unparalleled economic advance must, by present standards, be regarded as moderate . . . a time of rapid economic development out of a mainly agricultural setting is not necessarily the best for labor."[25]

It is customary to add the decline in hours which was at an annual compound rate of .25 percent over this period, to the rise in the real wage rate to get a "net" real wage change. This would give a real wage increase of 1.5 percent per year. However, this procedure, although in accord with organized labor's beliefs, introduces welfare considerations into the interpretation to an undesirably controversial degree. Although more time off the job per week and per day was preferred by workers, the released time did not necessarily represent decreased job-related input effort. For example, the intensity of labor during the remaining hours on the job may have increased. The spread of Frederick W. Taylor's "scientific management" system may have increased the tempo of work in manufacturing and the greater use of power-driven machinery certainly raised the proportion of serious job injuries. Also, commutation time may have increased to fill part of the new "leisure" hours, and it is debatable, as suggested by miners' demands for "portal-to-portal" pay, whether commutation to and from work is a leisure time activity. In any case, the question of relative shares of *output per unit of input effort* that is involved in this approach, is too complex to be approached here.

With respect to the period 1899 to 1914, when the rate of hours reduction was faster, Table 23 suggests that real annual earnings in the nonfarm sector rose at an annual rate of only .67 percent, whereas gross private domestic nonfarm output per person engaged sluggishly rose at about the same rate, again according to Kendrick. Thus nonfarm labor apparently fared *relatively* better than in the late nineteenth century, when real wages rose faster and hours reduction was slower. Indeed it at least seems to have maintained its comparative share of the productivity increment. (If one were to consider the hours decline, one would find an annual rise in labor's "net" real wage of 1.17 percent, since average weekly hours fell strongly at an annual rate of .5 percent.) Even the wages of farm workers increased, and as rapidly as the money wages of the average nonfarm workers between 1899 and 1914: from $239 to $351 per year.

The rise in real wages was no doubt due to a combination of factors whose relative weights are unkown. Paul Douglas counterfactually hypothesized many years ago[26] that the productivity increase in the quarter century after 1890 would have bequeathed to labor a rise in wages even in the absence of any unionization. Perhaps so, but it is also plausible that the "Progressive Years" of middle-class sympathy for labor, together with the more important lagged effects of labor's direct influence over the decades, also finally bore some fruit after 1909. Although incredible conditions, such as the twelve-hour day and the seven-day week, still prevailed in many manufacturing industries such as iron and steel, the long struggle leading toward the 40-hour week was well under way in many important sectors of the nonfarm economy.

But rising real wages and reduction of working hours were only two important components of the improvement in material conditions that, while leaving much to be desired, had already at the beginning of this period produced the highest average level of living in the world. This condition apparently was just as conducive to the growth of "pure and simple" trade unionism as absolutely increasing misery. Such trade unionism was destined to have a virtual monopoly of labor organization until massive misery struck the working classes with untold force in the 1930s.

One prominent form of improvement between 1870 and 1914 was in the area of education. Although the number of child laborers reached a peak in 1910, it was nevertheless also true that enrollment in public day schools of all persons 5 to 17 years of age rose from only 57 percent in 1870 to 74 percent in 1914. The average number of days attended per enrolled pupil also rose substantially, from 78 per year to 118 over the same period. The percentage of the population at least 17 years old who were high school graduates rose from only 2 percent to about 9 percent in 1910—a poor showing relative to the recent figures approaching 75 percent, but nonetheless an advance relative to the past.

A second powerful indicator of material advance is length of life and the expectation of life at various ages. A female's life expectancy at birth in 1850 in Massachusetts was only 40.5 years, but by 1909-1911 it was 53.1 years. Life expectancy at age twenty for females in 1850 was 40.2 years but by 1909-1911 it had advanced to 44.9 years. The greater advance for the former estimate—expectancy at birth—was due to the influence of the decline of the high rate of infant mortality. Of course, racial differences were scandalous: in 1914 the life expectancy at birth for white females in the United States was 57.5 years, but for nonwhite females it was only 40.8 years. This adverse ratio for nonwhites had risen only two percentage points since the turn of the century.

The improved life span to a significant extent reflected a gradual improvement in diet and in health services. Although the number of physicians per 100,000 population had *fallen* from 150 in 1870 to 144 in 1914, their "productivity," and more importantly the effort and productivity of health and sanitation workers, had risen. This was shown by the fact that the war against many diseases had scored numerous victories, such as sharply declining death rates from tuberculosis, typhoid fever, diphtheria, influenza, and pneumonia. In essence, while much advance was still needed in the sphere of peoples' health, education, and welfare, considerable progress could be recorded by 1914. But labor still had many welfare fronts on which to fight, including job safety and accident prevention, the coffee break, housing conditions, health and accident insurance, unemployment insurance, old age pensions, and of course the shorter workday.

NOTES

1. The most highly politicized farmers were those from the wheat-growing and cotton-growing areas; corn-hog farmers, dairy farmers, truck farmers, etc. were less active.
2. Irwin Unger, *The Greenback Era* (Princeton, N.J.: Princeton University Press, 1964), p. 202.
3. Ibid., p. 202.
4. Solon J. Buck, *The Agrarian Crusade* (New Haven, Conn.: Yale University Press, 1921), p. 54.
5. Rate data upon which the following discussion is based, are from Fred A. Shannon, *The Farmer's Last Frontier* (New York: Farrar and Rinehart, 1945), pp. 296-7.
6. See Sidney Ratner, *Taxation and Democracy in America* (New York: John Wiley & Sons, First Science Edition, 1967), pp. 55-6.
7. Ibid., pp. 196-9, *passim*.
8. See ibid., p. 261.
9. Ibid., p. 283.
10. The barriers to exit resided chiefly in the immobility of owner-operators long committed to farming. Outward immobility stems from (1) the low transferability of agrarian training (human capital) as well as of tangible farm capital to urban occupations, (2) the appeal of farmwork because of its flexibility and diversity together with a work regimen set largely by the operator, (3) the security of a partially self-produced food supply, (4) the appeal of the rural environment, and (5) devotion to "farming as a way of life."
11. Gerald Grob has claimed that in smaller communities labor often got the support of local government [see his *Workers and Utopia* (Evanston: Northwestern University Press, 1961)].
12. John R. Commons et al., *History of Labor in the United States* (New York: Macmillan, 1936), v. II, pp. 90, 99.
13. Philip Taft, *Organized Labor in American History* (New York: Harper and Row, 1964), p. 65.
14. Selig Perlman, *A History of Trade Unionism in the United States* (New York: Macmillan, 1929), p. 71.
15. See Selig Pearlman, "Upheaval and Reorganization," in John R. Commons et al., op. cit., pp. 339, 344.
16. Harry A. Millis and Royal E. Montgomery, *Organized Labor* (New York: McGraw-Hill, 1945), p. 65.
17. John R. Commons et al., op. cit., p. 423.
18. "The Development of Trades and Labor Unions," in Seymour Harris (ed.), *American Economic History* (New York: McGraw-Hill, 1961), p. 388.
19. Quoted in Foster Rhea Dulles, *Labor in America*, second revised ed. (New York: Thomas Y. Crowell, 1959), p. 201.

20. See Herbert Hill, "The Racial Practices of Organized Labor — The Age of Gompers and After," in Arthur M. Ross and Herbert Hill (eds.), *Employment, Race and Poverty* (New York: Harcourt, Brace, and World, 1967), p. 389.
21. John R. Commons et al., op. cit., p. 499.
22. See Selig Perlman and Philip Taft, *History of Labor in the United States, 1896-1932* (New York: Macmillan, 1935), pp. 138-9.
23. John W. Kendrick, *Productivity Trends in the United States*, National Bureau of Economic Research (Princeton, N.J.: Princeton University Press, 1961), p. 338, Table A-XXIII.
24. Estimates by Edward C. Budd, "Factor Shares, 1850-1910," in National Bureau of Economic Research, Conference on Research in Income and Wealth, *Trends in the American Economy in the Nineteenth Century*, Studies in Income and Wealth, v. 24 (Princeton, N.J.: Princeton University Press, 1960), pp. 365-89, particularly p. 373, show wages as percentage of industry income to have been 50.3 percent in 1869-1870 and 51.5 percent in 1899-1900. More recent work has made it more difficult, if anything, to discover the actual trends. In a discussion of "Factor Shares in the Long Term," National Bureau of Economic Research, Conference on Research in Income and Wealth, Studies in Income and Wealth, v. 27, *The Behavior of Income Shares* (Princeton, N.J.: Princeton University Press, 1964), Stanley Lebergott asks "what basis do we have for asserting that the share of wages in the national income prior to 1919 was in fact stable? The answer, in brief, is: very little" (p. 67).
25. Clarence D. Long, *Wages and Earnings in the United States, 1860-1890*, National Bureau of Economic Research (Princeton, N.J.: Princeton University Press, 1960), p. 118.
26. Paul Douglas, *Real Wages in the United States, 1890-1926*, Pollak Foundation for Economic Research, Publication No. 9 (Boston: Houghton Mifflin, 1930).

[12]

The balance of payments and foreign economic policy

Developmental Aspects of the Balance of Payments

The vast structural and functional changes within the U.S. economy in the half century under review, like rather similar changes in many of the international trading countries, wrought massive transformations in the balance of payments of the United States as well as in the country's policy relationships with other lands. We have already pointed out at various places in the earlier discussion that the country continued to be an international debtor throughout the period, although its future creditor status was already clearly discernible long before World War I. It has also been noted that there was a vast international migration to the United States, infusing the economy with what amounted to a very substantial investment in "human capital," and that this immigration era was to end soon after World War I. Furthermore, the trade balance became typically positive after 1875. U.S. manufacturing had grown to a notable extent through import substitution by the end of the century. Coincident with the ending of the frontier and the growth of industry, many private interests had acquired new stakes in foreign investment, accordingly committing the government to new efforts, many of those efforts having a distinct imperial complexion, to protect those investments. Finally, it has been seen that the economic foreign policy of the domestically laissez faire government of the United States was chronically and strongly protectionist, even though protection permitted the tariff to continue to perform a major revenue-raising function.

Probably all these changes made some positive contributions to the development of the private market system as that system was then constituted, for they all served in some way to bolster either the probusiness environment or the rate of return on, and therefore the flow of, new private investment in plant and equipment. The economy did not, except for cyclical depressions, notably in 1873-1877 and 1893-1897, confront a problem of chronically inadequate aggregate demand. Development policy at the time, insofar as one can speak of policy, was rather to facilitate industrialization and urbanization through restricting aggregate consumption and maximizing saving and investment. We have seen in the last chapter how the course of wages and the constriction of the wage share contributed to this. Both the economy's international connections and economic foreign policy also contributed.

It will be recalled that the U.S. international balance of payments summarizes the flow of all its transactions, both real and financial with the rest-of-the-world over any time period. The balance of payments has three sections: the current account, showing goods and services flows; the capital account, showing long term financial transactions; and the cash or gold account, showing the flows of short term credit or gold. The "gold account" under the international gold standard shows the extent of cash flows necessary to finance the net flows of the other two sections. It is the balancing flow that makes the total balance of payments always balance.

All transactions requiring a payment by the rest of the world are called exports, receipts, or credits (plus sign). All transactions requiring a payment to the rest of the world are called imports, payments, or debits (minus sign). The totals of all credits and all debits must be equal, i.e., must balance. In this sense a balance of payments always balances. If sections or subsections, such as total commodity trade do not balance, the difference must be made up somewhere. For example, during 1869-1873 the U.S. current account was, taken net, in deficit: the country purchased more goods and services from abroad than it sold. This was all made up

for by increasing U.S. indebtedness to foreigners. Getting loans from abroad is effectively "exporting" something, in this case IOUs, for which persons in the U.S. *receive a "payment"* (hence a credit). But the various items making up the balance of payments are compiled individually, separately, and from different sources. Hence we cannot "match" or link together specific transactions involving a receipt with other specific exchanges requiring payment. The data sources do not reveal any connections among the various items in the balance of payments.

Until the mid-seventies an import balance on merchandise account, the main component of the current account of the balance of payments, helped the economy consume, in capital goods and consumer goods, more than it produced. This trade deficit was happily financed partly by gold outflows (every year from 1862 to 1876!), and partly by net borrowings from abroad. The first row of Table 24, covering the years 1869-1873 illustrates certain aspects of this relationship insofar as it is reflected in the balance of payments. There the last historic five-year deficit period for the balance of trade is seen in col. (1) and the service charge on net international liabilities of $418 million in col. (2). In that five years, U.S. net liabilities to foreigners increased over $600 million. This shows that the United States was behaving like an immature debtor in those five years: the inflow of new loans exceeded the service charge on the total of accumulated liabilities. By contrast, during 1894-1898 total liabilities fell absolutely, while the service charges were very large. Such behavior was that of a mature debtor. As a mature debtor it was appropriate for the United States to have a positive balance of trade, since this helped provide the foreign exchange with which the excess of annual service charges over the annual inflow of new borrowings could be financed. Later on as a creditor after World War I, however, a positive trade balance could persist, other things equal, only if new loans outflow exceeded income on foreign investments, or the world's gold continued to flow (net) into the United States, undermining the international gold standard.

Col. (3) is positive through the seventies largely because the decaying U.S. merchant marine engaged in the foreign trade was still about 1.5 billion tons, which meant more transportation services provided by U.S. firms and less freight charges for shipments in foreign ships. Happily for foreign shippers and for the ability of foreigners to get some of the dollars to finance the persistently positive trade balance, the U.S. merchant marine continued to decline

TABLE 24

BALANCE OF PAYMENTS,
1869-1873 to 1909-1913
(Five-year totals, millions of dollars)

Period[1]	Merchandise, net (1)	Services: income on investments, net (2)	Other services (3)	Net unilateral transfers (4)	Current account balance (5)	U.S. capital[3] (6)	Foreign capital[2] (7)	Capital account balance (8)	Net change in monetary gold stock[3] (9)	Errors and omissions (10)
1869-1873	- 553	-418	+170	+ 16	- 785	0	0	+786	0	+ 1
1874-1878	+ 488	-459	+151	- 60	+ 120	0	0	- 48	- 71	- 1
1879-1883	+ 820	-418	- 16	- 52	+ 334	0	0	- 10	- 324	0
1884-1888	+ 278	-474	-311	- 137	- 644	0	0	+794	- 150	0
1889-1893	+ 290	-659	-176	- 237	- 782	0	0	+719	+ 63	0
1894-1898	+1316	-621	-114	- 243	+ 338	0	0	-191	- 148	1
1899-1903	+2612	-463	-179	- 487	+1483	0	0	-848	- 424	-211
1904-1908	+2500	-339	-565	- 786	+ 810	-454	+ 454	0	- 465	-345
1909-1913	+2265	-351	-937	-1034	- 57	-699	+1171	+472	- 249	-166

[1]Fiscal years through 1900; thereafter, calendar years.

[2]An outflow of funds is shown as negative.

[3]An increase is shown as negative.

Note: Through 1898 the capital account balance functions in effect in the same way as the errors and omissions item in subsequent periods, i.e., it is the current balance adjusted for so-called invisible flows, after taking account of changes in the monetary gold stock. Furthermore, from 1881 through 1899 the figures for change in the monetary gold stock are also included in the totals for the capital account balance.

Source: U.S. Census Bureau, *Historical Statistics of the United States, Colonial Times to 1957* (Washington: Government Printing Office, 1968).

in tonnage engaged in foreign trade until the very end of this period. In the last quarter century, U.S. ships carried an average of only about 10 percent of the total value of the country's foreign trade. But the chief foreign supply of dollars recorded in col. (3) especially after the 1870s, came from U.S. travelers abroad.

Although the whole current account balance 1869-1873, col. (5), was negative, and was not to shift permanently to positive until the late 1890s, immigrant remittances to Europe as seen in col. (4) were a credit for the last time in the first five years of this period. The reasons for this were a combination of the historically smaller numbers of foreign-born in the country and the comparatively high income levels of most of the northern Europeans who at that time comprised the overwhelming bulk of the immigrant population of about 5.5 million in 1870 (the Irish were an important exception).

The subsequent flow of immigrant remittances to families "back home" became very large as numbers became much greater and the composition of the immigrant population shifted toward southern and eastern Europeans with very much lower income levels. These ever growing unilateral transfers, like the interest, profit, and rent paid on the foreign debt [col. (3)], provided foreigners with some of the dollar exchange to finance the excess of merchandise exports over imports, shown in col. (1).

The merchandise export balance itself represented "net foreign investment" as it is peculiarly defined in our national income accounts. As such, it had fundamentally the same stimulative effect on total spending in the economy as domestic investment. It also, of course, gave a direct boost to sales in the specific export sectors. We can safely assume that the tariff contributed to this export surplus by restraining imports. If our general hypothesis about the strategic role of investment and savings in the development process is correct, there was another contribution of the tariff—that testifying to the incompleteness of its protective features, i.e., to the inelasticity of the demand for imports. This was its tendency to raise revenue in a form that restricted consumption and bolstered savings in the aggregate.

The capital account balance shown in col. (8) poorly represents what was happening to the U.S. position with respect to foreign investment, particularly from the end of the nineties. Foreigners were over the long run always investing more in the United States. For example, foreign investments in the United States increased from $3.4 billion in 1897 (mostly long term, portfolio) to $7.2 billion as of

June 30, 1914. But U.S. investment abroad (mostly long term, direct) rose over the same period from $700 million to $3.5 billion. "Netting out" the U.S. international capital position thus conceals a major development. By 1919 the magnitudes were almost precisely reversed! So it is important to note in this period the clear trend toward creditor status for the United States. Only the negative net capital account balances for 1894-1898 and 1899-1903 in col. (8) correctly show the trend. The negative balances for 1874-1878 and 1879-1883 reflect cyclical and episodic influences only, and the large positive balance for 1909-1913 was due to a temporary influx of long term portfolio funds that statistically inundated historically very large exports of long term capital by U.S. business firms.

The shift of the United States from an international debtor to creditor position performed a developmental role. It helped forestall a decline in the overall rate of return on investment by providing foreign offsets to savings for an economy grown rich with savings even as it was losing some of its internal offset prospects by virtue of the closing frontier. It must be remembered that public investment (spending) was not an acceptable alternative, given the laissez faire social consensus of the times.

Major Shifts in the Foreign Trade Pattern

The gross volume of foreign trade was always by far the largest single item in the balance of payments. For example, during the five years 1869-1873 exports averaged $418 million *per year*, and imports $549 million per year. Exports were thus about 5 percent of GNP, while imports were about 7 percent. Hence, while trade dominated the balance of payments, it was always moderately small in the United States relative to the total volume of economic activity. The trend in these export and import ratios, which if anything is downward slightly, may be seen in Table 25, cols. (1) and (2).

But foreign trade, while small in the aggregate, was important to certain sectors and industries. We know this from the history of tariff lobbying, for example. Exports were important to the farmer throughout the period, and particularly important to cotton, wheat, and livestock producers. U.S. wheat, for example, was the British "staff of life" for many years. Despite rebellious wheat farmers' complaints against the middlemen, as Morton Rothstein and others have pointed out, [1] the elevator system — inspection and

TABLE 25

MEASURES OF EXPORTS, 1869-1914

| Year | Ratio to gross national product (current dollars) | | | | Ratio of agricultural exports to | | Ratio of manufactured product prices to GNP deflator (1913 = 100) | | Ratio of U.S. export to import price indexes for manufactured products (1913 = 100) |
	Exports (1)	Imports (2)	Agricultural exports (3)	Manufactured exports (4)	Farm gross product (5)	Total exports (6)	Exports (7)	Imports (8)	(9)
1869	5.2%	7.1%	4.9%		12.5%	91%			
1879	9.0	6.1	7.5	1.0%	28.9	83	1.379	1.188	1.26[1]
1889	6.8	6.5	5.1	1.0	22.0	74	1.263	1.037	1.22
1899	7.6	4.9	4.8	1.7	24.5	63	1.185	1.087	1.09
1909	5.6	4.9	3.0	1.5	16.7	53	1.036	.918	1.13
1914	6.1	5.3	2.9	1.8	16.3	48	.935	.899	1.04

[1]1880—ratio of 1.16 for 1879 is unrepresentative for this early period.

Source: Robert E. Lipsey, *Price and Quantity Trends in the Foreign Trade of the United States*, NBER (Princeton: Princeton University Press, 1963), pp. 154, 157, 430-73 *passim*.

grading, transferable elevator receipts, bulk-handling, and futures trading—powerfully implemented on the domestic and international marketing side the farmers' dramatic production performance in wheat, giving the United States world trade leadership until the beginning of the twentieth century. Meanwhile, raw cotton continued to dominate farm exports, although it experienced a sharp long-run relative decline.

The dominance of farm products in the U.S. export trade until the very end of our period may be seen by comparing the ratios in col. (3) with those in col. (1) of Table 25, or by direct examination of col. (6). For the years selected, it is not until 1914 that farm exports fell below one-half the total. And even viewed as a sector aggregate [col. (5)], agricultural exports are seen to have been enormously important to the agricultural economy of the country in the whole period. It is notable that the comparative advantage of U.S. agriculture in many product lines sustained farm exports for decades after the end of the period. It was only after World War II that a neomercantilist policy of subsidy became a significant factor in sustaining such exports.

But industrialization of the economy also had a powerful impact on world trade, and the product composition of trade. The manufacturing sector was not only substituting domestic output for imported manufactures; it was contributing more and more to the volume of exports, to the diversification of the export product mix, and to the transformation in the composition of U.S. foreign trade as indicated by:

	unfabricated exports		fabricated exports
from	and	to	and
	fabricated imports		unfabricated imports.

Thus we have, by way of illustration, in round percentages for the beginning and the end of the period under study, approximately the following situation:

Year	Percentage of total exports		Percentage of total imports	
	Crude materials	Finished manufactures	Crude materials	Finished manufactures
1865	58%	15%	12%	41%
1914	31	31	35	22

The reversal by 1914 is most striking. It reflects the industrialization of the domestic economy and the commercial invasion of world markets, particularly European markets, by U.S. manufactures (although part of that invasion consisted of constructing plants in Europe to avoid their tariff walls).

The rising relative and absolute importance of imports of crude materials other than foodstuffs reflected the growing economic ties between the United States and the people of the less developed world. This shift toward crude materials from about one-tenth of all imports to about one-third between 1860 and the turn of the century was accompanied by large shifts in supply-source areas toward Asia, Oceania, the Middle East, and South America. Unfortunately, private investors in the United States, like those in all other developed countries, had more of a stake in inducing the less developed economies to focus on the development of their initial comparative advantage in primary products than it did in contributing to the sectoral diversification of production ordinarily necessary for their economic development. And in many cases the primary-product export was a major factor in the economic well-being of the less developed country. This fact, together with the monopsonistic role that U.S. buyers enjoyed and sometimes engineered, tended to place the whole commercial sector of the less developed economy in a noncompetitive position, with little means of insulating itself against adverse cyclical, technological, and institutional changes in the United States.

The United States sold some fabricated exports to the less developed countries, but mainly these were sold to Canada and other manufacturing nations. Likewise, the continued although declining relative importance of fabricated imports meant the United States was an important customer of the comparatively smaller European exporters. These market relationships, along with the abiding reliance of the United Kingdom and Europe on U.S. farm product exports, added up to the fact that the diversified industrialized countries were their own best customers. This showed that, in general, industrialized countries need not fear competition from the industrialization of the less developed, primary-product economies. The reason was that industrialization ordinarily involved vast product diversification, as in the U.S. case, and this left plenty of leeway for comparative advantage through specialization.

The export drive of U.S. manufacturers failed to gain much momentum before the 1890s as col. (4) of Table 24 suggests: the growth of such exports about kept pace with the growth of GNP. Since manufacturing output was a rising proportion of GNP, exports were not even keeping pace with manufacturing output before 1889. But thereafter the export rise was sufficient to sustain exports as a roughly constant percentage of manufacturing output and GNP. Manufactured exports from the turn of the century accounted for about 6 percent of total manufacturing value of product and 12 to 14 percent of value added. The former comparison is the more appropriate because of the way exports are evaluated.

The relative prices of manufactured imports and exports in the long run were mildly favorable to the substitution of U.S. exports for foreign goods in foreign markets, i.e., there was a decline in the commodity terms of trade "against" U.S. exports. Columns (7) through (9) of Table 25 show something about the appropriate price movements. In foregin markets as well as in the domestic market the ratio of U.S. export prices to prices for manufactured goods produced in other countries [col. (9)] moved moderately in favor of the U.S. products, insofar as buyers would have tended to substitute lower priced U.S. goods for others. Between 1869 and 1914 the ratio (terms of trade) in col. (9) declined over 17 percent; but it is vital to note that the bulk of the decline came after 1889. Assuming the import price indexes represented close to the prices foreigners received for their manufactured products in other markets of the world, then U.S. manufactured products must have become increasingly competitive in world markets beginning in the nineties. So far as the domestic U.S. market is concerned, if domestic prices followed export prices closely, then for the years selected, and ignoring quality considerations, after 1889 domestic producers were at a competitive advantage pricewise compared with foreigners, i.e., the terms of trade moved "against" the latter [cols. (7) and (8)].

This experience shows that talking about commodity terms of trade moving for or against a trading country can be as dangerous and misleading as references to "favorable" and "unfavorable" balances of trade. The commodity terms of trade are a two-edged sword: if a sector's productivity performance, for example, is superior to the rest of the economic world, then under competition, other things equal, its relative prices (terms of trade) with fall. But this will make it more competitive—its products will be substituted for those of the rest of the world. And if the demand is relatively price-elastic the sector's total receipts will rise.[2] This seems to have been the case in the aggregate for U.S. manufactures after the 1890s. While the terms of trade shown in Table 25, col. (9), for example, fell 8 percent between 1909 and 1914, the ratio of the *quantity* of (finished) manufactured exports to (finished) manufactured imports rose 24 percent. The United States had replaced England as the "workshop of the world."

Territorial Expansion and Imperialism

The Spanish-American war in 1898, together with the peace settlements, the American acquisition of former Spanish colonies, and the subsequent U.S. military interventions in a number of less developed countries, suggested that the United States was embarking upon an external imperial policy similar to that pursued by European powers of like economic, social, and political complexion. It is difficult to test such a hypothesis here because the nation's economic history after 1914 is essential to such an examination. Still, many historical phenomena are most clearly seen in the years of their genesis rather than when they have developed all the complexities of maturity or have changed their essential characteristics because of a new setting or new policy goals.

As is usual in economic history, we are concerned chiefly with the *economic aspects* of the hypothesis that the United States exhibited an imperial behavior pattern in its foreign policy in this period. Treatment of the economic aspects falls into two categories: (1) the demonstration that in certain cases the key decision-making groups in some other country were forced to make nonindependent decisions that entailed the acquisition of noncompetitive profits by U.S. private businesses, and (2) the demonstration that the development of the U.S. economy in this period brought into operation new factors adding to the assumed commitment of the Federal government to protect business interests abroad. Our concern here will be with the second category of the imperial hypothesis, as the presuppositions and the materials necessary for examination of the first are still in a highly controversial state.

Elaboration of the hypothesis need not emphasize the forms of diplomatic, political, and military behavior, such as the U.S. government's turning over in the early nineteenth century the public finances of Santo Domingo to Kuhn, Loeb and Company, aiding a revolution in Panama, the invasion of Haiti, or the occupation of Nicaragua. This has been ably done by diplomatic and military historians. Rather, our chief focus will be on the new economic content underlying the varied practices that tended to reduce or induce people in certain other lands, particularly less developed countries, to accept positions of subordination to U.S. power and in some occasions even to profit from that relationship.

However, an imperial policy, as most common-sense meanings suggest, involves the foreign policy of the central government. Hence, there is no purely economic imperialism: at a minimum it needs to be viewed as an economic-political matter. Indeed, the business-government partnership, so preeminently characteristic of laissez faire, is in no respect more prominent than in the sphere of foreign policy.

In a recent work Walter LaFeber breaks down the imperial phenomenon into two categories. He chooses to refer to U.S. "colonialism" as the policy that involved attemped formal political and economic control of an area for direct economic benefits, and "expansion" as the policy of developing trade and investment opportunities without formal political control. [3] LaFeber's substitution and classification seem useful, although it is often convenient to use the older term for simplicity.

LaFeber, like Harold U. Faulkner and others before him, enunciated a roughly similar interpretation to that we presented above in Chapter 5 in the discussion of the frontier. This interpretation suggests a connection between the terminating frontier in the United States and the acceleration of foreign colonialist and expansionist policies by business and government. LaFeber stresses the ending of the era of continental land annexation by the time of the Civil War, and finds the beginnings of foreign expansionism in the ensuing decades, even as the frontier was still in the ascendency. But this emphasis on export markets for U.S. products and raw materials subordinates the significantly new private capital outflows. These helped to distinguish, along with the emergence of a merchandise export balance and changing product mix of the merchandise trade, the U.S. balance of payments, as the century approached a close, from anything that had been experienced before. Thenceforth, the foreign policy of the United States would increasingly underwrite the profit-maximizing goals of private business firms that had actual or potential investment abroad. *An overlapping creditor interest had now been added on a major scale to that of the export commodity producers, merchants, and shippers.*

The expanding flow of private foreign loans, even as the frontier was still present (and aggregate domestic investment was still growing relative to output), suggests that the frontier merely slowed this new development for a time. Hence the causal connection between the closing of the frontier and the growth of large capital outflows involved merely acceleration of the latter by the former.

What was new, therefore, in the government's historical commitment to aid private business was that expansionism and colonialism in foreign policy were linked with the emerging international creditor role of the United States. While older behavior patterns connected with merchandise trade promotion continued to persist, the important thing that was distinctly recent was involvement with the web of international creditor-debtor relationships.

The new U.S. financial imperialism (as Harold U. Faulkner once called it) did not, in general and with a few exceptions, involve expansion of the land mass under direct American legal sovereignty. This aspect of U.S. expansionism was in the past. The new expansionism and colonialism were dedicated primarily, though not exclusively, to the enlargement of private investment abroad, and to its stimulation and protection by the Federal government. In the U.S. case, most private foreign investment was "direct," i.e., in the form of U.S. privately owned plant and equipment, together with a sizable American managerial staff. This was particularly true outside Europe. Investment in Europe was more heavily of the portfolio type, that is, in securities. Therefore, protection by the Federal government required surveillance over physical property and security for U.S. nationals in foreign countries, property and personnel that were tangible evidence to foreign populations of the alien American presence. While such tangibility was no doubt in many cases a source of admiration and respect, protective surveillance of this U.S. property and personnel, particularly in the less developed countries outside the orbit of European colonial possessions, was likely to involve the sharpest kind of action by both parties in the event of hostile developments. In the case of countries with low per capita incomes especially, the presence of an American, or any foreign, enclave of managerial people living under distinctly superior material conditions even when there were native elitist groups, helped to generate negative demonstration effects over the long run. From the U.S. government's viewpoint, the growing accumulation of property owned abroad created a commitment to assure the sanctity of private contracts in a new international context, especially when strategic materials were involved.

The situation was not the same as it was with internal U.S. debtor-creditor relationships. A world nominally adhering to the doctrine of national sovereignty elicited from Herbert Hoover the quip that "there is no court to which a government can appeal for collection of debt except a battleship."[4] This pointed to the fact that many debtor-creditor relationships, particularly those in which the debtor country was small and economically underdeveloped, as compared with the creditor, were endowed with imperialistic elements, i.e., elements of dependency and dominance. Dependency involved (1) deprivation, or reduction, of the power of independent decision making and (2) extraction of economic rents that would not have existed under free competition.

The emphasis on U.S. investment abroad as both the newest and the most important expansionary economic factor emerging after the Civil War must be checked against the role of other economic factors. Many years ago Eugene Staley treated this subject in a work entitled *War and the Private Investor*.[5] He dealt with the following economic considerations as relevant to the analysis of nationalistic imperialism, colonialism and expansionism: the search for trade outlets, the attempt to overcome tariff barriers, the search for sources of raw materials, the investment of "surplus capital," and population pressure on the level of living.[6] The first named is a very old story, and the last named would not be considered operative in the U.S. case. Of the remaining three, the second and third are closely connected with external capital flows. The first of the three highlights the rise of protectionism around the world in the latter part of the nineteenth century. This turned out to be in the long run an invitation to *direct* U.S. foreign investment precisely to hurdle those tariff barriers—a strategy of U.S. multinational business to get and keep a foothold in foreign markets that remains of continuing importance to this day, particularly in Western Europe. The securing of raw materials by direct investment in mining and plantation facilities, largely in low income countries, was also a major feature of the new expansionism and colonialism.

The growth of U.S. industrial output per se was not the root of the new trend. Manufactured exports by value were never more than 6.6 percent of the total value of domestically produced manufactured products and 1.7 percent of GNP at the census dates (Table 25), with no trend in the former between 1869 and 1909. The increase in manufactured exports between 1869 and 1909 may be calculated to have equaled only 5.3 percent of the increase in total manufacturing value of product. Thus, so far as current experience, as distinguished from anticipations of potentials, is concerned, U.S. manufacturers were getting much more growth mileage from import substitution than they were from export sales increase. Contrary to the belief of many traditional economic historians, the evidence for a great pressure of "surplus" manufactured products requiring export markets as industrialization proceeded, is extremely weak. But industrialization did affect the new trend in that many of the new multinational firms were manufacturing firms, and the growth of manufacturing did accelerate the need for additional (foreign) sources of raw materials.

The growth of manufactured exports and the relative decline of manufactured imports refers to *flows* of products. The balance of payments account show only flows. The rising national commitment was assumed by European as well as U.S. tradition to be a "natural" responsibility of the state, for the furtherance and protection of business interests abroad, but it was imperfectly reflected in the service charge item of the current account and the loan flows of the capital account of the international balance of payments, shown in Table 24. This relationship can be better uncovered by an examination of the rising *stock* of U.S. controlled wealth sited in foreign lands. According to Cleona Lewis, U.S. direct and portfolio investment abroad, which was about $80 million in 1869, had reached $685 million by 1897. Mira Wilkins [7] cites estimates that in 1914 the book value of U.S. investments abroad totaled $3.5 billion, of which $2.6 billion was direct in plant, land, equipment, and inventories, and $.9 billion was portfolio investment in securities. Since GNP in 1914 was $36.4 billion, this was over 9 percent of GNP, and direct investment was 7 percent of GNP. Wilkins points out that this latter percentage was already as high as it was to be in 1966!

This was a remarkable new trend, especially for a country that was still nominally an international debtor. The income from private U.S. investment aborad also exceeded the annual service charge paid foreigners on their investment in the United States for the first time in 1915. The rapid rise in the net indebtedness of the United States from the Civil War to about 1890, and the continua-

tion of net debtor status to the end of our period should not be permitted to suggest a misleading static interpretation of events. In
the first place the rise in debt leveled off distinctly before the big upsurge in U.S. long term capital exports, which was after 1897. In the
second place the bulk of the debt was the portfolio type and was in
the traditional but then rapidly maturing railroad sector. In relative terms the transformation from net debtor to immature creditor
between 1914 and 1919 consisted largely in the liquidation of
foreign holdings, chiefly portfolio, of U.S. property.

The governmental commitment to exercise its power in support
of U.S. private property located abroad also reflected the character
of industrialization of the domestic economy; almost none of that
property was controlled by small nonfarm enterprise, but was typically large scale, incorporated, and engaged in manufacturing or extractive activity.

It follows that the new expansionism and colonialism of the U.S.
government, so well documented elsewhere by general historians,
was not linked with the continuing importance of farm exports. The
latter had been important to certain farm producers, and to the
economy, as for example in the case of cotton, as far back as the
early nineteenth century. The rise of wheat and meat exports after
1860 brought no significant change in U.S. commercial policy, and
did not prompt State Department interference with the power of independent decision making by people in other countries.

Except for marketing and shipping concerns, multinational
direct-investment corporations, like purely domestic firms, in general located their foreign facilities in response to either market-
oriented or raw material supply-oriented considerations. Canada,
the leading recipient country in 1914, attracted firms for both purposes. Mexico, the second largest debtor, along with most areas of
interest in the low-income countries south of the border were attractive to U.S. business chiefly for their railroads, ores, and other raw
materials. The already large U.S. properties in Europe in 1914 ($573
million in direct investments) were concentrated in market-oriented
marketing and manufacturing activities. Most supply-oriented investment was in less developed countries where LaFeber's colonialist rather than the expansionist relationships were more likely to
obtain.

However, it is important to realize that historically considerably
less than half of U.S. foreign investment was sited in less developed
countries. This tended to greatly limit the magnitude, from the

U.S. perspective, of that portion of the government's protective commitment that possessed an imperial potential.

Given the generally small balanced government budgets of those times, private gross national saving had to be offset by the sum of private domestic investment and net lending to the rest of the world.[8] John Maynard Keynes, elaborating the anticipations of John Stuart Mill with respect to England, convinced many skeptics that as a country became rich, its people tended to save more than its business sector could invest remuneratively at home. Thus, modern industrial economies moved from immature international debtors to mature debtors and then to international creditors. The reasons were either that average rates of profit at home moved disadvantageously for investors compared to those obtainable abroad, or that foreign investment offsets to growing savings were treated by business as equivalent to domestic offsets. This dynamic model may be employed with respect to British investment in the United States for at least the years from the enunciation of the Monroe Doctrine in 1823 to World War I. The slowdown of new foreign investment in the United States that accompanied the decline of the frontier after the 1890s, the apparent decline in the rate of return on property between the 1870s and 1910, and the rising flow of U.S. funds to other lands all suggest the applicability of the Keynesian thesis to the U.S. experience between the 1880s and 1914.

The United States arrived late on the scene of international rivalry for colonies largely because of its absorption with continental frontier expansion. This tardy appearance occurred at a time when the leading European powers had already carved out empires in the less developed "Third World." Furthermore, popular sentiment in the developed countries and the rebellious spirit in the colonial world were about to make untenable the traditional forms of imperial domination, particularly the complete deprivation of political sovereignty. Henceforth, the old forms were to be thrown off, and colonial or quasicolonial domination was to develop generally through the use of arrangements more subtle than outright possession of another country. The professed disinterest of many U.S. leaders around the beginning of the twentieth century in the possession of an owned colonial empire may be understood in the light of this forthcoming change in the international situation. Such change, more clearly perceived through the benefit of hindsight, has been described with penetrating insightful, and apparently quite independently of LaFeber, by Martin Bronfenbrenner as the emergence of "neo-empire." Bronfenbrenner presents a most useful list of "symptoms of imperialism," half economic, half political-military, in which *"sovereignty*, which is the political counterpart of *ownership*, ordinarily is no longer involved."[9]

In the case of the more industrialized economies like Canada, and the highly industrialized economies like the European, the accompaniments of the creditor-debtor relationships moved to the other end of the LaFeber spectrum, away from colonialism through quasicolonialism to mild expansionism. The "American invasion of Europe," which began in the period under study, like the British portfolio investment in the United States during the nineteenth century, had little if any of the accoutrements of imperialism. In the case of Canada, Hugh G. J. Aitken argues that the U.S. investment pattern and related policies tended to perpetuate Canada's traditional staple-producing economy, but Wilkins emphasizes U.S. manufacturing investment. In any case, much of the capital influx and/or trade flow from the United States to the rest of the more economically developed world came from straight oligopolistic market rivalry operating across national boundaries strengthened by tariff walls. The multinational corporation with branch plants in semiadvanced and advanced countries was a variant of Secretary of State John Hay's "Open Door" policy projected in 1899 to keep the Chinese market open to U.S. business. It is nevertheless noteworthy that in most cases expansionism as well as colonialism entailed capital flows and the location of U.S. business property in foreign countries. Of the $3.5 billion of U.S. assets abroad in 1914, about $2.65 were direct investment.

How does the Spanish-American War of 1898 fit into this analysis? The answer is that it apparently does. However, it is not necessary to enter into the unresolved controversy among historians over that war's more immediate causes. In addition to the background of the depression of 1893-1897 with its attendent social unrest, the active human ingredients at the time involved such things as popular chauvinism, the yellow press, anti-imperialist Democrats and Populists, some business interests, the naval lobby, statesmen anticipating the future long run interests of the corporate community, and any number of additional mutually congenial prowar groups.

But the cross-currents of group policy at that time do not seem particularly relevant to the long run import of the war. To the economic historian a more relevant matter was the relationship of that war to the development of the economy. In the first place, the primarily naval war had but a minor impact on the economy at the time; there was no significant conversion from a civilian to a war economy, no notable wartime inflation, no jump in the Federal debt, no postwar slump, etc. In the second and more important place, the independence of Cuba and the cession of Puerto Rico, Guam, and the Philippines (for $20 million) to the United States, together with the annexation of Hawaii in 1898, coincided with the general developmental requirements of the economy, the traditional commercial objectives of certain segments of U.S. private enterprise, and their future long run needs in the foreign sphere. The maximization of profits of the concerned segment of U.S. business was served by the carving up of Samoa (1899) by England, Germany, and the United States, by the construction of the Panama Canal (1904-1914), and by the establishment of a U.S. protectorate over Panama (1903-1904).

Such extraterritorial acquisition was manifestly not destined to be the main form by which the United States was to externalize its investment frontier in the future. Yet a temporary swing toward the more traditional imperial methods around the turn of the twentieth century may be understood as a transitional behavior pattern modeled after the influential British and Western European methods that had dominated the nineteenth century. A probable prime example is the annexation of Hawaii. That country had for some time been economically incorporated into the U.S. market, but annexationists in the islands under American leadership failed to win their objective until the "expansionists of 1898" successfully exploited the rising imperialist sentiment to swing Congress in favor of annexation.

In any case, in the laissez faire climate of the times, economic development policy precluded a large role for government expenditures and deficits, and major reliance was placed on the growth role of private investment, given the associated laissez faire policy of leaving the private savings ratio alone. Hence, military action implemented, as in the case of the Spanish-American War, the policy of furthering private foreign investment to partially offset the community's high propensity to save.

Robert Zevin has been joined by others in arguing that the foreign investments being protected were a "relatively trival" portion of total business wealth, and that an interpretation of imperialist policy that draws heavily on such a trivial stake is sustainable only if the costs of pursuing that policy are equally trivial. As is well known, the latter were sometimes not trivial, although in the period under study as distinguished from after World War I, they would probably be considered such.

However, there has historically been no social constraint requiring that public costs of a private enterprise decision backed by government be equated to the private resources committed in connection with that particular decision. The costs of protection were diffused among taxpayers to whom they were often a trivial portion of total taxes, costs separated in time, and disconnected in the public mind, from the specific private decision for which the public costs were incurred. Even if an international police action or war were connected with specific private stakes in the public mind, the former was likely to be influenced by nationalism, chauvinism, or a "free enterprise" bias that contributed to an acceptance of inordinate social costs. It is more empirically useful, therefore, to posit a "period multiplier" relating the addition of a foreign private investment (or the putative value of a commercial connection) to the social protection costs functionally connected therewith through time. The tail could at times wag the dog. An example of this might be U.S. involvement in Cuba or in Central America in the early 1900s, indeed of "dollar diplomacy" in the Caribbean generally.

Specific interest groups such as large corporate industrial businesses, investment bankers, and the military bureaucracy itself were able to wield concentrated power and to expolit a devoted government to a degree all out of proportion to the size of any specific foreign financial or other commitment that they had. Hence the "foreign asset protection multiplier." ("Asset" includes a market prospect as well as direct investments in a foreign country.) The size of the asset(s) may have been "trivial," but the elicited government protective action was sometimes a major engagement. This provides a link between the micro and macro aspects of imperialism, a link showing that there was no necessary incompatibility between the aggregative economic results, the specifics of private enterprise foreign commitments, and the larger actions of the government in foreign affairs. It should be noted, however, that before the 1940s, and ignoring World War I, the only two important military engagements of the United States were the Spanish-American War and American support of the Panama revolution against Columbia in 1903. U.S. naval forces participated in the division of Samoa in 1899. It is not intended to deal adequately with the period thereafter.

Keynesian theory has shown economic historians that neither the older nor the more recent objectives for foreign intervention were necessary for domestic full employment and economic development. Herbert Schiller and others have pointed out that the "vestigial colonialist" powers that were formerly vast empire-holders and are now bereft of empire have managed to continue to develop. Had the United States between the Civil War and World War I rejected its laissez faire beliefs and adopted modern monetary and fiscal policies, i.e., the mixed capitalist form, it might have performed as well or better than it did in part through foreign expansionism and colonialism. For that matter, historians have believed for a long time that the social benefits of expansionism and colonialism fell far short of the social costs.

NOTES

1. See his "America in the International Rivalry for the British Wheat Market, 1860-1914," *Mississippi Valley Historical Review*, 47 (December 1960), pp. 401-18.
2. Economists avoid the confusion pertaining to the implications of the "favorable" and "unfavorable" commodity terms of trade by taking productivity into consideration in the concept "double factoral terms of trade."
3. Walter LaFeber, *The New Empire* (Ithaca: Cornell University Press, 1967), p. viii.
4. Address to the American Bankers Association, Chicago, December 10, 1920, reprinted in R. L. Wilbur and A. M. Hyde (eds.), *The Hoover Policies* (New York: Charles Scribner's Sons, 1937), p. 349.
5. Eugene Staley, *War and the Private Investor*, (Chicago: University of Chicago Press, 1935).
6. Ibid. As reprinted in part in Harrison M. Wright (ed.), *The "New Imperialism"* (Boston: D. C. Heath and Company, 1961), pp. 77-88 *passim*.
7. Mira Wilkins, *The Emergence of Multinational Enterprise: American Business Abroad from the Colonial Era to 1914* (Cambridge, Mass.: Harvard University Press, 1970), pp. 201-2.
8. This view of savings and investment is drawn from the so-called "flow-of-funds" social accounts, as distinguished from the more familiar "national product" accounts.
9. "Burdens and Benefits of Empire: American Style," in Leland Hazard (ed.), *Empire Revisited* (Homewood, Ill.: Richard D. Irwin, 1965), pp. 46-7.

[13]

Epilog: the design of development in production

"The story of productivity, the ratio of output to input, is at heart the record of man's efforts to raise himself from poverty," says John Kendrick.[1] The largest single input factor responsible for the long run growth of total output during the core years of our period, 1870-1910, was the labor of human beings. Next in importance was the striking increase in physical capital (plants and machinery) used in production. If capital investment is weighted according to some customary imputed contribution to the rise in output, then in the total economy it vied with technological and other productivity-raising factors for second place in the determination of GNP growth. Of course, physical capital, like labor, "embodies" new knowledge. So it is difficult to ascribe to capital with accuracy its precise contribution to output growth.

Nevertheless, if we recall the nineteenth century's traditional failure to appreciate the strategic role of labor in production, its overweening admiration for the contribution of saving and physical investment was not too badly misplaced. If there ever was a period during which capital formation was in some sense focal in the development process, it was during the nineteenth century. And in those decades of rapid urbanization the proposition would have to be applied to residential construction as much as to the production of business plant, equipment, and additional inventories.

The high level of the capital stock per worker helps to explain the high average and marginal product per worker in the late nineteenth century and after. The latter in turn helps to explain the comparatively high real wage rates in the United States, the strong attraction of the U.S. economy to European and other immigrants, and the high growth rates of the U.S. labor force.

Yet even in this period, for the economy as a whole the growth of the stock of capital fell slightly short of the growth of GNP. Table 26 shows that the latter rose over half a percentage point per year faster than the growth of the capital stock of about 4 percent. In other words, the national economy's output/capital ratio apparently drifted upwards even as the country was rapidly becoming the richest in the world in capital goods. If we interpret this ratio as output per unit of capital input, the upward drift in these decades was apparently the beginning of a long secular process in the same direction, a process to continue past the mid-twentieth century.[2] The historic significance of this pattern for a business economy geared to the accumulation of capital is scarcely appreciated even at the present time.

We pointed out in Chapter 3 that for the period here under review the growth of output was more heavily attributable to total input growth, and relatively less to all other determinants, than in the twentieth century. Col. (1) of Table 26 shows that, after making the highly conjectural imputations customary in the "neoclassical" production function,[3] technological, institutional, and other such "residual" changes accounted for 1.4 percentage points of the 4.6 percent of output growth per year in the national economy. Thus this productivity increment accruing to the owners of capital and labor (with land treated as capital) was 1.4/4.6, or about a third of the total explanation for output growth. In the twentieth century, as Edward Denison has attempted to show, the residual productivity increment, attributable largely to the growth of knowledge, has accounted for well over half the secular increase in output. And the role of private business investment has been further reduced. Of course, all this treats capital and labor purely quantitatively, ignoring their knowledge-embodying character.

As is well known, the U.S. worker operates with a large complement of capital, a feature of the production system that evolved dramatically in this period. Col. (1) of the table shows that while labor increased at 2.75 percent per year, the capital with which it

TABLE 26

ANNUAL GROWTH RATES
OF PRODUCTIVITY PARAMETERS,
1870-1910

Parameter	National economy (1)	Nonfarm economy (2)	Manufacturing sector (3)	Railroad sector (4)	Non-South farm sector (5)
Output	4.60%	5.50%	5.00%[2]	7.30%	2.50%
Capital input or stock	4.00	4.75[1]	6.50	4.50	2.25[3]
Labor input or labor force	2.75	3.50	3.25	5.00	1.00
Residual productivity increment	1.40	1.50	.80	2.50	1.12
Output/capital ratio	.60	.75	-1.50	2.80	.25
Output/labor ratio	1.85	2.00	1.75	2.30	1.50
Capital/labor ratio	1.25	1.25	3.25	- .50	1.25

[1]Private nonfarm, nonresidential, real capital stock. Inclusion of residential investment raises rate to 5 percent.

[2]From Frickey, *Production in the United States, 1860-1914.* Kendrick's estimate is no longer than GNP growth.

[3]Value of capital (other than land) in farms.

Note: All rates are compound annual. The residual productivity increment is calculated from a Cobb-Douglas production function. Weights for capital and labor respectively were: for the total economy and the nonfarm economy, .33 and .67; for the manufacturing sector, .23 and .77; for the railroad sector, .33 and .67; and for non-South agriculture .30 and .70.

Sources: Most of the data are from John W. Kendrick, *Productivity Trends,* appropriate appendix tables. The data for the railroad sector, however, are from Albert Fishlow, "Productivity and Technological Change in the Railroad Sector, 1840-1910," NBER, v. 30. Output for the national economy, an estimate that seems somewhat high, is from the growth table in U.S. Department of Commerce, *Long Term Economic Growth.* Estimates for the non-South farm sector were made by Mr. Carl H. Goebel and the author, and are based on Tostlebe's work in *Capital in Agriculture.*

worked rose much faster—4 percent per year. Thus the capital/labor ratio increased, and this has been an abiding feature of U.S. economic history as well as the history of other industrialized countries. Of the important sectors treated in the table, only the somewhat unusual railroad sector had a faster employment growth than capital growth, and this may be attributed to the earlier maturation of investment in road as distinguished from equipment. Equipment investment, according to Fishlow,[4] grew at an annual compound rate of over 6 percent between 1880[5] and 1910, and this was a whole percentage point faster than the growth in persons engaged. The so-called "productivity of labor"—a mere partial productivity ratio shown in Table 26 as the output/labor ratio—is highest for the railroad sector because of the phenomenal rise in railroad output, as noted in Chapter 7. But even that sector failed in this period to reach the average 3 percent growth rate for the output/labor ratio in the private economy for a time after World War II.

Other intersectoral comparisons stand out sharply in the table. For example, in the manufacturing sector the labor force growth rate is close to that for the whole nonfarm economy, but the ratio of capital growth is by far the highest for any sector shown. The high rate of investment and capital stock growth not only raised the capital/labor ratio in the manufacturing sector at a truly remarkable pace, but it also caused its output/capital ratio to fall and thus to go against the aggregative trend. Indeed the sector's trend is what one would have expected in the entire nonfarm economy, in view of the rising aggregate rate of capital formation through the 1890s. But the important railroads and other "regulated industries," with their exceedingly high production growth, pulled the nonfarm economy's output/capital ratio up. According to Kendrick's data, output in the communications and public utilities sector grew 9 percent per year from 1879 to 1909! In any case, manufacturing was on trend for the whole economy in the twentieth century; after World War I its output/capital ratio drifted upwards.

The productivity performance of the manufacturing sector is rather mediocre despite the substantial increase in the amount of capital with which its average worker labored. For example, its output/labor ratio rose at a rate only .25 percentage points faster than the non-South farm economy. Manufacturing's residual productivity increment, accounting for less than a fifth of the growth of output, made the smallest contribution of all the sectors shown, an estimate suggesting that the sector's production grew in the period under consideration, in contrast with the half century that was to follow, overwhelmingly because of the growth of factor inputs. This mediocre productivity record is consistent with the discussion in Chapter 3 of innovating caution on the part of manufacturing entrepreneurs. The output record itself was apparently, on a

most generous estimate, no more than a percentage point above the
GNP record. Hence, on the brute output criterion of industrialization, the railroad and other public utility sectors were a much better
indicator of the industrialization of the economy than manufacturing was. Of course, manufacturing is important as an indicator because its size was much greater than the former sectors combined.
(For example, in 1910 there were 8.2 million persons engaged in
manufacturing, but only 3.2 million in transportation and public
utilities.)

The important Northern farm sector, accounting for about two-
thirds of total U.S. farm gross income throughout the period, with
its low output and input growth, behaved much as would be expected. However, the productivity increment amounts to a surprising
45 percent of the total annual growth of production. In a technical
sense this heavy weight might be ascribed to the very low rate of
annual additions to the labor force. But in an economic sense it
must have been due to the embodiment of knowledge in fixed capital and labor, the increased use of working capital inputs such as
fertilizer (not registered in the equation underlying Table 26), and
the rise in the amount of land worked by the typical farmer. The
slow rate of labor growth, together with the good annual rise of the
capital/labor ratio, yielded a quite favorable increase in the sector's "productivity of labor." Southern agriculture's performance
was not as good on this score. While output rose slightly faster,
labor input rose much faster than in the North—over 1.6 percent
per year. Hence, output/labor in the South increased only about 1
percent per year.

The good performance of the national economy in terms of GNP
growth for the whole period was of course partly due to the "shift
effect" of the movement of resources out of agriculture and into the
more productive nonfarm economy. The influence of this shift effect
may be sensed by comparing cols. (1) and (2) of Table 25, where it is
seen at once that the nonfarm economy yielded higher growth rates
for the residual productivity increment as well as for the partial productivity ratios. Kendrick's estimates[6] yield an annual rise in
"total factor productivity" (output relative to both labor and capital input) of .75 percent for the U.S. farm sector and 1.38 percent for
the private domestic nonfarm sector. So all the shifting out of farming was raising total factor productivity in the economy as a whole.

There are of course deficiencies in the approach underlying the
calculations in Table 26. The productivity performance of an economy is a result of the entire culture of which it is a part, and no sim-

plistic equation with three or four variables will adequately represent the multitudinous influences of the total culture as it impinges upon productive activity. Furthermore, as was pointed out frequently earlier in this discussion, no treatment of development is at all complete without reference to the demand side. Nevertheless, analysis of the data in Table 26 tells us a great deal about the pattern of development as well as some of the major causal factors operating to produce that design. Simon Kuznets has shown that features such as these, characterizing the U.S. experience, are broadly similar to the experience of numerous other developed industrialized countries in the world. Whether these features can be expected to hold true for the future experience of the densely populated, less developed countries of the world remains a moot, exciting, and practical question confronting historians, social theorists, and development planners today.

Changes in the Design of Product Use

Many other striking changes in the structure of production, in the long run also a mirror of the altered structure of demand, occurred during these decades. Some have either not been mentioned or been insufficiently stressed.

The pace of sectoral development just surveyed tells nothing of the shifting composition of output and demand. Setting aside the foreign balance, treated in the preceding chapter, let aggregate domestic demand be subdivided into gross enterprise demand for investment goods and household demand for private and public consumption goods. Then using current dollars we find a mild trend in the way the community disposed of its total income:[7]

Period	Gross Investment	Consumption
1869-1878	17.3%	82.7%
1879-1888	18.7	81.3
1889-1898	20.0	80.0
1899-1908	21.0	79.0

The shift toward gross investment obtains whether one uses current dollar estimates or estimates in dollars of 1860 purchasing power. Since actual gross investment equals actual gross savings, the community was clearly saving relatively more and consuming relatively less. This development pattern, with total consumption a falling share of gross output, is apparently unquestionable for this period, but apparently does not continue into the twentieth century. Interpreters must note that consumption was at that time almost exclusively private. Kuznets has estimated that public consumption averaged only 4.4 percent of GNP during the years 1889-1908. [8] The downward drift is somewhat surprising in view of the fact that estimates of the consumption-linked service share of total income (i.e., wages and salaries as distinguished from property income) showed no trend, but rather was practically constant, according to E. Budd, [9] at about 64 percent. Perhaps property income receivers (i.e., receivers of interest, profit, and rent) were saving a higher percentage of their incomes as time passed, or inequality in the size distribution of income increased.

The structure of demand for investment goods by enterprises also experienced notable shifts. In general, the share of gross new construction of all types fell and that of manufactured producer durable goods rose. In 1860 prices, the latter increased dramatically from 31 percent of gross domestic capital formation in 1869-1878 to an average of 57 percent in the decade 1899-1908. [10] As remarked in an earlier chapter, this trend reflected in large part the maturation of the railroad industry and the leveling off of the growth rate of residential construction as urbanization slowed with the end of this period.

One important effect of the shift was to raise the proportion of replacement investment — reduce the proportion of net investment — in total gross investment as time passed. This secular fall in the net investment element in total capital formation, a continuing trend in the twentieth century, was of the greatest significance for the future career of the business economy.

Another important effect of the shift in enterprise demand toward producers' durable equipment was the greater potential for innovation that it generated. The growth of knowledge associated with the almost limitless proliferation and diversification of producers' durables far outran the growth of knowledge asociated with new plant design and construction.

The transformations in the structure of demand for consumer goods by households has been treated in part in the earlier discussions of the relative decline of agriculture and rise of industry. That discussion, and particularly the matter of the low income elasticity of demand for food, is relevant here. It largely explains the secular

decline in consumer outlays on food (current dollars) from an average of about 37 percent of the total of such outlays during the 1870s
to about one-third in 1904-1913. Clothing elasticity is also low, and
consequently the two together declined over the same period from a
dominant 57 percent to rather less than 50 percent. [11]

Additional information on the structure of consumer demand is
provided by breakdowns of expenditures, in current prices, according to the degree of durability and the commodity-services classification. Thus, as per capita total consumption rose from $185 per
year to $436 per year between the 1870s and the end of the period
under study, we have the distribution of total household consumption outlays as follows: [12]

Period	Perishables	Semidurables	Durables	Services
1869-1878	51%	17%	7%	25%
1899-1908	47	16	8	30
1904-1913	43	16	8	33

Trends emerge only in the cases of perishables (e.g., food, tobacco,
drugs, fuel) and consumer services. It will be recalled from the discussion in Chapter 7 that "final" services, most but not all of which
are consumer products, comprised about 45 percent of the total
output of all services, the remainder being purchased primarily as
"intermediate" products by the business sector. The secular decline in the share of the most important single category, perishables, is due primarily to the low income elasticity, the relative secular price decline of products in this category, and the shift of consumers from the farm to the city. Urban consumers spend a smaller
proportion of their outlays on food, especially unmanufactured
foods, than farm families. It is likely that *unmanufactured* perishables explains the decline, if pre-Civil War patterns continued
through our period, for Gallman has estimated that between 1839
and 1859 that class of perishables fell from 36 percent to 29 percent
of all goods flowing to consumers, whereas factory manufactured perishables rose from 16 percent to 20 percent. A continued
increase in the latter would be consistent with the production data
on the growth of manufactured foods.

The rise in the services flow to consumers, in current prices,
offsets the fall in the share of perishables. Its rise is consistent with
the parenthesized proportions for service sector output, calculated
from Gallman and Weiss, in Table 15, col. (8), Chapter 7. [13] Rural-

urban population shifts as well as income elasticity helps to explain the relative rise in consumer outlays for services, for urban dwellers spend proportionately more for both housing and for other services such as domestic help, transportation, health care, recreation, and education.

The semidurables and the durables were produced almost entirely by the manufacturing sector. As a combined category their share in current prices did not rise. But the share of gross manufacturing product in GNP, according to Table 17 of Chapter 7, did rise, from 21 percent to 27 percent between 1869 and 1909. We must therefore conclude that, with the exception of manufactured perishable foods, the increased share must have gone almost entirely into intermediate products — capital goods — to meet the demand of the enterprise sector.

This conclusion helps to clarify the discussion in Chapter 6 of the relative importance of intermediate and household demand elasticities in explaining the growth of the manufacturing sector. Apparently the income elasticity of demand by enterprise for manufactured products was higher, as implied by the Hoffman thesis, than that for households. Indeed, since total enterprise demand was considerably less than total consumer demand for manufactured products, its income elasticity must have been much greater than that for household consumers.

The failure of the share of consumer durables to rise noticeably may come as a surprise to some. However, it must be realized that the automobile industry was still in its infancy at the end of this period. Motor vehicle registrations exceeded 1 million for the first time in 1913. Also, the shift from agriculture to urban pursuits went against major durables, for such commodities were of greater importance on the farm than they were to city dwellers in those times.

The analysis of household demand has thus far proceeded in terms of current prices for consumer goods. If the various categories under discussion are estimated in dollars of constant purchasing power, all trends practically disappear. In other words, in terms of real product flows into the household sector, consumers apparently maintained a highly stable pattern with respect to the allocation of their outlays between perishables, semidurables, durables, and services. The only change that could not easily be attributed to estimating error is a rise in durables from 8 percent at the beginning of this period to 10 percent at the end. [14] With this possible exception, the results of deflation for differing relative price trends do not convey a clear or satisfying message. As Kuznets had remarked, "the extremely rough character of the price indexes leaves little confidence in the reliability of the differences," adding that the "results cannot be relied upon for significant inferences."[15]

In any case these trends, or the lack of them, in the pattern of product demand by firms and households generally seem to dovetail, as one would anticipate, with the changing pattern of production. The national product originated in the different production sectors of the economy, the money claims to that product were distributed as income according to each person's command over personal services and property, and the income was disposed of, either as spending for household consumption or for investment, or for additions to claims against other countries. The design of development was the reflection of the profusion of individual decisions by hundreds of thousands of suppliers and millions of demanders, coordinated by the private market mechanism in the larger context of the business society. On the whole, it would be hard to find a more apt descriptive phrase for our era than Schumpeter's "intact capitalism," although intimations of its termination were already clearly evident.

NOTES

1. John W. Kendrick, *Productivity Trends in the United States*, National Bureau of Economic Research (Princeton, N.J.: Princeton University Press, 1961), p. 3.
2. See, e.g., ibid., pp. 338-40, Table A-XXIII.
3. Kendrick defines a production function as "the notion that the physical volume of output depends on the quantities of productive services, or inputs, employed in the production process and the efficiency with which they are utilized" (ibid., p. 6). The use of an aggregate production function in the manner here applied has been viewed with profound skepticism by many economists, notably the English "Cambridge School."
4. Loc. cit., p. 626, Table 10: sources for Table 26.
5. To use 1870 as initial year for this calculation would entail risk of large error because the numbers for that year are so small.
6. Loc. cit., pp. 338-9 and 362-3.
7. Calculated from R. Gallman, "Gross National Product in the United States, 1834-1909," in National Bureau of Economic Research, Conference on Research in Income and Wealth, *Output, Employment, and Productivity in the United States After 1800*, Studies in Income and Wealth, v. 30 (New York: Columbia University Press, 1966), pp. 11-27 *passim*.
8. Simon Kuznets, *Modern Economic Growth* (New Haven, Conn.: Yale University Press, 1966), p. 237.
9. "Factor Shares, 1850-1910," loc. cit., p. 382, Table 7.

10. R. Gallman, loc. cit., p. 15.
11. These data are from Simon Kuznets, *National Product Since 1869* (New York: National Bureau of Economic Research, 1946), p. 106, Table II8, and p. 146, Table III 11 (Shaw estimates).
12. Estimates for the first two periods are from R. Gallman, "Gross National Product in the United States, 1834-1909," loc. cit., p. 18. For 1904-1913 the estimates are calculated from *National Product Since 1869*, loc. cit., p. 106. Per capita consumption is from ibid., p. 107.
13. The unparenthesized proportions show constancy, at least after 1879, and these are consistent with the lack of trend shown for commodity versus all other production, at current prices, in a recent discussion by R. Gallman and E. S. Howle, "Trends in the Structure of the American Economy Since 1840," in R. W. Fogel and S. L. Engerman (eds.), *The Reinterpretation of American Economic History* (New York: Harper and Row, 1971), p. 27, Table 2.
14. R. Gallman, loc. cit., p. 18.
15. Simon Kuznets, "Long Term Changes in the National Income of the United States of American Since 1870," *Income and Wealth of the United States, Trends and Structure* (Cambridge, Mass.: Bowes and Bowes, 1952), pp. 173-4.

Bibliography

General Works

Useful bibliographies may be found in most of the standard economic history texts and in several of the works listed here. There are also a number of bibliographies, such as H. M. Larson, *Guide to Business History*: *Materials for the Study of American Business History* (Cambridge, Mass.: Howard University Press, 1948), and the "Goldentree Bibliographies" under the editorship of Arthur S. Link, published by the Meredith Corporation (New York: Appleton-Century Crofts).

Two valuable collections of original materials were published many years ago, and are still exceedingly informative. These were: E. L. Bogart and C. M. Thompson, *Readings in the Economic History of the United States* (New York: Longmans, Green, 1916); and F. Flügel and H. U. Faulkner, *Readings in the Economic and Social History of the United States* (New York: Harper, 1929), of which Part III is relevant to the subject here treated.

For the most authoritative, voluminous, and invaluable collections of time series, the two publications of the U.S. Department of Commerce, *Historical Statistics of the United States, Colonial Times to 1957* (Washington: Government Printing Office, 1960), and *Long Term Economic Growth* (Washington Government Printing Office, October 1966), are unexcelled.

Two sources of quantitative and theoretical information representing the best in contemporary scholarship have been published under the aegis of the Conference on Research in Income and Wealth of the National Bureau of Economic Research. These are: *Trends in the American Economy in the Nineteenth Century* (Princeton: Princeton University Press, 1960), which is volume 24 of the Studies in Income and Wealth (hereafter referred to as "NBER, *Trends*") and *Output, Employment, and Productivity in the United States after 1800* (New York: Columbia University Press, 1966), volume 30 of the same Studies (hereafter "NBER, v. 30"). In these two rich collections one will find significant treatments of such matters as the volume of commodity output, gross national product estimates, interregional income and population differences, retail price trends and price deflators for final products, farm product and investment, income originating in trade, factor shares, property income payments, wage trends, the balance of payments pattern, estimates of the labor force (total and by sector), building in Ohio, the development of the major metal mining industries, the growth of the petroleum, coal mining, and machine tool industries, the diffusion of power in manufacturing, and productivity growth in grain production and the railroad sector. Many of these able discussions are relevant to the topics dealt with in the various chapters of the present work.

Collections of original documents and interpretive essays that treat in part the economic history of the period here under examination have burgeoned in recent years. Frequently they contain articles from the scholarly journals that are classics in their respective fields. Among the many, one might fruitfully consult the following: A. D. Chandler, Jr., S. Bruchey, and L. Galambos (eds.), *The Changing Economic Order* (New York: Harcourt, Brace, and World, 1968); S. Cohen and F. G. Hill, *American Economic History, Essays in Interpretation* (Philadelphia: Lippincott, 1966); J. A. Garraty (ed.), *The Transformation of American Society, 1870-1890* (New York: Harper and Row, 1968); William Greenleaf (ed.), *American Economic Development Since 1860* (New York: Harper and Row, 1968); William Letwin (ed.), *A Documentary History of American Economic Policy Since 1789* (Chicago: Aldine, 1961); G. D. Nash (ed.), *Issues in American Economic History*, second ed. (Lexington, Mass.: D. C. Heath, 1972); R. M. Robertson and J. L. Pate (eds.), *Readings in United States Economic and Business History* (Boston: Houghton Mifflin, 1966); and H. N. Scheiber (ed.), *United States Economic History: Selected Readings* (New York: Knopf, 1964). Here again, one will find in these volumes much original source material as well as creative analytical effort pertinent to the U.S. economic experience between the Civil War and World War I.

Two nontext collections are of particular interest because they present with reference to the U.S. field the innovative kind of work in both methodology and interpretation that is being done by the "new economic historians." These are: the highly selective anthology by R. L. Andreano (ed. and contributor), *New Views on American Economic Development* (Cambridge, Mass.: Schenkman, 1965); and the more comprehensive creation of R. W. Fogel and S. L. Engerman (eds. and contributors), *The Reinterpretation of American Economic History* (New York: Harper and Row, 1971), hereafter referred to as *Reinterpretation*. These works can provide the student with a splendid grasp of the new economic history together with a treatment of many substantive matters in this period. Discussions of straight methodological questions, contained in Fogel's introductory essay in the second of these two volumes, may be helpfully supplemented by: A. Fishlow and R. W. Fogel, "Quantitative Economic History: An Interim Evaluation, Past Trends and Present Tendencies," *Journal of Economic History*, 31, no. 1 (March 1971), 15-42; and S. Kuznets, *Modern Economic Growth, Rate, Structure and Spread* (New Haven: Yale University Press, 1966), a seminal book by the person who has perhaps made the greatest single contribution to the quantitative analysis of U.S. economic history.

In any treatment of general works, honorable mention should be made to the appropriate books in the eminent series published some years ago by Rinehart. These were: H. U. Faulkner, *The Decline of Laissez Faire, 1897-1917* (1951); E. C. Kirkland, *Industry Comes of Age; Business, Labor and Public Policy, 1860-1897* (1961); and F. A. Shannon, *The Farmer's Last Frontier, Agriculture, 1860-1897* (1945). Economic historians are still mining the valuable deposits contained in these scholarly contributions.

One stimulating work emphasizing Schumpeter's development thesis of the innovating entrepreneur is Louis Hacker, *The World of Andrew Carnegie: 1865-1901* (Philadelphia: Lippincott, 1968). A number of short general treatments of subperiods of the half-century here under study have also appeared. Among these, C.

N. Degler's *The Age of the Economic Revolution, 1876-1900* (Glenview, Illinois: Scott, Foresman, 1967) and S. P. Hays' *The Response to Industrialism: 1885-1914* (Chicago: University of Chicago Press, 1957) are stimulating and informative.

Of the many scholarly journals containing discussions of U.S. economic history topics, perhaps the most essential, with their abbreviations when used in this bibliography are: *Agricultural History (AH); American Economic Review (AER); American Historical Review (AHR); Business History Review (BHR); Economic History Review (EHR); Explorations in Entrepreneurial History,* in recent years titled *Explorations in Economic History (EEH); Journal of Economic History (JEH),* organ of the Economic History Association; *Journal of Economic Literature (JEL),* dealing with all economic periodical literature; *Journal of Economic and Business History (JEBH); Journal of Political Economy (JPE); Mississippi Valley Historical Review (MVHR),* in recent years the *Journal of American History (JAH);* and the *Quarterly Journal of Economics (QJE).* Of course, there are many other periodicals that occasionally carry articles pertaining to the subject.

The following allocation of books and articles to the various chapters is in many cases arbitrary and works are frequently notable for their spillovers into other chapter topics. In a few cases it has been thought desirable to repeat an item in the listings for two different chapters.

Chapter 1

Understanding the cross section of the Northern and Southern economies on the eve of the Civil War is best achieved by study of the nation's history during the years preceding the war. The bibliography for this phase of U.S. economic experience is too vast to be touched upon here. But brief panoramic views may be obtained from: C. H. Hession and H. Sardy, *Ascent to Affluence* (Boston: Allyn and Bacon, 1969), pp. 318-29, which also presents the "balance sheet" of North-South strengths on the eve of the conflict; G. R. Taylor, *The Transportation Revolution, 1815-1860* (New York: Rinehart, 1951), especially Chapters XI and XVII, dealing with manufacturing and the national economy in 1860; Taylor's lecture on the national economy before and after the war (mostly before) in D. T. Gilchrist and W. David Lewis (eds.), *Economic Change in the Civil War Era* (Greenville, Del.: Eleutherian Mills-Hagley Foundation, 1965), pp. 1-22. Additionally on manufacturing one finds in F. Bateman et al., "Large Scale Manufacturing in the South and West, 1850-1860," *BHR,* v. 45 (1971), pp. 1-17 the thesis that the scale was similar in the two areas prior to the war, and that perfect competition is an inappropriate model even at that early date. The similarity thesis is considered further in the same issue of *BHR* by A. Niemi, Jr., "Structural Shifts in Southern Manufacturing, 1849-1899." Also of a survey nature is Part II, Chapters VI through XII, of D. C. North's *The Economic Growth of the United States, 1790-1860* (New York: Norton, 1966). The reader of this work will receive a bonus, for North was, at the time of the original publication of the work by Prentice-Hall in 1961, not only one of the newer of the new economic historians, but, heretically from the standpoint of that group, also an advocate in this little book of the "leading sector thesis" that cotton was the prime mover of the U.S. development process from about 1820 to 1840. Finally, in the general survey group there is drawn from the Eighth Census of the United States the pamphlet by the U.S. Civil War Centennial Commission, *The United States on the Eve of the Civil War* (Washington, D.C.: Government Printing Office, 1963).

A brief and highly selective list of panoramic discussions of particular aspects of the economy on the brink of war might also include: Chapter 7, "The Influence of Pre-Civil War Railroads on the Patterns of Domestic Commerce," in A. Fishlow's

American Railroads and the Transformation of the Ante-Bellum Economy (Cambridge, Mass.: Harvard University Press, 1965); E. W. Martin's *The Standard of Living in 1860* (Chicago: University of Chicago Press, 1942); E. J. Stevens, "Composition of the Money Stock Prior to the Civil War," *Journal of Money, Credit and Banking*, 3 (February 1971), 84-101; a treatment of the last cyclical movement just before the war in G. W. Van Vleck, *The Panic of 1857* (New York: Columbia University Press, 1943); and J. G. Williamson and J. Swanson, "The Growth of Cities in the American Northeast, 1820-1870," *EEH*, second series, Supplement, 4, no. 1 (1966), together with Williamson's "Ante-Bellum Urbanization in the American Northeast," *JEH*, 25, no. 4 (December 1965), 592-608.

The concern with slavery has produced an almost limitless literary and research effort that has recently received a revival attendant upon the publication of A. H. Conrad and J. R. Meyer, *The Economics of Slavery and Other Studies in Econometric History* (Chicago: Aldine, 1964), a pioneering work in the use of economic analysis to test an old established hypothesis that slavery was not profitable. This work tells much about the Southern economy in 1860. Surveys of the ensuing controversy insofar as it impinged upon the economy will be found in: S. L. Engerman, "The Effects of Slavery Upon the Southern Economy: A Review of the Recent Debate," *EEH*, second series, 4, no. 2 (Winter 1967), 71-97; and in Hugh G. J. Aitken (ed.), *Did Slavery Pay?* (Boston: Houghton, Mifflin, 1971), which also reprints the Engerman article. There is also: the older, much used and misused study by U. B. Phillips, *Life and Labor in the Old South* (Boston: Little, Brown, 1929); the classic work by Kenneth Stampp, *The Peculiar Institution: Slavery in the Ante-Bellum South* (New York: Knopf, 1956); and more recently E. D. Genovese's "The Significance of the Slave Plantation for Southern Economic Development," *Journal of Southern History*, 28 (November 1962), 422-37. Slavery in relation to North-South farm efficiency and growth rates is treated in R. W. Fogel and S. Engerman, "The Relative Efficiency of Slavery: A Comparison of Northern and Southern Agriculture in 1860," *EEH*, 8, no. 3 (Spring 1971), 353-67. In addition there is the challenging end-product of the Fogel-Engerman research, *Time on the Cross*, 2 v. (Boston: Little, Brown, 1974), discussed in the text.

Finally, the active promotional role of state government, both North and South, before the war is emphasized in a famous essay by R. A. Lively, "The American System: A Review Article," *BHR*, 29 (March 1955), 81-96. Lively's bibliography elaborates the subject and adds to one's grasp of the 1860 economic panorama.

Chapter 2

The most detailed among all recent general sources on the Civil War period, economic as well as political and military, is J. G. Randall and D. Donald, *The Civil War and Reconstruction*, second ed. (Boston: Heath, 1961). Chapters 14, 15, 17-20, and 28-30 are valuable background.

More immediate and specific for present purposes is the collection of excellent conference papers edited by O. T. Gilchrist and W. D. Lewis, *Economic Change in the Civil War Era*, previously referred to under Chapter 1. An at least equally rich companion piece is R. Andreano (ed.), *The Economic Impact of the Civil War*, second ed. (Cambridge, Mass.: Schenkman, 1967). Both of these lively and indispensable volumes deal with the years surrounding 1861-1865 as well as the war experience proper, e.g., with the Reconstruction period.

The remaining bibliographical suggestions are more or less in the nature of elaboration of the *Economic Change* and *Impact* volumes. However, the latter do tend to neglect rail transport, except for a brief comment by A. D. Chandler in the *Economic Change* volume. This gap is well filled by two companion pieces: R. C. Black

III, *The Railroads of the Confederacy* (Chapel Hill: University of North Carolina Press, 1952); and T. Weber, *Northern Railroads in the Civil War, 1861-1865* (New York: Columbia University Press/Kings Crown Press, 1952).

A classic study of the Northern economy at the time is E. D. Fite, *Social and Industrial Conditions in the North during the Civil War* (New York: Macmillan, 1910, republished New York: Frederick Ungar, 1963). In Paul Gates, *Agriculture and the Civil War* (New York: Knopf, 1965), it is contended the South was defeated by food scarcity, military desertions, and a disastrous currency.

On the last point one should peruse: the rather too merely descriptive R. C. Todd, *Confederate Finance* (Athens: University of Georgia Press, 1954); or, more broadly, J. C. Schwab, *The Confederate States of America, 1861-1865; A Financial and Industrial History of the South during the Civil War* (New York: Scribner's, 1901). Further on finance, in this case for the North, there is the famous study of the first years of the Civil War "fiat" money, W. C. Mitchell, *A History of the Greenbacks, with Special Reference to the Economic Consequences of Their Issue: 1862-1865* (Chicago: University of Chicago Press, 1903). Mitchell's argument therein and in his later *Gold, Prices and Wages under the Greenback Standard* (Berkeley: University of California Press, 1908) that currency depreciation was responsible for cutting Northern real wages during the war is attacked by R. A. Kessel and A. A. Alchain in the Andreano volume on *Economic Impact.* In Bray Hammond, *Sovereignty and an Empty Purse: Banks and Politics in the Civil War* (Princeton: Princeton University Press, 1970), time is also taken to rebut the Mitchell thesis.

The best single discussion of Civil War fiscal policies, both North and South, is to be found in S. Ratner, *Taxation and Democracy in America* (New York: Wiley, 1942, 1967), Chapters 4-6. An older standard source on the new banking system is A. M. Davis, *The Origin of the National Banking System*, v. V, no. 1 (Washington: National Monetary Commission, 1910).

Chapter 3

Since this is a survey chapter, bibliographical references here will be confined to selected overall changes not elaborated under specific subjects that are treated in the ensuing chapters. In particular, the matters considered relevant here are general production growth, wealth and input growth, population and immigration, technology, income distribution, consumer demand patterns, and economic cycles.

The most recent and authoritative GNP estimates may be found in: R. E. Gallman "Gross National Product in the United States, 1834-1909." in NBER, v. 30, pp. 3-90; and annual estimates of five-year moving averages from 1871 to 1953 in current and 1929 prices were made earlier by S. Kuznets in his *Capital in the American Economy* (Princeton: Princeton University Press, 1961), pp. 561-64. This latter work is also the most comprehensive and scholarly on the capital stocks and flows, total and by sector, for this period. Straight annual estimates by Kuznets for 1869 to 1882 are presented in J. K. Kindahl, "Economic Factors in Specie Resumption: The United States, 1865-1879," in *Reinterpretation*, p. 474.

Other outstanding production estimates may be found in: A. F. Burns, *Production Trends in the United States since 1870* (New York: National Bureau of Economic Research, 1934); in E. Frickey, *Production in the United States 1860-1914* (Cambridge: Harvard University Press, 1947); in R. E. Gallman, "Commodity Output, 1839-1899," in NBER, *Trends*, pp. 13-67; and in E. S. Shaw, *Value of Commodity Output since 1869* (New York: National Bureau of Economic Research, 1947). An excellent brief overview is presented by S. Kuznets, "Notes on the Pattern of U.S. Economic Growth," in his *Economic Growth and Structure* (New York: W. W. Norton, 1965), 304-27.

A link between output and input growth, and the related matter of productivity, is provided by M. Abramovitz in "Resource and Output Trends in the United States since 1870," *Papers and Proceedings of the American Economic Association*, May 1956, pp. 5-23. A scholarly full length work on the same subject is J. W. Kendrick, *Productivity Trends in the United States* (Princeton: Princeton University Press, 1961).

On the growth of inputs, capital is exhaustively treated in the previously mentioned work by S. Kuznets, *Capital in the American Economy*. Human capital investment is examined by proxy in: A. Fishlow, "Levels of Nineteenth Century American Investment in Education, "*JEH*, 26, no. 4 (December 1966), 418-36; and L. Solmon, "Capital Formation by Expenditures on Formal Education, 1880 and 1890," *JEH*, 29 (March 1969), 167-72. A discussion of land, less statistical but challenging, is offered in W. R. Van Dersal, *The American Land: Its History and Its Uses* (London, New York: Oxford University Press, 1943). Estimates of the growth of wealth have been made by Raymond Goldsmith in "The Growth of Reproducible Wealth of the United States of America from 1805 to 1950," *Income and Wealth of the United States*, International Association for Research in Income and Wealth (Cambridge, Mass.: Bowes and Bowes, 1952), pp. 247-328. Power input and output is thoroughly examined in the contemporary study by S. H. Schurr and B. C. Netschert, *Energy in the American Economy, 1850-1955* (Baltimore: Johns Hopkins Press, 1960).

For population and labor force there are a number of important contributions. For population there is the comprehensive statistical study by E. S. Lee et al., *Population Redistribution and Economic Growth, United States, 1870-1950. I. Methodological Considerations and Reference Tables* (Philadelphia: American Philosophical Society, 1957). While R. Easterlin has a full length study, his journal article, "Long Swings in United States Demographic and Economic Growth: Some Findings on the Historical Pattern," *Demography*, 2 (1965), 490-507, serves as an introduction to this remarkable phenomenon. Two older careful treatises are available for the more assiduous student of population trends: C. Taeuber and I. Taeuber, *The Changing Population of the United States* (New York: Wiley, 1958); and W. S. Thompson and P. K. Whelpton, *Population Trends in the United States* (New York: McGraw-Hill, 1933). Finally there is for empirical material U.S. Bureau of the Census, *A Century of Population Growth from the First Census of the United States to the Twelfth, 1790-1900* Washington: Government Printing Office, 1909).

The growth and distribution of the labor force has received extended examination. Only a few leading contributions can be cited here. Most recently, labor force (and wage) estimates have been prepared by S. Lebergott in his *Manpower and Economic Growth* (New York: McGraw-Hill, 1964). Earlier contributions were: C. D. Long, *The Labor Force under Changing Income and Employment* (Princeton: Princeton University Press, 1958), with breakdowns for sex, age, and rural-urban; and the papers on the industrial and occupational composition of the labor force by S. Fabricant and D. Carson in *Studies in Income and Wealth, Volume Eleven* (New York: National Bureau of Economic Research, 1949), pp. 3-45 and 46-134, respectively. There is a cursory treatment of blacks in the labor force in G. Mydal, "Population and Migration," *An American Dilemma* (New York: Harper, 1944). For data one may turn to U.S. Bureau of the Census, *Negro Population 1790-1915* (Washington: Government Printing Office, 1918).

An introduction to the considerable literature on the economic aspects of immigration may be gotten from: O. Handlin, *The Uprooted: The Epic Story of the Great Migrations that Made the American People* (Boston: Atlantic Monthly Press, 1951); and more recently from M. A. Jones, *American Immigration* (Chicago: University of Chicago Press, 1960). S. Kuznets has examined with his usual originality the contribution of immigrants to the U.S. labor force in "Long-

Term Changes in the National Income of the United States of America Since 1870." *Income and Wealth of the United States*, International Association for Research in Income and Wealth (Cambridge, Mass.: Bowes and Bowes, 1952), pp. 196-204. Additional references to human migration will be found in the bibliography for the next chapter.

General discussions of technological change, as distinguished from the more numerous studies of particular industries or sectors, may be represented by: Nathan Rosenberg's *Technology and American Economic Growth* (New York: Harper, 1972); and the somewhat earlier and controversial work of H. J. Habakkuk, *American and British Technology in the 19th Century* (Cambridge, Eng.: Cambridge University Press, 1962). Rosenberg's footnotes furnish the reader with a valuable bibliography. Habakkuk's thesis is that U.S. innovations were generally labor saving (capital-intensive) and that this gave an added stimulus to further innovation. A fine treatment of special topics is Paul David's *Technical Choice: Innovation and Economic Growth* (Cambridge, Eng.: Cambridge University Press, 1975). P. Strassman's *Risk and Technological Innovation* (Ithaca: Cornell University Press, 1959), emphasizes the excessive caution of manufacturing entrepreneurs.

Income distribution and payments are examined by: E. C. Budd, "Factor Shares, 1850-1910," and A. J. Schwartz, "Gross Dividend and Interest Payments by Corporations in the Nineteenth Century," in NBER, *Trends*, pp. 365-406 and 407-48 respectively. Interest is treated in: Sidney Homer, *A History of Interest Rates* (New Brunswick: Rutgers University Press, 1963); and F. R. Macaulay, *The Movements of Interest Rates, Bond Yields and Stock Prices in the United States since 1856* (New York: National Bureau of Economic Research, 1938). Also relevant is: D. G. Johnson, "The Functional Distribution of Income in the United States, 1850-1952," *Review of Economics and Statistics* (May 1954); and Lee Soltow, "Evidence on Income Inequality in the United States, 1866-1965," *JEH*, 29, no. 2 (June 1969), 279-86. As S. Lebergott examines wage trends in the same volume, 449-98. Clarence D. Long's *Wages and Earnings in the United States, 1860-1890* (Princeton: Princeton University Press, 1960) will also reward perusal. A formidable collection of wage statistics, by occupation, is contained in the 574 page volume U.S. Department of Labor, *History of Wages in the United States from Colonial Times to 1928*, Bureau of Labor Statistics, bulletin no. 604 (Washington: Government Printing Office, 1934). Two other famous wage studies, emphasizing real wages, and arriving at quite different results, are: P. H. Douglas, *Real Wages in the United States, 1890-1926* (Boston: Houghton Mifflin, 1930); and A. Rees, *Real Wages in Manufacturing 1890-1914* (Princeton: Princeton University Press, 1961). Slightly more specialized but equally valuable is E. Abbott, "The Wages of Unskilled Labor in the United States," *JPE*, 13 (1905), 321-67.

Aggregate consumption estimates may be found in S. Kuznets, *Capital in the American Economy*, op. cit., the appendixes. Still empirical but also more analytical is R. Mack, "Trends in American Consumption and the Aspiration to Consume," *American Economic Review, Papers and Proceedings*, May 1956, 55-68. On expenditure patterns there is, for example: J. G. Williamson, "Consumer Behavior in the Nineteenth Century: Carroll D. Wright's Massachusetts Workers in 1875," *EEH*, 4, no. 2 (Winter 1967), 98-135; and the highly informative U.S. Bureau of Labor Statistics, *How American Buying Habits Change* (Washington: Government Printing Office, 1959).

Economic performance exhibited cyclical patterns throughout the period under study. The matter is touched upon in this chapter and in Chapters 10 and 11. Essentials from the bibliographical standpoint are: R. Fels, *American Business Cycles, 1865-1897* (Chapel Hill: University of North Carolina Press, 1959), the most sophisticated general work; the more popular C. Hoffman, *The Depression of the Nineties* (Westport, Conn.: Greenwood, 1970); one among the very many on the long swing,

S. Kuznets," Long Swings in the Growth of Population and in Related Economic Variables," *Proceedings of the American Philosophical Society* (February 1958), 25-52; and the older scholarly study by A. M. W. Sprague, *History of Crises under the National Banking System* (Washington: National Monetary Commission, Sen. Doc. No. 538, 1910). An unfortunately neglected but seminal discussion of the construction cycle is W. Isard, "A Neglected Cycle: The Transport-Building Cycle," *Review of Economic Statistics* (November 1942), 149-58. More comprehensive and equally theoretical on construction is C. Long, *Building Cycles and the Theory of Investment* (Princeton: Princeton University Press, 1940).

Chapter 4

There are four general treatments of regional changes that make up a minimum packet of sources on the subject: R. A. Easterlin, "Interregional Differences in Per Capita Income, Population, and Total Income, 1840-1950," in NBER, *Trends*, 73-140; E. S. Lee, A. R. Miller, C. P. Brainerd, and R. A. Easterlin, *Population Redistribution and Economic Growth, United States, 1870-1950* (Philadelphia: American Philosophical Society, v. I, 1957, v. II, 1960); H. S. Perloff, E. S. Dunn, Jr., E. E. Lampard, and R. F. Muth, *Regions, Resources and Economic Growth* (Baltimore: Johns Hopkins Press, 1960, reprinted by University of Nebraska Press, no date); and the older study by W. C. Thornthwaite, *Internal Migration in the United States* (Philadelphia: University of Pennsylvania Press, 1934).

More specialized regionally or topically are: L. J. Arrington, *The Changing Economic Structure of the Mountain West, 1850-1950* (Salt Lake City: Utah State University Monographs, v. 10, no. 3, June 1963); the controversial discussion of D. F. Dowd, "A Comparative Analysis of Economic Development in the American West and South," *JEH*, 16 (December 1956), 558-74; and on black migration, C. G. Woodson, *A Century of Negro Migration* (Washington: The Association for the Study of Negro Life and History, 1918).

Of the vast literature on the South one may fruitfully consult such contributions as: S. Engerman, "The Economic Impact of the Civil War," *EEH*, second series, 3, no. 3 (Spring-Summer 1966), 176-99, reprinted in R. Andreano, *Economic Impact, etc.*, op. cit.; J. H. Franklin, *From Slavery to Freedom: A History of American Negroes*, third ed. (New York: Knopf, 1967); the older pioneering work by E. Q. Hawk, *Economic History of the South* (New York: Prentice-Hall, 1934); R. Ransom and R. Sutch, "The Rise of Sharecropping in the American South, 1865-1900," *Tenancy, Farm Size, Self-Sufficiency, and Racism: Four Problems in the Economic History of Southern Agriculture 1865-1880*, Southern Economic History Project, Working Paper Series, VIII (Berkeley: University of California, Institute of Business and Economic Research, April 1970); B. I. Wiley, "Salient Changes in Southern Agriculture since the Civil War," *AH*, 13 (1939), 64-76; or, among the outstanding general historical writings, C. Vann Woodward, *Origins of the New South, 1877-1913* (Baton Rouge: Louisiana State University Press, 1951).

Chapter 5

No brief bibliography can begin to do justice to the enormous literature on this subject of agriculture and the agricultural frontier. One seriously interested should start with the excellent 269 page general historical and bibliographical work by N. Klose, *A Concise Study Guide to the American Frontier* (Lincoln: University of Nebraska Press, 1964). The best general economic treatment is still probably F. A. Shannon, *The Farmer's Last Frontier, 1860-1897* (New York: Farrar and Rinehart,

1945), which also contains a 34 page bibliography. Other general and somewhat older sources are: L. B. Schmidt and E. D. Ross, *Readings in the Economic History of American Agriculture* (New York: Macmillan, 1925); the very famous, seminal, and controversial F. J. Turner, *The Frontier in American History* (New York: Holt, 1950), containing his famous 1893 paper before the American Historical Association and twelve other pieces; and the classic by W. P. Webb, *The Great Plains* (Grosset and Dunlap, copyright by W. P. Webb, 1931). More recent on the heart of the Midwest is A. Bogue's, *From Prairie to Corn Belt: Farming on the Illinois and Iowa Prairies in the Nineteenth Century* (Chicago: University of Chicago Press, 1963).

Overall quantitative analysis is facilitated by perusal of: M. W. Towne and W. D. Rasmussen, "Farm Gross Product and Gross Investment in the Nineteenth Century," NBER, *Trends*, 255-312; the earlier contribution of F. Strauss and L. H. Bean, *Gross Farm Income and Indices of Farm Production and Prices in the United States 1869-1937*, U.S. Department of Agriculture, Tech. Bull. 703, 1940; and more recently A. S. Tostlebe, *Capital in Agriculture: Its Formation and Financing since 1870* (Princeton: Princeton University Press, 1957).

The literature on agricultural technology may be represented by: the older and most scholarly study of L. Rogin, *The Introduction of Farm Machinery in Its Relation to the Productivity of Labor in the Agriculture of the United States during the Nineteenth Century* (Berkeley: University of California Press, 1931); the discussion in Chapter 5 of R. B. Lave, *Technological Change: Its Conception and Measurement* (Englewood Cliffs, N.J.: Prentice-Hall, 1966); William Parker, "Sources of Agricultural Productivity in the Nineteenth Century," *Journal of Farm Economics* (December 1967), 1455-68; and by W. D. Rasmussen, "The Impact of Technological Change on American Agriculture, 1862-1962," *JEH*, 22, no. 4 (1962), 578-91.

Farm and land policy go far back in U.S. experience. Two able studies in that area are: the older classic by B. H. Hibbard, *A History of the Public Land Policies* (Madison: University of Wisconsin Press, 1965, first published by Macmillan in 1924); and the more recent work by M. R. Benedict, *Farm Policies of the United States, 1790-1950: A Study of Their Origins and Development* (New York: Twentieth Century Fund, 1953). Policy in other related areas, such as forestry and mining, must be omitted because of space limitations.

Exciting contributions in selected particular topics are: J. D. Black and R. H. Allen, "The Growth of Farm Tenancy in the United States," *QJE*, 51 (1937), 393-425; L. F. Cox, "The American Agricultural Wage Earner, 1865-1900," *AH*, 22 (1948), 95-114; and the trail-breaking critique of P. W. Gates, "The Homestead Law in an Incongruous Land System," *AHR*, 41 (1936), 652-81.

Considerable interest and research effort was aroused by: the important discussions of A. G. Bogue, *Money At Interest: The Farm Mortgage on the Middle Border* (Ithaca: Cornell University Press, 1955); and his joint article with M. B. Bogue, "Profits and the Frontier Land Speculator," *JEH*, 17, no. 1 (1957), 1-24. On the much discussed doctrine of the frontier as a labor safety valve, challenging illustrative analyses, in this instance a con and pro, are: F. A. Shannon, "A Post Mortem on the Labor-Safety-Valve Theory," *AH*, 19 (1945), 31-8; and G. G. S. Murphy and A. Zellner, "Sequential Growth, the Labor-Safety-Valve Doctrine and the Development of American Unionism," *JEH*, 19, no. 3 (September 1959), 402-21.

Chapter 6

Manufacturing was given careful descriptive examination many years ago in the standard source of its type by V. S. Clark, *History of Manufactures in the United*

States, *1860-1914* (New York: McGraw-Hill, 1928). Similar but more emphatically statistical is the U.S. Bureau of the Census, *Census of Manufactures, 1914*, I, II (Washington: Government Printing Office, 1918). S. Fabricant's *The Output of Manufacturing Industries, 1899-1937* (New York: NBER, *Trends*, 1940) covers the end of this period with a strongly empirical approach. The central and strategic phenomenon of power usage is examined in A. H. Fenichel "Growth and Diffusion of Power in Manufacturing, 1838-1919," in NBER, *Trends*, v. 30, 443-78.

On the theory of industrialization, two excellent recent discussions are: H. Chenery, "Patterns of Industrial Growth," *AER*, 50, no. 4 (September 1960), 624-54; and R. W. Fogel and S. L. Engerman, "A Model for the Explanation of Industrial Expansion During the Nineteenth Century: With An Application to the American Iron Industry," *Reinterpretation*, 148-62.

Studies of particular manufacturing industries would lead us far afield. Steel was of course the most important single great new industry in our period, and the text emphasizes the crucial role of machinery and machine tools. On these two, there is excellent recent work, i.e.: P. Temin, *Iron and Steel in Nineteenth Century America: An Economic Inquiry* (Cambridge, Mass.: M.I.T. Press, 1964); and two essays in NBER, v. 30: R. M. Robertson, "Changing Production of Metalworking Machinery, 1860-1920," pp. 443-78, and D. McDougall, "Machine Tool Output, 1861-1910," pp. 497-517. N. Rosenberg, "Technological Change in the Machine Tool Industry, 1840-1910," *JEH*, 23, no. 4 (December 1963), 414-43, reveals in this example the importance of the quantitatively unimportant. Perhaps electricity deserves equivalent attention, young as it was at the end of this period, and a reference is also justified by virtue of the breadth and high quality of the work by H. C. Passer, *The Electrical Manufactures, 1875-1900: A Study in Competition, Entrepreneurship, Technical Change and Economic Growth* (Cambridge, Mass.: Harvard University Press, 1953), a work concentrating upon entrepreneurial innovation and emphasizing the central role of the small firm in industrial advance.

Chapter 7

The sphere included here is all production in the domestic economy except agriculture and manufacturing. In order to delineate this, references will deal only with: transportation, i.e., steam railroads and inland waterways; the service sector in general; the public utility sector and some of its components; trade; mining, including petroleum; and government.

For the railroad map, one should consult the thorough study by G. R. Taylor and I. Neu, *The American Railroad Network, 1861-1890* (Cambridge, Mass.: Harvard University Press, 1956). By the end of the period covered the network was practically complete. In addition, two recent eminent contributions in econometric history are: A. Fishlow, "Productivity and Technological Change in the Railroad Sector, 1840-1910," NBER, v. 30, 583-646; and the trail-breaking critique of the thesis of railroad indispensability, R. W. Fogel, *Railroads and American Economic Growth* (Baltimore: Johns Hopkins Press, 1964). On inland waterways, two rich government sources are: U.S. Bureau of Corporations, *Report of the Commissioner of Corporations on Transportation by Water in the United States*, 3 v. (Washington: Government Printing Office, 1909-1913); and U.S. National Waterways Commission, *Final Report*, 62nd Congress, 2nd Session, Sen. Doc. No. 469 (Washington: Government Printing Office, 1912).

Transportation in general is quantitatively analyzed in H. Barger, *The Transportation Industries, 1889-1946: A Study in Output, Employment and Productivity* (New York: National Bureau of Economic Research, 1951). E. C. Kirkland's *Men, Cities and Transportation* (Cambridge, Mass.: Harvard University Press,

1948) is transport history, regional history, and economic history for New England, 1820-1900.

Fortunately for the present work, the fine and somewhat courageous study of services, R. E. Gallman and T. J. Weiss, "The Service Industries in the Nineteenth Century" in V. R. Fuchs (ed.), *Production and Productivity in the Service Industries* (New York: Columbia University Press, 1969), 287-381, was published in time. Despite admittedly varying degrees of reliability of the data and the absence of regional breakdowns, this work will remain invaluable to historians in search of empirical material for some time to come. T. Weiss has also contributed more recently "Urbanization and the Growth of the Service Workforce," *EEH*, 8, no. 3 (Spring 1971), 241-58, useful for Chapter 9.

The public utilities, which of course include railroads and waterways, receive careful statistical examination in M. J. Ulmer, *Capital in Transportation, Communications and Public Utilities: Its Formation and Financing* (Princeton: Princeton University Press, 1960). More specific but not to be neglected is the "street" and interurban railway: G. Hilton and J. F. Due, *The Electric Interurban Railways in America* (Stanford: Stanford University Press, 1960); and U.S. Bureau of the Census, *Special Report: Electric and Street Railways* (Washington: Government Printing Office, 1902).

For wholesale and retail trade, there is: an older study by H. Barger, *Distribution's Place in the American Economy since 1869* (Princeton: Princeton University Press, 1955); and the more recent sketchy essay by the same author, "Income Originating in Trade, 1869-1929," in NBER, *Trends*, 327-33.

Mining as a composite sector and with breakdowns for subsectors is treated statistically in H. Barger and S. H. Schurr, *The Mining Industries 1899-1939* (New York: National Bureau of Economic Research 1944). There are also two able and more recent essays, overwhelmingly quantitative, in NBER, v. 30: the more general is O. C. Herfindahl, "Development of the Major Metal Mining Industries in the United States from 1839-1909," pp. 293-346; and on coal, V. F. Eliasberg, "Some Aspects of Development in the Coal Mining Industry, 1839-1918," pp. 405-35. Petroleum receives extensive historical consideration in H. F. Williamson and A. R. Daum, *The American Petroleum Industry*, 2 v. (Evanston: Northwestern University Press, 1959, 1963), but there is a briefer, lucid economic presentation in H. F. Williamson, R. L. Andreano, and C. Menezes, "The American Petroleum Industry," NBER, v. 30, 349-403. The vital pipeline industry—a transportation activity just emerging at the close of this period—is excellently examined by A. J. Johnson, *Development of American Petroleum Pipelines: A Study in Private Enterprise and Public Policy, 1862-1906* (Ithaca: Cornell University Press, 1956).

The Federal government sector was still small, but its role was more significant than usually imagined. The government sector when taken at all levels was even quantitatively noteworthy. Two studies will provide a general introduction, i.e.: that of H. W. Broude, "The Role of the State in American Economic Development, 1820-1890," in H. G. J. Aitken (ed.), *The State and Economic Growth* (New York: Social Science Research Council, 1959), 4-25; and for the end of this period, S. Fabricant, *The Trend of Government Activity in the United States since 1900* (New York: National Bureau of Economic Research, 1952). Of course we are here concerned with government as a sector, not with the many facets of government policy. But this topic would be enriched bibliographically by reference to any of the standard financial histories, such as: P. Studenski and H. E. Krooss, *Financial History of the United States*, second ed. (New York: McGraw-Hill, 1963); or M. G. Myers, *A Financial History of the United States* (New York: Columbia University Press, 1970). For the same indirect reasons, S. Ratner, *Taxation and Democracy in America* (New York: Wiley, 1967), is relevant.

Chapter 8

This chapter deals in a broad sense with three overlapping topics: changes in structural conditions within the business sector, changes in business behavior and policy, and changes in the environment surrounding the business community with particular reference to certain aspects of government-business relations not treated elsewhere. This bibliography follows this loose classification.

The analysis of structural changes within the business sector is well reviewed in: A. D. Chandler, Jr., "The Beginnings of Big Business in American Industry," *BHR*, 33, no. 1 (Spring 1959), 1-31; and A. D. Chandler, Jr., (ed.), *The Railroads, the Nation's First Big Business* (New York: Harcourt, Brace, and World, 1965). Chandler's *Strategy and Structure: Chapters in the History of the Industrial Enterprise* (Cambridge, Mass.: M.I.T. Press, 1962) connects structural and behavioral change and provides valuable material for understanding individual enterprise growth and administrative coordination. T. Cochran's *The Age of Enterprise* (New York: Macmillan, 1942) appraises the rising industrial enterprise in the larger economic context. W. L. Thorp, *The Integration of Industrial Operation*, Census Monograph III (Washington: 1924) analyses the growth of central office firms with particular reference to manufacturing. The spread of the corporate form of business is portrayed in the quantitative work of G. H. Evans, *Business Incorporations in the United States, 1800-1943* (New York: National Bureau of Economic Research, 1948). The classic discussion of fixed costs and their impact on business decision making is J. M. Clark, *The Economics of Overhead Costs* (Chicago: Unviersity of Chicago Press, 1923).

Business sector changes are extensively dealt with in the business history literature, a literature overwhelmingly devoted to the individual firm. Two outstanding bibliographical works in this field are: the comprehensive listing (over 4,000 items) of H. Larson, *Guide to Business History* (Cambridge: Harvard University Press, 1948); and the short recent review by L. Galambos, *American Business History* (Washington: Service Center for Teachers of History, 1967). Some of the better histories of particular firms are endowed with sufficient generality and objectivity to contribute substantially to our grasp of structural and functional change in this period. Reference has already been made to H. C. Passer's *The Electrical Manufactures*. Other examples are: R. M. Hower, *The History of an Advertising Agency: N. W. Ayer and Son at Work, 1869-1939* (Cambridge, Mass.: Harvard University Press, 1939), which partly serves the need for a treatment of the rise of advertising as a business sector change; and R. and M. Hidy's *Pioneering in Big Business, 1882-1911* (New York: Harper, 1955), which is much more than a study of the important Standard Oil Company.

Changes in the financial subsector of the business sector are well covered by: Fritz Redlich, *The Molding of American Banking: Men and Ideas* (New York: Johnson Reprint Corporation, 1968); G. W. Edwards, *The Evolution of Finance Capitalism* (New York: Augustus M. Kelley, 1967, reprinted); M. Myers, *The New York Money Market*, v. I, Part II (New York: Columbia University Press, 1931); R. Sobel, *The Big Board* (New York: The Free Press, 1965); L. E. Davis, "The Investment Market, 1870-1914: The Evolution of a National Market," *JEH*, 25 (September 1965), 355-93; and T. R. Navin and M. V. Sears, "The Rise of a Market for Industrial Securities, 1887-1902," *BHR*, 29 (1955), 105-38.

Turning now to the second overlapping topic of changes in business behavior and policy, an older work of fine quality dealing broadly with the rise of oligopoly and nonprice competition is A. R. Burns, *The Decline of Competition* (New York: McGraw-Hill, 1936). More recently the same subject has been summarily but discerningly analyzed by J. S. Bain, "Industrial Concentration and Antitrust Policy," in H. F. Williamson (ed.), *The Growth of the American Economy*, second ed.

(Englewood Cliffs, N.J.: Prentice-Hall, 1951), 616-30. An older classic on business combination is H. R. Seager and C. A. Gulick, *Trust and Corporation Problems* (New York: Harper, 1929). The "rationalization" of the production process in the form of scientific management is broadly presented in H. G. J. Aitken, *Taylorism at Watertown Arsenal: Scientific Management in Action, 1908-1915* (Cambridge, Mass.: Harvard University Press, 1960). Various controversial views of the business leadership of this period may be found in: the famous work in the muck-raking tradition, M. Josephson, *The Robber Barons* (New York: Harcourt, Brace, and World, 1934 and 1962); and a later survey by P. d'A. Jones (ed.), *The Robber Barons Revisited* (Boston: D. C. Heath, 1968), which contains a bibliography. More general is W. Miller (ed.), *Men in Business* (Cambridge, Mass.: Harvard University Press, 1952). Finally, wide ranging but empirically oriented discussions of the role of the entrepreneur are offered in: T. Cochran, "The Entrepreneur in Economic Change," *EEH*, second series, 3, no. 1 (Fall 1965), 25-38; and also in his *America's Railroad Leaders*, 1845-1890 (Cambridge, Mass.: Harvard University Press, 1953).

With regard to the governmental environment surrounding the business community, the aspects not treated elsewhere are regulatory control, antitrust, the purely domestic aspects of the tariffs, and welfare legislation.

As to regulation, the railroads come first to mind. Of the very large literature on that subject one should peruse: the older study by W. Z. Ripley, *Railroads: Rates and Regulation* (New York: Longmans, Green, 1912); and the contemporary G. Kolko, *Railroads and Regulation, 1877-1916* (Princeton: Princeton University Press, 1965), which pursues the thesis that railroad leaders accepted regulation and preferred Federal to state controls. An excellent general historical and analytical survey is M. H. Bernstein, *Regulating Business by Independent Commission* (Princeton: Princeton University Press, 1955).

For antitrust, in additional to the Bain, and the Seager and Gulick, earlier cited, two outstanding contributions are: William Letwin, *Law and Economic Policy in America: The Evolution of the Sherman Antitrust Act* (New York: Random House, 1965); and H. B. Thorelli, *The Federal Antitrust Policy: Origination of an American Tradition* (Baltimore: Johns Hopkins Press, 1955). Thorelli argues that throughout the crucial nineties the Justice Department systematically undermined enforcement.

On the tariff, the older study by F. Taussig, *The Tariff History of the United States*, eighth revised ed. (New York: Capricorn Books, 1964), is still the standard source, but C. L. Miller, *The States of the Old Northwest and the Tariff, 1867-1888* (Emporia, Kansas: Emporia Gazette Press, 1929) gives a more intimate view of the ebb and flow of public pressures behind tariff setting, as does E. Stanwood, *American Tariff Controversies in the Nineteenth Century* (Boston: Houghton-Mifflin, 1903), and the Ratner work cited above.

A grasp of the social reform and social welfare currents, and the emerging legislative framework that was in the long run to tighten the network of controls within which business enterprise was to function, may be gleaned from: C. Eastman, *Work-Accidents and the Law* (New York: 1910); H. I. Clarke, *Social Legislation* (New York: Appleton-Century-Crofts, 1957); H. U. Faulkner, *The Quest for Social Justice, 1898-1914* (New York: Macmillan, 1931); S. P. Hays, *Conservation and the Gospel of Efficiency: The Progressive Conservation Movement, 1890-1920* (Cambridge, Mass.: Harvard University Press, 1959); J. D. Hogan and F. A. J. Ianni, *American Social Legislation* (New York: Harper, 1956); R. Lubove, *The Struggle for Social Security, 1900-1935* (Cambridge, Mass.: Harvard University Press, 1968); G. E. Mowry, *The Era of Theodore Roosevelt and the Birth of Modern America, 1900-1912* (New York: Harper and Row, 1958); and F. M. Stewart, *A Half-Century of Municipal Reform: The History of the National Municipal League*

(Berkeley: University of California Press, 1950). These works are also pertinent to much of the discussion in Chapter 11, and a number of them contribute particularly to the bibliography of the Progressive movement.

Chapter 9

There are several excellent general studies of urbanization. First, one should as a minimum examine the following four of a more theoretical nature: E. Lampard, "The History of Cities in the Economically Advanced Areas," *Economic Development and Cultural Change* (January 1955), 81-136; A. R. Pred, *The Spatial Dynamics of U.S. Urban-Industrial Growth, 1800-1914* (Cambridge, Mass.: M.I.T. Press, 1966), which is also strongly empirical; E. Smolensky and D. Ratajczak, "The Conception of Cities," *EEH*, second series, 2 (Winter 1965), 90-131; and W. R. Thompson, "Economic Growth and Development: Processes, Stages and Determinants," Chapter I of his *A Preface to Urban Economics* (Baltimore: Johns Hopkins Press, 1968), 11-60.

More empirically weighted are: the distinguished studies by W. W. Belcher, *The Economic Rivalry Between St. Louis and Chicago, 1850-1880* (New York: Columbia University Press, 1947), which provides a fine example of the several works on intercity competition in our period; C. N. Glaab, *The American City, A Documentary History* (Homewood, Ill.: The Dorsey Press, 1963), especially Chapter 3, "The Growth of Cities in the Late Nineteenth Century," pp. 173-263; the more comprehensive C. N. Glaab and A. T. Brown, *A History of Urban America* (New York: Macmillan, 1967), which, like the preceding reference, contains a bibliography; B. McKelvey, *The Urbanization of America, 1860-1915* (New Brunswick, N.J.: Rutgers University Press, 1963); the earlier eminent work of the noted general historian A. M. Schlesinger, *The Rise of the City, 1878-1898* (New York: Macmillan, 1933); R. Wade, *The Urban Frontier* (Cambridge, Mass.: Harvard University Press, 1959); and the much older pioneering descriptive presentation by E. F. Weber, *The Growth of Cities in the Nineteenth Century* (New York: Macmillan, 1899).

Ghetto formation is ably treated in two city case studies: G. Osofsky, *Harlem: The Making of a Ghetto* (New York: Harper and Row, 1966); and A. H. Spear, *Black Chicago: The Making of a Negro Ghetto, 1890-1920* (Chicago: University of Chicago Press, 1967).

Chapter 10

A number of works relevant to this subject have already been cited in the bibliographies for preceding chapters. Cases in point are: the financial and taxation histories by Myers, Studenski and Krooss, and Ratner; the work on banking history by Redlich; and the books on the business cycle by Fels, Hoffman and Sprague. These were cited earlier partly in order not to bias unnecessarily the treatment of business cycles herein toward the monetary school of theorists.

By far the most important single source for this chapter is the scholarly and exhaustive work by M. Friedman and A. J. Schwartz, *A Monetary History of the United States, 1867-1960* (Princeton: Princeton University Press, 1963). The specific theoretical approach used by Friedman and Schwartz warrants the concomitant study of a critique, however, and one such that is most competently done is R. Clower, "Monetary History and Positive Economics," a review of the Friedman and Schwartz book in *JEH*, 24, no. 3 (September 1964), 364-80. The *Monetary History* is extensively, and from a theoretical viewpoint sympathetically, supplemented by P. Cagan's *Determinants and Effects of Changes in the Stock of Money, 1875-1960* (New York: National Bureau of Economic Research, distributed by Columbia University Press, 1965). The standard data source on the subject is Board of Governors of the Federal Reserve System, *Banking and Monetary Statistics.*

Of the vast literature on particular aspects of the history of money and prices, most of which is referred to in Friedman and Schwartz, Cagan, or the financial histories, one might note especially: A. I. Bloomfield, *Monetary Policy under the International Gold Standard: 1880-1914* (Federal Reserve Bank of New York, October 1959); the older scholarly classic by the eminent I. Fisher with H. G. Brown, *The Purchasing Power of Money* (New York: Macmillan, 1911, 1922); G. Garvy and M. R. Blyn, *The Velocity of Money* (Federal Reserve Bank of New York, October 1969), upon which considerable reliance is placed by this chapter's text, and which offers a theoretical alternative to Friedman and Schwartz on velocity; J. G. Gurley and E. S. Shaw, "The Growth of Debt and Money in the United States, 1800-1950; A Suggested Interpretation," *Review of Economics and Statistics*, v. 39-40 (1957-1958), 250-62; R. Sylla, "Federal Policy, Banking Market Structure and Capital Mobilization in the United States, 1863-1913," *JEH*, 29, no. 4 (December 1969), 657-86, which develops a stimulating hypothesis regarding the respective competitive position of the state banks and the national banks as to the provision of loan funds; and finally, one of the older laudatory discussions, P. M. Warburg, *The Federal Reserve System: Its Origins and Growth* (New York: Macmillan, 1930).

Chapter 11

The most difficult task facing a bibliographer on this subject is to contain its size, for it is hard to find an able scholar of U.S. history who has not written something on it. This almost brutally brief bibliography will classify citations under three broad headings: the agrarian response, the labor response, and—overlapping but more extensive and diffuse—the general social response. Progressivism will be treated under the last named category.

The original scholarly work on the farmers' response was done by S. J. Buck and J. D. Hicks. Their classic contributions were: S. J. Buck, *The Granger Movement* (Cambridge, Mass: Harvard University Press, 1913); by the same author, *The Agrarian Crusade* (New Haven: Yale University Press, 1920); and J. D. Hicks, *The Populist Revolt* (Minneapolis: University of Minnesota Press, 1931). The fine survey by F. A. Shannon has been cited earlier. Another competent survey of farm discontent, emphasizing the market nexus, is C. C. Taylor, *The Farmers' Movement, 1620-1920* (New York: American Book Company, 1953). A more recent and specific analysis is that of G. H. Miller, *Railroads and the Granger Laws* (Madison: University of Wisconsin Press, 1971). The older thesis, now challenged by contemporary historians, that farmers were mercilessly exploited by the industrial, transport, and financial sectors, is well presented in T. Saloutos, "The Agricultural Problem and Nineteenth Century Industrialism," *AH*, 22 (1948), 156-74, reprinted in a fine old collection of readings, J. T. Lambie and R. V. Clemence, *Economic Change in America* (Harrisburg, Penn.: Stackpole, 1954). Examples of recent attacks on various aspects of the traditional thesis are: A. G. Bogue, *Money and Interest: The Farm Mortgage on the Middle Border* (Ithaca: Cornell University Press, 1955), dealing with lenders and speculation; and, with respect to grain marketing, M. Rothstein, "America in the International Rivalry for the British Wheat Market, 1860-1914," *MVHR*, 47, no. 3 (December 1960), 401-18.

Labor's response involves, among other matters, a study of the labor movement, which has of course received extensive treatment. Among the leading general histories are: John R. Commons et al., *History of Labour in the United States*, v. II, III (New York: Macmillan, 1935, 1936); Philip Taft, *Organized Labor in American History* (New York: Harper and Row, 1964); and L. Ulman, *The Rise of the National Trade Union: The Development and Significance of Its Structure, Governing Institutions, and Economic Policies* (Cambridge, Mass.: Harvard University Press, 1955). There are also a number of more specifically oriented studies, such as: on the short lived National Labor Union, G. N. Grob, "Reform Unionism: The National Labor Union," *JEH*, 14 (Spring 1954), 126-42; on the Knights of Labor, Chapters II-IX of N. J. Ware, *The Labor Movement in the United States, 1860-1890* (New York: Appleton, 1929 and Random House, Vintage, 1964); on the AFL, L. L. Lorwin, *The American Federation of Labor* (Washington: Brookings, 1933); P. S. Foner, *History of the Labor Movement in the United States, Vol. 3: The Policies and Practices of the American Federation of Labor, 1900-1909* (New York: International Publishers, 1964); and on the Industrial Workers of the World, P. F. Brissenden, *The I.W.W.: A Study of American Syndicalism*, second ed. (New York: Russell and Russell, 1957). Labor's relationships with the agrarian movement are surveyed in Chapter III of N. Pollack, *The Populist Response to Industrial America* (Cambridge: Harvard University Press, 1962), a work otherwise largely devoted to intellectual developments. A good review of unionism in the last two decades of this period, with stress on labor's political interests, is M. Korson, *American Labor Unions and Politics, 1900-1918* (Southern Illinois University Press, 1958 and Boston: Beacon Press, 1965). There are also a number of able studies on the larger strike actions, but for the nonspecialist a perusal of the *Encyclopedia of the Social Sciences* (New York: Macmillan, 1934), v. 14, the essay on "Strikes and Lockouts," pp. 419-26, including bibliography, should suffice.

Turning to the more diffused topic of the general social response to industrialization and its attendent economic changes, there are a number of significant contributions that should be added to the many relevant citations already listed under earlier chapter bibliographies, such as E. C. Kirkland's *Industry Comes of Age*. For example, L. Benson's *Merchants, Farmers and Railroads: Railroad Regulation and New York Politics, 1850-1887* (Cambridge, Mass.: Harvard University Press, 1955) emphasizes the influence of merchants and shippers, rather than farmers, in securing railroad regulation through the Interstate Commerce Act. N. Fine, *Labor and Farmer Parties in the United States, 1828-1928* (New York: Rand School of Social Science, 1928) describes manual workers' efforts, whether on the farm on in the city, to advance their interests in the face of the business power viewed as essentially monolithic. J. K. Kindahl, "Economic Factors in Specie Resumption: The United States, 1865-1879" in *Reinterpretation*, op. cit., pp. 468-79 argues the banker passivity thesis on the money stock during those years of monetary tumult. A. Martin in his prize-winning *Enterprise Denied* (New York: Columbia University Press 1971) returns to the railroad regulation theme to argue that industrial and agricultural shippers manipulated the "archaic Progressives" into securing constraining legislation such as the 1906 Hepburn Act and the 1910 Mann-Elkins Act that in the long run destroyed railroad profitability and ability to compete. G. Golko's counter-contribution on this subject has already been cited.

On the money question again, W. T. K. Nugent, *Money and American Society, 1865-1880* joins the "revisionists" to try to show that almost anybody could take almost any stand on the monetary controversies of the period. Slightly more in line with the "loose-knit socioeconomic group" approach to those controversies, generally adhered to in a more brittle fashion in this volume, are R. P. Sharkey, *Money, Class and Party* (Baltimore: Johns Hopkins Press, 1959) for the period ending with Reconstruction, and then I. Unger's exciting book, *The Greenback*

Era: A Social and Political History of American Finance, 1865-1879 (Princeton: Princeton University Press, 1964).

On the formidable topic of Progressivism, the most useful item for a solid introduction is the recent paperback volume by the general historian D. M. Kennedy (ed.), *Progressivism: The Critical Issues* (Boston: Little, Brown, 1971). In addition to the highly representative selections from persons traditionally believed to be Progressives, there are selections from eminent interpreters. Moreover, the book contains an excellent list of suggestions for further reading with brief comments. Among the more prominent works that have not been cited already in this bibliography, perhaps attention should be called to: E. Goldman's *Rendezvous with Destiny* (New York: Vintage Books, 1960); R. Hofstadter, *The Age of Reform: From Bryan to F.D.R.* (New York: Vintage Books, 1955), a companion piece to Mowry's *Era of Theodore Roosevelt*, cited above; G. Kolko's *The Triumph of Conservatism: A Reinterpretation of American History, 1900-1916* (Chicago: Quadrangle Books, 1963), which argues that Progressivism was conservative and probusiness; and C. C. Regier, *The Era of the Muckrakers* (Chapel Hill: University of North Carolina Press, 1932), dealing with that influential current of the culture at that time. Two works by R. H. Wiebe, *Businessmen and Reform* (Cambridge: Harvard University Press, 1962) and *The Search for Order, 1877-1920* (New York: Hill and Wang, 1967), advance the revisionist thesis that the business element was by no means a monolithic reactionary class. D. P. Thelen, in "Social Tensions and the Origins of Progressivism," *JAH*, 56 (1969), 323-41, completes the process of dismantling the traditional socioeconomic group framework and recommends abandoning the search for a pure model of the Progressives.

Chapter 12

Three very useful theoretical contributions on growth and the balance of payments are, for the United States: R. N. Cooper, "Growth and Trade: Some Hypotheses about Long-Term Trends," *JEH*, 24, no. 4 (December 1964), 609-28, with a discussion by J. Williamson; a famous world-oriented survey by F. Hilgerdt, *Industrialization and Foreign Trade* (Geneva: League of Nations, 1945); and a similarly general analysis by S. Kuznets, "Trends in International Interdependence," in his *Modern Economic Growth* (New Haven: Yale University Press, 1966), 285-358, which has strongly influenced the discussion of imperialism in the present volume.

Much factual information is available. In this category some of the outstanding studies are: J. G. B. Hutchins, *The American Maritime Industries and Public Policy, 1789-1914* (Cambridge, Mass.: Harvard University Press, 1941); the comprehensive work by R. Lipsey, *Price and Quantity Trends in the Foreign Trade of the United States* (Princeton: Princeton University Press, 1963), heavily relied upon in the present volume; M. Simon, "The United States Balance of Payments, 1861-1900," in NBER, *Trends*, 629-715, also invaluable as a data source; and on farm exports two able discussions, W. Trimble, "Historical Aspects of the Surplus Food Production of the United States, 1862-1902," *Annual Report of the American Historical Association* (1918), I, 222-39, and E. G. Nourse, *American Agriculture and the European Market* (New York: McGraw-Hill, 1924).

Largely descriptive on the export trade shift from crude materials and manufactured foodstuffs to semi and finished manufactures in the European trade is M. Simon and D. E. Novack, "Some Dimensions of the American Commercial Invasion of Europe, 1871-1914: An Introductory Essay," *JEH*, 24, no. 4 (December 1964), 591-605. Two additional special topic treatments are: H. G. Vatter, "An Estimate of Import Substitution for Manufactured Products in the U.S. Economy,

1859-1899," *Economic Development and Cultural Change*, 18, no. 1, Part I (October 1969), 40-3; and J. G. Williamson, *American Growth and the Balance of Payments, 1820-1913, A Study of the Long Swing* (Chapel Hill: University of North Carolina Press, 1964). The latter is critically and extensively reviewed by C. P. Kindleberger, "The United States Balance of Payments in the Nineteenth Century," *EEH*, 3, no. 1 (Fall 1965), 50-61.

Turning to foreign economic policy and imperialism, and bearing in mind that the tariff was dealt with earlier, there are two important older studies that demand attention: C. Lewis, *America's Stake in International Investments* (Washington: Brookings Institution, 1938), essentially informational on that aspect of the foreign balance; and B. H. Williams, *Economic Foreign Policy of the United States* (New York: McGraw-Hill, 1929).

The extensive and somewhat heated literature on imperialism can merely be touched upon here. We do not refer at all to the enormous literature on U.S. policy in various areas, such as Latin America. Viewpoints differ markedly on this general subject and the perspective presented in the present volume is only one among several. The "revisionist" trend among historians in recent times has in general attempted to refute the thesis of a business class interest in imperial expansion and to replace it with the notions (1) that other social groups have had equal or greater interest, and (2) that as a conceptual and empirical category, imperialism cannot be defined and should therefore, like "Progressive," be abandoned. This approach is well represented by Hans Daalder in his article on "Imperialism" for the *International Encyclopedia of the Social Sciences*, v. 7 (New York: Crowell, Collier and Macmillan, 1968), 101-8. First we have the strongly attitudinal study of D. Healy, *U.S. Expansion: The Imperialist Urge in the 1890's* (Madison: University of Wisconsin Press, 1970), focused on the crucial decade when "America turned outward," and a sort of companion piece by the revisionist P. S. Holbo, "Economics, Expansion, and Emotion: An Emerging Foreign Policy," in *The Gilded Age*, revised ed. (Syracuse: Syracuse University Press, 1970), which argues that the public was hostile toward economic expansionism. However, E. R. May in *American Imperialism: A Speculative Essay* (New York: Atheneum, 1968) tries to show how certain groups worked to get public support for such policies. M. Plesur, in *America's Outward Thrust: Approaches to Foreign Affairs, 1865-1890* (DeKalb: Northern Illinois University Press, 1970), attempts to show the background for the nineties, particularly the preparatory work of "far-seeing statesmen" as they moved against domestically focused public opinion.

A somewhat older valuable edited source, presenting many different views, including those of J. A. Hobson, V. I. Lenin and J. A. Schumpeter, is H. M. Wright (ed.), *The "New Imperialism": Analysis of Late Nineteenth-Century Expansion* (Boston: D. C. Heath, 1961). With this as conceptual background, one can fruitfully turn to such well-known works as: W. LaFeber, *The New Empire, An Interpretation of American Expansion 1860-1898* (Ithaca: Cornell University Press, 1963), cited frequently in this volume; R. W. Leopold, "The Emergence of America as a World Power: Some Second Thoughts," in J. Braeman, R. H. Bremmer, and D. Brody (eds.), *Change and Continuity in Twentieth Century America* (New York: Harper, 1969), 3-34, which stresses trade and associated diplomatic-strategic values in U.S. expansionism; R. W. Van Alstyne, *The Rising American Empire* (Oxford, Eng.: B. Blackwell, 1960); and W. A. Williams, *The Roots of the Modern American Empire* (New York: Random House, 1970), wherein it is contended that the trade interests of the farmers pushed the business element and national political leadership into an expansionist direction. Clearly, each of us has his favored socioeconomic group(s). This is no less true of the excellent analysis by R. Zevin, "An Interpretation of American Imperialism," *JEH*, 32, no. 1 (March 1972), 316-60, except that Zevin has different strategic groups at different times.

Chapter 13

The best accessible discussion of the neoclassical production function underlying the growth rate estimates calculated in this chapter is E. S. Phelps, "Tangible Investment as an Instrument of Growth," in his edited work, *The Goal of Economic Growth* (New York: W. W. Norton, 1962), pp. 94-105.

Empirical material chiefly drawn upon will be found in J. W. Kendrick, *Productivity Trends in the United States*, and S. Kuznets, *Capital in the American Economy*, both previously cited. There is also a new and currently unpublished paper by R. E. Gallman, "Change in Total U.S. Agricultural Productivity in the Nineteenth Century," a study presented at the University of Chicago, Workshop in Economic History on January 21, 1972.

Index

ABOUT THE AUTHOR

Harold G. Vatter is professor of economics at Portland State University. He received his B.A. from the University of Wisconsin, his M.A. from Columbia University, and his Ph.D. from the University of California at Berkeley. Professor Vatter's main interest is economic history. He has published several books and numerous articles dealing with United States economic history.